Hymns and Hymnody

Hymns and Hymnody

Historical and Theological Introductions

Volume 2: From Catholic Europe to Protestant Europe

Edited by

Mark A. Lamport
Benjamin K. Forrest
and Vernon M. Whaley

James Clarke & Co

James Clarke & Co
P.O. Box 60
Cambridge
CB1 2NT
United Kingdom

www.jamesclarke.co
publishing@jamesclarke.co

Paperback ISBN: 978 0 227 17721 1
PDF ISBN: 978 0 227 90722 1

British Library Cataloguing in Publication Data
A record is available from the British Library

First published by James Clarke & Co, 2020

Published by arrangement
with Cascade Books

Dedications

From Mark—To my wonderful aunt, Kay Sutton, longtime church organist; and dear friend, Mark E. Fitzgerald (1955–98), gifted classical organist/pianist. Lovers of music offered in praise of God and the mission of his church.

From Benjamin—To my grandparents, Bill and Joyce Seal, who began, many years ago, a legacy of worship that has extended from their example to a generation of grandchildren who know, love, and worship Jesus. Thank you for your prayers and faithful example!

From Vernon—To my friend, pastor, and coworker in ministry, Dr. Robert J. Morgan—Thank your for renewing my love of the hymns by faithfully telling their story.

Contents

Tables

Figures

About the Editors, Introduction Contributors, and Editorial Advisory Board

EDITORS

Mark A. Lamport (PhD, Michigan State University) is a graduate professor in the United States and Europe. He is coeditor of *Encyclopedia of Christianity and the Global South* (2 vols., 2018); *Encyclopedia of Martin Luther and the Reformation* (2 vols., 2017); *Encyclopedia of Christianity in the United States* (5 vols., Selected: "Notable Books of 2016"); *Encyclopedia of Christian Education* (3 vols., Winner, Booklist Editors' Choice: Adult Books, 2016).

Benjamin K. Forrest (EdD, Liberty University) is Professor of Christian Education and Associate Dean at the College of Arts and Sciences at Liberty University. He is coeditor of *A Legacy of Preaching* (2 vols., 2018), *Biblical Leadership: Theology for Everyday Leaders* (2017), and *Biblical Worship: Theology unto the Glory of God* (forthcoming).

Vernon M. Whaley (PhD, University of Oklahoma) is Dean of the Liberty University School of Music. His publications include, *Exalt His Name* (2018), *Worship Through the Ages* (2012), *The Great Commission to Worship* (2011), and *The Dynamics of Corporate Worship* (2001).

INTRODUCTION CONTRIBUTORS

Robin A. Leaver studied at Clifton Theological (now Trinity) College, Bristol, England, and holds a doctorate from the Rijksunversiteit Groningen, the Netherlands. He is Professor Emeritus, Westminster Choir College, Princeton; and Visiting Professor, Yale Institute of Sacred Music, New Haven; and Queen's University, Belfast, Northern Ireland. Leaver has an international reputation for research and writings in the areas of church music, theology, liturgy, and hymnology, especially in Luther and Bach studies.

Pedrito U. Maynard-Reid (ThD, MDiv, MA, Andrews University; MTh, Fuller Theological Seminary; BTh, Northern Caribbean University; LRSM, Royal Schools of Music; LTCL, ATCL, Trinity College London) is Assistant to the President for Diversity and Professor of Biblical Studies and Missiology at Walla Walla University. He is a specialist in music and worship, with special emphasis on African American, Caribbean, and Hispanic.

Paul Westermeyer is Professor Emeritus of Church Music, Luther Seminary, St. Paul, Minnesota. He received his PhD from the University of Chicago and studied under Martin E. Marty. Westermeyer books include *The Church Musician*; *Te Deum: The Church and Music*; *Hymnal Companion to Evangelical Lutheran Worship;* and the essays from 1850 to 1900 in *Church Music in the United States.*

EDITORIAL ADVISORY BOARD

Kimberly Hope Belcher (PhD, MTS, Theology—Liturgical Studies, University of Notre Dame, Notre Dame, Indiana) is the Tisch Family Assistant Professor of Theology at the University of Notre Dame, where her research includes sacramental and liturgical theology and ritual studies. She is especially interested in ecumenical dialogue and serves as a Catholic representative in the US Catholic-Methodist dialogue.

Alexandra Buckle (PhD, University of Oxford) is Lecturer in Music at St. Hilda's College, Oxford. She works on late medieval English music, with a special focus on institutions, iconography, and patrons. Buckle has published widely on fifteenth- and sixteenth-century English music and articles can be found in *Early Music*; *Plainsong and Medieval Music*; *Journal of Liturgical Studies*; and *BBC History Magazine.* Alexandra was on the committee for the reinterment of King Richard III at Leicester Cathedral in March 2015 and her research guided the ceremony. Alexandra enjoys speaking about her research in more popular outlets, on the radio, and has twice acted as a music consultant for English Heritage.

Jeremy Dibble (MA, Trinity College, Cambridge; PhD, Southampton University; FRSCM, FGCM) is a Professor of Music at Durham University. He has published monographs on C. Hubert H. Parry (Oxford University Press), Charles Villiers Stanford (Oxford University Press), and John Stainer

(Boydell Press) and numerous articles on church music, hymnody, and organ music of the Victorian and Edwardian eras. He is the musical editor of the *Canterbury Dictionary of Hymnology.*

Margot E. Fassler (PhD, Cornell) has recently published the textbook *Music in the Medieval West* and its *Anthology* (New York, 2014); the edited volume (with Katie Bugyis and Andrew Kraebel) *Medieval Cantors and Their Craft: Music, Liturgy, and the Shaping of History, 800–1500* (York, 2016); and the coauthored two-volume study (with Jeffrey Hamburger, Eva Schlotheuber, and Susan Marti) *Liturgical Life and Latin Learning at Paradies bei Soest, 1300–1425: Inscription and Illumination in the Choir Books of a North German Dominican Convent* (Munster, 2016). Fassler is a fellow of the Medieval Academy of America and of the American Academy of Arts and Sciences, and is currently Vice President of the Medieval Academy of America.

C. Michael Hawn (DMA, Music Education and Voice, Southern Baptist Theological Seminary; MCM, Musicology and Voice, Southern Baptist Theological Seminary; BME, Wheaton College) is University Distinguished Professor of Church Music and Director of the Sacred Music Program at Perkins School of Theology, Southern Methodist University. He conducts research in hymnody and publishes widely in this field, especially in the area of non-Western congregational song.

Joseph Herl (PhD, University of Illinois; MMus, North Texas State University) is Professor of Music at Concordia University, Nebraska. His 2004 book *Worship Wars in Early Lutheranism* was awarded the Roland Bainton Prize of the Sixteenth Century Society and Conference. More recently, he was coeditor of a historical companion to the *Lutheran Service Book.*

Lim Swee Hong (PhD, Drew University, New Jersey; MSM, Southern Methodist University, Texas) is Deer Park Associate Professor of Sacred Music and Director, Master of Sacred Music program at Emmanuel College of Victoria University in the University of Toronto, Canada. He is also the Director of Research for the Hymn Society in USA and Canada.

Pedrito U. Maynard-Reid (ThD, MDiv, MA, Andrews University; MTh, Fuller Theological Seminary; BTh, Northern Caribbean University; LRSM, Royal Schools of Music; LTCL, ATCL, Trinity College London) is Assistant to the President for Diversity and Professor of Biblical Studies and Missiology at Walla Walla University. He is a specialist in music and worship, with special emphasis on African American, Caribbean, and Hispanic.

David W. Music (DMA/MCM, Southwestern Baptist Theological Seminary) is Professor of Church Music in the School of Music at Baylor University. He served as editor of *The Hymn* (1991–96) and has written extensively on congregational song and sacred choral music.

Stephen Michael Newby (DMA, Music Composition, The University of Michigan at Ann Arbor; MM, The University of Massachusetts at Amherst) is Associate Professor of Music at Seattle Pacific University in Seattle, Washington. His recent publications include areas of theology of multiethnic music and worship, oratorio and musical theater works based upon the prophet Hosea, Civil Rights, and Underground Railroad Movements.

Iain Quinn (PhD, Historical Musicology, University of Durham; MM, Yale University; BM, University of Hartford) is Assistant Professor of Organ and Coordinator of Sacred Music at Florida State University. Publications include editions of Barber, Czerny, Elgar, and Goss, and books *The Highest Walks of Art—The Development of an English Organ Sonata* and *Saint or Siren? The Organist in Victorian Literature.*

Lester Ruth (PhD, University of Notre Dame; ThM, Candler School of Theology; MDiv, Asbury Theological Seminary) is the Research Professor of Christian Worship at Duke Divinity School. Prior to Duke, he taught at Asbury Theological Seminary and Yale Divinity School. His current research explores the non-musical aspects of the history of contemporary worship.

Jo-Michael Scheibe (BA/MM, California State University at Long Beach; DMA, University of Southern California) chairs the Thornton School of Music's Department of Choral and Sacred Music at the University of Southern California. He is in frequent demand nationally and internationally as a clinician, conductor, and adjudicator for choruses at the university, community college, community, and secondary levels. Future engagements include international presentations in Shanghai, Bangkok, and Salzburg; national concerts at Orchestra Hall in Chicago and Carnegie Hall in New York City.

Bryan D. Spinks (DD, University of Durham) is the Bishop F. Percy Goddard Professor of Liturgical Studies and Pastoral Theology at Yale Institute of Sacred Music and Yale Divinity School. His areas of specialism include Church of the East, Syrian Orthodox and Reformed worship as well as Anglican rites. His most recent book is *Do This in Remembrance of Me: The Eucharist from the Early Church to the Present Day* (2013).

Martin Tel (DMA, University of Kansas; MA, Calvin Theological Seminary; MM, University of Notre Dame) is the Director of Music at Princeton Theological Seminary where he directs the seminary choirs, facilitates the music ministry for daily worship, and offers courses in church music. His research focuses on psalmody and congregational song.

Karen B. Westerfield Tucker (PhD/MA, Theology/Liturgical Studies, University of Notre Dame; MDiv, The Divinity School, Duke University) is Professor of Worship at the School of Theology, Boston University, where she teaches courses in the areas of liturgical studies and church music. Her publications take up such topics as Methodist/Wesleyan liturgical history and theology, worship and ecumenism, and hymnody.

Mel R. Wilhoit (DMA, Southern Baptist Theological Seminary) served as Professor of Music and Department Chair at Bryan College, Dayton, Tennessee, for over thirty years. His popular and scholarly works on music have appeared in numerous traditional and online publications.

EDITORIAL CONSULTANTS

Jonathan L. Best (PhD, St. Thomas University, Miami, Florida) teaches online courses in religion and theological writing for St. Thomas University, and operates an editing company—Best Academic Editing. His book *A Postmodern Theology of Ritual Action?* is scheduled to be published by Pickwick in 2019. He explores theological and philosophical issues related to uncertainty, transition, and being in-between at www.liminaltheology.org.

Ron J. Bigalke (PhD, University of Pretoria; PhD, MTS, Tyndale Theological Seminary; MDiv, Luther Rice University; MApol, Columbia Evangelical Seminary) is Georgia State Minister for Capitol Commission, and Research Associate, New Testament Department, University of Pretoria, mission and ethics project.

Mark D. Eckel (ThM, Grace Theological Seminary; PhD, Southern Baptist Theological Seminary) is Professor of Leadership, Education and Discipleship, Capital Seminary and Graduate School, Washington, DC. Numerous publications include reviews, articles, curricula, books, and hundreds of essays at www.warpandwoof.org.

Benjamin D. Espinoza (MA, Asbury Theological Seminary) is a PhD Candidate and research assistant at Michigan State University. He currently serves as college pastor at Faith Church and as the senior associate editor of the *Journal of Youth Ministry*.

Virginia Gray completed her Doctor of Education at Southeastern Baptist Theological Seminary in December 2014. She also holds an MA in Christian Education from Mid-America Baptist Theological Seminary and a BA in Political Science from Arkansas State University.

Bryce F. Hantla (EdD, Southeastern Baptist Theological Seminary; MA, North Carolina State University) is Director of Institutional Research and Accreditation as well as Associate Professor for Christian Education and English at the College of Biblical Studies-Houston.

Mariana Hwang (PhD, Talbot Theological Seminary; MDiv, Fuller Theological Seminary) is Associate Professor of Christian Education at Lincoln Christian University. Her areas of interest are children's spiritual formation and identity formation, and publications include a book on parenting and several articles in the *Encyclopedia of Christian Education* (Rowman & Littlefield, 2015).

D. Joshua Pruden is research assistant at Northland International University. He is currently working on his MA in Biblical Studies also from Northland, where he has his BA in Biblical Counseling. Pruden has been involved in cross-cultural ministry in China as an English teacher.

Moriah Wilson (MA in Music Education) is a classically trained musician and has studied both piano and voice. Her publications include an honors thesis titled "The Suzuki Method: Influences of Shinichi Suzuki on Japanese Music Education."

Introduction to Volume 2

From Catholic Europe to Protestant Europe

Robin A. Leaver

The three hundred years between the beginning of the sixteenth century and the end of the eighteenth century were the most momentous for the development of congregational hymnody. At the beginning of the sixteenth century only those in Catholic religious communities sang hymns (in Latin) within the liturgy. By the end of the century many Protestant congregations were singing in various vernacular forms of worship across Europe in High and Low German, French, Danish, Swedish, English, etc., expressing theologies that were differently nuanced and confessionally expressed, such as Lutheran, Calvinist/Reformed, Anabaptist, Anglican, Bohemian Brethren, etc. But by this time Roman Catholics had also begun to sing vernacular hymnody, influenced by Protestant hymnody, in non-Eucharistic worship and privately. The seventeenth century was marked by a gradual expansion of the hymn repertories in each of these linguistic and confessional groupings that were significantly expanded during the eighteenth century, becoming the primary feature of the evangelical revival that brought into existence new denominations such as Moravian (in succession to the Bohemeian Brethen of earlier times) and Methodist, denominations in which hymnody predominated and was enthusiastically promoted, which in many ways shaped their theology and formed a major part of their liturgies.

Wittenberg under the leadership of Martin Luther was the catalyst for the development of vernacular hymnody in the early sixteenth century. But hymns in German, in the form of religious folk-songs, had been flourishing for many decades, especially being sung on major feasts and other celebrations of the church year. What Luther did was revise and expand some of these earlier hymns, often translations from Latin, made new translations of other Latin hymns and liturgical chants, as well as writing new strophic hymns. What was radical and really new was that in the past vernacular religious folk-songs were sung extra-liturgically, during the appropriate seasons of Advent, Christmas, Epiphany, Lent, Easter, etc., but Luther made such hymnody an integral part of worship. The hymns enshrined the new understanding of evangelical theology, as in the Scripture proofs of every line of Paul Speratus's hymns in their early imprints, and in the specific catechism hymns that Luther wrote. The key period was the winter of 1523/24 when many of the key hymns emanated from Wittenberg. But Luther did not work single-handedly, though he was clearly the leader and the most prolific. There was a significant group of colleagues who joined him (and Speratus) in writing new hymns, among them Elisabeth Cruciger, Michael Stiefel, Justus Jonas, Erhalt Hegenwalt, and Michael Agricola. A distinctive genre created by Luther, which was to have an enormous impact across Europe and beyond in the following centuries, was the psalm-hymn, or metrical psalm, that is, the substance of the biblical psalm in rhymed strophic form.

From 1523 the Wittenberg hymns, originally circulating on individual broadsides, were reprinted, almost immediately, in other towns and cities, and modest collections of these hymns were gathered together in small booklets. Notable among them were: Nuremberg, with its hymn-writers inspired by those in Wittenberg, such as Hans Sachs and Lazarus Spengler; Erfurt, where two printer/publishers vied with each other to publish collections of the Wittenberg hymns; Rostock, which published Low German and Danish versions of the Wittenberg hymns; and Malmö, which did the same for Lutheran hymns in Swedish. Strasbourg, then in a predominantly German-speaking area, reprinted the Wittenberg hymns as soon as they became available. But the Strasbourgers frequently set Luther's texts to their own melodies, notably by Matthias Greiter, together with new texts by Greiter and Wolfgang Dachstein. These new texts were mostly metrical psalms, following Luther's models, which became emulated elsewhere, contributing to the adoption of the metrical psalm as the primary hymnic form sung by generations of Protestants across Europe and beyond. Roman Catholics produced a number of hymnals, clearly modeled on Lutheran hymnals, in order to express their theology in corporate song, though the singing was usually restricted to the Offices rather than the Mass, or to domestic circles. Two prominent examples are the hymnals of Michael Vehe (Leipzig, 1537) and Johann Leisentritt (Bautzen, 1567).

Ulrich Zwingli in German-speaking Zurich directed that, on theological grounds, corporate singing was unnecessary and therefore worship comprised only the spoken word in German in and around Zurich—a state of affairs that continued until almost the end of the century. But this did not stop the Zurich publisher Christoph Froschauer publishing a hymnal for use in nearby Constance. The primary section of the various editions of this hymnal comprised more than eighty metrical psalms, with additional versions by Ludwig Oeler and Thomas Blaurer.

The pastor of the small French-speaking community in Strasbourg was Jean Calvin, who was charged by the magistrates to conform the worship of the French congregation to the content and form of the worship of the German congregations. This included metrical psalmody and thus Calvin created his first collection of French metrical psalms in Strasbourg in 1539. Two years later he was called to serve the churches in Geneva, where, working with Clement Marot and Theodore Beza, he created the Genevan Psalter, with the melodies successively composed by Louis Bourgeois and Claude Goudimel, published in its complete form in 1562. For Calvin the restriction to singing almost exclusively metrical psalms was a theological issue. For him these Scriptural songs, biblical psalms rendered into verse, were to be the primary, almost exclusive, song of the Reformed churches. The French Psalter emanating from Geneva became the model for Reformed churches throughout Europe, usually vernacular versions using the Genevan melodies for the respective psalms, notably in Dutch, German, and in the Scottish psalters (from 1564–65), which are closer to the Genevan model than the English psalter that appeared a few years earlier.

English hymnody following the Wittenberg tradition began in the mid-1530s with Miles Coverdale's *Goostly Psalmes*, translations of Wittenberg hymns with their associated melodies. But the political climate was unstable under Henry VIII, when Reformation theology was being considered, and the collection was probably not known much outside of London. When Edward VI succeeded his father as king in 1547 the Reformation became an open affair and one of the earliest publications that marked the changing climate was the publication of a small collection of metrical psalms by Thomas Sternhold. A few years later the collection was enlarged with psalms written by John Hopkins but any further development was curtailed when in 1553 Edward VI died at a young age, and his half-sister Mary came to the throne. She reversed all the Protestant gains of Edward's reign and also the few Protestant influences of the late Henry VIII years. Catholicism was reintroduced, and Protestants, if they wanted to survive, either went into hiding or into exile. Significant families chose exile in Germany and Switzerland, where they came into contact with the Genevan psalms sung in

French, German, and Dutch Reformed congregations. The exiles had taken with them their small booklets of the psalms of Sternhold and Hopkins, to which were added English versions of metrical psalms and hymns, which, when Mary died in 1558 and they could return, they brought back their expanded and revised editions of Sternhold and Hopkins. These formed the nucleus of the complete Psalter of 150 psalms, plus a few hymns, published in London in 1562. Although it did not use many of the Genevan melodies it nevertheless conformed to Reformed theology that required that the substance of each psalm—no more, no less—be expressed in strophic form. *The Whole Book of Psalmes* of Sternhold and Hopkins, in its numerous editions, became the only congregational song heard in Anglican parish churches for centuries. Indeed, it was thought that only such metrical psalms were legal in the worship of the Church of England, but it was a false assumption that was only fully revealed in the early nineteenth century. Over the generations the antique language and the generally poor poetry were criticized, as often as not by those who wanted their own versions of metrical psalms to be published. But there was a problem. Copyright of the Sternhold and Hopkins psalms was held by the Stationers' Company of London, and the company resisted any attempt to usurp a significant part of its income.

In the seventeenth century Europe was devastated during the Thirty Years War, especially in Germany, which was laid waste and took a long time to recover. When the world around you is being destroyed the compensation is to withdraw into your inner self. Many devotional books were published in Germany, much of them strongly influenced by medieval mysticism. At the same time a new form of intensive, highly personal hymnody flourished by such writers as Martin Rinkart, Johann Heermann, Johann Rist, and supremely Paul Gerhardt, whose texts were set to a new form of melody, especially by Johann Georg Ebeling and Johann Crüger, whose hymnal, *Praxis pietatis melica*, in its many editions, was the most widely used hymnal of the seventeenth century. Such personal hymns, set to somewhat freer melodies, led to the specific Pietist style of hymnody epitomized in the *Geist-reiches Gesangbuch* of Johann Anastasius Freylinghausen, first published in 1704, that was enormously influential throughout the eighteenth century.

In England the power of the Stationers' Company was circumvented by poets with royal connections: Nahum Tate, poet laureate, and Nicholas Brady, chaplain to King William III. They produced *A New Version of the Psalms of David* (1696/98), which was issued in effect with a royal warrant. The theological principle remained the same as that of the Sternhold and Hopkins psalter—thereafter known as the "Old Version"—that only the substance of the biblical psalms was to be expressed in poetic form. Although intended to replace the "Old Version" it was only used in parish churches in towns and cities; in rural areas the congregations continued singing the "Old Version" well into the nineteenth century. The New Version fostered a new kind of freer melody than the old psalm tunes, a development that continued throughout the eighteenth century.

Congregationalist (or Independents) were not as restricted as Anglicans thought they were, and thus they could freely sing hymns. But Isaac Watts went further than writing hymns—some of the finest in the English language—he also wrote metrical psalms that introduced a new theological hermeneutic. Watts argued that the Reformed tradition of reproducing the substance of the Hebrew psalms without reference to the New Testament was theologically unacceptable. So in his versions of the psalms he drew on the whole Bible. It was a revolution that did not go unchallenged. Anglicans would not sing either his hymns or his psalms, even though their quality was exceptional. But little by little, toward the end of the eighteenth century Anglicans became familiar with a few of Watts's psalms and hymns since a few of them were slipped into the supplements that were appended to the Tate and Brady psalms.

Watts's influence in the earlier part of the century was more than significant, since John Wesley and his Holy Club in Oxford sang the hymns and psalms of Watts. Then John Wesley went to Georgia, and on the ship taking him across the Atlantic he encountered the singing of German Moravians. Following their conversion both Wesleys, John and Charles, were influenced by the London Moravian church in Fetter Lane, and the distinctive hymnody heard there. Charles's response to his conversion was to begin to write hymns and poetry, a small stream that soon began as a river but then became an amazing flood. The evangelical revival in England in the eighteenth century in many ways emulated and was significantly influenced by European Pietism. The hymnody of Count Zinzendorf's Moravians had a great impact on the Wesley brothers who effectively created Methodism and produced their own hymns. The piety sounded the same, but the theology was different. Welsh Methodists, as well as many Anglican Evangelicals, were Calvinist in their theology and in their singing, whereas the Wesleyan Methodists were uncompromisingly Arminian in belief and song.

The three hundred years between 1500 and 1800 saw an astonishing expansion and diversification, as new poetic forms and different melodic styles came into use. But these poetic and musical forms were developed to express particular theologies that were expressed in the corporate singing. Even though different denominations borrowed hymns from each other, each adapted them to their own different theological environment and liturgical usage. This is the substance of the essays of this volume, in which the bare bones of this extraordinary three hundred years reviewed in this introduction are fleshed out in the detail of these insightful essays that follow.

Part 4

Sixteenth Century

Chapter 1

Costanzo Festa

Christina Labriola

HISTORICAL BACKGROUND

Costanzo Festa was a celebrated Italian composer of the High Renaissance of both secular and sacred music. Festa was a prominent member of the papal chapel choir[1] (the Cappella Sistina) in the generation before Palestrina, his (far more familiar) younger contemporary and fellow countryman, on whom, it has been asserted, he was an important influence.[2] Festa is chiefly remembered as one of the earliest madrigalists at a time when the genre was in its nascent stage, and as the composer of one of the first complete cycles of polyphonic hymns for the entire church year. The focus of this chapter will be on his hymn cycle, following a survey of his biography and historical context.

1. "It is clear . . . that the music of certain composers comprised the greatest percentage of the papal choir's repertorial traditions [in the fifteenth and sixteenth centuries]. The names of the composers regarded as traditional are well known and not unexpected: Josquin, Carpentras, Festa, Morales, Arcadelt, and ultimately Palestrina." Brauner, "Traditions in the Repertory," 173.

2. "Baini asserts that Palestrina studied Festa's works closely; nay, he considers Festa as the immediate predecessor, the model composer, in that noble style of church music which stamps the works of Palestrina as unique in form and idea." Ritter, *History of Music*, 152. Cf. "Men of Progress in Former Times."

While many details of Festa's biography are uncertain and indeed a matter of debate in the scholarly world, a rough sketch of his life can still be provided. He was born around 1485–90, possibly in Piedmont, near Turin (like his presumed relative, Sebastiano Festa, also a composer).[3] He was a cleric in the diocese of Turin, though he seems not to have been ordained a priest; evidence reveals that he certainly spent time early in his career in Piedmont.[4] A theory exists that Festa may have studied in France at the time of Louis XII, perhaps as an apprentice of the composer Jean Mouton.[5] His motet *Quis dabit oculis*, written to mark the death of Anne of Brittany, Queen of France (1514), and evidence in his work of Mouton's influence,[6] seem to reinforce this claim, though it has not be definitively proven.[7] We know from existing documents that Festa was employed on the island of Ischia, in the bay of Naples, as a music teacher for the sons of the noble family d'Avalos, at some point between 1510 and 1517. Festa visited Ferrara in March 1514, at which time he seems to have been already a composer of some renown. In 1517, he became a member of the papal chapel in Rome, in which capacity as singer and composer he lived out his remaining years (d. April 10, 1545).[8] Connections with Florence are discernible in his works and other documents, but do not necessarily place him there;[9] his service to two Medici popes, Leo X and Clement VII, is perhaps sufficient to explain them.[10] Very likely he resided in Rome through the whole of his twenty-eight-year tenure in the papal chapel choir.

A letter from Costanzo Festa to a patron[11] in September 1536 seeking the printing of his musical works refers to his hymns, *Magnificats* and *basse*. A petition from the composer two years later in March 1538 lists "masses,

3. Haar, "Festa, Costanzo," n.p.

4. Haar, "Festa, Costanzo," n.p.; Crawford, "Review of Costanzo Festa's Biography," 104.

5. Lowinsky first presents this position in "The Medici Codex," 93–98; and defends it in "On the Presentation and Interpretation."

6. Mouton was the leading composer at the French court.

7. Crawford, "Review of Costanzo Festa's Biography," 104–7. Festa's presence in Piedmont, a crossroads of French and Italian culture, may be enough to account for his taking Mouton as a compositional model; yet the matter remains inconclusive. (Haar, "Festa, Costanzo," n.p.)

8. Crawford, "Review of Costanzo Festa's Biography," 104–7.

9. Crawford, "Review of Costanzo Festa's Biography," 110–11.

10. Haar, "Festa, Costanzo," n.p.

11. Filippo Strozzi was the patron, a Florentine, godfather to Festa's child. Agee, "Filippo Strozzi," 231.

motets, madrigals, *basse*, *contraponti*, lamentations" and other works.[12] A Venetian privilege was granted him, giving him the right to have all of his music printed. His hymn cycle appears to have been published together with the *Magnificats* in the same year, as well as a book of his madrigals.[13] This establishes Festa as an important figure in the history of the development of printing and music publication. The printing of these works would have meant their wide dissemination and use. Festa's inclusion in a significant Renaissance musical manuscript, the Medici Codex (c. 1518), a choirbook of motets given to Lorenzo de' Medici as a wedding gift by Pope Leo X, who was an enthusiastic patron of music, places him alongside such names as Willaert, Josquin, and Mouton.[14] According to James Haar, Festa composed about one hundred madrigals between 1525–40, and sixty motets, from simple to quite elaborate, for three to up to eight voices.[15]

Upon his death, Festa was hailed in a papal document as a "most excellent musician and eminent singer."[16] He is often regarded as the finest composer of his generation, "the first great Italian composer of the High Renaissance."[17] Indeed, Festa's status as a native Italian composer of eminence in the time at which he lived, when Franco-Flemish polyphonists dominated the Italian scene, is rare and noteworthy.[18] He is, says Lowinsky,

> the first great Italian composer after Landini, the only Italian musician who had a share in the creation of the madrigal, the only Italian whose output of Masses, motets, hymns, lamentations, and Magnificats can compare with that of his Northern colleagues in quantity and in quality, and—above all—the

12. Agee, "Costanzo Festa's Gradus ad Parnassum," 1–2; Agee, "Filippo Strozzi," 235.

13. Haar, "'Libro Primo,'" 147–48.

14. Cf. Lowinsky, *Medici Codex*; Lowinsky, "Medici Codex"; Rifkin, "Creation of the Medici Codex"; Shephard, "Constructing Identities."

15. Haar, "Festa, Costanzo," n.p.

16. "[M]usicus eccelentissimus et cantor egregius vita functus est." Crawford, "Review of Costanzo Festa's Biography," 109.

17. Agee, "Filippo Strozzi," 228; or at least among the first, Haar, "Festa, Costanzo," n.p.

18. "Since music . . . lacked an indigenous Roman heritage, the musical life of Rome was remarkably cosmopolitan by 1500. From north of the Alps came French chansons and Franco-Flemish masses and motets; from Tuscany and the Po valley came the frottola, lauda, and vocal improvisations with the lira da braccio; from Spain came a new way of performing the Passion, exotic string instruments such as the vihuela and large viols, and perhaps also the technique of falsobordone recitations. During the reigns (1513–31) of the two Medici popes, Leo X and Clement VII, the madrigal was developed by Bernardo Pisano, Costanzo Festa and other Tuscan musicians working in Florence and Rome." Reynolds, "Rome," 86.

> only one whose mastery of all musical techniques of the time, especially of counterpoint, matches that of his Franco-Flemish contemporaries.[19]

If it is true that Festa's career was not as "international" as some theories propose, his status as a native Italian comes again to the forefront: "perhaps," says David Crawford, "the quality of his music emerges all the more impressive when seen as a product of Italian musicianship."[20] What is clear is that Festa produced music for both sacred and secular settings, which was not only highly serviceable but demonstrated an elegance and excellence on par with the distinguished northern polyphonists of the early sixteenth century. As an Italian composer of excellence, Festa proves for us, as Agee points out, that "Roman counterpoint did not begin with Palestrina."[21] He therefore stands as an important antecedent to the flourishing of works of impressive contrapuntal genius to come after him.[22]

THEOLOGICAL PERSPECTIVES

Costanzo Festa's cycle of thirty hymns[23] presents us with miniature compositional gems as exemplars of his style, and with a sense of his genius for long-term musical organization, and liturgical-mindedness and attentiveness. These "most celebrated of his sacred compositions"[24] were composed for Vespers in the Sistine Chapel, and seem to have been used regularly at the chapel, replacing Du Fay's hymns. Their appearance in five different manuscripts attests that they enjoyed wide usage in Italy during the century, wider even than those of Festa's contemporary, Carpentras, who composed a hymn cycle of his own.[25]

The cycle is comprised of hymns for the major feasts of the entire church year: the Proper of the Season, the Proper of the Saints, the Common

19. Lowinsky, "On the Presentation and Interpretation," 106.

20. Crawford, "Review of Costanzo Festa's Biography," 111.

21. Agee, "Costanzo Festa's *Gradus Ad Parnassum*," 33.

22. See the nineteenth-century article "Men of Progress in Former Times," which characterizes Festa as possessing the talent but lacking the zeal and courage to become the kind of musical reformer Palestrina was.

23. Glen Haydon's edition made Festa's thirty hymns available for the first time to a wider audience. He points out that Fr. X. Haberl first called attention to their presence in 1887–88, in a manuscript in the papal archives dating from 1538. Preface, *Hymni per totum annum*, xi; cf. Brauner, "Parvus Manucripts" 123–28.

24. Haar, "Festa, Costanzo," n.p.

25. Glen Haydon, Preface to *Hymni per totum annum*, xi.

of the Saints, and the Ordinary of the Office (for Sunday). The specific Latin texts of these Vespers hymns, along with their relative chant melodies, were assigned to specific Sundays and feast days in the liturgical year. Festa's cycle gives us an example of music that is wed to the liturgical year, intimately bound up with the temporal cycle of the Roman Catholic Church's worship, with its movements of seasons and feasts. Composed with the church year in mind, Festa's hymns never lose sight of their highly specialized purpose and their functionality—to be at the practical service of the worshipping community. At the same time, a high level of aesthetic beauty, creativity, and dynamic artistry is attained, so that the hymns are practically minded without becoming perfunctory.

The origins of the hymn texts set by Festa span back to the first newly composed (non-Scriptural) metered texts written for Christian worship in the Western church, to Hilary of Poitiers and especially Ambrose, in the fourth century, and the grand tradition of Latin hymnody.[26] With the development of monastic life (via the Rule of St. Benedict in the sixth century) came the Divine Office (or Liturgy of the Hours) with its set hymns, psalms, antiphons, responsories, readings, and prayers. The Liturgy of the Hours provided a structured liturgical response to the injunction to "pray without ceasing," sanctifying the day with prayer and praise, and consecrating time itself. Vespers, or Evening Prayer, together with Lauds, became one of the principle hours. While the *Benedictus* was associated with Morning Prayer, the *Magnificat* was sung during Vespers. The *Benedictus*, the Canticle of Zechariah, at the beginning of the day, sings of the coming of the Messiah as the breaking dawn, while the *Magnificat*, the Canticle of Mary, at the close of day, sings of the great things now accomplished through the Incarnation. While certain elements of Vespers, like the *Magnificat*, remained the same day after day, the psalms and hymns changed according to the feast. The hymns of Vespers, with their non-Scriptural texts, provided an opportunity to reflect more deeply on the feast being celebrated and its central mystery, in an artistically meaningful way, through metered Latin verse.

Festa's hymns are polyphonic after the style of the time—many voices, on independent melodic lines, made up of independent rhythmic figurations, are woven together. Polyphonic settings of Latin hymns for Vespers had been a regular feature of the liturgy since the fifteenth century.[27] His hymns follow the practice of alternating verses of chant with polyphony. Most frequently, he sets the even-numbered strophes, so that the chant melody in unison begins the hymn. Interestingly, in the majority of cases, he

26. Britt, *Hymns of the Breviary and Missal*, 21.

27. Ward and Caldwell, "Polyphonic Latin Hymns," n.p.

chooses to set the doxology of each hymn (the last verse, a formula of praise to the Trinity), even if it breaks the pattern of alternation. This reveals a tremendous sense of musical climax and progression,[28] as though to end the hymn on the monophonic chant melody after the rich texture of polyphony would be anticlimactic.

In keeping with early sixteenth-century motet style, the verses of each hymn Festa sets polyphonically are built around the original chant melody, which functions as a *cantus firmus*—i.e., a central melody, usually in longer note values, in one voice part, around which the other parts are woven. When we realize that Festa has used the same plainsong melody to create unique, compelling verse settings within the same hymn, we begin to realize the "range and resourcefulness of Festa's creative genius," for, "no two treatments bear more than a very general resemblance."[29] For a given hymn, depending on the number of verses, there are often three, four, or even five different settings based upon the same chant melody. Each polyphonic verse is imbued with the spirit of the original chant, since the polyphony is "steeped" in the chant melody, and motives are derived from it. Festa is endlessly inventive: transforming, embedding, interweaving, echoing, imitating, dissecting, and extrapolating from the chant melody in varied and ingenious ways. This use of the *cantus firmus*, together with imitative techniques, provide a profound sense of unity in diversity. The transformation of the chant melody, and the general principle of alternation between polyphony and chant, create a sense of balance between the old and the new: the ancient infuses and is always at the heart of the new; the new is always informed by, and always honors and incorporates, the old. Generally speaking, we might consider this balance between tradition and innovation, modeled so seamlessly in music, an important theological and pastoral question for the church.

Another way in which Festa demonstrates an intuitive sense of balance is through changing textures. On a large scale, the alternating polyphony and chant provide one level of contrast. Within the polyphonic verses of a given hymn, Festa, more often than not, changes the number of voices (between three and six) to produce contrast and a sense of climax by building toward the greatest number of voices in the final verse. Variation in number of voices also produces varying degrees of complexity and intricacy. (See table 1.1.)[30]

28. Haydon, "Hymns of Costanzo Festa," 106.

29. Haydon, "Hymns of Costanzo Festa," 105.

30. In creating this table, I rely upon Haydon's edition of Festa's hymns, cross-referencing general information on the assigned hymns for the major feasts with Britt, *Hymns of the Breviary and Missal*, and Ward and Caldwell, "Polyphonic Latin Hymns."

Table 1.1: Costanzo Festa's *Hymni per totum annum*

Title	Feast	Verses set and number of voices	Total number of verses
Conditor alme siderum	Sundays in Advent	2 (a 4), 4 (a 3), 6 (a 5)	6
Christe, Redemptor omnium	Christmastide	2 (a 4), 4 (a 3), 6 (a 4), 7 (a 6)	7
Hostis Herodes impie	Epiphany	2 (a 4), 4 (a 3), 5 (a 5)	5
Audi benigne Conditor	Weekdays of Lent	2 (a 4), 4 (a 3), 5 (a 5)	5
Aures ad nostras Deitatis preces	Sundays of Lent	1 (a 4), 3, (a 4), 5 (a 4), 7 (a 3), 9 (a 5)	9
Vexilla Regis prodeunt	Passion Sunday and the Exaltation of the Cross	2 (a 4), 4 (a 3), 6 (a 4), 7 (a 5)	7
Ad coenam Agni providi	Eastertide (until the Ascension)	2 (a 4), 4 (a 4), 6 (a 3), 8 (a 5)	8
Tristes erant Apostoli	Common of Apostles and Evangelists (during Eastertide)	2 (a 4), 4 (a 3), 6 (a 4), 8 (a 4), 9 (a 5)	9
Deus tuorum militum	Common of One Martyr (during Eastertide)	1 (a 4), 3 (a 4), 5 (a 5)	5
Rex gloriose Martyrum	Common of Several Martyrs (during Eastertide)	2 (a 4), 4 (a 5)	4
Jesu corona Virginum	Common of Virgins (during Eastertide)	2 (a 4), 4 (a 3), 5 (a 5)	5
Jesu nostra redemptio	Ascension	2 (a 4), 4 (a 3), 5 (a 6)	5
Veni Creator Spiritus	Pentecost	2 (a 4), 4 (a 3), 6 (a 4), 7 (a 5)	7
O lux beata Trinitas	Trinity Sunday	1 (a 4), 2 (a 5), 3 (a 6)	3
Pange lingua gloriosi	Corpus Christi	2 (a 4), 4 (a 4), 6 (a 5)	6
Ut queant laxis resonare fibris	St. John the Baptist	2 (a 4), 4 (a 4)	5

Aurea luce et decore roseo	Sts. Peter and Paul	1 (a 4), 3 (a 6)	3
Nardi Maria pistici	St. Mary Magdalene	2 (a 5)	2
Petrus beatus catenarum laqueos/ Quodcumque vinclis	St. Peter's Chains/ St. Peter's Chair	2 (a 5)	2
Ave maris stella	All Marian feasts	2 (a 4), 4 (a 3), 6 (a 4), 7 (a 6)	7
Tibi Christe splendor Patris	St. Michael	2 (a 4), 4 (a 5)	4
Christe Redemptor omnium	All Saints	2 (a 4), 4 (a 4), 7 (a 5)	7
Exsultet caelum laudibus	Common of Apostles	2 (a 4), 4 (a 3), 6 (a 5)	6
Deus tuorum militum	Common of One Martyr	2 (a 4), 4 (a 3), 5 (a 5)	5
Sanctorum meritis	Common of Several Martyrs	2 (a 4), 4 (a 3), 6 (a 5)	6
Iste Confessor	Common of Confessors	2 (a 4), 4 (a 3), 5 (a 5)	5
Jesu, corona Virginum	Common of One Virgin	2 (a 4), 4 (a 3), 4 (a 5)	5
Hujus obtentu, Deus alme, nostris	Common of Holy Women	2 (a 5)	2
Urbs beata Jerusalem	Dedication of a church	1 (a 4), 3 (a 3), 5 (a 5)	5
Lucis Creator optime	Sundays throughout the year	1 (a 4), 3 (a 3), 5 (a 5)	5

Festa achieves balance and unity in diversity at the melodic level as well. Individual lines generally have a well-balanced sense of phrase and melodic shape, so that each line has integrity and interest. "Musical rhyme" and assonance are achieved by repetition and imitation of chant-derived phrases, often at different pitch levels, and by means of staggered entrances.[31] Rhythmically, there is much independent movement, so that block-chord style is essentially nonexistent, and parts seldom come to rest at the same time.[32] Studying the contours of individual lines reveals that they tend to unfold

31. Haydon, "Hymns of Costanzo Festa," 106–7.

32. Haydon, "Hymns of Costanzo Festa," 105, 108.

in an "organic" rhythmic way: "phrases ordinarily begin with longer note values, achieve a rhythmic climax with shorter note values, and round off with longer values at cadences."[33]

Glen Haydon, who prepared a modern edition of Festa's hymn cycle, makes note of Festa's ability on display despite (or perhaps, to some degree, as a result of) the strictures accompanying the setting of these hymns for liturgical use, and comments on their regrettably unknown status today:

> Within the rather severe restrictions inherent in the nature of his task, Festa shows himself as a competent master of the technical resources of his time and as a composer of much distinction. . . . [The] conclusion seems inevitable that in their appropriate liturgical setting [these hymns] can hardly be other than extremely effective, and it is to be regretted that, in the vicissitudes of the history of ecclesiastical music, these interesting musical monuments should have passed into comparative oblivion.[34]

Theologically and pastorally speaking, then, a consideration of Festa's hymns reveal an emphasis on balance, proportion, unity in diversity, and holding the traditions of the past within the expressions of the present. The manner in which they were composed, and the specificity of the function which they serve, also speak to a sense of proportion and order: all things working in tandem, fulfilling their proper function—"To every thing there is a season, and a time for every purpose under heaven."[35] They do not exist for themselves but are very much in tune with the rhythms and movements of the liturgical year. The major feasts of the church year are accounted and provided for, with much care and thoroughness, within the framework of the Liturgy of the Hours, a form of prayer that tends toward the same general emphasis on structure and order. Festa's music reveals that order need not be a limitation or stumbling block to creativity, but under the right circumstances, can actually help to give shape and direction. Music which strives to create beauty through balance and proportion, like Festa's, can also lead one to contemplate the divine beauty of God, shaping creation, as the book of Wisdom has it, according to principles of "measure and number and weight."[36] For St. Augustine, music's proportionality and *numerositas* are related to these foundational principles of order, and so serve to reflect

33. Haydon, "Hymns of Costanzo Festa," 106.

34. Haydon, "Hymns of Costanzo Festa," 117.

35. Eccl 3:1.

36. Wis 11:20b.

God's transcendent beauty through God's handiwork, for, "the universe is at every level formed into beauty by the pervasive power of number."[37]

The diversity and range of expression captured by the hymn texts are indicative of the Catholic theological tradition from which they come. They picture a divinely ordered cosmos, and a vast company of the communion of saints, very much a part of the worship of the church on earth, interceding on her behalf and joining in her song of praise, thanksgiving, and petition. Celebrating the seasons of the liturgical year, the church participates in the worship of heaven while still on earth, singing with angels and saints, beginning now what will continue into eternity. Music, and the ministry of singers and musicians, serve an intermediary role in connecting the things of earth to things above. The image of God we might derive is the unchanging and transcendent Trinity, sustaining and incorporating all things, including time and the progression of seasons, into the divine plan. Though transcendent, this is a God who is made manifest in myriad ways, through the saints and the sublime mysteries of salvation, and who is to be glorified unceasingly, season after season sanctified by an ongoing song of praise—a song that has ever new manifestations but at its heart remains one—"ever ancient, ever new,"[38] to borrow Augustine's phrase. Time, sanctified, becomes a thin veil; and beyond: eternity.

CONTRIBUTION TO LITURGY AND WORSHIP

"The practice of singing of the Vespers hymns alternating polyphony and chant on the major feasts over the whole year dates from at least the fifteenth century," Mitchell Brauner tells us; "Festa's cycle . . . was certainly not the only one available to the singers" in the papal chapel.[39] It does, however, appear to have been one of the first of its kind by a single composer.

Festa's hymns are a gift for many reasons. As a complete cycle, they reveal remarkable thoroughness and attention to the liturgical needs of the church. They demonstrate inventiveness, resourcefulness, ingenuity, and technical mastery of the motet form, even within the restrictions of the task.[40] The way in which they balance old and new elements, and serviceability with beauty, is creative and even potentially theologically insightful. Finally, they reveal the composer's strong grasp of contrapuntal technique, and graceful ability to handle elements such as imitation, variation, melody,

37. O'Connell, *Art and the Christian Intelligence*, 67.

38. Augustine of Hippo, *Confessions* X, 27.38.

39. Brauner, "Traditions in the Repertory," 169.

40. Haydon, "Hymns of Costanzo Festa," 105.

rhythm, and harmony. They are important as signposts, pointing the way for works along the same vein that would come after.

While he tends to be overshadowed in the eyes of history by many of the distinguished polyphonists that would follow him, Festa's influence is undeniable, as one of the first great Italian masters of Renaissance polyphony, one of the very earliest madrigalists, a central figure in the Cappella Sistina under Medici Popes Leo X and Clement VII, and a highly-regarded composer whose works were widely performed and disseminated in his lifetime.

His moving motet *Super Flumina Babylonis* for five voices (included in the *Medici Codex*) is deserving of comment.[41] With effortless grace and mastery, Festa creates a tapestry of sound that wanders through changing harmonic landscapes, on a text derived from Ps 137 ("By the rivers of Babylon, we sat down and wept"), placing at the center of it the Requiem chant "Pie Jesu" on long note values in the tenor voice. It is an example of Festa's ability to handle different texts, melodies, and harmonies in a remarkably evocative, well-balanced, and affecting manner. The combination of the funeral text from the Requiem Sequence with the psalm's lament of the exiled people whose joyful music turns to bitter sorrow is striking. The psalm text is not followed strictly but interpolates other scriptural allusions and passages from Job, Maccabees, and Revelation, "which have in common the one theme how a tragic event turned the musician's gay sounds to lamentation and to the silence of mourning."[42] Perhaps the most haunting moment occurs on the text "vox musicorum conversa est in lamentum" ("the voice of music turned into lamentation"). The voices, which had been moving independently, fall into somber homophony on slower note values, on the alienating harmonic progression through C minor, B-flat major, F minor, and finally coming to rest on A-flat major. This wandering progression leads the ear to unknown and foreign territory, much like the exiles in a foreign land. The music effectively and innovatively paints the transformation taking place in the text, of music becoming lament. We can see once again in this example Festa's command of musical technique and his creative ability

41. Lowinsky proposes that it was composed by Festa for the funeral of Louis XII; *Medici Codex*, III, 48–50.

42. Lowinsky, "Medici Codex," 90–92; cf. Lowinsky, *Medici Codex*, III, 228; Lowinsky, "On the Presentation and Interpretation," 118; Main, "Maximilian's Second-Hand Funeral Motet," 179–83. The translation given by Lowinsky is: "On the rivers of Babylon there we sat and wept. On the poplars [*sic*] we hung our instruments. Our harp play turned to mourning and our organ play to dirges. The voice of music turned to lamentation. The sound of flutes, the voice of minstrels, the sound of your harps, shall not be heard any longer, for on the poplars we hung our instruments."

to combine diverse sonic and textual elements to create something beautiful and evocative, bringing together the old and the new.

NOTABLE HYMNS/WORKS

Aside from his cycle of hymns for the church year, among Festa's liturgical music composed for the worship of the Cappella Sistina are masses and mass movements, a cycle of *Magnificat* settings, and a set of Lamentations. His *Te Deum* with its antiphon was in use "as late as 1616" in the papal chapel on a regular basis.[43] His *Magnificat* cycle is significant in that it sets all verses polyphonically, on all 8 tones—another example, along with the hymns, of Festa's characteristic thoroughness, ingenuity, and love of creative variety. His secular music, especially his work as an early madrigalist, is highly noteworthy. An instrumental work, variations on the *bassedanse La Spagna*,[44] a monumental work of 125 *contrapunti* over a ground (repeating) bass melody, reveal another instance of Festa's genius for seemingly infinite creativity, "melodic invention and contrapuntal elegance,"[45] and deft handling of techniques such as canon, imitative counterpoint, and motivic development around a *cantus firmus*.

BIBLIOGRAPHY

Agee, Richard J. "Costanzo Festa's *Gradus Ad Parnassum*." *Early Music History* 15 (1996) 1–58.

———. "Filippo Strozzi and the Early Madrigal." *Journal of the American Musicological Society* 38.2 (1985) 227–37.

Anderson, Rick. "Sound Recording Reviews." *Notes* 60.4 (2004) 1013–17.

Brauner, Mitchell P. "Costanzo Festa's *Inviolata,integra et casta es Maria*: a Double Homage Motet." In *Critica Musica: Essays in Honour of Paul Brainard*, edited by John Knowles, 57–64. Amsterdam: Gordon and Breach, 1996.

———. "The Parvus Manuscripts: A Study of Vatican Polyphony, ca. 1535 to 1580." PhD diss., Brandeis University, 1982.

———. "Traditions in the Repertory of the Papal Choir in the Fifteenth and Sixteenth Centuries." In *Papal Music and Musicians in Late Medieval and Renaissance Rome*, edited by Richard Sherr, 167–74. Oxford: Oxford University Press, 1998.

Britt, Matthew, O.S.B. *The Hymns of the Breviary and Missal*. New York: Benziger Brothers, 1922.

43. Reynolds, "Rome," 87.

44. It was likely used to teach counterpoint. Agee, "Costanzo Festa's *Gradus Ad Parnassum*."

45. Anderson, "Sound Recording Reviews," 1013.

Ciliberti, Galliano. "Una nuova fonte per lo studio degli inni di Costanzo Festa e Giovanni Pierluigi da Palestrina." *Revue belge de Musicologie / Belgisch Tijdschrift voor Muziekwetenschap* 46 (1992) 145–62.

Crawford, David. "A Review of Costanzo Festa's Biography." *Journal of the American Musicological Society* 28.1 (1975) 102–11.

Dean, Jeffrey J. "The Repertory of the Capella Giulia in the 1560s." *Journal of the American Musicological Society* 41.3 (1988) 465–90.

Einstein, Alfred. *The Italian Madrigal.* Translated by Alexander H. Krappe et al. Princeton: Princeton University Press, 1949.

Festa, Costanzo. *Opera Omnia.* 8 vols. Edited by Alexander Main and Albert Seay. Corpus mensurabilis musicae 25. N.p.: American Institute of Musicology, 1962–79.

———. *Hymni per totum annum.* Transcribed and edited by Glen Haydon. *Monumenta polyphoniae Italicae,* Vol. III. Chapel Hill: University of North Carolina Press, 1958.

Fenlon, Iain, and James Haar. "A New Source for the Early Madrigal." *Journal of the American Musicological Society* 33.1 (1980) 164–80.

Haar, James. "Festa, Costanzo." *Grove Music Online; Oxford Music Online.* Oxford University Press. http://www.oxfordmusiconline.com

———. "The 'Libro Primo' of Costanzo Festa."*Acta Musicologica* 52.2 (1980) 147–55.

Haydon, Glen. "The Hymns of Costanzo Festa: A Style Study." *Journal of American Musicological Society* 12.2/3 (1959) 105–17.

Jeppesen, Knud. "Costanzo Festa." In *Die Musik in Geichichte und Gegenwart,* IV, col. 90.

Lowinsky, Edward E. "The Medici Codex: A Document of Music, Art, and Politics in the Renaissance." *Annales musicologiques* 5 (1957 [publ. 1960]) 61–178.

———. "On the Presentation and Interpretation of Evidence: Another Review of Costanzo Festa's Biography." *Journal of the American Musicological Society* 30.1 (1977) 106–28.

———, ed. *The Medici Codex of 1518; A Choirbook of Motets Dedicated to Lorenzo Medici, Duke of Urbino.* Chicago: University of Chicago Press, 1968.

Main, Alexander M. "Costanzo Festa, the Masses and Motets." PhD diss., New York University, 1960.

———. "Maximilian's Second-Hand Funeral Motet." *The Musical Quarterly* 48.2 (1962) 173–89.

"Men of Progress in Former Times: Costanzo Festa." *The Musical World* 47.33 (1869) 572–73.

O'Connell, Robert J. *Art and the Christian Intelligence in St. Augustine.* Massachusetts: Harvard University Press, 1978.

Pietschmann, Klaus. "A Motet by Costanzo Festa for the Coronation of Charles V." *Journal of Musicological Research* 21 (Taylor and Francis, 2002) 319–54.

Reynolds, Christopher. "Rome: A City of Rich Contrast." In *The Renaissance: From the 1470s to the End of the 16th Century,* edited by Iain Fenlon, 63–101. London: Macmillan, 1989.

Rifkin, Joshua. "The Creation of the Medici Codex." *Journal of the American Musicological Society* 62.3 (2009) 517–70.

Ritter, Frederic Louis. *The History of Music from the Christian Era to the Present Time.* Boston: Oliver Ditson & Co., 1883.

Shephard, Tim. "Constructing Identities in a Music Manuscript: The Medici Codex as a Gift." *Renaissance Quarterly* 63:1 (2010) 84–127.

Ward, Tom R., and John Caldwell. "Polyphonic Latin Hymns." In Warren Anderson, et al., "Hymn." *Grove Music Online. Oxford Music Online.* Oxford University. http://www.oxfordmusiconline.com.

———. "Polyphonic Hymns to 1600." *The Canterbury Dictionary of Hymnology.* Canterbury. http://www.hymnology.co.uk/p/polyphonic-hymns-to-1600.

Chapter 2

Martin Luther

Raising Up the Reformation Song

Scott A. Moore

HISTORICAL BACKGROUND

Arguably the single most recognized figure of the Protestant Reformation, Martin Luther contributed much to the shaping of this movement, which altered the face of the Western Church. Luther's life and context prepared him to become a great product of what the church at the beginning of the sixteenth century had become. It also, however, primed him, with his heartfelt conviction of the faith and his way with words, to be aptly suited to rise up as a leader, amidst the fray of the political and ecclesial tensions abounding in the Holy Roman Empire at the time. Throughout his entire adult life, Luther used these skills tirelessly to build up the faith of Christians. The written legacy of his preaching and teaching has fueled the tradition that bears his name for the past 500 years.

On November 10, 1483, in Eisleben, Germany, Hans and Margarete Luder welcomed their son into the world. On November 11, the feast day of St. Martin of Tours, from whom he got his name—as was the practice of the day, Hans took his one-day-old child, accompanied by a number of friends and soon-to-be Godparents, and walked a couple hundred feet up the street to St. Peter's church for him to receive the sacrament of holy baptism. This day was an ever-important one in the mind of Martin the future theologian, as the reality of his having been baptized gave him comfort and strength in the years to follow. The Luder family moved soon thereafter to nearby Mansfeld, and it was there that Martin entered school at the age of seven. While Martin indicated that he came from humble beginnings, Hans Luder was already proving himself to be an industrious and success-oriented man. Hans was a miner and subsequently a mining prospector, which meant he took a financial risk to set up a copper mining location including processing the ore on site. This mindset to rise up the social ladder was certainly a part of Hans Luder's desire to see young Martin receive the best education possible. After about six years in Mansfeld with a typically classical grammar school education of the time in Latin and comprised of classes in writing, rhetoric, and critical thinking, it was decided that Martin should move on. He was first sent to the cathedral school in the city of Magdeburg and one year later on to Eisenach, which is where his mother was from and where he had relatives, in order to prepare for university studies in a school led by Franciscans. His time in Eisenach was not only a continuation of his classical education, but it was there that Luther received education in music and poetry where he learned to play the lute and was exposed to other instruments, as well. In addition to that, he supported himself as many young pupils of his day did as a *Kurrende-Sänger* (trans. walking singer). Pupils would walk around in little groups from door to door singing for money or food or drink. This educational experience laid some of the essential groundwork for the hymn writer of later years.

In 1501, Martin began his studies in Erfurt, which were comprised of a classical education in the "free arts" taught in Latin including grammar, rhetoric, logic, and mathematics, arithmetic, music, and astronomy. The thoughts of great authors like Aristotle and Virgil were key inspirations in his education, and the University of Erfurt was known in that day as a more modern university. During this time, while recovering from a near fatal accident caused by his own knife, he used the opportunity to spend more time with his music by playing the lute. Martin completed this foundational degree of *Magister Artium* in 1505 and now had the prerequisites in hand in order to study one of the three main university disciplines of medicine, theology, or law. It was decided by Hans Luder that Martin would study the law, a choice that increased his chances to move upward in society and a definite investment in the Luder family's future security. Much to his parents' chagrin, however, Martin had other plans. In July of 1505, he was summoned home to Mansfeld to talk over his future prospects of studying or being given into marriage and on his return journey found himself in the middle of a terrible thunderstorm near the town of Stotternheim, the likes of which drove him to promise to St. Anne, "help me, St. Anne, and I will become a monk." The terrifying experience of one storm provided enough momentum for Martin to break away from the other storm of his life and his situation with his parents and retreat to the sanctuary of monastic life. Leaving his friends behind at the gate, Martin entered the monastery on July 16, 1505, first as a guest and then after some months of a trial period, for good. The Augustinian hermits, a strict reform branch of the Augustinians, were now his family. The next phase of his formation had begun.

Martin's new life in the Augustinian Monastery in Erfurt, not far from where he had spent the last four years as a student, was regimented and arduous. Hard work in the monastery, begging for alms in the city, time for study, and naturally seven prayer offices a day left little time for sleep. During his time early on, Martin was granted use of a Bible and encouraged to read it, which he did thoroughly from cover to cover, apparently committing much to memory. He took his life as a monk extremely seriously and strived his best to be the best monk he could be. Martin's own retrospection much later in life casts doubt on what a positive experience this time was for him. He was diligent and industrious. Martin found spiritual respite within the walls of the monastery, the work and prayer life, and the Bible. Martin learned the benefits of structure from the practice of the tradition and the joys of freedom gained in his growing faith in Christ as he discovered through his deep and long excursions in the Holy Scriptures. In 1507, Martin was consecrated a priest in a private ceremony in St. Kilian's chapel connected to the cathedral of Erfurt and a month later celebrated his first mass on May 2. This was a very public affair that was marked by anxiety and relief. Martin was terrified of mishandling something so holy and significant and required the physical support of the prior to see things through. Martin's father was there with a large party to witness the event and even donated money for the celebrations. It was a turning point in their relationship. Martin showed his father and God that he could do this and do this well.

Life continued for Martin among the Augustinian hermits. His status as a priest and his scholarly abilities opened up avenues for him to teach Bible and theology both in Erfurt and then in Wittenberg, where Martin moved in 1508 for further studies and to fulfill his assignment to teach at the newly established university there. In 1511–12, he was sent to Rome for a meeting on behalf of the Augustinian order. While in Rome, Martin saw the greatness of the Renaissance and the depravity of an institution that had, in many ways, become quite corrupt. He was saddened by the terrible state of the structure of St. Peter's in Rome. An assembly line practice of the faith including the rampant sale of indulgences along with other unsavory practices was in direct contrast to the rich history and tradition of the faith that he saw all around him. This experience was grist for the mill of Martin's future theological convictions and fuel for the fire of his desire to reform a church he dearly loved.

Upon returning to Wittenberg, Martin Luder's career continued to soar. In 1512, he took over Staupitz's professorship and was given many other responsibilities by him within the order, as well. It is fitting to note within the context of this volume that Martin's early lectures concentrated on Psalms, the song book of the Bible. Martin knew them intimately, since as a monk, if one prays all seven offices each day in a week, one will have sung through all 150 psalms, some of them more than once. Studying these "hymns" of the faith in Latin, Greek, Hebrew, and of course German, Martin continued to hone his sensibilities of a sung living faith as he found it in ancient Scripture. During this time, Martin also continued to develop his theology influenced by the church father, after which his order was named, St. Augustine. Augustine, the German mystical theology of Johannes Tauler, and the influence and interpretations of Staupitz all guided Martin's development. The years leading up to 1517 and beyond show a constantly developing thought that continued more and more to lift up the notion of the comfort to be found in faith in a forgiving, self-sacrificing Jesus Christ. This became more and more foundational to his theological filter: the good news of freedom found through faith in Christ. The year 1517 is generally seen as a marker for the beginning of the Protestant Reformation. This moment of "posting" the 95 Theses on the practice of the sale of indulgences has taken on mythical proportions.[1] The reality of a reforming movement is much more multifaceted, covers a longer period of time, and is comprised of many various steps along the way. In 1517, Martin Luder also decided to adopt the common practice among academics and adapt his name to Greek or Latin. Being the wordsmith that he was and playing off of his last name, Martin chose *elutherios/elutherius* (meaning the liberated one). That only held for a while and Martin decided to drop the pretense of a full Greek/Latin name but held on to the 'th' from *elutherios*. The young Professor Luther, along with his colleagues on the Wittenberg faculty, continued to teach, preach, and write. With the help of the advent of the printing industry, the teachings coming out of this young upstart university in Wittenberg, championed by the young Augustinian friar/priest, were gaining traction, and in some corners of Europe even notoriety. The tension, however, between Martin

1. For a thorough treatment of the discussion of the veracity of the posting the 95 Theses see, Leppin and Wengert, "Sources for and Against."

Luther and Rome over the sale of indulgences and over Luther's general critique of the scholastic theology of the day increased exponentially, and the situation eventually came to a head in June 1520. At this point, Rome had had enough with Luther, and Pope Leo X issued the papal bull *Exsurge Domine* (trans. Arise, O Lord), which gave him sixty days to recant the listed citations of his work or else be excommunicated. Luther's response was to publicly burn this letter from the pope, sealing his opposition to a blind acceptance of the authority of the church.

Amidst growing pressure, Elector Frederick the Wise, Luther's constant protector from above, was able to stave off a final decision by convincing the Emperor Charles V to wait until hearing out the case at the Imperial Diet of Worms in April of 1521. It was here that Luther made his final stand and refused in good conscience, unless otherwise convinced by Scripture or reason, to recant his writings. This left the emperor with no choice but to declare Luther's life forfeit and issue an imperial ban. Luther went into protective exile to the Wartburg Castle in Eisenach. During this time, he stayed in contact with Wittenberg primarily through letters, and translated the New Testament into German. After hearing that his colleague Andreas Bodenstein von Karlstadt was leading Wittenberg to a more radical reformation including iconoclasm in the churches in his absence, Luther decided to return to Wittenberg to take up the mantle of a teaching leader of the Reformation based in Wittenberg. Beginning with his famous Invocavit sermons of March 1522, Luther set out on a path of moderate reform. At this same time, other more radical voices in Germany, like that of Thomas Müntzer, were gaining popularity for their moves to make worship more relevant. Müntzer's attempts at translating the mass and many Gregorian chorales into German were met with initial success. Luther was forced to take on the central task of becoming a practical theologian—that is, a theologian who attended to the "practical" pastoral concerns, including worship. Now was the chance for Luther's musical and poetic education to find an expression.

THEOLOGICAL PERSPECTIVES

Luther had been honing his biblical, academic theology for years. Luther's own rediscovery of God's free grace in the person of Jesus Christ and his life, death, and resurrection shaped his theology and filled his writings. The prospects of causing a positive reforming effect as a part of the Roman church, however, were dwindling rapidly. The pope had excommunicated him, he had "excommunicated" the pope in response; the emperor had banned him, and now Luther was left to forge the way constructively and not just critically. His own colleague, Karlstadt, had left his scars on Wittenberg and Luther was now called upon to be a practical theologian with the task of providing a new reforming voice for the worshiping church. In response to the extreme actions of Karlstadt and others, Luther offered his understandings of how to engage in liturgical reform in the first half of 1523 with the pamphlet *Concerning an Order of Public Worship*.[2] Orderly reform was now beginning to take shape. Little did Luther know at that point what was soon in store. The reformer's own poetic voice was called into service just months after things started to settle in Wittenberg, and the first cry from this voice was a tribute to the first martyrs of the cause. On July 1, 1523, two monastic brothers from Luther's Augustinian order from the cloister in Antwerp were burned at the stake on the market square in Brussels for their treasonous heresy of confessing Luther's teachings. In Luther's mind, this should have been him rather than two of his adherents. "The personal and emotional shock and the desire to use the [tragic] events for Reformation propaganda"[3] led Luther to respond by picking up his pen and setting it to paper. It was popular at the time to write inspirational tributes in the forms of ballad for interesting figures seen as heroes or for saints and martyrs. This was certainly the case for Luther's very first foray as a hymn writer, *Ein neues Lied heben wir an* (Flung to the heedless winds).[4]

Ein neues Lied heben wir an is a ballad-battle cry for two martyrs of the church. Perhaps he was even experiencing some guilt over the fact that others were dying for this cause he led while he was safe and protected in Wittenberg. In a letter "to the Christians in the Netherlands" that accompanied the publication of this first hymn, Luther's sense of "survivor's guilt" can be discerned: "We up here in Germany have not yet been sufficiently deserving to become so precious and worthy an offering to Christ, though many of our members have not been, and still are not, without persecution."[5] Guilt or no guilt, the attribution of worthiness was Luther's way of shifting the meaning of their death from heretic to that of martyr. Tertullian's second century saying, "the blood of the martyrs is the seed of the church," was taken up

2. Luther, *Luther's Works*, 53:7–9.

3. Jenny, *Luther, Zwingli, Calvin*, 15.

4. Because hymns in translation often create confusion, this brief introduction will refer to Luther's hymns in their original German followed, at first mention, by one of the translated titles used in English-language hymnals in parentheses. For a thorough chart to aid in identifying the location of English translations of German hymns see Robin A. Leaver's recent work on congregational singing in Wittenberg in Luther's time. Leaver, *Whole Church Sings*, 173–77.

5. Luther, *Letters of Spiritual Counsel*, 193.

by Luther in the form of song. Their memory and their story of faith would be printed, disseminated, and sung throughout Germany among those no longer interested in the oppression of Roman Catholic doctrine and rule. Luther wrote hundreds of thousands of words and preached thousands of sermons in Wittenberg alone. All of this theology and expression of the Christian faith, while certainly effective, now had a new conduit. And the opportunity to turn passive hearers into active singing theologians was not lost on the theology professor and priest-preacher from Wittenberg. Luther turned his energies to the task of empowering the faithful with words and music they themselves could sing.

By the end of the year, Luther turned his attention back toward addressing positively what changes could and should be undertaken regarding the Latin mass. This led to the publication of *An Order of Mass and Communion for the Church at Wittenberg* in 1523.[6] In this guidebook of sorts, Luther made various suggestions of what to keep and what could be done away with in the liturgy. Toward the end of this writing, Luther also made known his thoughts concerning congregational singing:

> I also wish that we had as many songs as possible in the vernacular which the people could sing during mass, immediately after the gradual and also after the Sanctus and Agnus Dei. For who doubts that originally all the people sang these which now only the choir sings or responds to while the bishop is consecrating? The bishops may have these [congregational] hymns sung either after the Latin chants, or use the Latin on one[Sun] day and the vernacular on the next, until the time comes that the whole mass is sung in the vernacular. But poets are wanting among us, or not yet known, who could compose evangelical and spiritual songs, as Paul calls them [Col. 3:16], worth to be used in the church of God. . . . I mention this to encourage any German poets to compose evangelical hymns for us.[7]

In a letter to George Spalatin, at the end of 1523, we read how Luther asks for help in this task and we are given a glimpse of Luther's vision of how to write texts for congregational singing:

> I would like you to avoid any new words or the language used at court. In order to be understood by the people, only the simplest and most common words should be used for singing; at the same time, however, they should be pure and apt; and further, the sense should be as clear and as close as possible to the psalm.

6. Luther, *Luther's Works*, 53:10–21.

7. Luther, *Luther's Works*, 53:19.

> You need a free hand here: maintain the sense, but don't cling to the words; [rather] translate them with other appropriate words.[8]

The name of this theory or method of translation is known today as *dynamic equivalence*, and it was a guiding principle of Luther's that led him throughout his translations of the Old and New Testaments to find ways to bring passages of Scripture to life using imaginative and inventive language, which ended up codifying and in some cases even creating what has become modern German. He employed this skill in his hymn writing, as well. And he desired it of all those that he could win for the task of creating a sing-able faith for the people of God.

There were other German poets, but Luther's desire to provide the faithful with words and music for their voice of faith encouraged him to continue and he began composing hymns based on the psalms as some of his earliest work. He knew the psalms well and regarded them highly. What better place to continue his new mission than with these gems from Hebrew Scriptures. Around the beginning of 1524, Luther wrote rhyming translations of identical meter of four psalms: Ps 12, *Ach Gott, vom Himmel sieh darein* (O Lord, look down from heaven behold); Ps 14, *Es spricht der unweisen Mund wohl* (The mouth of fools doth God confess); Ps 124, *War Gott nicht mit uns diese Zeit* (If God had not been on our side); and Ps 130, *Aus tiefer Not schrei ich zu dir* (Out of the depths I cry to you). The standard meter used by Luther in these four hymns, sometimes referred to as a *Lutherstrophe*, allowed for flexibility of marrying accompanying tunes to the various texts as needed. These were set to a number of suitable tunes, and already in early collections there is a tradition of certain melodies being assigned to certain texts. The last of these four, *Aus tiefer Not schrei ich zu dir*, with its remarkable melody in the Phyrigian mode ascribed to Luther himself, is certainly one of Luther's better known and often musically cited melodies. In addition to these four psalm hymns, Luther also wrote metrical versions of the following psalms: 128, *Wohl dem, der in Gottesfurcht steht* (Happy the man who feareth God); 67, *Es woll uns Gott genädig sein* (May God bestow on us his grace); and 46, *Ein' feste Burg ist unser Gott* (A mighty fortress is our God). The last one listed has become, in many respects, the banner hymn of the Reformation, Lutheran and beyond. Just as the faithful throughout time have called upon God to protect them from whatever evil abounds, this hymn of Luther's gives praise to God's protection and names Jesus Christ as the hero, who comes to set us free from sin and the powers of the devil.

8. Luther, *Luther's Works*, 49:69.

The year 1524 saw the advent of the first hymnals among "Lutheran"[9] circles. The very first "Lutheran" hymnal, the *Achtliederbuch* (Book of Eight Songs), was published in Nürnberg, a significant city of the Reformation and Reformation printing. Four of the eight hymns were from Luther's hand, three of them from the aforementioned collection: *Ach Gott, vom Himmel sieh darein*, *Es spricht der unweisen Mund wohl*, and *Aus tiefer Not schrei ich zu dir*. Luther added *Nun freut euch, lieben Christen g'mein* (Dear Christians, one and all rejoice) to this collection. In 1524, in the city of Luther's alma mater and first cloister home, Erfurt, the immense need for new hymns in German was met by two different publishers in the form of the *Erfurt Enchiridion*[10] containing twenty-five hymns in one version, twenty-six in the other, with eighteen of them being from Martin Luther. This hymnbook was reprinted many times and serves as a fundamental source of many later hymnbooks throughout the centuries. The third "Lutheran" hymnbook was the collection titled *Eyn geystlich Gesangk Buchleyn* (Spiritual Hymn Booklet), published in Wittenberg also in 1524. This hymnal contains thirty-seven polyphonic chorales arranged by Johann Walter, thirty-two of the hymns are German, the other five being in Latin, and twenty-four of the collection are from Martin Luther. With this hymnal being the first overseen by Luther himself, we see his underlying practical, theological premise for this endeavor. He writes in the foreword, "That it is good and God pleasing to sing hymns is, I think, known to every Christian; for everyone is aware not only of the example of the prophets and kings in the Old Testament who praised God with song and sound, with poetry and psaltery, but also of the common and ancient custom of the Christian church to sing psalms."[11] Following St. Paul's example in his letter to early Christian congregations, he argues that the church should "sing spiritual songs and psalms heartily unto

9. "Lutheran" is in quotes to denote those who were in the tradition following Luther and the Wittenberg theologians, the term Lutheran was coined by Johann Eck in the Leipzig Disputation of 1519 as a derogatory name to denote those who follow the heretical teachings of Luther. Luther did not like that name but preferred *evangelisch* (evangelical). By the end of the sixteenth century, Lutherans were using the name to positively denote themselves as the true church.

10. Broderson, *Erfurt Enchiridion*, 1. The translation of the original title page is certainly telling of the intent of such works, "An Enchiridion or little handbook, for a present-day Christian very useful to have with himself/herself for a continuous practice and contemplation of spiritual hymns and psalms 1524." Below it a reference to an index and then the following, "With these and similar hymns you shall justly educate the young youth."

11. Luther, *Luther's Works*, 53:315.

the Lord so that God's word and Christian teaching might be instilled and implanted in many ways."[12] Furthermore, Luther informs the reader that,

> these songs were arranged in four parts to give the young—who should at any rate be trained in music and other fine arts—something to wean them away from love ballads and carnal songs and to teach them something of value in their place. . . . Nor am I of the opinion that the gospel should destroy and blight all the arts, as some of the pseudo-religious claim. But I would like to see all the arts, especially music, used in the service of Him who gave and made them.[13]

Not only do we get a sense of what Luther hoped to achieve with the words of hymns filling the mouths and the ears of the faithful, we also see Luther's love of music in service to God's word and theology clearly stated.[14] It is worth noting that scholarship on the Reformation movement has oscillated between two poles: a mythic sensationalism of Luther and all that was supposedly accomplished by him alone and the extreme degree of his reforms and the extreme downplaying of what was accomplished with accusations of Luther being merely responsive and quite conservative. The historical reality lies somewhere between. The same is true in the field of Luther's liturgical reforms.[15]

By 1525–26, the situation had progressed to the point where Luther was ready to take on the task of creating a mass in the German language. At this point there were already quite a number of versions, but Luther was determined to add his mark. Luther set out to create a template guided by the freedom of the Gospel, not a legalistic form to be followed exactly to the letter for all time.[16] Luther composed some new melodies with German

12. Luther, *Luther's Works*, 53:315.

13. Luther, *Luther's Works*, 53:316.

14. Luther's appreciation of music can also be seen in his poem in *Frau Musica* (Dame Music), in his *Vorrede auff alle gute Gesangb*ücher (Preface for All Good Hymnals), in Luther, *Luther's Works*, 53:318–19. See also, Preface to George Rhau's Symphonia iuncundae, in *Luther's Works*, 53:319–21. And for introductory and in depth scholarship on Luther and his relationship to music, see: Hough, "Martin Luther and Musically Expressed Theology," 27–49; Leaver, *Luther's Liturgical Music*, 65–106 and 173–90; and Antilla, *Luther's Theology of Music*.

15. For a balanced and scholarly glimpse into the field of Luther and his liturgical reforms, see both works by Leaver, *Luther's Liturgical Music* and *The Whole Church Sings*.

16. Leaver, *Luther's Liturgical Music*, 292–304. A thorough analysis and support of Luther's theological motives present in his creation of the *Deutsche Messe* of 1526. Evangelical freedom and faith in Christ are foundational to understanding Luther's input.

texts for various liturgical elements to be sung. There are four locations for the congregation to sing with suggested options, and by this point there was already a growing repertoire of possible psalms and hymns. The exception is Luther's very free, metrical rendition of the creed, *Wir glauben all an einen Gott* (We all believe in one true God). Luther's text can be seen as a catechetical summation and interpretation of both the Nicene and Apostles' creeds. Luther's decision to ritually separate the blessing of the bread with distribution followed by the blessing of the wine with distribution is what allows for two places for hymns with a "Sanctus-like" character, like Luther's own setting of Isa 6, *Jesaja, dem Propheten, das geschah* (Isaiah in a vision did of old). Options amidst traditional, familiar, yet at times new, liturgical movements is the underlying premise to the *Deutsche Messe*. It was created to be more inspirational than dictatorial.

Whether it is the God who creates and provides, Christ who saves us in his loving act of sacrifice on the cross, or the movement of the Holy Spirit in our lives, Luther's hymns were and are sung lessons in understanding the mysteries of the faith. If one knows his *Wir glauben all an einen Gott* (1524) and then reads his later expositions on the Creed in both his *Large* and *Small Catechisms*, one will see glimpses of the same Luther. In 1524, he also wrote *Dies sind der heilgen zehn Gebot*, (These are the holy Ten Commands) as an exposition of divine law. *Aus tiefer Not schrei ich zu dir* (1523/24) is Luther's understanding of Confession, and *Jesus Christus unser Heiland, der von uns* (Jesus Christ, our Savior, who turned [away God's wrath] from us—1524) is Luther's German adaptation of *Jesus Christus nostra solus* (Jesus Christ our Savior), attributed to John Hus, and an exposition of the real presence of Christ in the bread and wine of the Sacrament of Holy Communion. After he wrote his catechisms in 1529, Luther the teacher, for both clergy and the laity, set out to complement what he had already written in the first two years as a hymnist. This led to him later write two more hymns for the remaining sections of his catechisms: the Lord's Prayer *Vater unser im Himmelreich* (Our Father God in heaven above—1539) and Holy Baptism *Christ unser Herr zum Jordan kam* (To Jordan came the Christ, our Lord—1541/43), thereby creating a catechism one could sing and embody. Luther's hymn writing became a powerful tool for him to distill and disseminate the truths of God's word and provide a means to teach the growing evangelical (in the sense of Gospel oriented) understanding of the Christian faith in a way that was dear to him—through singing.

CONTRIBUTION TO LITURGY AND WORSHIP

Luther emphasized holding in tension those aspects of the liturgical tradition he inherited with innovation that was gospel centered. Luther significantly influenced the trajectory of the place of congregational strophic hymn singing that moved beyond the Gregorian chant. Texts beyond paraphrases of psalms, unlike the early Reformed tradition of Calvin and Zwingli, were created and took root in the minds and hearts of the faithful.

The liturgy is not created in a vacuum but neither is it bound by a sense of legalism. This is one of his lasting and strongest legacies. Luther's liturgical reforms and his thrust of congregational hymn singing had a fertilizing effect on the hymnody of his contemporaries. As Andrew Pettegree notes,

> although other ministerial colleagues would eagerly take up the charge, these original compositions of Luther always had a special status in the movement. . . . Luther's hymns were the stimulus for a vast outpouring of composition and publication that utterly defined his movement. In the course of the century, Germany's printers turned out over one thousand editions of the Germany hymnal.[17]

It is also important to note the lasting influence Luther's hymns had on significant composers of Western music. Heinrich Schütz, Johann Sebastian Bach,[18] Felix Mendelssohn, Johannes Brahms, and Max Reger all embraced the Lutheran chorale tradition and made it their own, with more or less attention to Luther's actual contributions. Through Luther's deep love of music and singing and his extreme proficiency of the word, he was able to offer a contribution of texts and in some cases melodies that have stood the test of the last five centuries.

NOTABLE HYMNS

Aside from what has already been mentioned, the following notable hymns have also contributed significantly to the worshiping faith and, in some cases, Western music.

Mit Fried und Freud ich fahr dahin (In peace and joy I now depart) is Luther's paraphrase of the *Nunc dimittis* (Luke 2:29–32). Considering Luther's appreciation of Mary, it is interesting to note that he seemed not to have written a metrical hymn version of the *Magnificat* (Luke 1:46–55). He

17. Pettegree, *Brand Luther*, 322.

18. See, Marshall, *Luther, Bach, and the Early Reformation Chorale*. Here is also an interesting explanation on Luther's use of the church modes.

assigned, instead, the *Tonus peregrinus* to the *Magnificat* for singing in worship. *Herr Gott dich loben wir* (Lord God we praise you) is Luther's rimed translation of the great hymn the *Te Deum* indicated to be sung antiphonally, whether this was two choirs or soloist and congregation with support by the choir or members of the choir.[19] This text along with his translation of the *Litanei* are both translations to be sung to plainchant and are not in a strophic form.

Erhalt uns Herr bei deinem Wort (Lord, keep us steadfast in your word) is noted as a song for children and could be among the catechetical hymns. It lifts up the desire to have God give us the strength against all adversities. A part of the original text is quite direct, however, as it encourages the demise of the enemies of the faith being the "Turk"—Muslims from the Ottoman Empire and the Pope.

The final five hymns all serve to emphasize major festivals of the church year. *Nun komm, der Heilden Heiland* (Savior of the nations, come) is Luther's hymn for Advent based on *Veni redemptor genitum. Vom Himmel hoch, da komm ich her* (From heaven above to earth I come), which is Luther's only contrafactum—reusing a secular tune *Ich kumm aus frembden Landen her* (I come from foreign lands) for a religious text. It was written as a children's hymn for Christmas Eve. Christmas Day was marked by *Gelobet seist du, Jesu Christ* (All praise to you, eternal Lord) is based on the sequence hymn for Christmas Eve midnight *Grates nunc omnes. Christ lag in Todesbanden* (Christ Jesus lay in death's strong bands) is Luther's Easter hymn inspired by *Victimae paschale laudes.* Luther had already codified a version of the already extant *Christ ist erstanden* (Christ is arisen) also from the same Latin sequence hymn. And finally, *Nun bitten wir den Heiligen Geist* (Now to the Holy Spirit let us pray) is Luther's hymn for Pentecost based on the sequence hymn *Veni Sancte Spiritus.*

BIBLIOGRAPHY

Anttila, Miikka E. *Luther's Theology of Music: Spiritual Beauty and Pleasure.* Berlin: De Gruyter, 2017.

Broderson, Christiane, and Kai Brodersen, eds. *The Erfurt Enchiridion: A Hymn Book of 1524.* Speyer: Kartoffeldruck-Verlag, 2008.

Hough, Adam. "Martin Luther and Musically Expressed Theology." *Illumine: Journal of the Centre for Studies in Religion and Society Graduate Students Association* 11:1 (2012) 27–49.

Jenny, Markus. *Luther, Zwingli, Calvin in ihren Liedern.* Zürich: Theologischer Verlag Zürich, 1983.

19. Luther, *Luther's Works*, 53:4–96.

Leaver, Robin A. *Luther's Liturgical Music: Principles and Implications*. Grand Rapids: Eerdmans, 2007.

———. *The Whole Church Sings: Congregational Singing in Luther's Wittenberg*. Grand Rapids: Eerdmans, 2017.

Leppin, Volker, and Timothy Wengert. "Sources for and Against the Posting of the Ninty-five Theses." *Lutheran Quarterly* 29 (2015) 373–98.

Luther, Martin. *Luther's Works*. Vol. 49, *Letters, II*. Edited by Gottfried G. Krodel, Gottfried G. Minneapolis: Fortress, 1972.

———. *Luther's Works*. Vol. 53, *Liturgy and Hymns*. Edited by Ulrich S. Leupold. Minneapolis: Fortress, 1965.

———. *Martin Luther: Letters of Spiritual Counsel*. Edited by Theodore G. Tappert. Louisville: Westminster John Knox, 2006.

Marshall, Robert L. *Luther, Bach, and the Early Reformation Chorale*. Atlanta: Pitts Theology Library, 1995.

Pettegree, Andrew. *Brand Luther: 1517, Printing and the Making of the Reformation*. New York: Penguin, 2015.

Chapter 3

Early Lutheran Hymnody (1550–1650)

Benjamin Kolodziej

HISTORICAL BACKGROUND

Although Martin Luther's death in 1546 would not leave the newly reformed church without theological direction, the church would have to forge an identity apart from the personality of the reformer, a particularly acute concern with politics ever threatening to distract the German populace from their newly reclaimed spirituality. The Schmalkaldic Wars (1546–47) would continue as both literal and metaphorical skirmishes between Catholics and Protestants until the Peace of Augsburg (1555) would firmly establish *Cuius regio, eius religio* ("whose region, his religion") as a legal principle in the Holy Roman Empire, permitting the local sovereign to determine the religion of his territory. The Counter Reformation, initiated by the Council of Trent (1545–63), consolidated the doctrinal positions of the Roman Catholic Church on the one hand, while initiating some reforms on the other, presenting a challenge to Protestants who might have found their identity only in contradistinction to Rome. To prevent geographic isolation from leading to the theological disunity that already had become manifest in oscillating "bodies of doctrine" (*corpora doctrinæ*) among the different Lutheran principalities, the "Formula of Concord" (1577) and then the *Book of Concord* (1580) were promulgated as precise doctrinal confessions of the Lutheran Church. In the realm of hymnody and liturgy, Luther still provided the exemplar for subsequent hymnic and liturgical contributions, even as these trajectories would increasingly branch in other directions. In his collection of sermons from 1569, colorfully and obsequiously entitled *Cithara Lutheri*, or "Luther's Harp," Cyriacus Spangenberg avers:

> Since the time of the Apostles, among all mastersingers [Meistersingers] Luther has been the best and the most ingenious one; in his texts and tunes one does not find any unnecessary word. Everything flows and moves in a most lovely and smooth fashion full of spirit and doctrine; each word is a sermon of its own and reproduces its own reminiscence. There is nothing which is forced, articifical, patched together and spoiled. The rhythms are light and good, the words are polished and selective, the idea is clear and comprehensible, the melodies and tunes are lovely and full of heart; to sum it up everything is magnificent and precious, full of juice and vigor.[1]

Sydney Moore claims that German writers composed 20,000 hymns by the end of the sixteenth century; whether this particular metric is accurate or not, Lutheranism certainly experienced a flourishing of new hymnody in the decades after the first *Gesangbücher*[2] were published in the 1520s.[3]

The earliest generation of hymnwriters following Luther included Nikolaus Herman (1500–1561), a church musician and teacher in Joachimsthal in Bohemia, who published in 1561 *Die Sonntags-evangelia über das Jahr in Gesänge verfasset für die Kinder und christlichen Hausväter* (*The Sunday Gospels through the Church Year Set to Singing for Children and Christian Fathers*), containing numerous hymns of his own as well as Luther's, all set to their original, unison melodies, and arranged according to the liturgical year, or more specifically, the lectionary. Herman, whose hymns include "Lobt Gott, Ihr Christen, Allzugleich" (Let All Together Praise Our God) and "Erschienen ist der Herrliche Tag" (Arisen is the Holy Day) writes in his preface of the great value of vernacular hymn singing for children, exhorting fathers in particular to teach the hymns to their children domestically, "particularly on festival days, which provide seemly opportunities to sing these hymns at home."[4] This hymnal's title perhaps speaks best to

1. Translated by Riedel, *Lutheran Chorale*, 38.
2. A "Gesangbuch" is the German term for hymnal, literally "Singing Book."
3. Moore, *Sursum Corda*, 21.
4. Herman, *Die Sonntags-evangelia über das Jahr in Gesänge verfasset für die Kinder und christlichen Hausväter*, 12. "Auch hab ich hiermit Christlichen Hausvetern, welche am Feiertag mit iren Kindern geistliche Lieder daheim zu singen pflegen, wollen zu

its intended use; although liturgical, corporate singing would have become normative by the mid-fifteenth century, there was still a strong tradition of domestic singing, hearkening back to the earliest applications of Luther's own hymns.

Paul Eber (1511–69) graduated from the University of Wittenberg in 1536 and next to Luther, was "the most notable writer of the Wittenberg poets. His hymns exhibit a meaningfully tender, childlike simplicity."[5] His seventeen attributed hymns include "Helft mir Gottes Güte preisen" (Help Me Praise God's Goodness) and "Wenn wir in höchsten Nöthen sein" (When in the Hour of Utmost Need). These chorales, as Lutheran congregational, unison, vernacular hymns were known, were intended as sung catechesis. Nicolaus Selnecker (1530–92) arranged his *Christliche Psalmen, Lieder und Kirchengesang* of 1586 in three parts: the first section is devoted to psalm paraphrases, the second section aims to teach the catechism through hymns, and the third provides hymns for the liturgical year.[6] Selnecker, both an organist and a minister, and known for his chorale "Ach bleib bei uns, Herr Jesu Christ" (Lord Jesus Christ, with Us Abide) included both German and Latin psalms, hymns, and chants. Luther's reverence for the scholarly and liturgical benefits offered by the use of Latin continued in this generation of hymnwriters, although the new material was largely vernacular.

Complex polyphony would develop, exemplified in Georg Rhau's (1488–1548) *Newe Deudsche Geistliche Gesenge* (1544), a collection of motets based mostly on chorales, but also including some Latin hymn arrangements, representing several dozen composers.[7] The congregational chorale, although monophonic and a cappella, inspired the polyphony that flourished in the choral stanzas, evidencing a high level of often fauxbourdon composition in the tradition of Josquin or Senfl, both of whom Luther himself had admired. But the intersection between Lutheran theological development and historically Roman liturgical performance practice would soon conflict, a result of the obscuring of the text which often resulted from imitating the intricate polyphony of the Netherlands school, of which the Lutheran composers were fond. Lukas Osiander the Elder (1534–1604), a musician and clergyman who had assisted framing the Fomula of Concord, published *Fünfzig Geistliche Lieder und Psalmen* in 1586, a volume in which the chorales are set to four-part harmony and the *cantus firmus* is moved

gefallen werden."

5. Koch, *Geschichte des Kirchenlieds und Kirchengesangs der christlichen*, 2:277. "Eber ist nächste Luther der bedeutendste unter den Wittenberger Dichtern. . . . In seinen Liedern giebt sich ein sinniges und zartes kindliches Gemüth kund."

6. Selnecker, *Christliche Psalmen, Lieder, und Kirchengesenge.*

7. *Newe deudsche geistliche Gesenge für die gemeinen Schulen.*

from the usual tenor to the soprano. Osiander realized the import of this monumental change and defends the practice in its preface:

> I understand well that composers have usually placed the chorale melody in the tenor. When one does this, however, the chorale melody is unrecognizable beneath the other voices: because of this, the average person does not understand which song it is and therefore can not sing. Therefore I have taken the melody to the soprano ["discant"] wherein it is clearly recognizable and everyone can sing.[8]

This is not to suggest a sudden countenancing of four-part congregational singing, as this particular volume was published in multiple part-books, clearly intended for a choir's use. Yet, its creation was motivated by a concern for the communal singing which had continued to develop since the early decades in Wittenberg.

This proliferation of congregational singing and the increase in the number of chorales necessitated an evolution of performance practice that gave instruments a more pronounced role in musical execution. Luther himself spoke little about the organ, and when he did, it was fairly negative, no doubt partially a function of the organ's primitive state at the time.[9] Yet, an account of the organ's use at the Pfarrkirche in Wittenberg in 1536 mentions the Ordinary sung by the choir, and that the organ also played at various times, most notably at the Introit, Kyrie, and Gloria, which were rendered in alternation with the choir, and that two hymns sung by the choir were preceded by an intonation.[10] By the end of the century, the faculty of the University of Wittenberg had virtually sanctioned the use of the organ liturgically. The *Notwendige Antwort* of 1597 asserts:

> What other than the organ can be implied by divine Scripture as a means to praise and honor God with instruments and harp. As the Holy Ghost instructs, particularly in Psalm 105, "Praise Him with trombones, praise Him with psalms and harps, praise

8. Osiander, *Fünfftzig Geistliche Lieder und Psalmen*, Vorrede to the "Discantus." "Ich weiss wol dass die componisten sonsten gewönlich den Choral im Tenor füren. Wann man aber das thut, so ist der Choral unter andern Stimmen unkenntlich: Dann der gemein Mann verstehet nicht was es für ein Psalm ist: und kan nicht mit singen. Darumb hab ich den Choral in den Discant genommen damit er ja kenntlich und ein jeder Leye [?] mit singen könne."

9. Koriath, *Music for the Church*, 158.

10. Kolde, *Analecta Lutherana*, 216ff. The account comes from Reformed representative Wolfgang Musculus during his attendance at the Wittenberg Concord.

> Him with drums and cymbals. . ." Our churches keep the use of the organ and singing, carefully used in the service.[11]

Unlike the Swiss reformers, Lutheran reformers were reluctant to jettison any more Roman Catholic liturgical tradition than was necessary. Johann Spangenberg's (1484–1550) *Cantiones ecclesiasticae latinae* (1545) contains monophonic chants arranged liturgically, in Latin, and in neumatic notation.[12] Luther himself, in his preface to Johann Walter's *Chorgesangbuch* of 1524, outlines an *Alternatimpraxis*, which mirrors medieval antecedents. Robin Leaver summarizes this early practice:

> The strategy of Luther and Walter was that the chorale melodies should first be learnt by the boys in the school. When they had mastered these melodies, they would then learn the part-settings in Walter's *Chorgesangbuch.* When these had been mastered, the school choir was then ready to lead the congregation in church. Here an alternation was practiced. After an improvised organ prelude on the melody, ending on the leading-note, the choir led the congregation in singing the chorale in unaccompanied unison. The second stanza was then sung by the choir alone, perhaps with instruments doubling the voice parts, in one of the *cantus firmus* settings of the chorale melody, with the congregational melody in the tenor voice-part. The third stanza would follow with choir and congregation singing in unaccompanied unison. Then would come a choral settings—and so on until the end of the hymn.[13]

Nonetheless, even with the advent of four-part chorales, "in the days of the Reformation the organ was rarely thought of in connection with hymn singing by the congregation; it was identified rather with the presentation of polyphonic music by the choir."[14] Organ composition, then, would continue to flourish in a similar genre as it had for the past century; namely, in the alternation of organ intonations with sung iterations of the melody. Pre-Reformation or otherwise Roman Catholic composers such as Arnolt Schlick, Konrad Paumann, and Paul Hofhaimer would provide a compo-

11. *Notwendige Antwort*, 208–10. "Von Orgeln." "Was sonst die Orgeln sind wir aus geistlicher Schrifft gewiss das man Gott auch mit Instrumenent und Seitenspiel lobet und preiset. Wie uns der Heilige Geist lehret sonderlich im 105. Psalmen: Lobet ihn mit Posaunen, lobet ihm mit Psalter und Harffen, Lobet ihn mit Paucken und Reigen. . . . Neben dem kan man in unser Kirchen wol alle zeit verschaffen das mit dem Orgeln und singen mas gehalten und gnugsame zeit an den Gottesdienst selbst gewendet werde."

12. Spangenberg, *Cantiones ecclesiasticae latinae,* 1545.

13. Leaver, *Luther's Liturgical Music,* 135.

14. Koriath, *Music for the Church,* 157.

sitional basis for Lutheran composers Hans Kotter and Elias Ammerbach, among others.

From the most important composer in the Lutheran tradition between Johann Walther and J. S. Bach, Michael Praetorius's (1571–1621) multi-volume *Musae Sioniae* (1605–10) contains over 1,200 musical settings of the chorale repertoire. Praetorius, whose minister father had been a student of Luther in Wittenberg and a colleague of Walter in Torgau, composed settings of chorales which ranged from simple cantional arrangements to complex polychoral motets utilizing multiple ensembles to original compositions, including "Es ist ein Ros' Entsprungen," which he set in 1599 to an existing Marian text. His later compositions, including a collection entitled *Polyhymnia* (1619–21), would synthesize Italian influences into the Germanic chorale form, all "while pursuing a concern for the preservation of the chorale and for providing a large repertoire of music for the Latin Mass . . . simultaneously embrac[ing] the gradual use of the newer musical devices and style of his day."[15] He would eventually write a musicological treatise (*Syntagma musicum*) and a description of the musical instruments of the turn of the century in *De organographia*. Friedrich Blume calls Praetorius "the most vigorous representative of Lutheran orthodoxy in the whole history of church music."[16] Praetorius's musical treatment of each stanza in a multi-stanza chorale demonstrates the sonoric potential inherent within the *alternatim* style, and would presage the baroque settings of Schütz, Buxtehude, and Bach.

The original tunes of the chorale repertoire were frequently sprightly and dance-like, reflecting the changing meters of Renaissances dance and art music. Luther and his successors often composed utilizing the Ionian or hypoionian modes (the latter which was recognized as a legitimate mode by Swiss theorist Glareanus a year after Luther's death), reflecting contemporary use of this major mode by the Italian and French composers.[17] Cyriacus Spangenberg had reason to brand Luther a Meistersinger, and his compositional successors would continue to bear that mantle intentionally, indirectly extending that medieval musician's guild well beyond its Germanic confines. In the Meistersinger tradition, the composer of a tune and a text were generally the same person—a musical generalist rather than specialist. A certain element of the Meistersinger's art was honing the ability to compose a text to a pre-existing tune, a skill not infrequently employed by

15. Schalk, *Key Words in Church Music*, 122; "Michael Praetorius," *The Canterbury Dictionary of Hymnology*, https://hymnology.hymnsam.co.uk/m/michael-praetorius.

16. Blum, *Protestant Church Music*, 159.

17. Riedel, *Lutheran Chorale*, 49–50.

the early Lutheran hymnists. Bartholomäus Ringwaldt (1532–99), author of over two hundred hymns including "Es ist Gewisslich an der Zeit" (The Day is Surely Drawing Near)[18] and Ludwig Helmbold (1532–98), writer of the chorale, "Von Gott will ich nicht lassen" (From God will I Not Depart) not only both hailed from Mühlhausen, but likewise were considered skilled musicians, although their training was for the ministry.[19] The Meistersingers had fostered the development of the simple Bar form, championing songs with an AAB (*Stollen, Stollen, Abgesang*) musical schema. The Bar form predominates in Luther's hymnic corpus, just as it does in the work of his followers.

Hans Sachs (1494–1576), arguably the most famous Meistersinger even had he not become the subject of Richard Wagner's later opera, certainly influenced the development of chorale tunes.[20] Their tunes and poetic texts, each invented according to prescriptions set forth in a *Tabulatur,* were often reworked, adapted, or borrowed for subsequent tunes.[21] Sach's "Silberweise" ("Silver Tone") bears similarities to several Lutheran chorales.[22]

18. Koch, *Geschichte des Kirchenlieds und Kirchengesangs der christlichen*, 181ff.

19. Koch, *Geschichte des Kirchenlieds und Kirchengesangs der christlichen*, 234ff.

20. Ameln, "Die 'Silberweise' von Hans Sachs," 132–37. Ameln posits a contrary opinion as to whether Luther consciously borrowed this tune.

21. Christiansen, "Implications of the Meistersinger Tabulatur."

22. "Lieder Archiv," https://www.lieder-archiv.de/lieder/solo1/300763.png.

Figure 3.1: Music Sheet of *Silberweise*

Distributed around 1513, there are certainly similarities between this melody and "Ein Feste Burg," (A Mighty Fortress) both melodically and rhythmically, particularly in the ascending motif at the beginning of the second half and the driving, triple meter.[23] If the connection between this unaccompanied tune and Luther's is tenuous, Phillip Nicolai (1556–1608) was less subtle, taking this melody as the basis for what would become the King and Queen of Chorales. In 1599, Nicolai published *Freudenspiegels,* a devotional volume largely dealing with eschatological themes, to which the two chorales "Wachet Auf, Ruft Uns die Stimme" (Wake, Awake! For Night is Flying) and "Wie Schön Leuchtet der Morgenstern" (O Morningstar, How Fair and Bright) are modestly appended. Nicolai's tunes bear more than passing similarity to Sach's "Silberweise," particularly in the *Abgesang* and generally in the final cadences, which gravitate downwards (similar to the final phrases of Luther's "Ein Feste Burg" and "Vom Himmel Hoch" [From Heaven Above]).[24]

23. Riedel, *Lutheran Chorale,* 38.

24. "Lieder Archiv," https://www.lieder-archiv.de/lieder/solo1/211000.png.

Figure 3.2: Music Sheet of King of Chorales: *Wachet Auf!*

The melody to this "King of Chorales" exhibits the text painting characteristic of later sixteenth-century chorales, a straightforward process when composer and text writer were still the same person. Although Nicolai has made few alterations to the *Abgesang* of the Silberweise, he commences the *Stollen* with an ascending triad, reminiscent of tower brass sounding forth the beginning of the day. Nicolai's second hymn, the "Queen of Chorales," bears similar hallmarks:

Figure 3.3: Music Sheet of Queen of Chorales: *Wie schön leuchtet der Morgenstern*

Nicolai's opening motif still outlines a major triad, but the final phrase of the *Stollen* mirrors closely the same phrase in Sachs, while the final cadence is likewise a descending octave, with the descending perfect fourth found in a similar position in Sachs's original. Nicolai's tune, however, is largely in duple time, with only forays into triple meter in the *Stollen* in which he directly quotes Sachs. With both tunes, Nicolai provides only an unharmonized melody.[25]

As noted, Osiander's hymnal of 1586 had begun the process of migrating the *cantus firmus* to the soprano position permanently as he harmonized each melody in four parts. Seth Calvisius (1556–1615), a musician, mathematician, astronomer, and Kantor at Thomaskirche in Leipzig, first published his *Harmonia cantionum ecclesiasticarum* in 1597, a single-volume

25. Nicolai, *Freundenspiegels des ewigen Leben*, 409.

consisting of a few Latin hymns, but mostly of harmonized chorales. Calvisius's treatment of the chorale tunes themselves portends their next stage of musical development: the melodies have begun to shift from highly rhythmic to isorhythmic, in which the duple/triple meters tend to even out. Luther's original "Ein Feste Burg" becomes in Calvisius:

Figure 3.4: Music Sheet of *Ein Feste Burg (A Mighty Fortress)*

He subjects Luther's Phyrigian-mode tune to "Aus Tiefer Noth" to similar treatment, although admittedly this was already a meditative chorale that Luther had conceived in more introspective terms with fewer rhythmic intricacies.

Calvisius's successor to the Kantorship at St. Thomas in Leipzig, Johann Herman Schein (1586–1630), would publish his own *Cantional oder Gesangbuch Augspurgischer Confession* in 1627, not only solidifying the cantional style, but also adding figured bass for the benefit of the "Organist, instrumentalists, or lutenists."[26] In the preface, Schein encourages these chorales to be sung both at home and in church, for although the chorale had found liturgical currency in its first hundred years and had become a fundamental feature of Lutheran worship, hymn writers still sought to preserve its domestic applicability. The late sixteenth-century chorale bore its own character, a character of middle-class German art music set to didactic texts profoundly shaped theologically by Luther himself, largely unencumbered by the unique cultural, political, and theological pressures that would beset Germany by the seventeenth century.

THEOLOGICAL PERSPECTIVES

The first generation of Lutheran hymnists produced a *corpus* of didactic and even polemical chorale repertoire, a pedagogical apparatus to proclaim a renewed theology of Law and Gospel; put more simply, they were sermons

26. Schein, *Cantional oder Gesangbuch Augspurgischer Confession*, "Vorrede."

in song. Yet, the generations following Luther's death dealt with a unique set of concerns:

> Largely because of the theological instability of Philipp Melanchthon, Lutheranism became fearful during the era of the Counterreformation. It was attacked and beleaguered by Roman Catholicism on one side and by crypt-Calvinism on the other. . . there was much trepidation and lack of the sturdy faith of a Martin Luther among Lutheran people and their theologians in the second half of the sixteenth century. Lutherans learned to resort to prayer more than ever before, and the result was that this became a great era of prayer hymns for the church.[27]

These prayer-hymns were further imbued with an eschatological tone, imploring security among the waves of diffidence and anxiety. Bartholomäus Ringwaldt's reworking of the Latin chant *Dies Irae* in his "Es ist Gewisslich an der Zeit," published in his *Handbüchlin: Geistliche Lieder und Gebetlein* (1586), encapsulated the apprehension of the era:

> The day is surely drawing near when Jesus, God's annointed,
> In all His power shall appear as judge whom God appointed.
> Then fright shall banish idle mirth, and flames on flames shall ravage earth as Scripture long has warned us.
> The final trumpet then shall sound and all the earth be shaken, and all who rest beneath the ground shall from their sleep awaken. But all who live will in that hour, by God's almighty, boundless pow'r, be changed at His commanding.[28]

Even given that he is borrowing imagery from the *Dies Irae,* Ringwaldt here employs language more stark and ominous than in Luther's third stanza of "A Mighty Fortress," which deals with the "old, evil foe" who "on earth has no equal." The literal translation is even more direct: Mirth ("Lachen") shall give way to fire ("Wenn alles wird vergehn in Feu'r") of which Peter has so written ("Wie Petrus davon schreibet.")[29]

In his 1581 volume entitled *Evangelia, Auff alle Sontag unnd Fest, Durchs ganze Jahr,* (Gospels for Every Sunday and Festival Through the Year) Ringwaldt had translated this eschatological concern into a prayer: "O Holy Spirit, grant us grace that we our Lord and Savior in faith and fervent love embrace and truly serve Him ever. The hour of death cannot bring

27. Koriath, *Music for the Church,* 243.

28. *Lutheran Service Book,* #508.

29. *Kirchen-Gesangbuch,* #433.

loss when we are sheltered by the cross that canceled our transgressions."[30] Like the earlier generations of hymnists, these texts bore a Christocentricity even when their tone suggested despair, each elucidating the condemnation of the Old Testament law before inevitably articulating the Gospel. Eugene Brand suggests that all sixteenth-century Lutheran liturgical expressions were united in their need to "show their affinity for 'justification by grace through faith,' the synoptic theology of the Lutheran protest."[31] Returning to Ringwaldt's interpretation of the *Dies Irae*, the final stanzas clearly announce this Gospel of justification by faith:

> My Savior paid the debt I owe and for my sin was smitten.
> Within the Book of Life I know my name has now been written.
> I will not doubt, for I am free, and Satan cannot threaten me;
> there is no condemnation!
>
> May Christ our intercessor be and through His blood and merit read from His book that we are free with all who life inherit. Then we shall see Him face to face, with all His saints in that blest place which He has purchased for us.[32]

These hymns suggest a kind of inevitability of strife and stress within life, and that peace and redemption is found only in Christ, and then only after death. Yet, there can be little doubt that Luther and his followers had the same concern, as death was certainly imminent from either plague or pope, certainly a looming reality after 1523 and the execution of Johann Esch and Heinrich Voes for their profession of Lutheran doctrines. What motivated the first generation to compose didactic hymn texts motivated these later writers prayerfully to meditate on eschatology and their own death.

Martin Schalling's (1532–1608) "Herzlich Lieb hab' ich zu dir," published in 1571, represents a developing strand of *Sterbelied*, or songs for the dying, which served to provide evangelical hymns of comfort to supplement (if not replace) the aforementioned *Dies Irae* and other Latin chants that stressed the justice of God and Christ as *Pantokrator*. The text is personal and emotive, set in the first person.

30. *Lutheran Service Book*, #693. See also "Bartholomäus Ringwaldt," *The Canterbury Dictionary of Hymnology*, https://hymnology.hymnsam.co.uk/b/bartholomaeus-ringwaldt.

31. Brand, "Lutheran Worship," 251.

32. *Lutheran Service Book*, #508.

Figure 3.5: Music Sheet[33]

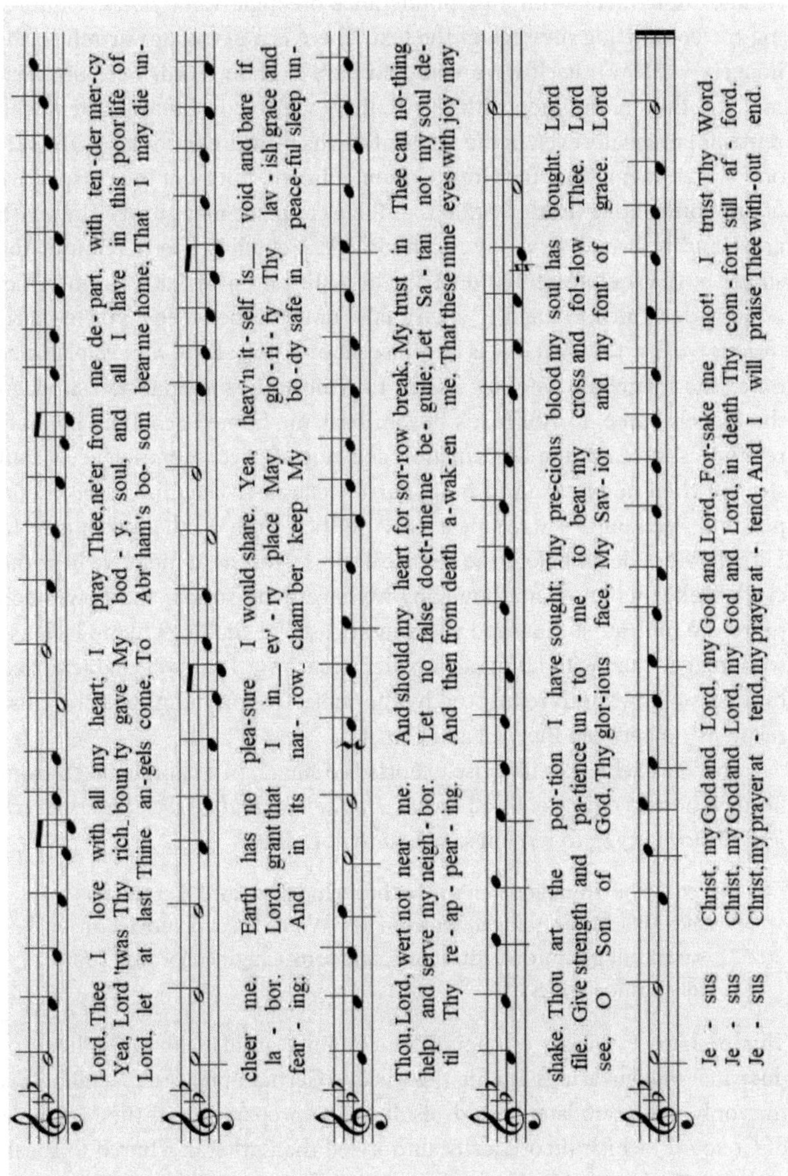

33. This transcription is of personal creation taken from *Lutheran Service Book*, #708, which notes that text and tune are both public domain. Setting is copyright Baerenreiter.

The anonymous, bar-form tune from the 1570s conveys solidity in its steady, duple meter with a preponderance of single-value notes, reinforcing the comforting message of the text. There is a personal warmth in the imagery—"Heav'n itself were void and bare if Thou, Lord, were not near me." It is this communion with Christ, then, which constitutes heaven, who remains personally even in the midst of earth's pleasure or sorrows. The second stanza exemplifies the Great Commandment, but from the perspective of one confronting death: "Grant that I in ev'ry place may glorify Thy lavish grace and help and serve my neighbor." Yet, Schalling subtly reminds the singer of that quintessential doctrine of justification by faith, urging, "Let no false doctrine me beguile," such a false doctrine being any type of meritorious works. The final line is reminiscent of a *Kyrie Eleison* in its plaintive tone. The hymn's eschatology comes to fruition in the final stanza, when the "angels come, to Abr'ham's bosom bear me home." Schalling possibly references the common Reformation doctrine of psychosomnolence ("soul sleep") when he prays, "And in its narrow chamber keep my body safe in peaceful sleep until Thy reappearing. And then from death awaken me." In Luther's view, death before the resurrection is, "Just as at night we hear the clock strike and know not how long we have slept, so too, and how much more, are in death a thousand years soon past."[34] Schalling's hymn is dense with imagery and with Lutheran-imbued preaching, but is yet characterized by a personal warmth reinforced by the subjective pronouns and the close relationship between the soul and Christ.

Nicolas Selnecker likewise exhorts the singer, in a chorale taken from his devotional volume entitled *Passio: Das Leiden und Sterben unsers Herrn Jesu Christi* (1572), to remain steadfast in doctrine:[35]

> Let me be Thine forever, my faithful God and Lord. Let me forsake Thee never nor wander from Thy Word. Lord, do not let me waver, but give me steadfastness, and for such grace forever Thy holy name I'll bless.[36]

This perhaps expresses a longing for certainty amidst the multiplicity of doctrinal maneuverings among the various German princes, machinations that only five years later would result in the preparation of the "Formula of Concord," which theoretically authorized the Lutheran Church to speak with a unified confessional voice.

34. Martin Luther, *Predigten 1533/34*. WA, 37.191.

35. "Nikolaus Selnecker," *The Canterbury Dictionary of Hymnology*, https://hymnology.hymnsam.co.uk/n/nikolaus-selnecker.

36. *Lutheran Service Book*, #698.

Just as doctrinal formulations failed to lessen eschatological fervor, Lutheran orthodoxy would contemporaneously develop a mystical strand, represented in Philipp Nicolai's "Wachet Auf" (1599):

> "Wake, awake, for night is flying," the watchmen on the heights are crying: "Awake, Jerusalem, arise!" Midnight hears the welcome voices and at the thrilling cry rejoices: "Oh, where are ye, ye virgins wise? The Bridegroom comes, awake! Your lamps with gladness take! Alleluia! With bridal care yourselves prepare to meet the bridegroom who is near."[37]

Probably composed during a plague of 1597 during which Nicolai was required daily to encounter death and to communicate pastoral comfort to his people, the text derives from the parable of the foolish and wise virgins found in Matt 25, utilizing marriage imagery. In this case, the soul is the bride and Christ is the bridegroom, reinforcing the theology of the mystical union of Christ and his church. Nicolai introduces both of his hymns (the other being "Wie schön leuchtet der Morgenstern") as "A Spiritual Bridal Song of the Faithful Soul for Christ, its Heavenly Bridegroom."[38] Although eschatological and no less impassioned, these hymns are not in the same character as Schalling's *Sterbelied.* They anticipate the uniting of Christ with his church on the final day, but do so in a corporate sense. Both cases, however, foreshadow Pietism as it develops through the seventeenth century, in which subjectivity and poetic license arguably will take precedence over objective doctrinal proclamation.

CONTRIBUTION TO LITURGY AND WORSHIP

Hymnody during the late sixteenth century owes its existence to the first-generation Lutheran hymnists who had empowered the laity to participate musically in the liturgy. A gradual process through the century, corporate hymn singing developed an important corollary industry. Luther's own writings and translation of the Bible had fortuitously corresponded with the development of the printing press, of which he took full advantage. Publishers soon found that printing *Gesangbücher* (hymnals) could be lucrative, and the relatively inexpensive volumes were easy to procure and to use by clergy and congregants alike. This, of course, induced the composition of more chorales, springing from different regions in Germany and reflecting slightly different theological stances. Much like the applications of

37. *Lutheran Service Book,* #516.

38. Nicolai, *Freudenspiegels,* 409.

twenty-first century social media, this economy of hymnological materials only increased the pace at which development could then occur. Osiander's transferring of the *cantus firmus* from the tenor to the soprano as well as his setting the chorales in a homophonic, four-part, cantional style, heralded the practice of all subsequent hymn-singing, whether or not music was printed with the text in any given instance. If Osiander's observation in his preface is correct, this seemingly "modern" development of moving the tune to the uppermost voice likely did result in healthier congregational participation, if subsequent centuries' practices are any indication. This cantional style subsequently fostered the development of instrumental music in the liturgy; whereas instruments had previously been used to double the choir parts on stanzas of an *alternatim* chorale, they could now begin to "lead" rather than accompany. The unison, monophonic chorale would over two centuries transform into a four-part, congregational hymn, which could be supported ably by an organ, lute, or various consorts of instruments. As the chorale became more accessible to sing corporately, the rugged, dance-like tunes that had been inherited from the medieval Meistersingers began to favor the isometer that would characterize their standard performance well into the twentieth century, before a mid-century liturgical renewal. So successful was this implementation of corporate singing that, as Gracia Grindal claims, "Lutheran piety tends to be located in the sermon and the hymns, not the liturgy."[39]

NOTABLE HYMNS

"Wake, Awake, for Night is Flying" and "O Morningstar, How Fair and Bright" remain the most important chorales of this era, with the church having bestowed on them the appellation of the "King" and "Queen" of chorales, respectively. Their phrases were quoted in literature and in art, and will sometimes appear stenciled on the walls in old homes. Expressing the eschatological concerns of the era are Ringwaldt's "The Day is Surely Drawing Near" and Selnecker's "Lord Jesus Christ, with Us Abide." Nikolaus Herman (1500–1561), one of the musician/pastors from early in the era, is known for his "Let All Together Praise Our God," one of many of his melodies that inspired either cantata stanzas or organ settings. Johann Lindemann (1549–1631) represents the later era in his hymn text "In Thee is Gladness" (1598), which he arranged for an energetic dance-tune borrowed from an Italian madrigal. Conversely, Martin Schalling's plaintive "Lord, Thee I Love with All My Heart" has become the quintessential Lutheran

39. Grindal, "Rhetoric of Martin Luther's Hymns," 184.

funeral hymn. One of the most important collections of hymnody from the time was assembled by Theodoric Petri of Nyland (c. 1560–c. 1630), a Finnish aristocrat educated in Rostock, who in 1582 published *Piae Cantiones*, a collection of Latin hymns modified appropriately for Lutheran theology. Although at the time only on the periphery of the Lutheran chorale tradition, the hymns contained therein enjoyed centuries of popularity and lent themselves often to German chorale texts.[40] Among the many familiar melodies popularized by this collection include "Puer Nobis Nascitur," "In Dulci Jubilo," "Personent Hodie," "Resonet in laudibus," and "Divinum mysterium." That these hymns come from the Latin repertory exhibits that desire, even so late in the century, to locate the Lutheran Church within the *catholic* Church Universal and conservative since Luther's earliest liturgical reforms. The veritable explosion of hymnody during the second half of the fifteenth century, and the particular musical and theological character of that hymnody, would imbue Lutheranism with a uniquely catechetical *corpus* of Christian hymnody.

BIBLIOGRAPHY

Ameln, Konrad. "Die 'Silberweise' von Hans Sachs—Vorlage evangelischer Kirchenlieder?" *Jahrbuch für Liturgik und Hymnologie* 21 (1977).

Blum, Friedrich. *Protestant Church Music*. New York: W. W. Norton, 1974.

Brand, Eugene. "Lutheran Worship." In *A Dictionary of Liturgy and Worship*, edited by J. G. Davies. London: SCM, 1972.

Brown, Christopher Boyd. *Singing the Gospel: Lutheran Hymns and the Success of the Reformation*. Cambridge: Harvard University Press, 2005.

Calvisius, Seth. *Harmonia cantionum ecclesiasticarum*. Leipzig: Jacobi Apel, 1597.

The Canterbury Dictionary of Hymnology. Edited by J. R. Watson and Emma Hornby. Norwich: Canterbury, 2013. https://hymnology.hymnsam.co.uk/.

Christiansen, Heinz. "Implications of the Meistersinger Tabulatur." Master's Thesis, Rice University, 1967.

Grindal, Gracia. "The Rhetoric of Martin Luther's Hymns: Hymnody Then and Now." *Word and World* 26 (2006) 178–87.

Herl, Joseph. *Worship Wars in Early Lutheranism: Choir, Congregation, and Three Centuries of Conflict*. New York: Oxford University Press, 2004.

Herman, Nikolaus. *Die Sonntags-evangelia* über *das Jahr in Gesänge verfasset für die Kinder und christlichen Hausväter*. Edited by Rudolf Wolkan. Vienna: F Tempsky, 1895.

Kirchen-Gesangbuch: für Evangelisch-Lutherische Gemeinden. Ev.-luth. Synode von Missouri, Ohio u. a. Staaten. St. Louis, MO: 1862.

Kolde, Theodore. *Analecta Lutherana: Briefe und Actenstücke zur Geschichte Luthers*. Gotha: Friedrich Andreas Perthes, 1883.

40. "Piae Cantiones," in *The Canterbury Dictionary of Hymnology*, https://hymnology.hymnsam.co.uk/p/piae-cantiones.

Koch, Eduard Emil. *Geschichte des Kirchenlieds und Kirchengesangs der christlichen, insbesondere der deutschen evangelischen Kirche*. Stuttgart: Belser, 1867–68.

Koriath, Kirby, ed. *Music for the Church: The Life and Work of Walter Buszin*. Fort Wayne: Concordia Theological Seminary Press, 2003.

Leaver, Robin. *Luther's Liturgical Music: Principles and Implications*. Grand Rapids: Eerdman's, 2007.

Luther, Martin. *Predigten 1533/34*. American Edition. 55 vols. Edited by Jaroslav Pelikan and Helmut T. Lehman. Philadelphia: Muehlenberg and Fortress, 1955–86.

Lutheran Service Book. St. Louis: Concordia, 2006.

Moore, Sydney Herbert. *Sursum Corda: Being Studies of Some German Hymn Writers*. London: Independent, Ltd, 1956.

Newe deudsche geistliche Gesenge für die gemeinen Schulen. Wittemberg: Georgen Rhau, 1544.

Nicolai, Philipp. *Freundenspiegels des ewigen Leben*. Frankfurt: Johann Spies, 1599.

Notwendige Antwort. Wittenberg: Paul Gräbern, 1597.

Osiander, Andreas. *Fünfftzig Geistliche Lieder und Psalmen*. 4 vols. Nürmberg, 1586.

Riedel, Johannes. *The Lutheran Chorale: Its Basic Traditions*. Minneapolis: Augsburg, 1967.

Schalk, Carl. *Key Words in Church Music: Definition Essays on Concepts, Practices, and Movements of Thought in Church Music*. St. Louis: Concordia, 1978.

Schein, Johann Hermann. *Cantional oder Gesangbuch Augspurgischer Confession*. Leipzig: Timotheo Ritzschon, ed., 1645.

Selnecker, Nicolaus. *Christliche Psalmen, Lieder, und Kirchengesenge, in welchen die christliche Lehre zugefasset u. erkleret wird*. Leipzig: Beyer, 1587.

Spangenberg, Cyracius. *Cantiones ecclesiasticae latinae*. 1545.

———. *Cithara Lutheri*. 1569–71.

Chapter 4

John Calvin and the Complete French Psalter

Corneliu C. Simuț

HISTORICAL BACKGROUND

The influence John (Jean) Calvin (1509–64) had on ecclesiastical worship is inextricably connected with the singing of psalms, which turns out to be a fundamental feature not only of the liturgy but also the life of French Protestants.[1] Having acquired historical fame in the early decades of the sixteenth century, the French Protestants—also known as Huguenots—built their religious experience on the singing of psalms. Later, all the psalms sung by the Huguenots were gathered in special collections of liturgical hymns also known as psalters. The most famous such hymnal was the French psalter which, given the alternate name of French Protestants, went down in history as the Huguenot psalter. Regardless of whether one uses the phrase French psalter or Huguenot psalter, it must be clarified that both titles point to two distinct issues. Thus, the French or Huguenot psalter may first refer to a range of phenomena with ecclesiastical and artistic connotations associated with the singing of psalms by the French Protestants in various social and political contexts, like for instance public marches as

1. Engelhard, "Les traductions en vers du psaume 84 entre 1542 et 1562," 265.

display of communal faith or even as demonstration of personal faith before execution. In this respect, the French psalter does not refer to a specific published work, but to the psalms that were sung by the Huguenots either as they marched in various cities to publicly show their faith and defend it in battle against Catholics or as they were executed by Catholics having been accused of heresy.[2]

From this context, therefore, the earliest historical reference to the French psalter can be associated with the execution of Jean Leclerc in 1524 when this Protestant pastor from Meaux started to sing various verses from Ps 115 as he walked to the place where he was to be burned at the stake. The flame of the pyre took many other French Protestant lives as executions increased in numbers: Wolfgang Schuch met his death in Nancy in 1525, Aymon de la Voye in 1542, a Protestant known only as Nicholas in 1548, Macé Moreau from Troyes in 1550, Pierre Millet in 1550, Étienne Gravot in 1553, Jean Filleul and Julien l'Éveille in 1555, Jean Bertrand in 1556, and Jean Rabée in 1556.[3] Regardless of whether they used melodies invented on the spot like Leclerc or established tunes known to entire Huguenot congregations, they are all reported to have joyfully sung psalms shortly before they were executed. Secondly, the French psalter refers to the sum of the printed editions of various psalters published in France and Switzerland—specifically in Lyon, Strasbourg, Lausanne, and Geneva—even if, in the end, the phrase was gradually associated with the Genevan psalter published in various editions between 1539 and 1562 under Calvin's theological supervision.[4] Interestingly, the Genevan psalter went through a number of editions between 1539 and 1562 and so did Calvin's *Institution de la religion chrétienne* between 1536 and 1559; it is thus fair to say that the French psalter and Calvin's magnus opus were interwoven in a joint theological development.[5]

The most important names that emerge in connection with the French psalter are those of Clément Marot (1496–1544), Louis Bourgeois (1510–61), Claude Goudimel (1505–72), Théodore de Bèze (1519–1605), and Jean Calvin. While Marot was in charge of versification—a task taken over by de Bèze after Marot's departure from Geneva—Bourgeois dealt with the rhythm and melodies followed by Goudimel,[6] while Calvin was responsible for the theology behind the whole psalter, an instrument that proved

2. Brooks, "France, ii: 1560–1600," 177.
3. Douen, *Clément Marot et le psautier Huguenot*, 2–6.
4. Hackett, "Politics and the 'Heauenly Sonnets,'" 363.
5. Gilmont, *John Calvin and the Printed Book*, 257–60; van 't Spijker, *Calvin*, 56.
6. Gangwere, *Music History during the Renaissance Period*, 290.

extremely powerful in the wide range of actions taken by the Huguenots against their Catholic opponents. One of the most frequent such actions was the singing of psalms as protest against Catholic faith and practice, which often took the shape of processions meant to disrupt Catholic church services; events of this particular nature unfolded a number of times in Lyon and increased in frequency after 1560,[7] when the Huguenots not only appropriated unused Catholic churches in Agen and Montauban, but also rioted in the streets of Paris, Rouen, and Beauvais, as well as pillaged churches, attacked processions, destroyed relics, crashed images, and even murdered priests in Montpellier.[8]

Since interrupting Catholic services was not enough, the Huguenots would fight against Catholics whenever they were provoked or even without being incited to violent responses. Daniel Toussain, a Huguenot pastor, is a notorious example in this respect because he forfeited his life alongside a group of French Protestants when they were surrounded by a Catholic army at Montargis in 1569.[9] In the face of death, Toussain and his fellow Huguenots sang Ps 124 as proof that leaving this world was nothing but genuine freedom; the same psalm was used numerous times by the Huguenots in Orléans who were convinced that God deserved all praise for protecting them from Catholics.[10] Protection was indeed what the Huguenots needed since Catholics often accused them not only of being heretics, but also of proselytizing in the language of the common people in spite of the fact that in the midst of the sixteenth century the Jesuits employed the very same tactics as they tried to convince Protestants to join their cause—and in doing so returned to the bosom of the Catholic church.[11] Such a return was not common. The French Protestants and Catholics were at war. While the former continued to take over Catholic monasteries, burn down cathedrals, and tread on the eucharistic host, the latter massacred Protestants whenever they had the chance.[12] In sixteenth century France, Catholics were the religious majority while Protestants were perceived not only as a reactionary minority but also as a hostile population who refrained from everything pertaining to Catholic faith and practice.[13]

7. Carbonnier-Burkhard, "Calvin dans des recueils de prières «nicodémites»?"139–40.

8. Durant and Durant, *Age of Reason Begins*, 340.

9. Nakam, *Au landemain de la Saint-Barthélemy*, 62.

10. Diefendorf, "Huguenot Psalter," 41.

11. van Orden, "Children's Voices," 226.

12. Durant and Durant, *Age of Reason Begins*, 340.

13. Knecht, *French War of Religion, 1559–1598*, 52.

In a time when religious toleration, or any other sort of toleration for that matter, was virtually absent, the Huguenots needed to find a source of spiritual strength and they did so in the psalms. As a constantly persecuted community, they not only focused on the singing of psalms but it was this personal and ecclesiastical practice that allowed them to be convinced that persecutions were trials sent by God in order to test his people, his elect church, as the French Protestants considered themselves. Persecution also offered the Huguenots various opportunities to compare their religious communities to the early church.[14] While persecution was mutual for French Catholics and Protestants, since the latter were a minority the harshness of such punitive measures was more severe for them and the loss of life considerably more terrible in their camp. This historical truth was demonstrated on August 24, 1572, when the so-called Night of Saint Bartholomew claimed thousands of Huguenot lives—commoners, nobles, as well as political and military leaders such as admiral Gaspard de Coligny—in Paris and other major cities. The murderers had been instigated by members of the Catholic nobility and most likely ordered by the king himself, a situation that turned the whole affair into a state crime with war-like connotations.[15]

Despite such horrific events, the singing of psalms helped the Huguenots deal with similar situations of intense and terrible persecution as the psalms were not only sung in personal or communal worship but also quoted, in rather large portions, during the delivery of regular sermons. This explains why the measures taken by Catholics against Protestants in France focused on limiting the freedom of worship and banning the singing of psalms.[16] These actions, however, proved largely ineffective since Huguenot churches continued to grow as new converts fled in the French Protestant camp dominated by the singing, reading, memorization, and proclamation of psalms; for instance, Nicholas Pithou from Troyes is said to have heard Ps 13 in his mind as he suffered from serious illness but he later confessed that he was healed the very same day, which convinced him and his wife to quit France for Geneva in order to study Reformed theology in more detail.[17] This event demonstrates the paramount importance of psalms not only for conversion but also for dedication to ecclesiastical service; in the following years, Pithou returned to Troy and became the spiritual leader of the local Huguenot church.[18]

14. Recaut, "Religious Polemic and Huguenot Self-Perception," 29.

15. Jouanna, *Saint Bartholomew's Day Massacre*, 123.

16. van Ruymbeke, *From New Babylon to Eden*, 13.

17. Benedict, *Rouen during the Wars of Religion*, 141.

18. Diefendorf, "Huguenot Psalter and the Faith of French Protestants," 44–45.

Pithou is famous not only for hearing Ps 13 in his mind, but also for hearing it in de Bèze's translation, although other translations were available, such as that of Louis Budé, a famous Protestant scholar with an exceptional grasp of the Hebrew language. This not only proves the enormous influence of de Bèze's translation—who continued Marot's work—but also shows that psalms had become the very heart of Huguenot piety in the first half of the sixteenth century. The extremely powerful impact of psalm singing was recognized by the Catholic doctors of the University of Sorbonne who issued an interdiction of psalm singing in France,[19] an academic measure with potential ecclesiastical implications that was ignored by both Protestants and Catholics. The situation became inflammatory after 1550, when Bèze's translation became available to the public, alongside the publication of the Genevan psalter in the early 1560s.[20] Nevertheless, years before the publication of the Genevan psalter public confrontations between Protestants and Catholics had been serious enough to convince King Henry II that psalm singing should be forbidden in public, a decision staunchly refused by the Huguenots who remained adamant in their practice to sing psalms in public and private worship.[21]

When placed against the tragic events of the Night of Saint Bartholomew, the French psalter acquires a double function: first, it was a means to invoke God's protection, a message the Huguenot church in Paris heard from Calvin in 1557 and from pastor Pierre Merlin in 1567;[22] and second, in the aftermath of the mass assassinations inflicted upon the Huguenots on August 24, 1572, it became an instrument to strengthen the faith of Huguenot communities not only by assuring them of God's providence, but also by convincing the lapse to return to the Protestant faith. Thus, the French psalter was accompanied by a series of theological tracts meant to support the militant message of Psalms in an attempt to persuade the Huguenots of God's love in spite of persecution so that those who remained in the Protestant camp after the massacres should find comfort while those who joined the Catholics should return to God's elected few. To give just a few examples: Daniel Toussain's *L'exercise de l'âme fidèle* (1582) shows how God preserves his inheritance in spite of severe persecution, while Jean de l'Espine's *Traicté de l'apostasie* (1583) and *Traité consolatoire* (1584) defended not only the idea that the events of the Night of Saint Bartholomew were God's fatherly punishment meant to discipline his elect in France, but also the conviction

19. Arnade, *Beggars, Iconoclasts, and Civil Patriots*, 69.

20. Old, *Worship*, 45.

21. Schmitt, *La Réforme catholique*, 228.

22. Barker, *Protestantism, Poetry, and Protest*, 40n107.

that God extends his infinite love to the lapsed should they rejoin the fellowship of Huguenot churches.[23] The French psalter therefore carries with it the message of God's unfailing love, parental protection, fatherly discipline, as well as divine preservation extracted from the Old Testament through the lens of the New Testament to be delivered to Huguenot churches under Calvin's careful systematic oversight and his astute theological acumen.

THEOLOGICAL PERSPECTIVES

Calvin's theology of worship is dominated by his interest in God and what he has to say to humanity by means of his word; hence, his focus on psalms as part of God's word that must play a central role in Christian worship, including worship through words/psalms and hymns.[24] The text, therefore, is much more important than music because whenever believers worship God they must understand that they stand before God ("devant Dieu/apud Deum") and it is before God that the whole reality of worship should be performed. Before God, however, one cannot stand idle and empty; this is why worship must originate in the believer's innermost depths of the heart lest the benefits of worship be nullified. In Calvin, the heart is not just feelings; it is a human's entire spirituality[25] that must always be connected to the mouth—or with lips and throat—if worship is to go beyond the mere mechanics of vocal physiology into trustworthy spirituality. Worship devoid of sincere spirituality may provoke God's anger against such worshippers who, in not involving the heart in singing, will eventually abuse God's most holy name and thus mock his majestic greatness. Worship, therefore, must permanently be accompanied by the feelings of the heart, by the sincerest spirituality of each believer based on God's words, so the singing of psalms has the capacity to elevate man's heart to God.[26]

When engaged in worship, man's heart becomes a temple, which is an indication that in Calvin's theology the venue of true worship is man's innermost spirituality, although this must be coupled with public and communal worship, as commanded by God.[27] While man's interior temple is the foundation of worship, Calvin points out that such type of worship does

23. Diefendorf, "Huguenot Psalter and the Faith of French Protestants," 47–52.

24. Dominicé, *La Réforme et nous*, 57.

25. Millet, "Influence and Reception," 25.

26. Calvin, *Institution de la religion chrétienne*, 418; Grosse, *Les rituels de la cène*, 166.

27. Leith, *Introduction to the Reformed Tradition*, 152; Calvin, *Institution de la religion chrétienne*, 417–18.

not stand alone. Believers must come together in worship in special public places that Calvin designates as "temples"; it is here that each individual believer must have fellowship with other believers because they are all part of God's people, so the very idea of temple juxtaposes individual and communal worship.[28] In Calvin, believers must join together in praises to God, so there is no excuse for those claiming to practice true worship by isolating themselves in their private rooms in order to avoid praising God together with other believers.[29]

True worship, Calvin points out, must aim at glorifying God through words and songs,[30] and there is no better way to praise God than by using his own words, hence the Huguenot conviction that genuine worship is based on singing God's praises through psalms, an assurance also used by Calvin with a view to spiritual edification.[31] Such worship truly honors God because all believers come together before God in worship sharing the same spirit and the same faith, a vital connection in Calvin's theology.[32] The church must have one voice in everything, worship included, so praising God by reciting or singing psalms is the best way to make sure that the church speaks with the same voice as believers confess their faith and, in so doing, they are both edified and enabled to follow their confession of faith.[33]

Calvin is careful to highlight that psalm singing is no novelty for the church; on the contrary, hymn singing based on psalms is an old ecclesiastical practice going back in history to the time of the apostles. As far as Calvin is concerned, the apostles promoted a worship pattern based on the interweaving of spirit and mind, reason and feelings, as showed by the apostle Paul in 1 Cor 14:15: "[I] will sing with [my] spirit, but [I] will also sing with [my] understanding"—or, in the French translation of the Latin original, "I shall sing with my mouth, but I shall also sing with my intelligence/mind/reason—and in Col 3:16. In the latter text, believers are urged to exhort each other by hymns, psalms, and spiritual songs. In doing so, believers sing to the Lord in their hearts with grace,[34] an attitude which, in Calvin's theology, does not originate in man's heart, but rather in God's being, and it is

28. Gerrish, "Preface," 4.

29. Calvin, *Institution de la religion chrétienne*, 417.

30. Bürki, "Reformed Tradition in Continental Europe," 445.

31. Pak, *Judaizing Calvin*, 78.

32. Milner, *Calvin's Doctrine of the Church*, 162.

33. Calvin, *Institution de la religion chrétienne*, 419; Pidoux, *Le psautier Huguenot du XVIe siècle*, xiii–xiv.

34. Calvin, *Institution de la religion chrétienne*, 419.

dispatched by God to believers when their worship is anchored in God's word, a clear reference to psalms and psalm singing.[35]

True worship, which in Calvin is performed before God and his angels, must also be characterized by earnestness, a key feature meant to bestow elegance and authority upon the church's praises to God because earnestness not only points to the relationship between God and believers,[36] but is also a piece of adornment ("ornament") that embellishes the community of believers as they praise God.[37] Thus, worship—including singing and especially psalm singing—strengthens the believer's heart and in so doing prepares it for prayer which, in turn, fills the believer's heart with increasing spiritual enthusiasm.[38] Such enthusiasm, Calvin warns, must never lose sight of the spiritual meaning of words, notably of psalms as God's words, in favor of music; the text, therefore, is always more important than music.[39]

In Calvin, another key feature of ecclesiastical singing moderation is that it not only provides worship with balance[40] but also enriches it with holiness and healthy spirituality. Church singing must never aim at pleasing the ear because the purpose of worship is never to emphasize the greatness of the church but the greatness of God himself. Music for the sake of music—or singing for man's own pleasure and senses[41]—and not for lifting up praises to God is surely going to displease God profoundly.[42] Consequently, in church music aesthetics must never prevail over spirituality and nor should music do over the meaning of the text which, in Calvin, is God's word from psalms.[43]

When believers pray and sing, they come before God for the edification of the whole church, an indication that, in Calvin, the main function of worship and psalm singing is to fortify believers in their faith.[44] Through worship, however, the church reaches for those who are not believers and do not comprehend what happens in the church when the faithful sing God's praises; hence, worship must be simple for everybody to understand, but in simplicity it must disclose love ("charité/caritatis") and civility ("humanité/

35. Kim, "At Work and Worship," 49.
36. Chapell, *Christ-Centered Worship*, 48.
37. Witte, "Moderate Religious Liberty," 1130.
38. Calvin, *Institution de la religion chrétienne*, 420.
39. Trocmé-Latter, "Psalms as a Mark of Protestantism," 7.
40. Haas, *Concept of Equity in Calvin's Ethics*, 89–90.
41. Rokseth, "Les premiers chants de l'église calviniste," 7.
42. Calvin, *Institution de la religion chrétienne*, 420
43. Eire, *War against the Idols*, 201.
44. Leith, *Introduction to the Reformed Tradition*, 177.

humanitatis") towards non-believers. The simplicity of worship is not meant only to explain the details of songs and prayers, music and preaching, but also to point to the relationship between the believer and Christ.[45] In this respect, worship with prayer, singing, and preaching must be performed in the language of the people so that everybody catches the meaning of what happens. Comprehension is crucial; without it the tongue and lips cannot be connected to the heart and worship—regardless of whether it is public or private—becomes empty while its outcome is far from pleasing God.[46]

In the end, worship must bring man closer to God and in particular the believer to the Lord; it is impossible though to achieve such an endeavor unless the will is moved toward this end. In Calvin, therefore, the heart expresses itself in and through the will to the point that the latter becomes inflamed beyond expression. In other words, the mechanics of worship is only an instrument that serves the purpose of drawing believers closer to God, but what lies beneath the reality of worship is the even deeper reality of the heart, the ardor of the believer's love for God.[47] Calvin's insistence on the role of the heart, or spirituality in worship, originates in his conviction that Catholic worship is heartless,[48] or devoid of spirituality, so whoever wants truly to praise God, then he or she should sing the very words of God. Hence the idea of the psalter, as there are no better words to express one's love for God than those revealed to the church by God himself in Scripture and can be understood by the entire worshipping community of saints irrespective of whether they pour their hearts before God in private or in public.[49]

CONTRIBUTION TO LITURGY AND WORSHIP

The greatest contribution of the French psalter to liturgy and worship is its focus on God's word. Everything in the psalter was meant to point to what God has to say both through the words of the psalms themselves and the words of the sermon delivered by the minister. Having had a humanist education,[50] most of the people involved in the production of the psalter—but notably Marot and de Bèze—were concerned that the word of God be understood by everybody regardless of whether people in the pew were educated or not, as it was the case most of the times. This is why in composing

45. Canlis, *Calvin's Ladder*, 130.
46. Calvin, *Institution de la religion chrétienne*, 420–22.
47. Calvin, *Institution de la religion chrétienne*, 420–22.
48. Trull, "Theise dearest offrings of my heart," 41.
49. Millet, "Influence and Reception," 413.
50. Jinkins, "Theodore Beza," 137.

the versified version of the psalms in French they used simple phrases, loads of parallelisms, as well as textual and melodic symmetry, catchy metaphors and rich imagery—all meant to facilitate the memorization of psalms and implicitly God's word.[51] Becoming easily familiar with the psalms was aided by composing verses that remained faithful to the original text of the French translation of the Bible; this particular aspect imbued the French psalter with a compelling poetic message, easy to follow lyrics, critical teaching exhortations, and evident antithetic images which assisted believers in learning as much as possible of God's word by heart. The simplicity of such liturgical devices turned the memorization of psalms into a vital feature of the Huguenot's Protestant identity of reformed confession.[52] At the same time, the juxtaposition of syllables and musical keys made the psalter not only accessible and easy to understand, but also appealing and fast to assimilate by believers and non-believers alike. Originally monodic but polyphonic in later editions despite Calvin's aversion to polyphonic singing,[53] the French psalter literally transformed Huguenot liturgy into one of the most unvarnished, engaging, and captivating types of Protestant worship, as well as perhaps one that comes the closest to being thoroughly faithful to God's word.

Although different in form, Huguenot public and private worship was one single reality in spirit. Encompassing the whole of life, worship was considered a modus vivendi to the point that psalm singing became a normal feature of the Huguenot's daily existence.[54] Ecclesiastical liturgy and family worship were not different regarding the singing of psalms, a spiritual activity that was the backbone of Huguenot spirituality irrespective of whether French Protestants went to fight in a war or to pray in a church. The French psalter therefore has the huge merit of extending church liturgy into the daily life of the Huguenots while, at the same time, turning the normality of everyday life into divine liturgy. Consequently, the French psalter instilled a rather strict discipline into ecclesiastical and personal dealings, which was evident in the Huguenots' preoccupation to carry their printed psalters to worship and sing together with the rest of the congregation. For the French Protestants, the liturgy was extremely important and participation as well as personal involvement were mandatory. For instance, everybody was required to sing in the church under serious ecclesiastical penalties enforced

51. Linder, "Calvinism and Humanism," 1790.

52. Lebranc, *Les paraphrases françaises des psaumes a la fin de la période baroque, 1610–1660*, 157.

53. Genre, *Le culte chrétien*, 76.

54. Sandberg, *Warrior Pursuits*, 155.

by means of church discipline as confirmed by various Reformed synods like those held in Figeac and La Rochelle. The singing of psalms as worship by means of God's very words become so crucial to Huguenot liturgy that other local synods—notably Montpellier—decided to forbid the singing of only one or two stanzas and enforced the singing of entire psalms with only a few hymns being allowed as part of the liturgy.[55]

One of the most peculiar features of the French psalter that consolidated not only Huguenot ecclesiastical liturgies but also private worship beyond regular church liturgies into French Protestants' homes and their various gatherings—to wage war, to face persecution, or otherwise just to spite Catholics—for their common "cause" was its remarkably compelling capacity to keep people focused on God's word in the church during the various components of the liturgy.[56] It must be emphasized here that sixteenth century church services were not held only on Sundays, but every day through the week with ecclesiastical services aimed at engaging as many people as possible before or after working hours; thus, having people in churches every day despite the non-centralized and anti-hierarchical system of the French Protestants[57] was indeed a considerable achievement. In Geneva, for instance, the first church service of the day started at four or five o'clock in the morning while the second was available at eight. The city cathedral was open every evening for prayer followed by a sermon—based on the Gospels for Sunday sermons and other texts from Scripture for the rest of the week—but what appears to have kept the Huguenots together during these many liturgies was the singing of psalms from the French psalter. This extremely popular work succeeded in coagulating not only the entire Huguenot liturgy—with its prayers, confessions, readings of Scripture, exhortations, communions, sermons, and closing benedictions[58]—but also the hearts, minds, and wills of the vast majority of French Protestants who decided to remain firm in their faith and confession despite the horrible realities of war, persecution, and death.

NOTABLE HYMNS

The most famous Huguenot song is Ps 68, also known as the *Marseillaise* of French Protestants: "Let God arise, let his enemies be scattered," a piece of Scripture often used in battle to spread terror amongst their Catholic

55. Nichols, *Corporate Worship in the Reformed Tradition*, 58–59.

56. McKee, *John Calvin on the Diaconate*, 234–35.

57. Garrioch, *Huguenots of Paris*, 4.

58. Nichols, *Corporate Worship in the Reformed Tradition*, 59.

enemies; this may well have been the case when thousands of Huguenots sang verse 23 ("Bathe your feet in blood, that the tongues of your dogs may have their portion from the foe") as they marched against Catholic armies.[59] Psalm 118, "For the Lord is good, his mercy endures forever," was the source of encouragement for the soldiers of Henri de Navarre,[60] while Ps 124, "If it had not been the Lord who was on our side," was sung by the French Protestants as they seized the city of Bourges.[61] Huguenot martyrs, like those in Meaux and Lyon, used to sing Ps 79, "Let the groans of the prisoners come before thee, according to thy great power preserve those doomed to die!," and Ps 9, "The Lord is a stronghold for the oppressed."[62] Other psalms used by the Huguenots for encouragement in face of various trials or personal disappointment were 119, "How blessed are those upright in their way"; 13, "How long, o, Lord, wilt Thou forget?"; and 130, "Out of the depths of sadness."[63]

BIBLIOGRAPHY

Arnade, Peter J. *Beggars, Iconoclasts, and Civil Patriots: The Political Culture of the Dutch Revolt*. Ithaca, NY: Cornell University Press, 2008.

Barker, Sara K. *Protestantism, Poetry, and Protest: The Vernacular Writings of Antoine de Chandieu, c. 1534–1591*. Farnham, UK: Ashgate, 2009.

Benedict, Philip. *Rouen during the Wars of Religion*. Cambridge: Cambridge University Press, 1981, reprinted in 2003.

Brooks, Jeanice. "France, ii: 1560–1600." In *European Music, 1520–1640*, edited by James Haar, 171–81. Woodbridge, UK: Boydell, 2006.

Bürki, Bruno. "The Reformed Tradition in Continental Europe: Switzerland, France, and Germany." In *The Oxford History of Christian Worship*, edited by Geoffrey Wainwright and Karen Westerfield Tucker, 436–62. Oxford: Oxford University Press, 2006.

Calvin, Jean. *Institution de la religion chrétienne*, livre 3, chapitre 20, tome second, in Guilielmus Baum, Eduardus Cunitz, Eduardus Reuss, éds. *Ioannis Calvini opera quae supersunt omnia*, volumen IV. Brunsvic: C. A. Schwetschke et fils éditeurs, 1866.

Canlis, Julie. *Calvin's Ladder: A Spiritual Theology of Ascent and Ascension*. Grand Rapids, MI: Eerdmans, 2010.

Carbonnier-Burkard, Marianne. "Calvin dans des recueils de prières «nicodémites»?" In *Jean Calvin et la France*, edited by Bernard Cottret and Oliver Millet, 129–52.

59. Lindberg, *European Reformations*, 283.

60. Rice and Huffstutler, *Reformed Worship*, 104.

61. Diefendorf, "Huguenot Psalter and the Faith of French Protestants," 41.

62. Lindberg, *European Reformations*, 284.

63. Hotoran, "Psalmii hughenoți în contextul Reformei Protestante," 394–95.

Genève, Switzerland: Droz et Société de l'Histoire du Protestantisme Français, 2009.

Chapell, Bryan. *Christ-Centered Worship: Letting the Gospel Shape Our Practice*. Grand Rapids, MI: Baker Academic, 2009.

de l'Espine, Jean. *Traicte de l'apostasie fact par M. I. D. L., Ministre de la parole de Dieu en l'Eglise d'Angers*. 1583.

———. *Traitte consolatoire et fort vtile, contre tovtes afflictions qui aduienent ordinairement aux fideles Chrestiens. Composé nouuellement par I. De Spina, Ministre de la Parole de Dieu: et adressé à vn grand Seigneur de France*. A Lyon, 1584.

Diefendorf, Barbara B. "The Huguenot Psalter and the Faith of French Protestants in the Sixteenth Century." In *Culture and Identity in Early Modern Europe, 1500–1800*, edited by Barbara B. Diefendorf and Carla Hesse, 41–64. Ann Arbor, MI: University of Michigan Press, 1993.

Dominicé, Max. *La Réforme et nous*. Genève, Switzerland: Labor et Fides, 1972.

Douen, Orentin. *Clément Marot et le psautier Huguenot: Étude historique, littéraire, musicale et bibliographique contenant les mélodies primitives des psaumes et des spécimens d'harmonie*, tome premier. Paris: L'Imprimerie Nationale, 1878.

Durant, Will, and Ariel Durant. *The Age of Reason Begins: A History of European Civilization in the Period of Shakespeare, Bacon, Montaigne, Rembrandt, Galileo, and Descartes, 1558–1648*. New York: Simon and Schuster, 1961.

Eire, Carlos M. N. *War against the Idols: The Reformation of Worship from Erasmus to Calvin*. Cambridge: Cambridge University Press, 1989, originally published in 1986.

Engelhard, Eliane. "Les traductions en vers du psaume 84 entre 1542 et 1562." In *Les paraphrases bibliques aux XVIe et XVIIe siècles. Actes du Colloque de Bordeaux des 22, 23, et 24 septembrie 2004*, edited by Véronique Ferrer and Anne Mantero, 265–87. Genève, Switzerland: Librairie Droz, 2006.

Gangwere, Blanche. *Music History during the Renaissance Period, 1520–1550: A Documented Chronology*. Westport, CT: Praeger, 2004.

Garrioch, David. *The Huguenots of Paris and the Coming of Religious Freedom, 1685–1789*. Cambridge: Cambridge University Press, 2014.

Genre, Ermanno. *Le culte chrétien. Une perspective Protestante*. Genève, Switzerland: Labor et Fides, 2008, originally published in 2004.

Gerrish, Brian A. "Preface." In *John Calvin: Writings on Pastoral Piety*, edited by Elsie Anne McKee, xiii–xviii. Mahwah, NJ: Paulist, 2001.

Gilmont, Jean-François. *John Calvin and the Printed Book*. Translated by Karin Maag. Kirksville, MO: Truman State University Press, 2005.

Grosse, Christian. *Les rituels de la cène. Le culte eucharistique réformé à Genève, XVIe–XVIIe siècles*. Genève, Switzerland: Droz, 2008.

Haas, Guenther H. *The Concept of Equity in Calvin's Ethics*. Carlisle, PA: Paternoster, 1997.

Hackett, Kimberley J. "Politics and the 'Heauenly Sonnets': George Wither's Religious Verse, 1619–1625." *History* 94.315 (2009) 360–77.

Hotoran, Anamaria M. "Psalmii hughenoţi în contextul Reformei Protestante." In *Psaltirea renascentistă franceză. Versificare în limba română a psalmilor pe melodiile hughenote cu ocazia împlinirii a 450 de ani de la apariţia Psaltirii renascentiste franceze*, edited by Mircea V. Diaconescu, Ştefan Bratosin, and Iacob Coman, 393–96. Bucureşti, Romania: Editura Academiei Române, 2012.

Jinkins, Michael. "Theodore Beza: Continuity and Regression in the Reformed Tradition." In *Evangelical Quarterly* 64.2 (1992) 131–54.

Jouanna, Arlette. *The Saint Bartholomew's Day Massacre: The Mysteries of a Crime of State*. Paris: Gallimard, 2007.

Kim, Julius J. "At Work and Worship in the Theater of God: Calvin the Man and Why I Care." In *With Calvin in the Theater of God: The Glory of Christ and Everyday Life*, edited by John Piper and David Mathis, 31–52. Wheaton, IL: Crossway, 2010.

Knecht, R. J. *The French War of Religion, 1559–1598*. 3rd ed. London: Routledge, 2014.

Lebranc, Paulette. *Les paraphrases françaises des psaumes a la fin de la période baroque, 1610–1660*. Paris: Presses Universitaires de Frances, 1960.

Leith, John H. *An Introduction to the Reformed Tradition*. Atlanta, GA: John Knox, 1977, reprinted in 1981.

Lindberg, Carter. *The European Reformations*. Oxford, UK: Blackwell, 1995.

Linder, Robert D. "Calvinism and Humanism: The First Generation." *Church History* 44.2 (1975) 167–81.

McKee, Elsie A. *John Calvin on the Diaconate and Liturgical Almsgiving*. Genève, Switzerland: Droz, 1984.

Millet, Olivier. "Influence and Reception." Translated by Randi H. Lundell. In *The Calvin Handbook*, edited by Herman J. Selderhuis, 397–428. Grand Rapids, MI: Eerdmans, 2008.

———. "Le Bruit et la Musique dans le Cinquième Livre." In *Études rabelaisiennes. Le Cinquiesme Livre*, tome XL, edited by Franco Giacone, 252–364. Genève, Switzerland: Droz, 2001.

Milner, Benjamin C., Jr. *Calvin's Doctrine of the Church*. Leiden, The Netherlands: Brill, 1970.

Nakam, Géralde. *Au landemain de la Saint-Barthélemy. Guerre civile et famine*. Paris: Anthropos, 1975.

Nichols, James H. *Corporate Worship in the Reformed Tradition*. Eugene, OR: Wipf and Stock, 2014.

Old, Hughes O. *Worship: Reformed according to Scripture*. Rev. and exp. ed. Louisville, KY: Westminster John Knox, 2002.

Pak, G. Sujin. *The Judaizing Calvin: Sixteenth-Century Debates over the Messianic Psalms*. Oxford: Oxford University Press, 2010.

Pidoux, Pierre, ed. *Le psautier Huguenot du XVIe siècle, mélodies et documents recueills par Pierre Pidoux*. Premier volume: Les Mélodies. Bâle: Édition Baerenreiter, 1962.

Recaut, Luc. "Religious Polemic and Huguenot Self-Perception and Identity, 1554–1619." In *Society and Culture in the Huguenot World, 1559–1685*, edited by Raymond A. Mentzer and Andrew Spicer, 29–43. Cambridge: Cambridge University Press, 2002.

Rice, Howard L., and James C. Huffstutler. *Reformed Worship*. Louisville, KY: Geneva, 2001.

Rokseth, Yvonne. "Les premiers chants de l'église calviniste." *Revue de musicologie* 36 (1954) 7–20.

Sandberg, Brian. *Warrior Pursuits: Noble Culture and Civil Conflict in Early Modern Europe*. Baltimore: Johns Hopkins University Press, 2010.

Schmitt, Paul. *La Réforme catholique. Le combat de Maldonat, 1534–1583*. Paris: Beauchesne Éditeur, 1985.

Toussain, Daniel. *L'exercise de l'âme fidèle, assauoir prières et méditations pour se consoler en toutes sortes d'afflictions*. Frankfurt, Germany, 1582.

Trocmé-Latter, Daniel. "The Psalms as a Mark of Protestantism: The Introduction of Liturgical Psalm-Singing in Geneva." *Plainsong and Medieval Music* 20.2 (2011) 145–63.

Trull, Mary. "Theise dearest offrings of my heart": The Sacrifice of Praise in Mary Sidney Herbert, Countess of Pembroke's Psalmes." In *English Women, Religion, and Textual Production, 1500–1625*, edited by Micheline White, 37–58. Farnham, UK: Ashgate, 2011.

van 't Spijker, Willem. *Calvin: A Brief Guide to His Life and Thought*. Translated by Lyle D. Bierma. Louisville, KY: Westminster John Knox, 2009.

van Orden, Kate. "Children's Voices: Singing and Literacy in Sixteenth-Century France." *Early Music History* 25 (2006) 209–56.

van Ruymbeke, Bertrand. *From New Babylon to Eden: The Huguenots and Their Migration to Colonial South Carolina*. Columbia: University of South Carolina Press, 2006.

Witte, John, Jr. "Moderate Religious Liberty in the Theology of John Calvin." In *Religious Liberty in Western Thought*, edited by Noel B. Reynolds and W. Cole Durham, Jr., 83–122. Grand Rapids, MI: Eerdmans, 2003, originally published in 1996.

Chapter 5

English Language Metrical Psalters of the Sixteenth Century

J. Michael Morgan

HISTORICAL BACKGROUND AND THEOLOGICAL PERSPECTIVES

Throughout the history of worship—in the Jewish tradition, in the daily offices of the Roman Catholic Church, and since the beginning of the Reformation—the book of Psalms has been known by many names, including the "hymnbook" of the Bible, the "prayer book" of the Bible, and the "worship book" of the Bible.

One is hard-pressed to think of a more readily accessible way of involving a congregation in verbalizing Scripture than through the singing of a psalm. The prose text may be sung to a harmonic "mantra" as in Anglican chant; performed with a recurring refrain, or antiphon, as a dialogue between cantor and congregation; or paraphrased in verse, as a hymn, and sung to a familiar tune.

Richard Rolle, the fourteenth century English divine, defined the Psalter with lyrical abandon in the preface to his own translation of the book of Psalms:

> Psalm singing chases fiends, excites angels to our help, removes sin, pleases God. It shapes perfection, removes and destroys annoyance and anguish of soul. As a lamp lighting our life, healing of a sick heart, honey to a bitter soul, this book is called a garden enclosed, well sealed, a paradise full of apples![1]

Walter Brueggemann says much the same thing in more contemporary terms:

> The book of Psalms provides the most reliable theological, pastoral, and liturgical resource given us in the biblical tradition. In season and out of season, generation after generation, faithful women and men turn to the psalms as a most helpful resource for conversation with God about things that matter most. The psalms are helpful because they are a genuinely dialogical literature that expresses both sides of the conversation of faith.[2]

Such a conversation between God and the community of faith underscores the fulfillment of the ancient covenant through which we have become the adopted sons and daughters of God—children who honor and claim the goodness and grace of a loving parent. "I am yours, you are mine," God has promised; "I am with you always," and it is through our worship, both in our congregations and in our own hearts, that we keep the conversation alive.

Falling between Rolle and Brueggemann, the seventeenth century Scottish divine David Dickson spoke of the psalms as being a blend of "crosses and sweet comforts," which in a few words is a biography of our lives.[3] At the dawn of the Reformation, one of the requirements of the Protestant churches was that the Bible be translated into the language of the people. It was through the Scriptures in the vernacular that the protests of the new churches were supported, in opposition to the established teachings and real and perceived prejudices of the medieval Roman Catholic Church.[4]

The Mass was also translated from the Latin, first into a close German translation by Luther, then a French version for the congregation in Geneva, and finally into English as represented in the Book of Common Prayer (1549). The other Catholic observances of worship were consolidated and rendered into the vernacular, primarily as Morning and Evening Prayer services, as well as individual prayers for special occasions.

1. Rolle, *Psalter*, 3.
2. Brueggemann, *Message of the Psalms*, 15.
3. Dickson, *Brief Explication* 3.
4. Brown, *Oxford Handbook of the Psalms*, 570.

Music in Worship at the Reformation

Music in worship also went through phenomenal reforms as ownership passed to the people who filled the naves every Sunday morning. Three leaders in the early history of the Protestant movement—Martin Luther in Germany, Ulrich Zwingli in Zurich, and John (Jean) Calvin in Geneva—each recognized the power of music to underscore liturgy, transform theology, and propel congregational worship. Martin Luther was the broadest in his approach to incorporating music into worship. He paraphrased some of the psalms, translated a number of old Latin hymns into German, and wrote some new ones, always seeking to bring a Christian perspective to the Old Testament. Zwingli, on the other hand, understood the power of music to transform, but out of his fear of what it could accomplish, initially banned it from his worship in all forms, from instrumental interludes to congregational song. John Calvin struck a middle ground, and allowed only metrical psalms to be sung in worship. Like Luther, he saw music as one of God's gifts to us, to be returned to God through our congregational singing of the psalms. Calvin had a profound reverence for Scripture which caused him to insist that public praise in church should be confined to the language of the Bible, adapted to the minimum extent required for congregational singing. He believed that the only songs worthy of our returning to God were the songs God gave to us, namely the psalms. He also was quite clear that there should be no other music in the liturgy, and that psalmody should be accompanied neither by choir nor by instruments.

In the first decades of the sixteenth century the Catholic Church was in supreme power, but it rapidly began to take a strong defensive stance against the growing aggression of the Protestant forces. The 1520s through the 1540s saw the decline of royal support for Rome and King Henry's anointing of the Church of England. Young King Edward, through his advisors, left England with a liturgy in the vernacular, and the church situation appeared to be moving ahead, though at a slower pace than during his father's reign.

The first collection of hymns and psalms in English, published between 1539 and 1546 as *The Gude and Godlie Ballates*, was the work of the three Wedderburn brothers—James, John, and Robert—who, from a diversity of talents, answered both of the initial aims of metrical psalmody. One of the brothers, James, produced a number of tragedies and comedies, including a play on the beheading of John the Baptist, and was forced out of the church (and ultimately his homeland) for secularizing the divine. The middle brother, John, became a priest, but fell under suspicion of heresy and fled to Wittenberg in 1539, where he became associated with Luther and Melanchthon. Robert, the youngest of the three, was ordained and subsequently served as vicar of Dundee. It was because of his more stable reputation that their collection of texts became known as the *Dundee Psalter*. The title page for the *Gude and Godlie Ballates* composed by the Wedderburn brothers reads in its entirety: *A Compendious Book of Godly Psalms and Spiritual Songs Collected Further of Sundry Parts of the Scripture, with Diverse Other Ballads, Changed out of Profane Songs into Godly Songs, for Avoiding of Sin and Harlotry.*[5]

Edward's early, though not unexpected, death in 1553 at age fifteen ignited a wildfire of confusion as to who would become the next monarch. His sister Mary seemed to be the natural choice, since she was the elder daughter of Henry VIII, but her uncompromising defense of the Catholic Church cast a shadow over her coronation. His sister Elizabeth was the preferred candidate of the Protestants, but many questioned her legitimacy as the heir to the throne of England, gained only through the divorce of her father in order to marry her mother, Anne Boleyn. Their cousin, Lady Jane Grey, stepped in at the request of King Edward to be crowned as queen, but the Catholic forces succeeded in executing her and establishing Mary as the new ruler.

At Elizabeth's accession, many of the Catholic Church leaders feared that she would attack their congregations with the same aggression that Queen Mary had exercised, and a new seminary was established at Rheims, France, to train priests and missionaries to return to England once the Reformation had passed.

The English Church had become a separate body from that of Rome, through the act of Henry VIII in 1532, which replied to the Pope's censure of Henry's divorce of his first wife by designating the British Sovereign as the "Supreme Head" of the Church of England. The next nearly forty years were spent in constituting that church and fashioning it into what is now known as the Church of England.[6]

Even when the first "official" version of the metrical psalms in English appeared in 1562, published by Sternhold and Hopkins, the following phrase defined the dual purpose for singing the new songs: *Newly Set Forth and Allowed to Be Sung in All Churches, of All the People Together, Before and After Morning and Evening Prayer, as Also Before and After the Sermon,*

5. Lang, *Compendious Book of Psalms.*

6. Routley, *Music of Christian Hymns* 35.

and Moreover in Private Houses for Their Godly Solace and Comfort, Laying Apart All Ungodly Songs and Ballads, Which Tend Only to the Nourishing of Vice, and Corrupting of Youth.[7]

Since the English and Scottish churches were so much involved in establishing who they were in opposition to the Catholic Church in terms of theology and practice, it would not be until 1562 that psalm singing became such a vital part of their existence. The setting of the twenty-third psalm by the Wedderburn brothers was innocent enough, and the Catholic Church probably would have found nothing offensive in having a congregation sing it in worship:

> The Lord God is my Pastor good,
> abundantly me for to feed;
> then how can I be destitute
> of any good thing in my need?

Even if the Roman Catholic clergy were not particularly offended by such religious texts, except for the fact that they were in the language of the people, they could never support the work of poets who, along with their psalms, would turn the impending crisis between Protestants and Papists into such a troublesome ballad as:

> The Pope, that pagan full of pride,
> he hath us blinded long;
> for where the blind the blind doth guide,
> no wonder they go wrong.

Miles Coverdale, a Protestant clergyman and the translator of the first complete English Bible to be published (1535), published his rather small volume entitled *Goostly Psalms and Spiritual Songs* around the same time as the Dundee Psalter. Though considerably shorter than its predecessor (it contained only forty-one texts), Coverdale's work reflects three distinct characteristics: his reliance on Luther for a number of his sources, his stronger disdain for the Roman Catholic Church, and his stronger skills as a translator rather than a poet.

He included translations of several of Luther's hymns and psalms. Luther's *Ich ruf' zu dir, Herr Jesu Christ* becomes "I Call on Thee, Lord Jesu Christ," and the immortal *Ein Feste Burg Ist Unser Gott* (Ps 46) is rendered "Our God Is a Defense and Tower, a Good Armor and Good Weapon." Coverdale's attacks on the Established Church are for the most part his own poetry, and substantially more amusing in the light of the Reformation. Using the image of one of Lucas Cranach's illustrations in Luther's 1545 Bible,

7. Sternhold, *Whole Booke of Psalmes.*

which depicted the Pope as the gaudily clad "whore of Babylon," he invited us to sing:

> Let go the whore of Babylon,
> her kingdom falleth sore;
> her merchants begin to make their moan,
> the Lord be praised therefore.
> Their war is naught, it will not be bought,
> great falsehood in found therein;
> let go the whore of Babylon, the mother of all sin . . .
> Ye hypocrites, what can ye say? Woe be unto you all!
> Ye have beguiled us many a day; heretics ye did us call . . .
> For now we see God's grace freely
> in Christ offered us so fair;
> let go the whore of Babylon, and buy no more her ware.

In 1546, Henry VIII put the *Gude and Godlie Ballates* on the list of prohibited books, and church leaders in both England and Scotland began to look ahead to a much more acceptable version of the psalms, interspersed with appropriate hymns. The Scots did not ban the singing of the Wedderburn psalms and hymns (since they were Scots themselves), and Coverdale's version had never received enough familiarity to merit such a dubious honor.

The "Old Version" of Sternhold (1549–62) and the Scottish Psalter (1564)

The inception of English metrical psalmody, which was the only legal vehicle of public praise until hymns were formally authorized in 1821, was founded by Thomas Sternhold, and the circumstances were curiously parallel to those in which Marot became the first poet of Geneva. Sternhold, Groom of the Royal Wardrobe at the end of Henry VIII's reign and through that of Edward VI, began metricizing psalms for the edification of the young new king who was ten years old when he came to the throne in 1547, and sixteen when he died in 1553.[8]

According to tradition, young King Edward was strolling through the halls at Windsor Castle when he heard organ music and singing coming from the chapel. Stopping by, he learned the source was Sternhold singing some of his own psalm paraphrases; liking very much what he heard, he encouraged Sternhold to write more.

8. Routley, *Music of Christian Hymns*, 35.

The strong Puritan strain in him, which sought to replace the trivial secular music that was the court's normal entertainment with easily sung sacred songs, led him to versify certain psalms to be sung to familiar tunes, and by the time of his death in 1549 Sternhold had completed thirty-seven psalm versions. These psalm settings did not yet find a home in the liturgy, however. Even though the *Book of Common Prayer* was completed in the same year, no effort was made to introduce metrical psalms into the church, not so much due to any strong objection to the principle as to the fact that no complete psalter was yet available.

The entire psalter, *The Whole Booke of Psalmes*, was completed in Geneva in 1562—the same year as the French Genevan Psalter—and was brought back to Britain after the tumultuous reign of Mary Tudor, infamously remembered as "Bloody Mary" for her violent actions against Protestants and their church, which she detested.

Mary was a maniacal Roman Catholic and sought at once to reverse all that had been achieved up to then by the new Protestants. The "Great Bible" of her father, Henry the Eighth, which had been authorized as the first English Bible for reading in public worship, was removed from churches and cathedrals, and the Book of Common Prayer, completed in 1549 and revised in 1552 as the first English liturgy, was forbidden to be used in Anglican congregations. The Latin Mass was reintroduced in a "resurrected" Roman Catholic Church.

During the five years of her reign (1553–58), many English church leaders fled to the continent of Europe, while the rest, if they were in sympathy with the new church, went into retirement or hiding. Many found their way to Geneva, where they found Calvin's church structure fully developed—with which they disagreed—and the 1551 Genevan Psalter in use, which they clearly loved.[9]

When Mary died, her Protestant sister Elizabeth was the only survivor of Henry the Eighth to succeed to the throne. The Protestant refugees who had fled from the wrath of Queen Mary—especially John Hopkins, William Whittingham, William Kethe, and Robert Wisedom—returned and built upon the work of Sternhold, bringing back to England with them a new translation of the Bible, greatly influenced by the French Protestant theologians in Geneva, especially Theodore Beza, and a complete English psalter. The English version was perhaps not as poetically excellent as the French text sung in Geneva, but it was an unmatched gift for the restored Church of England, replete with many tunes composed by Louis Bourgeois originally for Calvin's psalter.

9. Routley, *Music of Christian Hymns*, 36.

The Scots, always wanting to maintain some degree of independence from their English "cousins," were reluctant to authorize an identical psalter. The work on their version was begun while John Knox was minister to the congregation in Geneva, and was completed after he returned to Great Britain to become a "thorn in the flesh" to the newly crowned Queen Elizabeth. The first Scottish psalter, completed in 1564, substituted about a third of its texts from Scottish poets.[10]

As an example of how certain psalm texts differed between the English and Scottish psalters, consider these two settings of Ps 47. The English version was composed by John Hopkins, and the Scottish version by William Kethe. The English text is in the standard "common meter" (8.6.8.6.D), while the Scottish text was written to be sung to a distinctively rhythmic tune—a "Geneva jig"—from the French Genevan psalter.

> The English Version (1562)
> Ye people all in one accord, clap hands and eke[11] rejoice:
> Be glad and sing unto the Lord, with sweet and pleasant voice.
> For high the Lord and dreadful is, with wonders manifold,
> a mighty king he truly is, in all the earth extolled.
>
> The Scottish Version (1564)
> Let all folk with joy clap hands and rejoice,
> and sing unto God with most cheerful voice.
> For high is the Lord and feared to be,
> the earth over all a great king is he
> in daunting the folk, he hath so well wrought,
> that under our feet, whole nations are brought.

While Queen Elizabeth was never overly critical of the texts in the "Old Version," many of the tunes with their unusual rhythms—especially those borrowed from the French Genevan psalter—prompted her to label them as "Geneva jigs," but that did not impede their acceptance and vitality as congregational songs.

Later Psalters of the Sixteenth Century

The "Old Version" preceded the great era of Elizabethan poetry, and the quality of the metrical paraphrases varied significantly from one author to the next. But there could be no argument about the sincerity and dedication of those authors to their cause. The Reformation had brought some degree

10. Brown, *Oxford Handbook of the Psalms*, 573.

11. "eke" = "also"

of denominational independence to the Protestant churches in England, Scotland, and across the European continent, each of which had to compile new liturgies, establish new principles of faith and governance, and determine how best their congregations could be drawn into a full participation in the worship of God. There weren't very many places for them to turn beyond their own integrity and creativity; they were literally part of a "new creation," which needed to be identified and celebrated.

The name Matthew Parker is virtually unknown today, except by staunch Anglican historians. Very few church musicians can identify his connection with congregational song, but his psalter—completed around 1557, though not printed until 1567—left its enduring mark in the psalm-singing tradition. While it was never actually published, the version of the psalms by Parker, who became Queen Elizabeth's Archbishop of Canterbury, must be mentioned here. Its value is not based on its poetic merit, but for the inclusion of tunes by Thomas Tallis. Here, the famous "Canon" appears here for the first time, as well as the "Ordinal" and the "Third Mode Melody" made famous by Ralph Vaughan Williams. Matthew Parker could not have found a more capable "co-conspirator" for his psalter than Thomas Tallis. Parker remained in England during the reign of Mary Tudor, spending his time hiding in the countryside and, among other things, paraphrasing the psalms. As the English and Scottish refugees flocked back to Britain when Elizabeth came to the throne, they brought with them the "Old Version" of Sternhold and Hopkins and the 1564 Scottish psalter. Parker realized that his version could not compete with these two well-established collections and privately printed a few copies of his own psalms to present to friends and colleagues.

Parker was right about the challenging competition of texts among the available psalm versions, for who among the worshipers in the pew would choose to sing, instead of Kethe's immortal text, Parker's version of Ps 100:

> O joy all men terrestrial,
> Rejoice in God celestial,
> I bid not Jews especial,
> But Jews and Greeks in general!

The tunes, however, contributed by Thomas Tallis are worth noting and remembering, even if the poetry was not. Tallis's tunes include eight psalm tunes in four parts (mean, contra-tenor, tenor, and bass) and a ninth tune, known as Tallis's "Ordinal," which sets the text of the old Latin hymn "Veni Creator Spiritus" in four parts as well. The famous Tallis "Canon" is the eighth tune, in which each line of the tune is repeated, and the canon appears between the "mean" and the "tenor." In 1621, Thomas Ravenscroft in his harmonized collection of tunes removed the repeats and reduced the tune from eight to four lines, as we know it today. The "Canon" is paired with Parker's paraphrase of Ps 67.

> God grant with grace, he us embrace,
> in gentle part, bless he our heart;
> with loving face, shine he in place;
> his mercies all on us to fall,
> that we thy way may know all day,
> while we do fail this world so frail;
> Thy health's reward is nigh declared,
> as plain as eye, all Gentiles spy.

As the century of conflict came to an end, the most noteworthy of the scarce attempts to paraphrase the psalms, with no intention of their becoming congregational songs, was begun by Sir Philip Sidney and completed by his sister, Mary Sidney Herbert, in 1599 (though it was not published until 1823). Upon examining Sir Philip's beginning of his paraphrase of the 23rd Psalm it is obvious that his meter was not conceived with a simple tune in mind:

> The Lord, the Lord my shepherd is,
> And so can never I taste misery.
> He rests me in green pasture his:
> By waters still, and sweet
> He guides my feet.

New Musical Settings of the Earlier Texts

Closing out the sixteenth century focuses not on other textual paraphrases of the psalms, but a series of harmonized settings of psalm tunes—William Daman, John Cosyn, Thomas Est, and Richard Allison. It was the tunes, not the texts, that came to the forefront as people were encouraged to learn to sing, and to choose sacred songs over secular ditties. From their respective titles, it is clear these composers and arrangers sought to make the tunes and harmonies accessible for household prayers and domestic recreation.

John Bull's edition of Daman's psalter (1579) asserted that the tunes were "to the use of the godly Christians for recreating themselves, instead of fond and unseemly ballads." Cosyn's title page (1583) stated that he was publishing the tunes "for the private use and comfort of the godly, in place of many other songs neither tending to the praise of God, nor containing anything fit for Christian ears." Est's edition of the "Old Version" of the psalms (1592) proclaimed on the title page that it was "compiled by sundry authors, who have so labored herein, that the unskillful with small practice may attain to sing that part, which is fittest for their voice."[12] Richard Allison brought out his simply harmonized version (1599) "for the use of such as are of mean skill, and whose leisure least serveth to practice."[13] Their primary audience was domestic, and they witnessed to the pleasure as well as the duty that the metrical psalms served for the common people.[14]

CONTRIBUTION TO LITURGY AND WORSHIP

The sixteenth century was an epoch of exploration and discovery, of conflict and resolution, both in political and religious arenas. The Tudors shaped what Great Britain and her expanding colonial realms would be for centuries to come. The conflicts between Roman Catholics and Protestants, which reached their turning point in 1517 with Martin Luther's ninety-five theses, continued through the sixteenth and seventeenth centuries, passing from one faith to the other and back again, depending on which church owned the fidelity of and power over the reigning monarch. Neither sought to emphasize what they shared in common, but instead aggressively promoted the differences.

One of the first innovations in the Reformation movement was to transform members of the congregation from passive observers to active participants in the ritual of praise. For too long, worshipers sat or knelt in silence while cantors chanted the songs and prayers, and choirs of monks, priests, or nuns sang the responses. The dialogue with God in liturgy and song moved closer to being a reality as congregations celebrated the presence of God among them.

Perhaps the most definitive catalyst in achieving Reformation is to be found in two isolated verses from that biblical source that had for millennia exemplified for Jews and Christians alike how we should express who God is and how God should be glorified—the book of Psalms:

12. Est, *Whole Booke of Psalmes.*
13. Allison, *Psalmes of David in Meter.*
14. Quitslund, *Reformation in Rhyme*, 248–49.

> Sing praises to God, sing praises: sing praises unto our King, sing praises.
>
> For God is the King of all the earth: sing ye praises with understanding. (Ps 47:6–7)

The key phrase is "sing with understanding," to offer our praise to God in a language we can speak and read and comprehend for ourselves, in the vernacular of our everyday existence.

Martin Luther's love of music and appreciation for the power that music could lend to worship, especially congregational singing in the language of the people, inspired him to make it an integral part of worship in the German church. In addition to metrical psalms like his own setting of Ps 46, "Ein Feste Burg Ist Unser Gott" ("A Mighty Fortress Is Our God"), he allowed many hymns not based in the psalms, and kept the liturgy close to the order of the Latin Mass.

John Calvin in the French Protestant Church established the singing of psalms as the only musical gifts worthy for a congregation to offer up to God. Hymns were considered inferior songs of human composition, though Calvin permitted and even encouraged the writing of metrical paraphrases, which he believed still carried the same sanction as the prose psalms found in the Bible.

> In England and Scotland the influence of Calvin prevailed over that of Luther and determined among other things the form of church song. The Scottish Church, under John Knox's influence, adopted the Genevan system of metrical psalmody into its constitution. The English Church adopted metrical psalmody just as effectively, but less formally, as something not provided for in the Prayer Book system, but yet "allowed" to adhere to the margin of that system. Practically, both English-speaking churches entered upon an era of psalm singing which was to be little disturbed through two centuries.[15]
>
> As one author has reflected, The musical practices of the Christian Church growing out of the Reformation in all of their contextual complexity and diversity present a fund of such provisional achievements that may substantially challenge, enrich, and renew our on-going constructions of Christian worship.[16]

15. Benson, *English Hymn* 26.
16. Flynn, "Liturgical Music," 788.

NOTABLE HYMNS

William Kethe's setting of Ps 100 from the "Old Version" represents well the transformation necessary to adapt ancient tradition to contemporary experience. It is the only example, text and tune, which has endured 450 years of evolution:

> All people that on earth do dwell
> sing to the Lord with cheerful voice;
> Him serve with fear, his praise forth tell,
> come ye before Him and rejoice!

The phrase "Him serve with fear" originally did not imply terror or anxiety, but awe and wonder. A century later we began to sing "Him serve with mirth," which removed the negative connotation and even better proclaimed the gladness with which the psalmist calls us to serve our God. The last stanza in retrospect acknowledges not the turmoil of the Reformation in the sixteenth century but the lasting faith we have inherited over the centuries through the church. The middle stanzas entreat us to praise the God who cares for us as a shepherd, to recognize him as our creator, and to approach him with joy. The closing stanza begins with the question "Why?" and then moves into what we learned from the Reformation, whether we are Catholic or Protestant:

> For why? The Lord our God is good,
> his mercy is forever sure;
> his truth at all times firmly stood,
> and shall from age to age endure."

William Kethe was a Scottish clergyman who settled initially in Frankfurt, Germany, but moved to Geneva with John Knox and the English and Scottish refugees who settled there in 1557. He contributed twenty-five psalm texts to the Anglo-Genevan Psalter of 1561. Only ten of his paraphrases were reprinted in the final version of the English Psalter in 1562, though all twenty-five were retained in the first Scottish Psalter in 1564.

The tune known to us as "Old Hundredth" was composed by Louis Bourgeois for the French psalter, originally set to Ps 134.

In the sixteenth century Anglican and Scottish traditions it was more the musical settings—tunes, harmonizations, canons, anthems—than the texts that survive today. The evolution of the English language, especially in worship, and the development of the Protestant Church itself in theology and practice probably account for the deficit of enduring texts from the sixteenth century, and Kethe's Ps 100 set the tone for generations to come.

BIBLIOGRAPHY

Allison, Richard. *The Psalmes of David in Meter.* London: William Barley, 1599.

Benson, Louis F. *The English Hymn: Its Development and Use in Worship.* Richmond, VA: John Knox, 1962.

Brown, William P. *The Oxford Handbook of the Psalms.* New York: Oxford University Press, 2014.

Brueggemann, Walter. *The Message of the Psalms: A Theological Commentary.* Minneapolis: Augsburg, 1984.

Dickson, David. *A Brief Explication of the First Fifty Psalms.* London: Thomas Johnson, 1655.

Est, Thomas. *The Whole Booke of Psalmes: With Their Wonted Tunes.* London: Thomas Est, 1592.

Flynn, William T. "Liturgical Music." In *The Oxford History of Christian Worship*, edited by Geoffrey Wainwright and Karen B. Westerfield Tucker, 769–92. Oxford: Oxford University Press, 2006.

Lang, David. *Compendious Book of Psalms and Spiritual Songs, Commonly Known as "The Gude and Godlie Ballates."* Edinburgh: W. Paterson, 1868.

Quitslund, Beth. *The Reformation in Rhyme: Sternhold, Hopkins and the English Metrical Psalter, 1547–1603.* Aldershot, England: Ashgate, 2008.

Rolle, Richard. *The Psalter or Psalms of David and Certain Canticles, with a Translation and Exposition in English by Richard Rolle of Hampole. Edited from Manuscripts by the Rev. H. R. Bramley.* Oxford: Clarendon, 1884.

Routley, Erik. *The Music of Christian Hymns.* Chicago: G.I.A., 1981.

Sternhold, Thomas. *The Whole Booke of Psalmes, Collected into English Metre.* London: John Daye, 1565.

Chapter 6

Catholic Reformation Hymnody

Anthony Ruff

HISTORICAL BACKGROUND

With the rapid spread of Reformation ideas across Europe after Martin Luther's call for church reform in 1517, a response was called for by the Roman Catholic authorities. This response has often been called the "Counter Reformation." The Council of Trent (1545–63) was noted for its defensive attitude. The Catholic bishops at Trent condemned Protestant teachings, defined Catholic teachings, and defended them strongly, with an emphasis on what divided Catholics and Protestants rather than what united them.

But scholars have increasingly noted that efforts to reform the Catholic Church predate the Protestant Reformation and continued throughout the sixteenth and successive centuries independent of it. Hence, while the term "Counter Reformation" continues to be used, it has become more common to speak of the Catholic Reformation.[1] It is this term that is used in the present work. It refers to the entire complex of efforts to renew the Catholic Church, including the founding of new religious orders such as the Jesuits, the creation of seminaries, efforts to improve preaching and catechetical

1. Lampe and Soergel, "Counter Reformation."

instruction, publication of religious works of all sorts, standardization of liturgical practice with the issuing of the missal in 1570 for the rite of the Mass, and most important for our purposes, the development of hymnody and the publication of hymnals.

The term "Counter Reformation" has some accuracy in that the life of the Catholic Church came to be characterized by resistance and opposition to Protestant ideas and practices. This attitude began to soften only gradually with Catholics movements of renewal in the nineteenth and especially the twentieth century. These movements culminated in the Second Vatican Council (1962–65), which marks a turning point in the direction of less defensiveness, greater respect for other Christian traditions, and explicit advocacy for ecumenical dialogue toward the goal of eventual reunion of divided Christians. With the Second Vatican Council the era of the Catholic Reformation in the sense of a "Counter Reformation" drew to a close and the Catholic Church undertook an internal reform of a markedly different character.

It is well attested that people sang religious hymns and songs in vernacular extensively in the Middle Ages, and that at least in some cases, this vernacular singing was brought into an otherwise Latin and clericalized liturgy.[2] It was the work of Martin Luther to give much greater emphasis to congregational vernacular hymnody and make it a central feature of Protestant worship.[3]

In response to the popularity of Protestant hymn-singing, some Roman Catholic figures were skeptical of hymnody because of its association with "heretical" movements. But the more common Catholic reaction—especially in German-speaking countries, Hungary, and Slavic lands—was to make greater use of vernacular hymnody.[4] This was done in part to counter the spread of Protestant movements, but it was also done out of recognition of the positive value of hymnody in itself.

An early hymnal of the Catholic Reformation is the Czech Catholic hymnal of 1529, *Pisničky Velmi Pěkné a Přikladné* ("Good and Exemplary Hymns"). It contained vernacular hymns based on the Epistles and Gospels assigned to the various Sundays of the liturgical year and the Vespers hymns.[5]

The first significant hymnal of the German Catholic Reformation was issued by Michael Vehe in 1537 in Halle, Germany: *Ein new Gesangbüchlin*

2. Please see chapter 15 in volume 1: "Western European Vernacular Song."

3. Reynolds and Price, *Survey*, 26.

4. Ruff, *Sacred Music*, 576–92.

5. Ducreux, "L'Hymnologie," 171.

geistlicher Lieder ("A New Little Hymnal of Spiritual Hymns"). It included, in addition to hymns borrowed from Protestant sources, eight German metrical psalms, German versions of the Our Father and Hail Mary, hymns based on canticles such as the *Te Deum* and the *Magnificat,* and German versions of Latin hymns such as "Pange Lingua." Based on the layout of the hymnal, it is very possible that Vehe intended for vernacular hymns to be sung at Mass. As a contemporary, Georg Witzel, wrote in 1542, "On the high feasts of the year one already knows, based on the custom of the Church, what is to be sung in German."[6]

Georg Witzel's *Psaltes Ecclesiasticus* ("The Church Musician") of 1550 contains many Latin hymns in translation, with indications for their extensive use at High (i.e., fully sung) Mass. For example, it says above the vernacular hymn "Christ ist erstanden": "At this point the entire church shouts out with resounding high voice and unutterable joy."[7]

Johann Leisentritt of Bautzen issued the hymnal *Geistliche Lieder und Psalmen* ("Spiritual Hymns and Psalms") in 1567. It contained approximately 260 texts set to 175 notated melodies, many borrowed from Protestant sources. It was reissued in 1573 and 1584. Leisentritt stated explicitly his desire to bring people back to the Catholic Church who had defected to Protestantism.[8] Leisentritt wrote in the forward to his hymnal that vernacular hymns could be sung at Offertory and Communion "without harm to the substance of the Catholic religion."[9]

The first diocesan synod in Dilingen, Germany, in 1567 stated, "We permit ancient and Catholic vernacular hymns, especially those which our praiseworthy German forebears employed on the major feast days of the church, and we approve that they be retained in church and in processions." The influential Salzburg provincial synod of 1569 issued a similar decree.[10]

The Diocese of Bamberg issued its first diocesan hymnal in 1576. It stated that no elements of the official Latin liturgy were to be omitted because of the vernacular hymns. This perhaps suggests a doubling in which a proscribed Latin element of the liturgy was followed by a vernacular piece.[11]

A Czech Catholic hymnal of 1580 titled *Písně na Evangelia* ("Hymns on the Gospels") had sixty-seven hymns based on the Gospel readings and fifty hymns based on the Epistles of the church year, with the second half

6. Gülden, *Johann Leisentrits,* 59–60.

7. Harnoncourt, *Gesamtkirchliche,* 323.

8. Wetzel and Heitmeyer, *Johann Leisentrit's Geistliche Lieder.*

9. Harnoncourt, *Gesamtkirchliche,* 329n93.

10. Ruff, "Metrical."

11. Schmidt, "Kirchenlied," 112.

of the book based on the Christian life and the life of Christ.[12] A 1581 German-language hymnal, issued in Prague by Christoph Hecyrus, provided seasonal hymns to be sung after the first reading, strophic stanzas of the *Kyrie* and *Gloria* that follow the Latin text very closely, and hymns for the Offertory and the Our Father.[13]

In France, the *Paraphrase des Hymnes* ("Paraphrases of Hymns") of Michel Coyssard, first printed in 1592 and reprinted into the middle of the seventeenth century, is an example of French translations of Latin hymns and antiphons.[14]

A particularly interesting hymnal of the Catholic Reformation is the one issued in 1602 in Graz, Austria, by Nicolaus Beuttner.[15] Beuttner spent three years in outlying villages around Graz listening to popular hymns and songs known by memory by older people that otherwise had almost died out during the years when the areas were predominantly Lutheran. The hymnal also includes Protestant material: its first hymn is Luther's "Nun komm, der Heiden Heiland" ("Savior of the Nations, Come"). The hymnal speaks of replacing Latin chant with congregational hymnody, and Beuttner lists seven vernacular hymns for singing at Mass during Communion.

A *Cantual* issued in Mainz and Hildesheim in 1605 is a striking example of extensive use of vernacular hymnody at Latin High (i.e., sung) Mass. It provided for vernacular hymnody at the Gradual, Sequence, or Alleluia, after the Gospel, after the Homily, at the Offertory, at the Elevation, during the Communion procession, and after the final blessing. At Low (i.e., recited) Mass, nearly uninterrupted vernacular hymnody was permitted, with pauses only for the Gospel, the consecration of the bread and wine, and the final blessing.[16] In 1661, Archbishop Johann Philipp von Schoenborn published a hymnal in Mainz with "Evangelienlieder" ("Gospel Hymns") for every Sunday and feast day.[17]

Benedictine Abbot David Corner issued the *Groß catholisch Gesangbuch* ("Large Catholic Hymnal") in Nurnberg in 1625/1631, with further printings in Vienna under the title *Geistliche Nachtigal der catholischen Teutschen* ("Spiritual Nightingale of the Catholic Germans") from 1631 on.

12. Ducreux, "L'Hymnologie," 171.

13. Harnoncourt, *Gesamtkirchliche*, 330.

14. Launay, "Aprés," 413.

15. Harnoncourt, *Gesamtkirchliche*, 343–45; Harnoncourt, "Das Gesangbuch"; Lipphardt, "älteste"; Ruff, "Unity."

16. Harnoncourt, *Gesamtkirchliche*, 348–51.

17. Schmidt, "Kirchenlied," 115.

The second edition had almost 500 hymns.[18] *Davidische Harmonia* ("Davidian Harmony") was first printed in Vienna in 1659, then reprinted and enlarged as *Rheinfelsischen Gesangbuch* ("Rheinfels Hymnal") in Augsburg in 1666. It was of three-fourths Protestant origin.[19]

There are numerous witnesses to vernacular hymnody sung at Latin High (i.e., sung) Mass in Germany. In 1677 the bishop of Munster authorized vernacular hymns at High Mass at the Introit, Gloria, after the first reading, before the Homily, at the Offertory, Elevation, Agnus Dei, during Communion, and after the blessing.[20] The foreword to a Munster hymnal contains a directive from the prince ordering German hymns at High Mass as appropriate to the season.[21] A 1687 hymnal from Friedrichstadt, provided for the Kyrie, Gloria, Credo, Sanctus, and Agnus Dei (i.e., the "Ordinary") to be sung in vernacular strophic settings, with the Introit, Offertory, and Communion to be replaced by vernacular metrical psalmody.[22]

Metrical psalmody is genre in which the text of psalms are rhymed and put into a meter with a regularly recurring pattern of syllables in each line of a strophe. This allows the strophes of text to be sung to a hymn tune in the same meter. While metrical psalmody has been developed especially in Protestant traditions, at was also part of Catholic practice in various places beginning in the sixteenth century.[23]

Catholic priest Kaspar Ulenberg issued a collection of all 150 psalms in meter in Cologne in 1582. It was often reprinted into the nineteenth century.[24] In Poland, Jan Kochanowski set the entire psalter in rhymed meter, and this was set for four voices by Mikołaj Gomółka and published in 1580. It was used widely by Catholic and Protestant congregations.[25] Metrical psalmody was also sung in Catholic Bohemia.[26]

In Hungary, the 1676 *Cantionale Catholicum* of János Kájoni (1629–87) had 60 psalm hymns among its 545 Hungarian hymns. Fifty-two of these were of Protestant origin, including a Hungarian version of Luther's

18. Harnoncourt, *Gesamtkirchliche*, 346–47.
19. Bäumker, *Katholische*, vol. 1, 232, 182–86, 411.
20. Heinz, "Jesuiten," 161–62.
21. Schmidt, "Kirchenlied," 112.
22. Heinz, "Jesuiten," 162–65.
23. Ruff, "Metrical."
24. Harnoncourt, *Gesamtkirchliche*, 331; Fornaçon, "Kaspar Ulenberg."
25. Witkowski, "Die polnischen."
26. Ducreux, "L'Hymnologie," 172.

famous paraphrase of Ps 46, "A Mighty Fortress is Our God." Later Hungarian Catholic hymnals also included metrical psalmody.[27]

In France, the 1551 translation of the psalter by the Protestant Marot was popular also among Catholics. Other translations were approved by Catholic officials, and in 1648 the *Paraphrases des Psaumes* was issued by Bishop Godeau of Grasse. In 1686 a royal council prohibited this translation because the popularity of the psalms was seen to draw people away from the Latin liturgy.[28]

The eighteenth-century Enlightenment, with its emphasis on rationality, brought with it a catechetical and didactic thrust in hymn texts. Sentiments emblematic of the era were expressed by a Catholic leader in Breslau:

> The people should be *actual participants* of what occurs in the assembly, and not idle spectators, or worse, just staring in admiration at what is happening. . . . The actual participation of the members of the community in the communal worship of God is only conceivable when every member is conscious and remains conscious of what the servant of the altar undertakes in the name of Christ or in the name of the community.[29]

The Enlightenment brought the development of the *Singmesse*—literally the "sing-Mass." This was a series of strophic hymns to be sung throughout Mass, intended to help Catholics understand what was happening in the Latin liturgy.[30] In Austria, Empress Maria Theresia decreed in 1755 that a *Singmesse* be used throughout Austria.

An influential hymnal of the Enlightenment era was issued in Landshut in 1777, *Der heilige Gesang zum Gottesdienst in der römisch-katholischen Kirche* ("Sacred Song for Worship in the Roman Catholic Church"). This hymnal included a *Singmesse* by Johann Kohlbrenner, later set to music by Michael Haydn, which is still in use today in Europe in various languages.[31] The practice of singing hymns throughout Mass spread from Germany and Austria eastward to Slavic and Hungarian lands.[32] For a time it was in use in northern Italy as well.[33]

27. Holl, "Das Psalmlied"; Csomasz and Papp, "Abriss," 19–31.

28. Launay, "Après," 411–13.

29. Ruff, *Sacred Music*, 582.

30. Harnoncourt, *Gesamtkirchliche*, 352–54; Kurthen-Weidesheim, "Zur Geschichte."

31. Brenninger, "Das Landshuter."

32. Csomasz and Papp, "Abriss," 26–28; Ropitz, "Slowenischer," esp. 45; Sehnal, "Der tschechische,"

33. Cattaneo, *Il Culto*, 477n57.

Borrowing from Protestant sources, which is found already in the sixteenth and seventeenth centuries, increased in the Enlightenment era. The *Katholische Gesangbuch zum allgemeinen Gebrauch bei öffentlichen Gottesverehrungen* ("Catholic Hymnal for General Use at Public Worship of God") issued by Kaspar Anton von Mastiaux in Munich in 1810, for example, took over half of its 800 hymn texts from Protestant sources.[34]

Count von Zinzendorf of the Church of the Brethren is best known for his influence upon Protestant hymnody in Europe and the US.[35] Less well known is his *Christ-catholisches Singe- und Bet-Buechlein* ("Christian Catholic Booklet for Song and Prayer"), issued for Catholic use in Breslau in 1727, with approximately 150 Protestant hymns.[36] It is reported that this hymnal was "truly received with joy by many honorable and open-minded people of the Catholic Church, and used with blessings for their hearts."[37]

A study of eighteen Czech Catholic hymnals from 1588 to 1762 showed an average of approximately 30 percent of their contents of Protestant origin, with only one hymnal less than 20 percent (13 percent in 1601) and a 1652 hymnal being of 77 percent Protestant origin.[38]

In the nineteenth century, the German reformist Cecilian movement attempted to eliminate vernacular hymnody from High (sung) Mass and preserve the exclusive use of Latin. Though a decree from Rome of 1894 prohibited vernacular hymnody at High Mass,[39] this did not prevent the continued use of vernacular hymns there.[40] At Low (recited) Mass, it was undisputed that vernacular hymnody was permitted, and figures in the Cecilian movement worked hard to provide high quality hymnals for this use as well as at devotional exercises.

As already noted, it was primarily in German-speaking regions and in regions further east that vernacular hymn singing occurred at Mass. But some examples from other regions are also to be found. In 1598, a council at Avignon had permitted vernacular hymns to be sung in church at Christmas, most likely during the liturgy. But another council prohibited the practice in 1725.[41] In 1725, a Roman provincial council under Pope Benedict XIII decreed that a hymn be sung every Sunday at High Mass after

34. Bretschneider, "Pädagogische."
35. Reynolds and Price, *Survey*, 42–43.
36. Baümker, *Deutsches*, vol. 3, 144; Teuscher, "Jesus," 40.
37. Müller, *Hymnologisches*, 25.
38. Ducreux, "L'Hymnologie," 173.
39. Hayburn, *Papal*, 456; Romita, *Jus Musicae*, 206–7.
40. Ruff, *Sacred Music*, 93–105.
41. Romita, *Jus Musicae*, 70, 87.

the sermon.[42] A late nineteenth-century children's hymnal printed in Paris, *Cantique Parouissial,* also includes vernacular hymns for use during Mass, with indications above some hymns for singing at the elevation of the host and chalice and at communion.

There is a long history of vernacular singing at both High Mass and Low Mass in Brittany.[43] There are reports of vernacular hymnody being used at Mass and other liturgies in England and America in the early nineteenth century before being suppressed.[44] A decree from Toledo, Spain, in 1850 allowed for vernacular singing at First Communion, Confirmation, and other particular days of the year.[45]

Especially at the beginning of the twentieth century, efforts to involve people more actively in Catholic worship developed into the "Liturgical Movement."[46] In the decades before the Second Vatican Council (1962–65), popes gave increasing emphasis to the value of congregational hymn singing.[47] There was a marked increase in the production of congregational hymnals across the entire Catholic Church. This extensive movement need not be documented in detail here, for it belongs, by way of anticipation, more to the reforms affirmed by the Second Vatican Council than to the spirit of the Catholic Reformation issuing from the sixteenth-century Council of Trent.

THEOLOGICAL PERSPECTIVES

In appraising theologically and liturgically the hymnody of the Catholic Reformation, two distinctions should be kept in mind: that between liturgy and devotions, and that between High Mass and Low Mass. These distinctions played a role in the function of the congregational hymnody used in worship and prayer.

First, the liturgy of the Catholic Church consists primarily of the Mass (the service of Holy Communion) and the daily cycle of Scripture-based offices (such as Lauds, Vespers, and Compline) in the Liturgy of the Hours.[48] These texts for these liturgies are found in officially approved books issued by Rome or, in some cases, by religious orders under Rome's supervision. Up until the Second Vatican Council, the Latin language was used exclu-

42. Jungmann, *Mass*, vol. 1, 155.
43. Abjean, "Chant" 579.
44. Higginson, *History*, 13.
45. Pons, *Droit*, vol. 4, 59.
46. Ruff, *Sacred Music,* 194–242.
47. Ruff, *Sacred Music,* 293, 313.
48. Ruff, "Gregorian," 24–40.

sively in these books. In the case of Mass, all the texts officially part of the liturgy were found in the missal, to be read or sung by the ordained priest.

In a less important category are devotions. These communal services are more popular in character, vary regionally in their content, and are less regulated by church authorities. The have often emphasized aspects of the Catholic faith less centrally important than the Mass and the Office, such as prayers to Mary and the saints or adoration of the eucharistic host put on display. But because these services have largely been in vernacular, they have often had a disproportionate attraction for the Catholic people compared to the more important services of the officially regulated Mass and Office.

There has been little dispute historically that vernacular hymnody befits devotional services. As a result, there is a large body of devotional hymnody sung historically by Catholics. This explains why there is to this day so much Catholic Marian hymnody, though the Blessed Virgin Mary is entirely subordinate to God and Jesus Christ in Catholic teaching.

As the historical survey above shows, there is also a long history of vernacular hymnody being sung at the Latin liturgy, particularly in German-speaking and Slavic regions. This vernacular singing seems to have been permitted at the officially Latin liturgy as a salutary byproduct of an overly clergy-dominated view of liturgy. Because the official liturgy was done by the ordained priest rather than the congregation, it did not much matter what the congregation did—for example, sing vernacular hymns—parallel to the Latin liturgy of the priest. Though congregational vernacular hymnody was not central to the liturgy, and its legitimacy was always somewhat unstable and susceptible to critique, it was nevertheless in use—in some times and places, quite extensively.

To understand the use of congregational hymnody in the Latin liturgy, the second distinction is important: between High Mass and Low Mass. In High Mass, the primary public texts of the liturgy were all sung by the priest, with a choir singing Latin responses in alternation with the priest. In Low Mass, such texts of the priest were recited, with an acolyte or altar boy reciting the choral responses. The significance of this distinction for vernacular hymnody is that, at least in theory, singing vernacular hymns was not permitted at High Mass. But as history shows, such singing nevertheless was widely practiced, especially in German-speaking countries. Reformist efforts to purge High Mass of vernacular hymns did not meet with success. By 1943—this was in the wake of the expanding Liturgical Movement—Rome officially decreed that in Germany and Austria vernacular hymns could be sung at High Mass, though it was canonically illegal.

At Low Mass, by contrast, it was never disputed that vernacular hymns could be sung. While the priest quietly said his official Latin texts alone or in alternation with a server, the congregation could sing hymns. These locally chosen hymns might be more closely related to the content of the Latin liturgy or more removed from it. Though this practice was permitted, it was not equally practiced everywhere. It was less common in Romance countries and among English-speaking Catholics in England and Ireland.

The upshot of all this is that the inheritance of Catholic Reformation hymnody varies widely in its relationship to the central aspects of the Catholic faith celebrated in the official liturgy. Some of the hymnody, in some times and places, has helped Catholics understand and participate in the most important rites of their religion. But much of it has put undue emphasis on secondary aspects of the faith.

An important theological aspect of Catholic Reformation hymnody is the ecumenical sharing it witnesses between Catholic and Protestant traditions. Many cases have been noted above in which Catholic hymnals drew extensively upon Protestant repertoires. This might not have been expected, given the defensive posture of the Council of Trent noted earlier. The Catholic Reformation is known for its polemical, anti-Protestant stance. Fortunately, this stance was counterbalanced by the impulse among at least some Catholic musicians and publishers to make use of worthy repertoire from Protestant sources. One could perhaps speak of a "practical ecumenism" in musical matters long before the rise of the ecumenical movement in the twentieth century.

CONTRIBUTIONS TO LITURGY AND WORSHIP

The tradition of Catholic Reformation hymnody has produced an extensive repertoire that has enriched and continues to enrich the worship of the churches. There is an ecumenical dimension to this, since hymns coming from the Catholic Reformation are typically found in the hymnals of most Christian traditions today. But a central contribution of this tradition is the way in which it affected the worship of the Catholic Church itself in the era between the Council of Trent in the sixteenth century and the Second Vatican Council in the twentieth century.

Catholic worship in this era is generally described as highly centralized, uniform, regulated down to the most minute detail, inaccessible to the faithful because of the Latin language, and dominated by clergy to the exclusion of lay people.[49] Each of these tendencies, all of which are unfortunate in various ways, were mitigated and counterbalanced by the presence of vernacular congregational hymnody.

49. White, *Roman Catholic.*

Catholic Reformation hymnody was highly localized, with much regional variance. There was little uniformity from one region to another. Because hymnody was not considered to be an integral part of the Latin liturgy, it was not highly regulated by church officials for the most part. There are instances in Germany of diocesan hymnals approved by bishops, but these are an exception to an overall tendency toward great freedom and personal initiative. Vernacular hymns helped make the liturgy more accessible to lay people by facilitating their comprehension and participation. This allowed for a significant role for lay people in a liturgy that otherwise would have been the exclusive domain of clergy.

NOTABLE HYMNS

Because congregational hymn singing has been cultivated more strongly among Protestants than Catholics historically, and only came to find strong, explicit Roman approval in the decades before the Second Vatican Council, many hymns of the Catholic Reformation have been in use more among Protestants than among Catholics in the English-speaking world. Several examples can be named of hymns commonly found in hymnals of various Christian traditions today.

From Catholic hymnals in Cologne come two widely used tunes: *Es ist ein Ros,* commonly sung with "Lo, How a Rose," of 1599, and *Lasst uns erfreuen,* commonly sung with "All Creatures of Our God and King," of 1623. *Paderborn,* commonly sung to "Ye Servants of God, Your Master Proclaim," comes from that city from 1765. *Grosser Gott,* commonly sung with "Holy God, We Praise Thy Name," comes from a Catholic hymnal of 1775 in Vienna. *Ellacombe,* sometimes sung with "I Sing the Almighty Power of God," comes from an Enlightenment era hymnal of 1784 from Wurtemberg.

Two hymn tunes in Catholic use are *Gott Veter sei Gepriesen* and *Ich glaub' an Gott.* The first is often sung with "O God, Almighty Father" and comes from Limburg in 1838. The second is often sung with "To Jesus Christ, Our Sovereign King" and comes from an 1870 hymnal from Mainz.

As is well known, the beloved Christmas carol "Silent Night" / *Stille Nacht* comes from Catholic Austria in 1818.

In a separate category are hymn melodies from France not treated above because they were originally conceived as tunes for use with Latin Office hymn texts rather than congregational vernacular texts.[50] Because of the way chant hymns were then sung, however, these tunes have the character of congregational hymns. They readily lend themselves to congregational

50. Pocknee, *French Diocesan.*

singing and are used as such today in many hymnals. Three examples in widespread use in many church traditions, with characteristic Latin names, are the tunes *Christe sanctorum* of 1681, *Iste confessor* of 1746, and *Deus tuorum militum* of 1753.

BIBLIOGRAPHY

Abjean, Roger. "Chant Liturgique en Bretagne." *Encyclopédie des Musiques Sacrées*, vol. 3, 579–80.

Bäumker, Wilhelm. *Das katholische deutsche Kirchenlied in seinen Singweisen von den frühesten Zeiten bis gegen Ende des 17.* Jahrhunderts. 1883–1911. Hildesheim: Olms-Verlag, 1962.

Brenninger, Georg. "Das Landshuter Kirchengesangbuch von 1777—Ein Bestseller der Aufklärungszeit." In vol. 1 of *Liturgie und Dichtung: Ein interdisziplinäres Kompendium*, edited by Hansjakob Becker and Reiner Kaczynski, 811–20. St. Ottilien: Eos-Verlag, 1983.

Bretschneider, Wolfgang. "Pädagogische Bedeutung und Funktion des deutschen Kirchenliedes zwischen Aufklärung und Restaration—Dargestellt am Werk des Kaspar Anton von Mastiaux (1766–1828)." Diss., University of Bonn, 1980.

Cattaneo, Enrico. *Il Culto Cristiano in Occidente: Note Storiche.* Roma: Edizioni Liturgiche, 1984.

Csomasz, Kálámn, and Géza Papp. "Abriss der Geschichte des ungarischen Kirchenliedes." *I.A.H. Bulletin* 11 (1983) 6–31.

Ducreux, Marie-Elizabeth. "L'Hymnologie Catholique Tchèque de la Contre-Réforme." *Jahrbuch für Liturgie und Hymnologie* 29 (1985) 169–79.

Fornaçon, Siegfried. "Kaspar Ulenberg und Konrad von Hagen." *Musikforschung* 9 (1956) 206–13.

Gülden, Josef. *Johann Leisentrits bautzener Meßritus und Meßgesänge.* Münster: Aschendorff, 1964.

Harnoncourt, Philipp. "Das Gesangbuch des Nikolaus Beuttner (Graz 1602) auf dem Hintergrund der religionsgeschichtlichen Situation in der Steiermark." *Musik und Altar* 22 (1969/1970) 116–20.

———. *Gesamtkirchliche und teilkirchliche Liturgie: Studien zum liturgischen Heiligenkalender und zum Gesang im Gottesdienst unter besonderer Berücksichtigung des deutschen Sprachgebiets.* Freiburg im Breisgau: Herder, 1974.

Hayburn, Robert. *Papal Legislation on Sacred Music 95 A.D. to 1977 A.D.* Collegeville, MN: Liturgical, 1979.

Heinz, Andreas. "Die Jesuiten als Förderer deutscher Messlieder." *Liturgisches Jahrbuch* 35 (1985) 158–67.

Higginson, J. Vincent. *History of American Catholic Hymnals: Survey and Background.* Springfield, OH: Hymn Society of America, 1982.

Holl, Béla. "Das Psalmlied und die katholische Kirchengesangs-Tradition in Ungarn." *Jahrbuch für Liturgie und Hymnologie* 34 (1992–93) 114–18.

Joseph Ropitz. "Slowenischer Kirchengesang." In *Kirchenchöre Österreichs*, edited by Johann Trummer, 44–50. Graz: Universal Verlag, 1987.

Jungmann, Joseph. *The Mass of the Roman Rite.* 2 vols. Translated by Francis A. Brunner. 1955; Westminster, MD: Christian Classics, 1986.

Kurthen-Weidesheim, Wilhelm. "Zur Geschichte der deutschen Singmesse" ("On the History of the German Singmesse"). *Kirchenmusikalisches Jahrbuch* 26 (1931) 76–110.

Lampe, E. I., and P. Soergel. "Counter Reformation." In *New Catholic Encyclopedia*, 4. 2nd ed. Washington, DC: Catholic University of America, 2003.

Launay, Denise. "Après le Concile de Trente, la Contre-Réforme en France." In *Encyclopédie des Musiques Sacrées*, 2. Paris: Éditions Labergerie, 1968–71.

Lipphardt, Walther. "Die älteste Ausgabe von Beuttners Gesangbuch—Graz 1602." *Jahrbuch für Liturgie und Hymnologie* 8 (1963) 143–52.

Müller, Joseph. *Hymnologisches Handbuch zum Gesangbuch der Brü*dergemeine. 1916; Hildesheim: Olms-Verlag, 1977.

Pocknee, Cyril E. *French Diocesan Hymns and Their Melodies*. Manchester, UK: Faith Press, 1954.

Pons, André. *Droit ecclésiastique et Musique sacrée*. St. Maurice: Editions de l'Oeuvre St. Augustin, 1958–64.

Reynolds, William J., and Milburn Price. *Survey of Christian Hymnody*. Revised by David W. Music and Milburn Price. Carol Stream: Hope, 2010.

Romita, Florentius. *Jus Musicae Liturgicae*. Roma: Edizioni Liturgiche, 1947.

Ruff, Anthony. "Gregorian Chant and Polyphony." In *So You Want to Sing Sacred Music*, edited by Matthew Hoch, 23–53. Rowman & Littlefield, 2017.

———. "Metrical Psalmody of the Catholic Reformation." *G.I.A. Quarterly* 10/2 (Winter 2005) 16–19, 42–45.

———. "Unity in Song and Sacrament in Early Seventeenth-Century Catholicism." *G.I.A. Quarterly* 8.2 (1997) 16–18, 41.

———. *Sacred Music and Liturgical Reform: Treasures and Transformations*. Chicago: Liturgy Training Publications, 2007.

Schmidt, Hans. "Kirchenlied (Katholisch)." In *Musik in Geschichte und Gegenwart*, 8. Kassel: Bärenreiter-Verlag, 1949–86.

Sehnal, J. "Der tschechische Messgesang im 17. und 18. Jahrhundert." *I.A.H. Bulletin* 18 (1990) 127–35.

Solzbacher, Joseph. "Die Psalmen Davids, in allerlei deutsche Gesangreime gebracht durch Kaspar Ulenberg, Köln 158.2." *Kirchenmusikalisches Jahrbuch* 34 (1950) 41–55.

Teuscher, Gerhard. "'Jesus, Still Lead On': Count von Zinzendorf (1700–1760): Poet and Master-Singer of the Moravian Church." *Hymn* 47 (1996) 32–41.

Vehe, Michael. *Ein new Gesangbüchlin geistlicher Lieder*. 1537; Repr. Walther Lipphart, Mainz: B. Schott's Söhne, 1970.

Wetzel, Richard D., and Erika Heitmeyer. *Johann Leisentrit's Geistliche Lieder und Psalmen, 1567: Hymnody of the Counter-Reformation in Germany*. Vancouver: Fairleigh Dickinson University Press, 2012.

White, James. *Roman Catholic Worship: Trent to Today*. Collegeville, MN: Liturgical, 2004.

Witkowski, Leon. "Die polnischen Psalmen von Jan Kochanowski und Mikolaj Gomolka aus dem Jahre 1580." *I.A.H. Bulletin* 5 (1977) 36–40.

Chapter 7

Tomas Luis de Victoria

ALEXANDER BLACHLY

HISTORICAL BACKGROUND

ESPECIALLY IN ITALY, RENAISSANCE composers of polyphonic hymns tended to follow a set pattern, embedding paraphrased versions of plainchant hymn melodies in a fabric of contrapuntal voices. Such settings alternated polyphony with chant, stanza by stanza, in what is known as an *alternatim* practice. Although medieval chant manuscripts transmit nearly a thousand Latin hymns with melodies,[1] *alternatim* hymn composers drew on only about fifty of these.

Cycles of polyphonic hymns for the church year always started with Advent and continued with Christmas and other major feasts in the Temporale until Pentecost or Corpus Christi, then concluded with various saints' days from the Sanctorale and some commons. This had been Guillaume Du Fay's practice in the fifteenth century (twenty-three settings from ca. 1433–35), and it is found consistently in the collections by Elzéar Genet Carpentras (Avignon, 1534), Costanzo Festa (Sistine Chapel, 1535), Adrian Willaert (Venice, 1542), Francesco Corteccia (Florence, 1543), Orlande de Lassus (Munich, 1580), Francisco Guerrero (Rome, 1584), Giovanni

1. The Cantus manuscript database of Latin chants (http://cantus.uwaterloo.ca) lists 905 hymns with melodies.

Pierluigi da Palestrina (Rome, 1589), Juan Navarro (Rome, 1590), and others. In contrast to Du Fay's practice, however, in which all of the polyphonic stanzas were sung to the same music, the sixteenth-century collections provided separate musical settings for each polyphonic stanza, often with reduced voices for one or two middle stanzas and with increased voices for the final polyphonic stanza.

Some smaller collections of polyphonic hymns appeared between those by Du Fay and Carpentras, but these do not systematically follow the church year. Two such examples are the eleven hymns by Johannes Martini (d. 1497) and seven by Adam von Fulda (d. 1505).

The dates of the larger sixteenth-century collections just mentioned, and the fact that they originated in Rome and other Catholic cities, mostly in Italy, and furthermore were settings of Latin poetry, show that they belong to the Counter-Reformation. Both in style and purpose they were opposed to the congregational chorales and metrical psalms of the Protestant churches north of the Alps. In light of *alternatim* hymns' elaborate polyphony, it should come as no surprise that modern hymnals, which favor simpler chordal textures, do not include these elegant Latin pieces.[2]

It has become commonplace to speak today not just of the hymns, but also the motets, Masses, Magnificats, sequences, and other sacred works from sixteenth-century Italy as the "Golden Age" of polyphony, that is, of imitative writing in which the voice-parts of the choir sing independent melodies that echo each other to form a harmonic web. It is intricate music, intended for professionals to perform and for the congregation to listen to as devotional music, as though at a sacred concert. Whereas the Protestant hymn generated enthusiasm through participation, the purpose of the high-art polyphony from the Golden Age was, by means of dazzling counterpoint and skillful feats of execution, to impress, to inspire, and to persuade. To quote Noel O'Regan, complex polyphony served the sixteenth-century Catholic Church as "a potent weapon in the fight for souls."[3]

Spanish composer Tomás Luis de Victoria was born 1548 in, or near, Ávila and died in 1611 in Madrid. Through his appealing music, he made an important contribution to the recasting of ancient texts in modern musical garb that constituted one branch of the Counter-Reformation. In 1581, Victoria published thirty-two four-voice hymns in Rome,[4] a city where he resided from 1565 to 1587. He then returned to the country of his birth

2. The stark difference in approach that existed between Catholic and Protestant hymns during the later Renaissance is obscured in modern Catholic hymnals, which include a significant body of Protestant hymns that can be sung by the congregation.

3. Noel O'Regan, "Tomás Luis de Victoria's Roman Churches," 406.

4. Victoria, *Thomae Ludovici a Victoria Abulensis*, 158.

to live out the remainder of his life as a priest, composer, choir director, and organist at the Monasterio de las Descalzas Reales in Madrid. At the time of the 1581 print, he was associated with the Roman church of S. Girolamo della Carità, gaining a chaplaincy there a year later. As the title page of his collection makes clear, the melodies of the hymns follow the versions sung in sixteenth-century Rome. However, the thirty-second hymn in the collection is a second setting of *Pange lingua . . . corporis* is labeled "*More Hispano*" ("Spanish manner," referring to the traditonal Spanish melody), so that in fact only thirty-one of the hymns follow the use of Rome. (Victoria's *Officium Hebdomadae Sanctae* of 1585 includes his second setting of the hymn *Vexilla regis prodeunt*, also labeled "*More Hispano*").

Victoria provided the rationale for his 1581 collection of hymns in the dedication to Pope Gregory XIII:

> When I noticed that the harmonizations (*modos*) of the sacred hymns in diverse volumes as they had been created by diverse writers were sought out at great expense for churches and irritation (*taedio*) to singers—and so that, as much as I could, I might relieve the inconvenience for both and might obtain the favor of both—I collected and embellished the hymns present here in one volume in pleasing harmonizations.[5]

The texts of almost all of the hymns he selected date from the fourth to tenth centuries. Authors include Ambrose, Pope Gregory the Great, Venantius Fortunatus, Caelius Sedulius, Prudentius, Paulinus of Aquileia, Rabanus Maurus, Paulus Diaconus, Odo of Cluny, and Thomas Aquinas, plus anonymous poets from the fifth to the tenth centuries.[6] Aquinas's *Pange lingua . . . corporis* from ca. 1264, the year Pope Urban IV officially established the feast of Corpus Christi to which this hymn belongs, is the most "modern" of the hymns set by Victoria, and more recent than any of the others by approximately three centuries. Yet these ancient hymns should not have been difficult to find: both texts and melodies were frequently copied into the antiphoners and breviaries owned by nearly every church in Victoria's day.

As mentioned above, the collections listed earlier drew on the same core repertoire of chant hymns as Victoria's. For example, of the twenty-three hymns set by Du Fay, twenty-one were also set by Victoria; of the

5. "*Cum enim sacrorum modos hymnorum ut à diversis auctoribus factos ex diversis voluminibus magno tum ecclesiarum dispendio, tum cantorum taedio peti animadverterem, ut, quoad possem, utrique incommodo mederer, & gratiam ab utrisque inirem, eos hymnos volumine uno collectos in praesenti congruentibus modis excolui & exornavi.*"

6. Whether the melodies of the hymns are as old as the texts cannot be determined, since the earliest chant manuscripts with notation that specifies pitches date from the eleventh century.

eleven hymns set by Martini, ten were set by Victoria; of the thirty hymns set by Festa, twenty-seven were set by Victoria; of the twenty-eight hymns set by Carpentras, twenty-three were set by Victoria; of the thirty-eight hymns set by Lassus, twenty-eight were set by Victoria, etc. Moreover, all of Victoria's hymns but two, No. 14, *Doctor egregie* for the Conversion and Commemoration of St. Paul, and No. 30, *Huius obtentu Deus* for a single Martyr, are included in the printed *Breviarium Romanum* of 1568,[7] which Pius V that year decreed was to be observed "in all churches, monasteries, orders and even exempt places in the whole world, in which the Office must be said or has customarily been said."[8]

From the evidence just cited, we may conclude that it was not the original plainchant hymns, but rather some aspect of their polyphonic elaborations transmitted in manuscript that "irritated" Victoria's singers and that churches found "expensive." The wording in Victoria's preface, though not as specific as we might wish, suggests that it may previously have been the practice for his singers to copy out their own parts from manuscript anthologies rented from ecclesiastical institutions nearby. Victoria's newly printed set was inexpensive, easily available, and required no copying of parts by the singers.

Victoria's older friend Guerrero published his own hymn settings in Rome three years after Victoria's (twenty-four hymns, all of which Victoria had set in his collection), followed five years later by Palestrina, whose collection of seventy-two hymns (many in multiple settings) included all thirty-one set by Victoria. A year later, in 1590, Juan Navarro published fifty-nine polyphonic hymns in Rome. The printing of so many *alternatim* hymns in such a short time indicates their popularity in the Eternal City. They were all for unaccompanied voices, and all in the elevated style of the Golden Age. Guerrero's and Palestrina's, following the model of Festa's, challenged singers by incorporating canons and other contrapuntal puzzles.

Listed in a 1608 inventory belonging to the Roman church of S. Maria di Monserrato, where Victoria served as *cantor y sonador del órgano* from 1569 to 1575, is a manuscript containing "various hymns by Costanzo Festa and others."[9] There is no indication of when it came into the church's pos-

7. *Breviarium Romanum, ex decreto Sacrosancti Concilii Tridentini restitutum, Pii V Pont. Max. jussu editum (Romae: Apud Paulum Manutium, M.D.LX.VIII)*

8. Cited in Zager, "Post-Tridentine Liturgical Change," 42–45. There are, however, numerous small differences in the texts of Victoria's hymns and the texts printed in the 1568 breviary, indicating that the breviary itself was not Victoria's source. Since, in any case, the breviary does not include the hymn melodies, it is clear that Victoria had to have another source for these.

9. Reported by O'Regan, "Tomás Luis de Victoria's Roman Churches," 408.

session. Perhaps Victoria's singers had been copying their parts from this manuscript, among others, years before the 1581 print. The same inventory includes Victoria's own printed collection of hymns, dating from six years after his employment at the church had ended.

On August 28, 1575, Victoria celebrated his ordination to the priesthood, at which time he left S. Maria di Monserrato, never to return. During the period from then until 1582, when he was granted the chaplaincy at S. Girolamo della Carità, his employment in Rome remains unclear, but these were his most productive and creative years, when he had the opportunity to devote his energies to composing. In the period leading up to 1581, he focused on music for Vespers. In addition to the publication of his thirty-two hymns, 1581 saw his separate publication of Magnificats in all the tones. The hymn print itself ends with four Vespers psalms for eight voices arranged for double choir. All of the hymns are in *alternatim* format, with the first stanza and subsequent odd-numbered stanzas sung in chant. They are printed in a single large book in "choirbook" arrangement, with Cantus and Tenor on a verso, Altus and Bassus on the facing recto, and with the chant stanzas sometimes at the bottom of a verso, beneath the Cantus and Tenor (e.g., first stanza of No. 1, *Conditor alme syderum*), sometimes at the bottom of a recto beneath Altus and Bassus (first stanza of No. 6, *Ad preces nostras Deitatis*), often between the Cantus and Tenor on a verso (first stanza of No. 22, *Christe redemptor . . . conserva*; see figure 7.1). The various placements of the chant in successive openings of a given hymn can be confusing if one doesn't keep in mind that on any given opening the chant is always to be sung before the polyphony, and that each opening contains exactly one chant stanza and one polyphonic stanza.[10]

10. No. 22, *Christe Redemptor . . . conserva*, represents the sole exception to this rule. Here, the third and fifth stanzas, sung in chant, are notated on the same opening; on the next opening, the polyphonic sixth stanza is to be sung before the final stanza, which is sung in chant.

Figure 7.1: Music Sheet of *De Nativitate Domini*

Polyphonic Latin hymns provided composers with the unusual opportunity of writing for chorus one of the most popular forms of sixteenth-century instrumental music—theme and variations, many sixteenth-century examples of which survive for organ, harpsichord, vihuela, lute, and viola da gamba. Unlike a through-composed motet, which rarely referred to the melody of a chant hymn even if it used a hymn's words as its text, *alternatim* hymns normally projected, in every polyphonic stanza, a paraphrase of the complete hymn melody in one or more voices. This was most often the Tenor, but sometimes it could be the Cantus, Bassus, or even Altus. Typically, the paraphrase moved in slower notes than the surrounding voices. According to sixteenth-century convention, as mentioned earlier, every polyphonic stanza of an *alternatim* hymn required its own separate harmonization, with the result that a six-stanza Latin hymn would give the effect of a plainchant "theme" stated three times, alternating with three polyphonic "variations." Victoria was adept at honoring the notes of the Gregorian melody in his paraphrased versions, which, with only a few exceptions, faithfully follow the pitches of the melodies printed in plain view of each polyphonic stanza. One does occasionally see the addition of a sharp to a single note of the chant, most often at a cadence, and once or twice Victoria abbreviates or decorates the source melody slightly.

Nine of Victoria's hymns are notated in "high clefs," i.e., treble, mezzo, alto, baritone: No. 2, *Christe Redemptor . . . ex Patre*; No. 3, *Salvete flores martyrum*; Nos. 12 and 32, *Pange lingua . . . corporis* (both versions); No. 16, *Ut queant laxis*; No. 18, *Lauda mater ecclesia*; No. 20, *Quicumque Christum quaeritis*; No. 21, *Tibi Christe splendor*; and No. 22, *Christe redemptor . . . conserva*. High clefs in the course of the sixteenth century served to indicate downward transposition, often of a third or a fourth. Various explanations for the practice, which has been known since the eighteenth century as *chiavette*, have been advanced in recent years.[11] In Victoria's hymns, the reason seems to have been two-fold: 1) a wish to notate each Gregorian melody in the same position on the staff as it occurs in chantbooks; and 2) a concomitant wish to avoid using key signatures with sharps or more than one flat. If one ignores the intended downward transposition, Victoria's high-clef hymns appear to call for sopranos to sing high G's and A's and for basses to avoid any notes lower than an octave below middle C. It is as though these pieces call for a different choir from the one for which the hymns in the normal clefs (soprano, alto, tenor, bass) were intended.[12]

11. See the detailed discussion of *chiavette* by Patrizio Barbieri in *Grove Music Online*.

12. It should be noted that the 1581 print shows the chant of No. 12, *Pange lingua . . . corporis* (Roman version) incorrectly with an F-clef instead of C-clef, with the result that the chant appears to sound a fifth lower in the odd verses, with a final on D, than in its paraphrased form in the even stanzas, where the paraphrased melody has a final on A. The Solesmes *Hymnarium* and *Antiphonale monasticum* show the melody of *Pange lingua . . . corporis* with A final and C-clef, as it should be in Victoria's print, while the Solesmes *Liber usualis* shows it with D final and F-clef and a key signature of one flat. The lack of a flat for the chant in the Victoria prints exacerbates the clef problem,

Victoria's polyphonic stanzas were reprinted in partbooks in Venice in 1600. Unlike the earlier edition, this one includes only the first phrase of the first stanza in chant, usually in the Tenor partbook, sometimes in the Bassus. It omits any indication of subsequent chant altogether. The 1581 print, it will be recalled, notated each chant stanza completely—both words and melody, and on the same opening as the following polyphonic stanza.[13] The 1600 edition also omits the four eight-voice Vespers psalms. To approximate the look of quadratic chant neumes, both editions employ black breves from the font of mensural note shapes.[14]

It seems possible that the two prints from Victoria's lifetime reflect differing local practices for performing polyphonic hymns in Rome and Venice. The inclusion of the complete chant stanzas in the 1581 Roman print implies that at least some of the singers who were gathered around a single choirbook to sing the polyphony also sang the chant. The 1600 Venetian partbooks, on the other hand, may include only a chant incipit—just enough to identify each hymn—because the printer anticipated a different performance arrangement, in which one choir sang polyphony and a separate choir sang the chant stanzas, reading from a local antiphoner or hymnarium.

Pedrell's 1908 edition of Victoria's hymns always shows both chant and polyphony at the notated pitch of the sixteenth-century prints. In No. 18, *Lauda mater ecclesia* for the feast of Mary Magdalene, Nancho Alvarez's undated online edition recognizes that transposition is implied by the

---

with the chant melody now appearing to include an impossible melodic tritone. Both Felipe Pedrell's pioneering modern edition of 1908 and Nancho Alvarez's more recent but undated online edition of the Victoria hymns fail to correct the original print's error. (Further evidence that the F-clef is a mistake can be seen in Victoria's No. 30, *Urbs beata Hierusalem,* which uses the *Pange lingua . . . corporis* melody. Here both the chant and its paraphrases are notated on D with a B-flat key signature.)

13. In both prints, a hymn with a final stanza to be sung in chant occasionally gives only the beginning words of the doxology (e.g., "Præsta Pater ut supra" in No. 5, *Lucis creator optime*), with the expectation that the singers could find the remaining words elsewhere in the volume and sing them to the melody at hand. In this case, however, the words "Præsta Pater" are found nowhere else in the book—one of several such mistakes in the print. "Tu esto nostrum ut supra" in No. 9, *Jesu nostra redemptio* for ascension, represents another blind cue. The direction "Quæsumus auctor omnium ut supra" for the fifth stanza of No. 24, *Tristes erant Apostoli* for the Nativity of Apostles in Paschal Time, refers to words that do occur "above," namely, as the seventh stanza of No. 8, *Ad cenam agni providi,* for the Octave of Easter to Ascension. Both hymns are sung to the same chant melody but have different polyphonic settings of the even stanzas, except for Stanza 8. The eighth stanza, "Gloria tibi, Domine" is set to identical polyphony yet is printed in full for both hymns.

14. For the single phrase of chant of *Pange lingua . . . corporis* printed in the 1600 edition, the same mistake of F-clef for C-clef is retained.

high clefs and also that a different, independent transposition of the chant is needed in order for unadorned chant and paraphrased chant in the polyphonic stanzas to agree on their final. Alvarez transposes the polyphony of *Lauda mater ecclesia* down a third from F final to D final with a key signature of two sharps, while transposing the chant, notated with C final, up a step to D final, also with two sharps. He makes the same type of transpositions in No. 21, *Tibi, Christe, splendor Domini* for St. Michael, again matching chant and paraphrase finals with key signatures of two sharps. This seems to be the only reasonable way for these pieces to be performed. One wonders how sixteenth-century singers dealt with instances like these, where the final of the chant and the final of its paraphrase in the polyphonic stanzas must be reconciled in performance.

Victoria often reduces interior polyphonic stanzas to three voices (never less than three) but refrains from expanding the concluding polyphonic statement beyond four to five or six, as found in the hymn settings by Festa and, later, Guerrero and Palestrina. Nor does Victoria introduce canons or other manipulations of the chant melodies, although he does occasionally have the paraphrased chant migrate away from the Tenor, and frequently a voice other than the one singing the paraphrase will briefly anticipate each new phrase of the paraphrased melody.

Offsetting the compositional modesty of his approach, Victoria enriches the polyphonic stanzas with masterful counterpoint that often includes strong, modern-sounding, V-I cadences. No. 8, *Ad cenam agni providi,* for the Octave of Easter to Ascension, may serve as a case in point. The chant melody is in the Mixolydian mode on G, with its entire range extending up only a fifth to encompass the notes G to D. There are no mode-defining F-naturals. While for the polyphonic stanzas Victoria does include in the surrounding counterpoint some occasional F-naturals (notes that belong to the chant's implied mode), he notates so many F-sharps at cadences that the result sounds like modern G major colored by only occasional hints of Mixolydian. (In keeping with a common late-sixteenth-century practice, most accidentals are notated in both prints, leaving almost none to be supplied according to the rules of *musica ficta.*) In the second stanza, at the words "Cruore eius roseo," the music cadences briefly and unexpectedly on an E-major triad, placing a clear emphasis on "his red blood" before continuing with "Gustando vivimus Deo" ("in tasting which we live in God"). Though Victoria's hymns contain several other such effects, for him clothing the ancient Gregorian melodies with uniform but richly imitative counterpoint seems to have been a higher compositional priority than creating expressive rhetorical moments à la Lassus.

Many listeners today are struck by what they perceive to be the "sincerity" of Victoria's music, which may derive from his belief, stated in the preface to his *Missarum Liber Duo* of 1583, that music "describes the very being of God."[15] In one important respect Victoria differed from his great composer contemporaries Lassus, Palestrina, and Guerrero: he was a priest. This perhaps explains why he never sets final stanzas of his hymns in canon or otherwise manipulates the foundational musical material. Such respect for the original melodies could also partly explain why only occasionally does Victoria relinquish the contemplative polyphony that prevails through most of the collection to set a final polyphonic stanza in chordal texture in a lilting triple meter. He makes just such an exception for No. 8, *Ad cenam agni providi,* with notes of the doxology faster by a third than in the preceding stanzas. The same triple-meter doxology is used twice more for Nos. 24 and 27, both of which use the same melody as *Ad cenam agni providi* but have different polyphony for the even stanzas. Victoria writes different triple-meter doxologies for Nos. 12, 21, and 32. Aside from these six triple-meter polyphonic final stanzas, all thirty-two hymns show extraordinary consistency in setting even-numbered stanzas in duple-meter polyphony. Another sign of Victoria's focus and consistency of approach throughout his life: he wrote no secular or instrumental music, not even music for organ, despite being employed as an organist for most of his career.

Different in effect from *Ad cenam agni providi* is No. 7, the setting of the noble Dorian melody of the sixth-century poem by Venantius Fortunatus, *Vexilla regis prodeunt.* Here we encounter a majestic mood of dark intensity in keeping with Fortunatus's meditation on the cross, "a shining tree adorned with purple of the King." Stanza 4 reduces to three voices, with the chant melody in slow motion in the Cantus, accompanied by lower voices moving in minims and semiminims—almost exactly the same texture one sees in Stanza 4 of Festa's *Conditor alme siderum,* the first hymn in his collection. We should recall that the 1608 index from S. Maria di Monserrato referred to above listed a manuscript containing Festa's hymns in the possession of the church. Possibly it was acquired before Victoria left in 1575. It is tempting to think that Victoria knew Festa's settings, which are so similar to his own from forty-six years later.

One other observation on high clefs is in order: for No. 3, *Salvete, flores martyrum,* Victoria scores Stanza 2, the only polyphonic one, for two high voices (Cantus I and Cantus II, both notated with treble clefs) plus Altus

15. Cited by Stevenson, "Tomás Luis de Victoria," 34.

(mezzo clef) and high Tenor (alto clef). Possibly, this arrangement specifies a performance by very high voices as a means of recalling the voices of young children (*Salvete, flores martyrum* is sung on the Feast of Holy Innocents). More likely, however, is that transposition down by three or four steps is intended, as in the other high-clef hymns, which would still give the effect of high voices, but ones singing in the same ranges employed in the other hymns in the collection.

THEOLOGICAL PERSPECTIVES

To discover the theological perspectives communicated by Victoria's hymns, we recall that his source for the texts was most likely an antiphoner that contained the same hymns as the *Breviarium Romanum* of 1568 but that included the melodies as well. Many of these hymns had changed little since the Middle Ages, with the result that Victoria's collection proclaims a theology expressed by poets from many centuries earlier.

The Counter-Reformation goal of propagating a theology that had been articulated in the first millenium of Christianity moved into new territory with the advent of highly expressive and often overwhelming paintings, sculptures, and architecture as the sixteenth century progressed, yet the beliefs themselves remained essentially constant. First and foremost was the fact of the Trinity. In the late ninth century, there had been some controversy over the phrase "Te trina Deitas" ([We entreat] you, three-fold God), in the hymn *Sanctorum meritis*. In his treatise "De una et non trina Deitate" of 857, Archbishop Hincmar of Reims objected to the implication of a three-fold God, which he found blasphemous. By the time of Du Fay's hymns in the early fifteenth century, the offending phrase had been changed to "Te summa Deitas unaque" ([We entreat] you, greatest and sole God), which is how it appears in the sixteenth-century *alternatim* hymns as well, including Victoria's No. 26.

Traditionally, every hymn included as a final stanza a doxology praising the Trinity, mirroring in this respect the Christian practice of ending every psalm with a doxology. But whereas psalms used a single textual formula for this purpose, hymns showed endless inventiveness. Victoria's thirty-one hymn texts have nineteen different doxologies, with only six of these occurring in more than one hymn.

The texts of Victoria's hymns take for granted that many significant events in the New Testament were prefigured by parallel events in the Old.

Ad cenam agni providi, Victoria's No. 8, refers in Stanza 1 to the crossing of the Red Sea, in which those "in white robes sing to Christ the Prince at the feast of the providing lamb." The explanation in this case comes from 1 Cor 10:1–4, where Paul declares that the Red Sea crossing represents baptism. Thus, God's saving of the Israelites from Egyptian enslavement by the parting of the Red Sea prefigures Christ's saving of Christians by baptism from the slavery of sin. The hymn continues with references to events immediately preceding the Red Sea crossing, including the horror of a devastating angel who slays every firstborn son in Egypt except in households marked with lamb's blood on the door. Those households are Jewish, and the blood on the door allows the angel, by recognizing this, to "pass over" such homes. The hymn compares Christians to Jews "rescued from Pharaoh's cruel empire," meaning, for those singing the hymn, rescued from Satan's cruel empire: Christ "rises from the tomb and casts down the tyrant in chains, opening up paradise." J. M. Neale identified those mentioned in white robes in the first stanza as catechumens newly baptized, awaiting their first communion.[16]

The pattern of citing Old Testament events as prefigurations of ones in the New Testament (understood as a metaphor for modern times), can also be found in Venantius Fortunatus's famous *Vexilla regis prodeunt*, Victoria's No. 7, which makes prefiguration explicit. "Faithful David's prophecy, that on a tree our God has reigned, is now fulfilled" refers to the words "dicite in nationibus Dominus regnavit a ligno" of Ps 95:10 as translated in the Old Latin *Psalterium Romanum*. In *Quicumque Christum quæritis*, Victoria's No. 20, Prudentius states that Jesus is "the King of the Gentiles and King of the Jews, promised by the Father to Abraham and to his seed forever. He is the one indicated by the prophets' testimony and by witness of the same, whom the Father commanded we should hear and believe."

More common than references to the Old Testament are references and allusions to the New. The anonymous seventh- or eighth-century author of *Urbs beata Hierusalem*, Victoria's No. 31, draws on ideas from Eph 2:20 (the hymn's "built in heaven out of living stones" = "built on the foundation of the apostles and prophets, with Christ Jesus himself as the chief cornerstone"), Pet 2:5 (same phrase = "ye also, as living stones, are built up a spiritual house"), and Reve 21 ("newly come from heaven in the nuptial chamber, prepared like a bride to be joined to the Lord" = "I saw the Holy City, the new Jerusalem, coming down out of heaven from God, prepared as a bride beautifully dressed for her groom").

J. M. Neale observes that in No. 3, *Salvete flores martyrum*, Prudentius alludes to Revelation when he speaks of the slain children "innocently

16. Neale, *Short Commentary on the Hymnal*, 26–29.

playing before the altar" ("aram ante ipsam simplices"), which echoes "I saw under the Altar the souls of them which were slain for the Word of God" (Rev 6:9).[17]

Caelius Sedulius's *Hostis Herodes impie* for Epiphany, Victoria's No. 4, cites various events in the Gospels as manifestations of Christ's Godhead: the arrival of the Magi who "acknowledge God by gifts"; his baptism in a "pure stream" as the "heavenly Lamb" who "brought no sins but washed us clean"; and his transformation of water into wine at the wedding in Cana, revealing a "new kind of power."

Paul the Deacon's eighth-century hymn to John the Baptist, *Ut queant laxis,* Victoria's No. 16, recounts in four quatrains the saint's early history as told in Luke 1—starting with the announcement to Zechariah, John's father, by Gabriel ("a messenger coming swiftly from Olympus") that he and Elizabeth, though very old, would have a son who would grow to be great in the sight of the Lord and would be named John. It continues to mention incidents from Luke's account until the moment at the Visitation six months later when John in Elizabeth's womb recognizes Jesus in Mary's womb ("Lying hidden in the womb, you sensed the King dwelling in the bridal chamber").

Odo of Cluny's hymn to Mary Magdalene, *Lauda, mater ecclesia,* Victoria's No. 18, draws on material in the Gospels of Mark, Luke, and John. The first stanza alludes to the statements in Luke 2:8 and Mark 16:9 that Mary had seven demons cast out of her by Jesus' "sevenfold grace," a term that recalls the seven gifts of the Holy Spirit that Rabanus Maurus mentions in the third stanza of his Pentecost hymn, *Veni Creator Spiritus* (Victoria's No. 10): "You, by your sevenfold gifts, are the finger of God's right hand." In the second stanza, Odo calls Mary Magdalene "the sister of Lazarus," thereby converging her identity with that of Mary of Bethany, who, according to Luke 10:38 and John 11 and 12, was the sister of Martha and Lazarus. In the fourth stanza, with the words "she runs to the healer bearing an aromatic vase," Mary Magdalene appears to be identified with the unnamed woman in Luke 7:36–50, a "sinner" who brought an alabaster jar of ointment for Jesus' feet as he was dining with a Pharisee. In the sixth stanza, Odo alludes to the statement in Mark 16:9 and the implication in John 20:18 that Mary Magdalene was the first to see Jesus after he had risen from the tomb: "She sees Jesus rising in victory from hell, and she merits these first joys, who loved him more than the rest," this final statement referring back to the unnamed woman with the jar of ointment. Of her Jesus had said to the Pharisee that a person forgiven a great debt loves the forgiver more than

17. Neale, *Short Commentary on the Hymnal,* 16.

one who is forgiven only a minor debt. *Tristes erant Apostoli,* Victoria's No. 24, recounts the narrative of Matt 28:5–8, in which an angel tells Mary Magdalene and "the other Mary" that Jesus would soon be seen in Galilee. They run to tell the apostles.

Some of the hymn texts make no reference to biblical narratives, focusing instead on dogma: Mary's purity (No. 15, *Ave maris stella*); the eternal nature of Jesus as "begotten" and as the "only-born of the Father before the world began" (No. 2, *Christe, redemptor omnium . . . ex Patre*); Christ's great power, at which "every celestial and terrestrial knee is bent" (No. 1, *Conditor alme syderum*); the miraculous power of a confessor, at whose tomb "the limbs of the sick are restored to health, and those weighted down with any sickness are restored" (No. 28, *Iste confessor Domini*); and the ability of apostles to "close heaven and open its locks with a word" (No. 23, *Exultet cælum laudibus*).

The 1581 and 1600 prints assign *Aurea luce et decore,* Victoria's No. 17, to *Sancto Petro,* but the text reveals that it is actually for both Peter and Paul: "Gate-keeper of heaven and doctor on earth, judges of the world, illumining the world: one triumphed on a cross, the other by a sword, and they earned the exalted company of the laurel life."[18]

CONTRIBUTIONS TO LITURGY AND WORSHIP

Like most *alternatim* hymn collections in Counter-Reformation Italy, Victoria's 1581 collection was specifically designed to fulfill the needs of the liturgy. His hymns seem particularly well suited to each liturgical occasion, perhaps because they were composed with a priest's sensibility. Like the other sixteenth-century polyphonic hymn cycles, they follow the church year from Advent to Corpus Christi, plus some important saints' feasts and commons, and each hymn provides a heading over its several pages identifying the occasion to which it belongs.[19] Is there a place for Victoria's hymns in to-

18. The references here are to the traditions that Peter was crucified upside down on a cross, while Paul was decapitated by the blow of a sword.

19. Victoria's thirty-two hymns, showing the liturgical occasion to which each is assigned in the 1581 and 1600 prints, followed by the author of the medieval hymn text (not indicated in the prints):

1. *Conditor alme syderum*, De adventu Domini, *anon. (7th cent.)*
2. *Christe redemptor. . .ex Patre*, De nativitate Domini et infra Octavam, *anon. (6th cent.)*
3. *Salvete, flores martyrum*, De Innocentibus, *Prudentius (384–413)*
4. *Hostis Herodes impie*, De Epiphania, *Caelius Sedulius (5th cent.)*
5. *Lucis Creator optime*, In Dominicis per annum, *attr. Pope Gregory I (ca. 600)*
6. *Ad preces nostras*, Dominica in Quadragesima, *anon. (10th-century)*

day's church? Of all the *alternatim* hymn settings by Counter-Reformation composers, Victoria's present probably the fewest technical challenges and provide the most immediate rewards for a choir of moderate skill. With some instruction, the chant verses could be sung by a congregation. The juxtaposition of congregation and choir for the chant and polyphony would then approximate the sixteenth-century practice of alternating a chant schola with a polyphonic choir. As high art, of course, these works are at their most compelling when both chant and polyphony are performed by highly skilled singers. Victoria undoubtedly envisioned such performances, and in Madrid, with his famous choir in the Monasterio de las Descalzas Reales, no doubt achieved them, as he likely did earlier in Rome as well, where he was repeatedly hired to lead various choirs for special occasions during a residence of over two decades.

---

7. *Vexilla regis prodeunt*, Dominica in Passione, *Venantius Fortunatus* (530–609)
8. *Ad cenam agni providi*, In Octava Paschae usque ad Ascensionem, *attr. Ambrose* (340–397)
9. *Jesu nostra redemptio*, In Ascensione Domini, *anon. (probably 7th or 8th cent.)*
10. *Veni, Creator Spiritus*, In Pentecoste, *attr. Rabanus Maurus* (776–856)
11. *O lux beata Trinitas*, In Festo Sanctissmae Trinitatis, *attr. Ambrose* (340–397)
12. *Pange lingua . . . corporis*, In Festo Corporis Christi, *Thomas Aquinas* (1225–1274)
13. *Quodcumque vinclis*, In Cathedra Sancti Petri, *attr. St. Paulinus of Aquileia (8th cent.)*
14. *Doctor egregie Paule*, In Conversione et Commem. S. Pauli, *H. Elphis (d. 493)*
15. *Ave maris stella*, De Beata Virgine. *anon. (9th cent.?)*
16. *Ut queant laxis*, In Festo S. Ioannis Baptistae. *attr. Paulus Diaconus (8th cent.)*
17. *Aurea luce*, De Sancto Petro. *attr. H. Elphis (d. 493)*
18. *Lauda mater ecclesia*, De Sancta Maria Magdalena. *Odo of Cluny* (879–942)
19. *Petrus beatus*, In Festo Sancti Petri ad Vincula (*same music as Quodcumque vinclis*). *Paulinus II Aquil. (ca. 800)*
20. *Quicumque Christum quæritis*, In Transfiguratione Domini. *Prudentius* (384–413)
21. *Tibi, Christe, splendor Patris*, De Sancto Michaele. *Rabanus Maurus* (776–856)
22. *Christe redemptor . . . conserva*, In Festo Omnium Sanctorum. *attr. Rabanus Maurus* (776–856)
23. *Exultet cælum laudibus*, In Natali Apostolorum. *anon.* (*10th-century*)
24. *Tristes erant apostoli*, In Natali Apostolorum Tempore Paschali. *attr. St. Ambrose* (340–397)
25. *Deus, tuorum militum*, De Uno Martyre. *anon. (6th cent.?)*
26. *Sanctorum meritis*, De Pluribus Martyribus. *attr. Rabanus Maurus* (776–856)
27. *Rex gloriose martyrum*, Pro Martyribus Tempore Paschali. *anon.* (*6th cent.?*)
28. *Iste confessor*, In Festo Confessorum. *anon.* (*8th cent.*)
29. *Jesu, corona virginum*, De Virginibus. *ascr. St. Ambrose* (340–397)
30. *Huius obtentu Deus*, Pro Martyre tantum, et pro nec Virgine nec Martyre. *anon. (8th cent.)*
31. *Urbs beata Hierusalem*, In Dedicatione Ecclesia. *anon. (7th or 8th cent.)*
32. *Pange lingua . . . corporis*, De Corpore Christi (*More Hispano*). *Thomas Aquinas* (1225–1274)

NOTABLE HYMNS

All of Victoria's hymn settings stand out for their contrapuntal skill and colorful harmonies, but four are especially appealing: No. 1, *Conditor alme syderum*; No. 8, *Ad cenam agni providi*; No. 10, *Veni Creator Spiritus*; and No. 31, *Urbs beata Hierusalem*. In these a memorable plainchant melody becomes the basis for calmly unfolding harmonic motion marching to a final cadence, sometimes with colorful accidentals along the way. Though not as flashy as Lassus's hymns, or as ingenious as Palestrina's, these four are especially notable for their transparent counterpoint and long-range harmonic inevitability.

BIBLIOGRAPHY

Alvarez, Nancho, ed. *Tomás Luis de Victoria, [Opera omnia], Hymns*. www.uma.es/victoria.

Britt, Matthew. *The Hymns of the Breviary and Missal*. London: Burns Oates & Washbourne Ltd, 1922.

Cantus Manuscript Database of Latin Chants. http://cantus.uwaterloo.ca.

Neale, J. M. *The Hymnal Noted, Or, Translations of the Ancient Hymns of the Latin Church, Set to Their Proper Plainsong Melodies*. London: Novello, Ewer & Co., 1851; repr. Glendale, CO: Lancelot Andrewes, 2010.

———. *A Short Commentary on the Hymnal Noted from Ancient Sources*. London: Joseph Masters, 1853; repr. Lexington KY: Ulan, 2017.

O'Regan, Noel. "Tomás Luis de Victoria, Francisco de Soto and the Spanish Archconfraternity of the Resurrection in Rome." *Early Music* 22 (1994) 279–95.

———. "Tomás Luis de Victoria's Roman Churches Revisited." *Early Music* 28 (2000) 403–18.

———. "Victoria in Rome." *Leading Notes* 8 (1998) 26–30.

Pedrell, Philippo, ed. *Thomae Ludovici Victoria Abulensis Opera omnia*. Vol. 5. Leipzig: Breitkopf und Härtel, 1908.

Stevenson, Robert. *Spanish Cathedral Music in the Golden Age*. Berkeley: University of California Press, 1961.

———. "Tomás Luis de Victoria: Unique Spanish Genius." *Inter-American Music Review* 12 (1991) 1–100.

Tavard, George A. *Trina Deitas: The Controversy between Hincmar and Gottschalk*. Milwaukee: Marquette University Press, 1996.

Victoria, Tomás Luis de. *Ludovici a Victoria Abulensis: Hymni totius anni secundum Sanctae Romanae Ecclesiae consuetudinem qui quattuor concinuntur vocibus*. Rome: Domenico Basa.

Zager, Daniel. "Post-Tridentine Liturgical Change and Functional Music: Lasso's Cycle of Polyphonic Latin Hymns." In *Orlando di Lasso Studies*, edited by Peter Bergquist, 41–63. New York: Cambridge University Press, 1999.

Chapter 8

Giovanni Pierluigi da Palestrina

Polyphonic Music as Devotional Expression

David W. Music

HISTORICAL BACKGROUND

Giovanni Pierluigi da Palestrina was born ca. 1525–26, probably at Palestrina (near Rome), which gave him the name by which he became known. His musical education was achieved at least partly by service as a choirboy at Ste. Maria Maggiore Church in Rome, and in 1544 he received his first professional position, that of organist at St. Agapito church in Palestrina. He left this position in 1551 and returned to Rome as singing master (and later chapel master) at the Cappella Giulia, the Vatican choir that sang for services not officiated by the pope. In 1555, he became a member of the pope's personal musical chapel, the Sistine Cappella, though he was a married man and thus technically ineligible for the position. Later that year, upon the accession of a new pope, Palestrina was dismissed from the Cappella, though he continued to receive a pension for the service he had given. He went on to hold a succession of musical positions, including the churches of St. Giovanni Laterno (1555–60) and Ste. Maria Maggiore (where he had been trained, 1560–65), and the Seminario Romano (1566–71). In 1571, Palestrina returned as choirmaster of the Cappella Giulia and retained this appointment for the rest of his life. In addition to these regular positions, he served periodically as music director for Cardinal Ippolito II d'Este at his estate in Tivoli, and provided music for processions and other activities of the Roman confraternities, which were religious organizations founded by/for lay persons, that grew out of the Counter-Reformation. After the death of his first wife in 1580 Palestrina considered entering the priesthood but instead married the widow of a wealthy fur merchant in 1581. He continued to pursue his musical activities but added to these investment in the fur business and real estate in Rome. He died in Rome on February 2, 1594.

A key event during Palestrina's lifetime was the meeting of the Council of Trent between 1545 and 1563. Called in part to counter the Protestant Reformation, the council made very few pronouncements about music, except to admonish composers, organists, and churches to avoid using secular tunes in worship and to give the words of sacred music greater prominence and intelligibility. Palestrina's exact relationship to the council (if any) is not now evident. The fact that the composer wrote a Mass for Pope Marcellus II (the *Missa Papae Marcelli*), one of the reforming popes of the period, led to a legend that the council sought to return to the sole use of Gregorian chant in the church but that Palestrina and his Mass "saved" church music (i.e., polyphony). This legend, however, has no historical basis. Indeed, much of Palestrina's music broke the council's strictures: some of his Masses were based on previously existing secular pieces and the frequent use of imitation often obscured the words. On the other hand, the "Palestrina style" was certainly in keeping with the spirit of the reforming movement in its careful text declamation and objective nature, and it has often become synonymous with "Roman Catholic religious music," at least for music that goes beyond unison singing, such as Gregorian chant.

THEOLOGICAL PERSPECTIVES

Insofar as is known, Palestrina never left a written statement about his theological convictions, apart from a few scattered references in publication dedications and letters in which he acknowledged his trust in God's grace, and since he was a composer and not a poet, there are no hymn texts to analyze. Even the (mostly Latin) texts he chose to set are not necessarily a trustworthy guide to his theology, since many of them were standard liturgical texts that any Roman Catholic church composer of the time would employ and others were specific commissions by churches or individuals.

Still, some inferences, based upon the music he wrote, are observable. It is not claimed that his compositions provide any sort of detailed description of Palestrina's theological views, but rather that his works—like those of any other thoughtful composer—reflect certain overall views of God, creation, and the church.

The objective nature of Palestrina's music seems more commonly to mirror the transcendence of God than his immanence. This feature can be seen in a variety of ways. For one thing, the composer showed a marked preference for setting the unvarying words of the Mass Ordinary over the broader array of texts that could be used for motets. While many portions of the Mass Ordinary text are subjective in nature—the cry for mercy of the *Kyrie eleison* or the crucifixion and burial of Jesus in the Credo, for instance—much of it is made up of relatively straightforward statements of praise or belief: there is little in it of personal testimony or individual emotion. Furthermore, the frequent repetition of the Ordinary texts—which were sung every time Mass was celebrated—tended to give even the more subjective portions a sense of objectivity that might not be reflected in a simple one-time reading of the words.

While it was not uncommon in the Renaissance for composers to make numerous settings of the Mass Ordinary, the number of times that Palestrina returned to it suggests something beyond mere convenience, commissions from patrons, personal challenge, or the like. It surely reflected also a view of God as one who is not subject to adequate depiction by humans; in other words, God is one who is "other." The frequent resetting of the unvarying Ordinary text implies the unvarying nature of God himself.

The objective nature of Palestrina's musical style also suggests this "otherness." The seamless, continuously unfolding counterpoint or alternation between voices can be seen as representative of the eternity of God and his continued acts of creativity, and of his variety of actions within a unity of essence. The homogenous sound that is often found in Palestrina's music suggests that, while God is constantly on the move, he is steadfast and unified in his purposes. This homogeneity, formed by the frequent imitation, overlapping of text, equality of parts, moderate ranges, smooth vocal lines, careful preparation and resolution of dissonance, and other features creates a body of sound that directs attention away from the individual word, note, or voice toward the corporate and universal. Even when Palestrina highlights a particular word or phrase through musical rhetoric, the device is seldom exaggerated and almost invariably stays within the context of the body of sound as a whole. Thus it is not the individual word but the general mood and message of the text that is emphasized by Palestrina. In that sense, his is an affective theological methodology rather than one that is completely tied to written revelation.

As with Gregorian chant, the music of Palestrina calls little attention to itself—and, by extension, to the singer or listener—but rather to God. The music is not intended to make a person "feel" anything except that one is in the presence of the Holy and that the best way to listen to it is on one's knees (figuratively, if not literally). This is not to say that Palestrina's sacred music lacks emotion or appeal to the singer/listener; as H. K. Andrews observed in *An Introduction to the Technique of Palestrina*, the composer "covered the whole range of emotional expression from intense jubilation to penitential sorrow with complete technical mastery of his medium and consummate restraint."[1] The key word in Andrews's analysis is "restraint," for the God Palestrina honored with his music is one who should be approached on his own terms rather than human ones. In this sense, at least, Palestrina might be compared to John Calvin, though the outcomes of their philosophies and approaches were radically different.

Palestrina's theology on the nature of God reflects order, perfection, and beauty. The symmetrical phrasing, interweaving of themes, and overall equilibrium of a Mass movement or motet bespeak a creator whose work is not haphazard or arbitrary but fits into a well-conceived plan in which each element supports another. Palestrina's God is one who is in complete control. The intricacy of Palestrina's musical imitation (like the complexity of nature) coalesces into beautiful harmonies that reflect a creator who lovingly guides the creation to its final destination. Dissonance certainly happens in nature (and in human nature), but the composer's handling of this musical element implies that, while such discords will occur, God can lead them to a successful and satisfying conclusion, restoring the balance of nature.

Another perspective that is suggested by Palestrina's sacred music is the durability and continuity of the church. For the composer, a Roman Catholic often working in the heart of the Vatican, the church was the "ark of faith" through which Christ's salvation was mediated to the world, and it had an unbroken history going back to the time of Jesus and Peter. Just as in his music, that history was made up of different themes, with the end of one period overlapping with the beginning of another (sometimes with dissonance along the way), but the whole creating a continuous narrative that demonstrated the strength and resilience of the church. The large number of settings of the Mass Ordinary, the official service of the Roman Catholic church, also hints at this idea.

1. Andrews, *Introduction to the Technique*, 7.

Finally, it can be said that much of Palestrina's music seems to be couched in the spirit of prayer and contemplation. While expression of the text is uppermost, the music creates an atmosphere that allows the mind to probe spiritual depths beyond those communicated by the words alone. In this sense, the comparison of Palestrina's music with Gregorian chant is an apt one.

Exceptions to these generalizations can, of course, be found throughout Palestrina's works, and some of the same sorts of ideas can be seen in the music of his contemporaries. On the whole, however, these concepts probably hold true more consistently for this composer than for any other. As a result, Palestrina's music has often been—and frequently still is—held up as the ideal of polyphonic music written for the purposes of devotion.

CONTRIBUTION TO LITURGY AND WORSHIP

Palestrina published his first book of Masses, containing five works, in 1554. He continued pursuing this genre until the end of his life (several collections were published posthumously), ultimately composing at least 104 such works, more than his renowned contemporaries Orlande de Lassus, Tomás Luis de Victoria, and William Byrd combined.

The bulk of Palestrina's works in this genre were cantus firmus Masses, in which the music was founded upon a preexisting composition. More than half of the Masses were of the "parody" or "imitation" type, with both melodic and harmonic features of an existing polyphonic model (usually a motet or madrigal) being adapted to new surroundings by adding or subtracting voices, combining the voices in new ways, rewriting parts, and interspersing new material. The model was sometimes the composer's own work but was often a piece by another musician, which gave scope either to honor the earlier person or to show how the later composer could expand or improve upon the compositional materials. An example of the technique can be seen in the Kyrie of the *Missa Veni sponsa Christi*, based on Palestrina's own four-voice motet. The motet uses four musical themes, the first two of which serve as the basic material for the Kyrie I and Christe, respectively, while the third and fourth themes are employed for Kyrie II. However, the borrowed "themes" are not just melodies but also vertical sonorities derived from the motet, varied and intermixed with new harmonies.

Another important technique employed in about a third of Palestrina's Masses is paraphrase, in which a single preexisting melody is used to develop themes for contrapuntal elaboration in the voice parts of each movement; the *Missa Aeterna Christi munera*, based on a Gregorian hymn, is such a work. The remaining pieces are tenor Masses (a borrowed melody appearing in the tenor part of each section in relatively unadorned fashion), hexachord Masses (a newly invented melody that served as the theme for each section), polychoral Masses, or were freely composed; counted among the latter is his most famous work in this genre, the *Missa Papae Marcelli*.

In addition to the Masses, Palestrina wrote more than 300 motets based on introits, graduals, antiphons, and other biblical and liturgical texts, as well as numerous hymns and offertories. In this context, a "hymn" was not a piece for congregational singing but a setting of a metrical text as opposed to the prose text of most other liturgical items. Palestrina's music also included choral settings of Lamentations, Magnificats, litanies, and more than 140 madrigals, both spiritual and secular; however, no authentic instrumental works by the composer are known.

Pervading Imitation

The theological perspectives of Palestrina's music are intimately bound up with his style of composition. This style was based on that of the Franco-Flemish composers of the previous generation. In this approach, a phrase of the text was given its own musical theme, which would then be subjected to imitative writing between the voices, building what is often called a "point of imitation." The next phrase would be given a new theme that would be worked out in similar fashion. Once a new theme was introduced, the previous one would typically not be heard again in the course of the piece. The ending of one section of music frequently overlapped with the beginning of the next one (employing a new theme), creating "pervading imitation," a continuous unfolding of music.

In Palestrina's hands, the pervading imitation style achieved a remarkable sense of balance and proportion. Short phrases of text were subjected to numerous points of imitation or melismatic passages that extended their length, while longer phrases received fewer repetitions or were set more syllabically; thus the sections with short texts and those with longer ones would typically be of similar length.

This procedure can be clearly seen in the two parts of the four-voice motet *Sicut cervus*, a setting of a baptismal tract that is based on Ps 42:1–3 (Ps 41:2–4 in the *Vulgate*). Part one of the motet sets thirty syllables of text, while the text of part two is more than twice as long at sixty-eight syllables. Nevertheless, the musical settings of the two sections are almost identical in length (fifty-eight breves vs. fifty-nine) because the imitative themes of the first part are given more repetitions and tend to use longer note values and melismatic passages.

Similar proportions—though not as precise as those between the two major divisions of the motet—are also found within each part. For example, the first phrase of part one (*Sicut cervus . . . aquarum*) contains fourteen syllables, the second phrase (*ita desiderat*) six syllables, and the third (*anima mea ad te Deus*) nine syllables. If these lines were set syllabically and with no repetition, the first phrase of music would normally be twice as long as the second and the third half again as long as the second. However, if measured from the sounding of the first syllable to the final statement of the last syllable in each phrase of text, the first phrase covers twenty-five breves, the second twenty-two breves, and the third nineteen breves. Thus, the second phrase, which contains fewer than half the syllables of the first, is musically almost as long as the initial phrase. Of course, the beginning of each new phrase overlaps with the conclusion of the former one, as can be clearly seen (for example) at the twenty-second breve, where the cadence that ends the opening portion of the motet (*Sicut cervus . . . aquarum*) is overlapped by the beginning of the next section (*ita desiderat*): the bass part enters with the new section of text and musical theme while the soprano part is still holding *[aqua]rum* and the alto is continuing with a melismatic passage on the same word.

This motet demonstrates other characteristic features of Palestrina's technique: each important grouping of words in a textual phrase is given its own distinctive subtheme. The opening textual phrase, *Sicut cervus desiderat ad fontes aquarum*, employs two musical subthemes, one for *Sicut cervus* that is syllabic and in long note values and the other for *desiderat ad fontes aquarum*, which is more melismatic and with shorter note values. While the two subthemes are usually employed as a single unit, at the eighteenth and nineteenth breves the second subtheme and its associated text appear in the tenor and bass parts divorced from the beginning of the theme.

Palestrina's handling of imitation is creative and varied. Sometimes the voices enter at regular intervals, but often one or more of the voices enters "early" or "late," giving the music a certain amount of unpredictability. For example, in the opening of *Pueri Hebraeorum*, in which the first soprano enters a breve after the second soprano, the alto comes in only half a breve later and the tenor not for another four breves. Imitative themes also occasionally appear in inversion, as in the motet *Surrexit Pastor bonus*. Here, the second tenor begins with a leap up of a fifth while the bass entry leaps down a fifth, with the following notes also inverted from the original statement; the alto pattern duplicates that of the second tenor and the first tenor that of the bass.

Other Techniques

While Palestrina is justly famous for his use of pervading imitation, this was far from the only approach he employed. Some works, such as the motet *Alma Redemptoris Mater*, are mainly homophonic, while a surprisingly large number of motets and several Masses, particularly ones apparently dating from his later life, are written in a polychoral idiom. Some of these works show characteristic features of the incipient Baroque style, including slightly greater prominence of the uppermost voice and passages in which the bass voice moves principally by fifths and fourths. This is reflected in the triple-time section concluding Kyrie II of the *Missa Hodie Christus natus est* or the end of the *Osanna* in the *Missa Ascendo ad Patrem*; both works are derived from motets of Palestrina's own composition.

A technique that was often used by the composer, particularly in works involving more than four but fewer than eight voices, was to group voice parts in various combinations during the course of a piece. This creates a continually shifting kaleidoscope of tonal colors. *O magnum mysterium*, a Nativity responsory for six-part S1/S2/A1/A2/T/B choir, is such a piece. The work opens with a statement sung by S1/S2/A2/T (ignoring a single "O" in A1 and B; see ex. 1), followed by the groupings S2/A1/A2/B, S1/S2/A1/T, S1/A1/A2/T/B, S2/A2/T, S1/A1/A2/B, and so on throughout the motet.

In many of his works, especially longer ones such as the Masses, Palestrina made use of several of these techniques in the course of the composition. The shorter-texted movements of the Mass (Kyrie, Sanctus, Benedictus, Agnus Dei) principally employed imitation, while the longer-texted ones (Gloria, Credo) included more homophonic writing or voice groupings (see the *Missa Brevis*). An exception is the *Missa Papae Marcelli*, in which there is almost no imitation of the sort seen in *Sicut cervus*, the composer instead relying principally upon voice groupings and homophonic writing. The variety of approaches also shows up in individual pieces, as in the five-voice antiphon motet *Ascendo ad Patrem*, which begins in an imitative fashion (with the entries grouped into SA + T1/T2/B), moves to continually shifting combinations of voices with brief polychoral-like sections, and includes a single very short homophonic passage.

Balance and proportion were also achieved by the composer's treatment of melodic contour, voice ranges, rhythm, and dissonance. Imitative themes tend to trace an arch in their appearance on the page, rising to the middle of the phrase and falling toward the end (see the first soprano part in *Tu es Petrus*). Individual voice parts usually proceed step-wise or with only small leaps; when a skip (whether large or small) does occur, the line typically turns back on itself by step-wise motion. Voice ranges are generally moderate, exploring neither the upper nor lower extremes. The voice parts most often proceed in adjacent rhythmic values; for example (expressed in modern terms), a half note is seldom followed by an eighth note without an intervening quarter note, the result being a smooth transition from one rhythmic value to another. Changes of meter and general rhythmic movement within a composition are largely restricted to moving from duple to triple meter for words of a joyous character such as "alleluia," and sometimes back to duple again. Dissonances are carefully prepared and just as carefully resolved.

Other important factors that go into making up the "Palestrina style" are his harmonic structure and treatment of the words. The harmony is derived from the contrapuntal interplay of the voices, which are largely independent of one another, but the vertical sonority is obviously an important concern for the composer. A distinguishing feature of this sonority is a tendency toward the use of full chords (i.e., chords containing thirds), especially at cadence points. The motet *Quia vidisti me, Thoma* ("Because you have seen me, Thomas"), for example, opens with an imitative passage between the soprano and alto that contains several open fifths and unisons as well as passing-tone dissonances. However, once the tenor voice enters, there is seldom a chord that does not have a third or a suspension in it, even when the texture is reduced to only two voices. This gives the piece a rich sonority and warmth of sound. Even works in which "incomplete" chords might have been used for expressive purposes, such as the Lamentation settings, make extensive use of full chords.

Palestrina's works are somewhat conservative in their tendency toward diatonicism and the infrequent use of accidentals. For example, the Pentecost motet *Loquebantur variis linguis* ("Speaking various languages") covers approximately 100 breves but contains not a single chromatic sign, perhaps suggesting the plainness and clarity with which the message of the apostles was received by their hearers. Admittedly, there are places in the motet where *musica ficta* would almost certainly have been applied, and in some works the composer gave more chromatic indications than in this one, such as the opening of *O magnum mysterium*; however, this use of chromatic harmony was usually done for some special purpose (see below).

A special characteristic of Palestrina's music is its careful text declamation. Generally speaking, Palestrina linked stressed syllables with long note values, notes that are higher in pitch, or melismas, while unstressed syllables most often occur on shorter or lower pitched notes and are sung syllabically or with very short melismas. Speech rhythm (one note per syllable of text) occurs frequently, particularly in the head-motives of themes. The composer customarily sets each complete textual phrase to a single musical theme. When the text includes a lengthy phrase, it might be broken up into two or three portions, each with its own musical theme, but the overall comprehension of the words is never compromised. Thus in the Palm Sunday motet *Pueri Hebraeorum* Palestrina separates the opening line of text into three segments: *Pueri Hebraeorum—portantes ramos olivarum—obviaverunt Domino clamantes* ("The children of the Hebrews—bearing olive branches—went to meet the Lord, crying out"). A different musical theme and compositional procedure is assigned to each segment. In this and other cases, the breaks made in the text are natural ones that show careful attention both to the meaning of each sub-phrase and to the phrase as a whole.

Palestrina followed the practice of most Renaissance composers in using word painting, the illustration of specific words by means of musical devices, reflecting obvious meanings of words or at least not contradicting their natural implications. For instance, the first word of the motet *Ascendo ad Patrem* ("I ascend to my Father") is depicted by an upward leap of an octave, and the beginning of *O magnum mysterium* expresses the "great mystery" of the Incarnation through a "musical mystery," obscuring the modal center of A minor (Aeolian) by moving from an opening E major chord through A major and D major chords to G major within the space of four breves.

However, while making full use of such devices, Palestrina is generally more concerned with keeping the overall message and mood of a text than with illustrating individual words. Even when he does musically underline a particular word it is often for a larger purpose. Thus in the opening of part one of *Sicut cervus*, the word *aquarum* ("water") is depicted through melismas of up to seventeen notes, a procedure that another Renaissance composer might employ as an illustration of flowing water. However, the word painting has a function for Palestrina beyond mere playfulness with musical sounds, for this emphasis on "water" highlights the liturgical use of this text as a baptismal tract. Furthermore, the largely stepwise nature of the melismas, their centering in the middle of the singers' ranges, and the fact that at least two other voices are singing at the same time means that they are not foregrounded to the listener.

On the other hand, the word *desiderat* ("desires"), which could likewise be symbolized either by melismatic writing or by extended note values (emphasizing the longing of the deer for water) receives no special attention. Indeed, the drawn-out notes that suggest longing do appear in the musical theme, but on the words *Sicut cervus* rather than *desiderat*. Palestrina has given the overall message of the deer's longing without resorting to the painting of an individual word.

But this instance also demonstrates the composer's sense of balance in text setting, for the word *desiderat* occurs again in the next phrase, *ita desiderat anima mea* ("so my soul desires"), and here it *is* set melismatically. As the new musical theme unfolds, it becomes evident that the composer had saved his illustration of "desire"—now referring to human desire—for this point in the piece. In setting the second phrase of text, Palestrina used both devices to symbolize the desire of the singer for God, long notes and a melisma, but since both devices are used, they do not call undue attention to themselves individually. Indeed, the musical procedure for the first two words of this phrase is remarkably similar in overall approach to that of the opening of the motet, several long notes followed by shorter note values and a melisma, musically suggesting the textual comparison that is made between the longing of the deer for water and that of the soul for God.

Similarly, in *Surrexit Pastor bonus*, the inversion of the opening imitative theme described above serves as a musical interpretation of the text, *Surrexit Pastor bonus qui animam suam posuit* ("The good Shepherd who laid down his life arose"): the descending fifth reflects the laying down of the Shepherd's life and the ascending fifth the Shepherd's resurrection. Since both the ascending fifth and the descending fifth appear on the word *surrexit* ("arose"), it is evident that Palestrina was aiming at an illustration of the entire line, not just a single word.

While the meaning of the word painting in works such as *Ascendo ad Patrem*, *O magnum mysterium*, *Sicut cervus*, and *Surrexit Pastor bonus* is self-evident, it is also true that these devices are worked into the composition so that they are seldom allowed to interrupt the flow of sound or the general spirit of contemplation. As stated above, it is the overall mood and message of the text that is of most importance to Palestrina, not the individual word. In this sense, his music is similar to Gregorian chant in its general ambience.

NOTABLE WORKS

The *Missa Papae Marcelli* and *Sicut cervus* are undoubtedly the best known and most often performed of the composer's Masses and motets, respectively, and both are worthy of this status, even if they are not entirely typical. The *Missa Brevis* and the motets *Exultate Deo*, *O magnum mysterium*, *Adoramus te Christe*, and *Alma redemptoris Mater* are also important for the number of performances and recordings they receive (the last two at least in part because of their relative simplicity). Other works mentioned in the discussion above—particularly among the motets—and many others like them have proven to be appropriate and useful for various liturgical occasions.

BIBLIOGRAPHY

Alwes, Chester. "Palestrina's Style: The Art of Balance." *Choral Journal* 35.1 (August 1994) 13–17.

Andrews, H. K. *An Introduction to the Technique of Palestrina*. London: Novello and Company, 1958.

Coates, Henry. *Palestrina*. London: J. M. Dent and Sons, 1938.

Early Music 22.4 (November 1994). Entire issue dedicated to the quatercentenary of Palestrina's death.

Fellerer, Karl Gustav. "Church Music and the Council of Trent." *Musical Quarterly* 39.4 (October 1953) 576–94.

Jeppesen, Knud. *The Style of Palestrina and the Dissonance*. Translated by Margaret W. Hamerik. London: Humphrey Milford, 1927; 2nd ed., New York: Dover, 1970.

Lockwood, Lewis, ed. *Giovanni Pierluigi da Palestrina: Pope Marcellus Mass. An Authoritative Score, Backgrounds and Sources, History and Analysis, Views and Comments*. New York: W. W. Norton, 1975.

Lockwood, Lewis, and Jessie Ann Owens. "Palestrina." In *The New Grove High Renaissance Masters: Josquin, Palestrina, Lassus, Victoria, Byrd*. New York: W. W. Norton, 1984.

Lockwood, Lewis, Noel O'Regan, and Jessie Ann Owens. "Palestrina, Giovanni Pierluigi da." *Oxford Music Online; Grove Music Online*. http://www.oxfordmusiconline.com/grovemusic/view/10.1093/gmo/9781561592630.001.0001/omo-9781561592630-e-0000020749.

Mahrt, William. "Palestrina's *Sicut Cervus*: A Motet Upon a *Parallelismus Membrorum*." *Sacred Music* 141.1 (Spring 2014) 34–41.

Marvin, Clara. *Giovanni Pierluigi da Palestrina: A Guide to Research*. New York: Routledge, 2002.

Music, David W. "O Magnum Mysterium: Three Mystical Renaissance Settings." *The American Organist* 40.11 (November 2006) 75–78.

Novack, Saul. "Tonality and the Style of Palestrina." In *Music and Civilization: Essays in Honor of Paul Henry Lang*, edited by Edmond Strainchamps and Maria Rika Maniates, 428–43. New York: W. W. Norton, 1984.

Owens, Jessie Ann. "Palestrina at Work." In *Papal Music and Musicians in Late Medieval and Renaissance Rome*, edited by Richard Sherr, 270–95. Oxford: Clarendon, 1998.

Pyne, Zoë Kendrick. *Giovanni Pierluigi da Palestrina: His Life and Times*. London: John Lane, 1922.

Roche, Jerome. *Palestrina*. Oxford Studies of Composers 7. London: Oxford University Press, 1971.

Part 5

Seventeenth Century

Chapter 9

British Hymnists

J. Christopher Holmes

HISTORICAL BACKGROUND

With few exceptions, the metrical psalm was the dominant form of church music in Britain from the Reformation until the eighteenth century. Even as hymns began to appear in the seventeenth century, very few congregations would have been comfortable with singing them in a corporate worship setting. Incremental but significant changes occurred in those turbulent years, which provided the transition from exclusive psalmody in worship to the incorporation of sung hymnody.[1] A number of individuals contributed to this remarkable shift in church music, many more than can be presented here, but this chapter details some of the most pivotal British hymnists of this period, both in terms of the hymns they penned and their passion to see hymn singing become a normative practice for congregational worship. Most of these writers were committed churchmen, regardless of denominational differences.

The impetus for the development of British hymnody almost certainly was the increase in the influence and accessibility of the English Bible. The Reformation had asserted the Word of God as the foundation of the

1. Benson, *English Hymn*, 45.

church—and the basis of its worship—which anchored the songs of the church in the trustworthiness of Scripture.[2] The Word of God contains not only inspired psalms fit for singing but also texts, narratives, and doctrines capable of serving as platforms for hymns and songs. During the seventeenth century, the breadth of congregational song began to widen substantially as the whole canon of Scripture steadily was deemed suitable to be sung by God's people.

In the early sixteenth century, the Reformation influence of John Calvin upon public worship in Britain had resulted in an almost exclusive adoption of metrical psalmody. The underlying theological conviction that drove Calvin was his unswerving commitment to Scripture and his adherence to the regulative principle. He would not endorse anything in the worship of the church that could not locate its foundation in the authority of Scripture. While congregational singing was certainly referenced in God's Word, in Calvin's thinking, anything to be sung had to be taken directly from the Bible. Any texts of human composition, Calvin believed, must depart at some point from biblical truth. He concluded that only the God-inspired psalms of Scripture were suitable for public worship.[3]

This embrace of metrical psalmody was a departure from the historic Latin hymnody. Consequently, the predominance of psalms tended to negate interest in the creation of hymns. Although the conversion of the Latin hymns into English might have seemed a likely method for the evolution of British hymnody, this route was not pursued, and metrical psalmody not only endured but also deepened in the latter decades of the sixteenth century.[4]

British hymnody developed slowly throughout the seventeenth century as a growing dissatisfaction with psalmody emerged. Exclusive psalmody no longer seemed sufficient to provide the full range of Christian expression, and relaxing the rigid manner with which it had been employed no longer seemed to violate the conscience of many worshippers. As well, other aspects influenced the movement toward hymns from metrical psalms. The literary character of the authorized psalters was poor and needed to be updated and improved. Their lackluster artistry had been tolerated for many years and would no longer be endured. In addition, seventeenth-century worshippers faced a host of difficult and challenging circumstances that warranted greater accommodation and acknowledgement in public worship than the sixteenth-century psalm texts could provide. Finally,

2. Julian, *Dictionary of Hymnology*, 345.

3. Benson, *English Hymn*, 23.

4. Benson, *English Hymn*, 63.

congregational song was confined to the language only available in the Old Testament psalms, but many were increasingly open to the possibility that other biblical texts—as much the Word of God as the psalms—could also be paraphrased and incorporated into congregational singing. These aspects, along with the significant increase in devotional poetry, eventually resulted in the emergence of hymnic forms.[5]

When George Wither (1588–1667) issued *The Hymns and Songs of the Church* (1623), it was among the earliest English-language hymnbooks. A remarkable publication, it contained both Scripture paraphrases, which were conventional, as well as true hymns for special occasions. Wither had petitioned James I for permission to publish the work, in order to bypass the monopoly held by the Stationers' Company to permit the publishing of books. Wither suspected the hymnic content would be controversial—he desired his book to be bound with every copy of the metrical psalter, so it would be used concurrently with them after morning and evening prayer, but not as a part of the liturgy. Although the book did receive a royal patent, almost immediately the company was able to suppress Wither's work, because of their alliance with the Puritans who favored the exclusive use of psalms. The patent had to be withdrawn.[6] Had the book been successful, original hymns might have developed nearly a century earlier within the established church, rather than emerging toward the end of the seventeenth century among the nonconformists. Wither's work resulted in persecution and financial loss rather than personal accolades and profit.[7]

These intermediate years of the seventeenth century in Britain were turbulent, and conflict was evident in nearly all religious, political, and social contexts. The hymns that appeared in this period reflected both the environment in which they were produced and the varied convictions of their authors. The writing and publishing of hymns in the seventeenth century marked at least a developing literary interest in that art form; nevertheless, the practical introduction of hymn singing into the churches alongside the long-established metrical psalmody proved particularly difficult.

Another significant individual from this period was George Herbert (1593–1633). One of the metaphysical poets, Herbert was particularly skilled, and various lines from his poems were later extracted as hymn texts. The source of these texts was *The Temple* (1633), his collection of poems published posthumously, which include some of the most remarkable poetry

5. Benson, *English Hymn*, 45–56.
6. Watson, *English Hymn*, 57.
7. Julian, *Dictionary of Hymnology*, 347.

in the English language.[8] Herbert and the other devotional poets produced ground-breaking compositions clearly intended to enhance private devotion; however, establishing English hymnody was neither the goal nor the result.[9] Herbert did not compose texts for congregational singing; thus, many of his most beautiful and substantial poems could not be adapted for that setting. Over a century later, John Wesley endeavored to convert many of these texts into hymns, but his success was limited.[10]

Shortly following the Restoration of Charles II in 1660, the Clarendon Code was ratified, and the various dissenting sectors of Christian worship outside the Church of England—Baptists, Presbyterians, Congregationalists, Quakers, etc.—found themselves under a significant threat of persecution. Each group addressed the matter of public singing in accord with their own convictions.[11] These strenuous years did not encourage the production of hymns among nonconformists, since those who chose to sing risked signaling their whereabouts and facing the unpleasant consequences of persecution. Others, such as the Quakers and some Baptists, believed the practice of psalm singing was altogether inappropriate for corporate worship.[12] Nevertheless, the transition from psalmody to hymnody is most obvious in the latter half of the seventeenth century. This development is especially evident among the Particular (Calvinistic) Baptists and Congregationalists.

One important exception is Thomas Ken (1637–1711), who completed his education at Winchester College in 1651. Firmly committed to the Church of England and possessing a reputation for utter faithfulness, Ken served in multiple church roles over the next several years. Ken returned to Winchester College in 1665 and later published *A Manual of Prayers for the Use of the Scholars of Winchester College* (1674), which encouraged students to sing his "Morning," "Evening," and "Midnight" hymn texts apparently already in use at the college. These hymns were appended to the *Manual* in 1695, and they are significant in that they did not develop from a Puritan model.[13] Ken's hymns from the *Manual* reflect his saintly personality and do not compare to his other hymns.[14] Ken exhorted, "Be sure to sing the Morning and Evening Hymn in your Chamber devoutly, remembering that the Psalmist, upon happy Experience, assures you that it is a good thing to

8. Eskew and McElrath, *Sing with Understanding*, 128.

9. Benson, *English Hymn*, 67.

10. Gregory, *Hymn-Book of the Modern Church*, 110.

11. Benson, *English Hymn*, 74.

12. Julian, *Dictionary of Hymnology*, 348.

13. Benson, *English Hymn*, 69–70.

14. Julian, *Dictionary of Hymnology*, 349.

tell of the loving Kindness of the Lord early in the Morning and of his Truth in the Night season."[15]

In the context of British hymnody, the renown of Benjamin Keach (1640–1704) rests squarely on the introduction of hymn singing to his congregation and his public defense of its practice.[16] Although he enjoyed considerable religious freedom in his early years, those liberties were radically restricted after 1660. Like many other Baptists following the Restoration, Keach suffered severely for his nonconformist beliefs. After publishing a book for the education of children that included his Baptist convictions, he was targeted for persecution in his home in Buckinghamshire.[17] Seeking a new beginning, Keach moved to London in 1668. Soon afterward, he embraced Calvinistic doctrine and eventually became the pastor of a Particular Baptist congregation in Southwark, where he remained for thirty-five years.

In 1688, the Glorious Revolution ushered in a new monarchy that brought a measure of toleration for the nonconformists and some freedoms from the previous penalties. The new religious environment provided opportunities to publish one's convictions more freely. In 1691, Keach published his first hymn collection, *Spiritual Melody*, which contained three hundred hymns. Not all these texts were written by Keach, but the sharing of material was a common practice at that time. *Spiritual Melody* may have been the first English hymn book to be used in congregational worship. It was almost certainly the first *Baptist* hymn book. Keach later published *A Feast of Fat Things Full of Marrow* (1696), which included another one hundred hymns. Virtually all of his hymns have been absent from modern use.[18]

If each hymn component is counted separately, the total number of hymns that Keach published is nearly five hundred. He did borrow or edit the work of other authors, drawing especially from John Mason. Nevertheless, the bulk of the hymns that Keach published were his own compositions.[19] Many of his texts possessed little artistry. While they were faithful in theological content and metrical arrangement, their beauty was often lacking, rendering them neither attractive nor singable. Nevertheless, Keach's efforts paved the way for future hymn writers.

After a long and tumultuous century, the labors of many faithful men began to bear lasting fruit—hymns began to be embraced as appropriate for

15. Ken, *Manual of Prayers*, 6.

16. Music, "Hymns of Benjamin Keach," 153.

17. Julian, *Dictionary of Hymnology*, 610.

18. Julian, *Dictionary of Hymnology*, 610.

19. Clarke, "Hymns, Psalms, and Controversy," 23. See also Music, "Hymns of Benjamin Keach," 148–52.

public worship. British hymnody began to flourish in the early eighteenth century with the advent of prominent hymn writers such as Isaac Watts, the Wesleys, etc. Although Anglicans did not widely utilize hymns until the nineteenth century, many others began to employ them with increasing regularity, and often they were composed with greater skill and artistry.[20] Hymnists from various denominational streams contributed to the ongoing transition from psalms to hymns as the principal mode of congregational song. As prominent as the metrical psalms had been, the labors of the seventeenth-century hymnists were sufficient to encourage the consideration and ultimately the embrace of hymns in regular church services. What had once been limited to the privacy of individual devotion was greatly expanded to the public assemblies of corporate worship. Hymns were no longer believed to be inappropriate but capable of faithfully conveying the truth of God's Word in the midst of the gathered saints.

THEOLOGICAL PERSPECTIVES

While the hymns that emerged in the seventeenth century reflected the distinctive theological convictions of their authors, they were still profoundly biblical in the way they conveyed doctrine and practice.

George Wither

In his attempt to preserve a faithful reading and interpretation of Scripture in his hymn texts, George Wither explored simultaneously the possibilities of using figurative language in the expression of devotion and the application of religious principles to daily life. Wither's *Halelviah or, Britans Second Remembrancer* (1641), in particular, is a rich collection of texts for personal and household worship. His original hymns and single-minded focus anticipated the hymnology of the later seventeenth century.[21]

His "Come, O come, with sacred lays" is a preface to his *A Preparation to the Psalter* (1619) and is a beautiful appeal for all of creation to offer its fullest praise to God.[22]

Come, O come, with sacred lays,
Let us sound the Almighty's praise.

Let such things, as do not lie,
In still music praises give.

20. Watts, *Dissenters*, 308–9.

21. Watson, *English Hymn*, 63, 68–69.

22. Wither, *Preparation to the Psalter*, xi–xii. The spelling of the hymn text has been updated.

Hither bring in true consent,
Heart, and voice, and instrument.
Let the orphurion sweet
With the harp and viol meet.
To your voices tune the lute:
Let nor tongue or string be mute;
Nor a creature dumb be found,
That hath either voice or sound.

Lowly pipe, ye worms that creep
On the earth, or in the deep.
Loud, aloft, your voices strain,
Beasts and monsters of the main.
Birds, your warbling treble sing.
Clouds, your peals of thunder ring.
Sun and moon, exalted higher,
And you stars, augment the choir.

Come, ye sons of human race,
In this chorus take your place:
And, amid the mortal throng,
Be you masters of the song.
Angels, and celestial powers,
Be the noblest tenor yours.
Let (in praise of God) the sound
Run a never-ending round;
That our holy hymn may be
Everlasting, as is He.

So shall He, from heaven's high tower,
On the earth His blessing shower:
All this huge wide orb we see,
Shall one choir, one temple be.
There our voices we will rear,
Till we fill it everywhere;
And enforce the fiends that dwell
In the air, to sink in hell.
Then, O come, with sacred lays,
Let us sound the Almighty's praise.

This striking text calls upon the inhabitants of God's universe to herald his praise. The hymn summons a variety of participants and instruments, loosely following the days of creation in Genesis, insisting that God's praise should be "everlasting, as is he." In one way or another, all that God has made has a voice, a means to utter praise. The hymn resounds the biblical mandate of Ps 150:6 that everything that has breath should praise God. This combined symphony is not limited to the earth and its inhabitants, but it includes the "angels and celestial powers." With a singular focus, all extol the matchless worth and majesty of God.

George Herbert

George Herbert's interest in writing devotional poetry was very personal and corresponded with his delight in using sacred song for private worship. His connection with hymnody did not arise until over sixty years after his death, when *Select Hymns from Mr. Herbert's Temple* (1697) appeared.[23] The modification of devotional poems into hymn texts is important in the

23. Benson, *English Hymn*, 66–67.

history of hymnody, especially as they included individual and reverential connections to the biblical paraphrases. As is apparent in the metaphysical poets and others, an increasing engagement with the Scriptures resulted in a greater grasp of the ways in which language, specifically tropes and figures, could be utilized to voice religious truth. Throughout the seventeenth century, an intense and excited interest in biblical metaphors steadily developed.[24]

One of the best known of Herbert's hymn texts is "Let all the world in every corner sing," which was included in *The Temple* (1633). He named this selection "Antiphon," the name for a verse or prose composition that consists of passages or verses sung alternatively by two choirs. The text is usually modified as follows to create two similar stanzas.[25]

Let all the world in every corner sing,	Let all the world in every corner sing,
My God and King.	My God and King.
The heavens are not too high,	The Church with psalms must shout,
His praise may thither fly;	No door can keep them out;
The earth is not too low,	But above all, the heart
His praises there may grow.	Must bear the longest part.
Let all the world in every corner sing,	Let all the world in every corner sing,
My God and King.	My God and King

Herbert's text is a call to worship. All are constrained to acknowledge God as creator and sovereign. The hymn's instruction resembles the imperative of Ps 107:2, that those who are redeemed of God must declare it. Certainly the praise of God's people will reach him in the heavens; he is not too distant. As well, as the church proclaims God's glory, their song will penetrate every barrier—"no door can keep them out." Herbert's focus on the human heart is visible in the second stanza, for the heart will continue to praise God throughout eternity.[26]

Samuel Crossman

The contribution of Samuel Crossman (1623–84) to hymnody is small but significant. Although he sympathized with the Puritan cause, he did conform to the Church of England and was ordained as a minister about the time he published his *The Young Man's Meditation* (1664). This short work

24. Watson, *English Hymn*, 75.
25. Herbert, *Temple*, 45.
26. Watson, *Annotated Anthology of Hymns*, 94.

contained nine poems that were fashioned in the same metrical patterns as the psalms and obviously were intended to be used as hymns.[27]

Doubtless, Crossman's best known hymn is "My song is love unknown," which is based on Gal 6:14 and insists the only basis for boasting is in the cross of Jesus Christ. It is written in a vein similar to Herbert's "The Sacrifice."[28] The text affirms the cross of Christ as an example of ultimate love and ultimate grief. This outstanding hymn on the crucifixion has been incorporated into many hymn collections.[29]

My song is love unknown,
My Saviour's love to me,
Love to the loveless shown,
That they might lovely be.
O who am I,
That for my sake
My Lord should take
Frail flesh and die?

He came from his blest throne,
Salvation to bestow,
But men made strange, and none
The longed-for Christ would know.
But O my friend,
My friend indeed,
Who at my need
His life did spend!

Sometimes they strew his way,
And his sweet praises sing,
Resounding all the day
Hosannas to the King.
Then 'Crucify!'
Is all their breath,
And for his death
They thirst and cry.

Why, what hath my Lord done?
What makes this rage and spite?
He made the lame to run,
He gave the blind their sight.
Sweet injuries!
Yet they at these
Themselves displease,
And 'gainst him rise.

They rise, and needs will have
My dear Lord made away;
A murderer they save
The Prince of Life they slay.
Yet cheerful he
To suffering goes,
That he his foes

In life no house, no home,
My Lord on earth might have;
In death no friendly tomb
But what a stranger gave.
What may I say?
Heaven was his home;
But mind the tomb

27. Benson, *English Hymn*, 69.

28. Watson, *English Hymn*, 87.

29. Watson, *Annotated Anthology of Hymns*, 109–10. The text is found in Crossman, *Young Man's Meditation*, 8–10.

From thence might free. Wherein he lay.

Here might I stay and sing,
No story so divine:
Never was love, dear King,
Never was grief like thine!
This is my friend,
In whose sweet praise
I all my days
Could gladly spend.

Crossman begins the text with multiple uses of "love," signaling the theme of the hymn. He inserts several theological concepts, including the incarnation of Christ, human depravity, and substitutionary atonement. John 1:11 is in mind as Crossman laments that "none the longed-for Christ would know." The hymn assembles rich expressions and deep emotion as it conveys the unfathomable sacrifice of Jesus—"They rise, and needs will have my dear Lord made away." Near the end, he affirms the merciful juxtaposition that the death of Christ transformed heaven into Crossman's home, while the tomb—which had been Crossman's dwelling—held the Savior instead.

John Bunyan

John Bunyan (1628–88) is best known for his unusually successful allegory, *The Pilgrim's Progress* (1678), which includes the poem, "Who would true Valour see." Bunyan wrote both the poem and the allegory while in prison for his Baptist convictions. With few alterations, this poem appeared as a hymn in 1873. Percy Dearmer's modernized version, "He who would valiant be," was included in the *English Hymnal* (1906). The hymn's underlying concepts of virtue and courage have enabled it to transcend its origins in dissent. It has even been considered the most non-denominational hymn, since the *pilgrim* metaphor is grasped by all those on life's toilsome journey.[30] Bunyan packed a remarkable amount of human experience into the hymn's three stanzas. The text summarizes fully the message of Bunyan's allegory.[31]

30. Watson, *Annotated Anthology of Hymns*, 107–8.

31. Watson, *English Hymn*, 127. The hymn text is found in Bunyan, *Pilgrim's Progress*, 172–73.

Who would true Valour see,
Let him come hither;
One here will constant be,
Come Wind, come Weather.
There's no Discouragement
Shall make him once relent,
His first avowed Intent
To be a Pilgrim.

Whoso beset him round
With dismal Stories,
Do but themselves confound;
His Strength the more is.
No Lion can him fright;
He'll with a Giant fight,
Be he will have a Right
To be a Pilgrim.

Hobgoblin, nor foul Fiend
Can daunt his Spirit;
He knows, he at the End
Shall Life inherit.
Then Fancies fly away,
He'll fear not what Men say,
He'll labour Night and Day
To be a Pilgrim.

The initial stanza displays a single-minded purpose to possess "true valour" regardless of any disappointment, distraction, or "discouragement." Bunyan then insists that those who attempt to burden or dissuade pilgrims by focusing on the hardships of the world "themselves confound." God's Word declares in 2 Cor 12:9 that his grace is sufficient, and his power is perfected in our weakness. Encountering a "lion" or "giant" should not result in crippling fear, for God is able to deliver. Bunyan discloses finally that eternal life is far more worthwhile than earthly "fancies." God's Word, not men's words, will empower the pilgrim, and as long as his trust is in God, nothing "can daunt his spirit."

Thomas Ken

Doubtless, Thomas Ken's hymns had a substantial influence upon English hymnody, but as with many other hymnists, their impact was not immediate. Some believe that Ken best represents the development of congregational song in the latter half of the seventeenth century. Each of Ken's three "Winchester hymns" concluded with a doxology, four ending lines that have likely been sung more than any other four lines in the English language.[32]

32. Eskew and McElrath, *Sing with Understanding*, 130.

Ken wrote these hymns before 1674 and edited them prior to their publication in 1695.[33]

The "Morning Hymn" is especially popular, and is known for its plainness and neatness, employing Ken's "octosyllabic couplets" to summarize the discipline of the daily Christian life with both purpose and humanness. As well, man's earthly existence is placed in the context of the greater life yet to come.[34] This hymn consists of fourteen stanzas and falls into three sections that are addressed to the soul, to the angels, and to God.[35]

Awake, my Soul, and with the Sun,
Thy daily Stage of Duty run;
Shake off dull Sloth, and early rise,
To pay thy Morning sacrifice.

Thy precious Time misspent, redeem,
Each present day thy last Esteem,
Improve thy Talent with due Care,
For the Great Day, thy self prepare.

I would not wake, nor rise again,
Ev'n Heaven it self I would disdain,
Were not thou there to be enjoy'd,
And I in Hymns to be employ'd.

Direct, controul, suggest this Day,
All I design, or do, or say,
That all my Powers with all their Might,
In thy sole Glory may Unite.

Praise God, from whom all Blessings flow,
Praise Him all Creatures here below,
Praise Him above ye Heavenly Host,
Praise Father, Son, and Holy Ghost.

The hymn begins with remarkable imagery comparing the soul and its tasks to the sun and its daily course. The sun is constant in its movement from one horizon to another; similarly, believers are to pursue their responsibilities with comparable diligence. Of the soul's regular priorities, Ken includes the essential desire to redeem the time, as Paul writes in Eph 5:16. Coupled with this task must be the realization that earthly life is temporal and judgment is coming, as Heb 9:27 makes clear. Near the end of the hymn, the author affirms that without the joy of God's presence, not only would life hardly be worth living but he would despise even heaven itself. Prior to the concluding Trinitarian doxology, the hymn asks God to exercise

33. Julian, *Dictionary of Hymnology*, 618.

34. Watson, *Annotated Anthology of Hymns*, 114. See also Watson, *English Hymn*, 94.

35. Ken, *Manual of Prayers*, 130–33. The stanzas included here are among the most familiar.

his sovereignty such that all that the believer does that day will result in God's greater glory.

CONTRIBUTION TO LITURGY AND WORSHIP

In addition to those who wrote hymns, some served to promote the singing of hymns in public worship. Both of these aspects were vital to the development of British hymnody in the seventeenth century. In particular, two nonconformists were instrumental in this effort.

John Bunyan's *The Pilgrim's Progress* contained poetic material, but the lyrics were not originally intended for congregational singing. As a hymnist, then, Bunyan's direct contributions were few; however, his convictions regarding corporate hymn singing were very important. Bunyan believed that psalmody and hymnody were altogether appropriate forms of expression, that they had received God's approval, and that they ought to receive the church's. To him, church song was critical for relieving the discomfort and pain of man's daily struggle in the world.[36]

In two of his tracts, *A Treatise of the Fear of God* (1679) and *Solomon's Temple Spiritualized* (1688), Bunyan related his conviction that hymns should function as necessary elements of public worship. Bunyan was personally involved in the hymn singing debate, a significant source of controversy between the Particular (Calvinistic) and General (Arminian) Baptists.[37] In *Solomon's Temple Spiritualized*, Bunyan enlarged his argument in favor of singing in the context of public worship. Citing biblical texts such as Pss 33, 40, and 96, Bunyan asserted that God had commanded specifically that "new songs" were to be sung.[38] He stated, "To sing to God, is the highest worship we are capable of performing in heaven; and it is much if sinners on earth, without grace, should be capable of performing it according to His institution, acceptably. I pray God it be done by all those that now-a-days get into churches, in spirit and with understanding."[39]

Benjamin Keach had become convinced that Christ had ordained corporate singing that included hymns, and he endeavored to practice that belief within his church.[40] As early as 1664, Keach began inserting hymnic material into some of his published works, and his congregation began to sing hymns in public worship as distinct from psalms perhaps as early as

36. Rogal, "John Bunyan," 118–20, 125.

37. Rogal, "John Bunyan," 118.

38. Rogal, "John Bunyan," 120.

39. Bunyan, *Solomon's Temple Spiritualized*, 102.

40. Keach, *Spiritual Melody*, v.

1673.[41] Keach accomplished this by introducing hymns slowly but regularly at the close of each observance of the Lord's supper. In his multi-volume work, *Tropologia, a Key to Open Scripture Metaphors* (1681–82), Keach affirmed that congregational singing was a duty for believers. Additionally, he felt there was no more reason "to object against compiling *Sacred Hymns* to be sung out of the Word of Christ, than there is to object against precompiled Sermons that are to be preached."[42] Thus, Keach believed that hymns sung congregationally were to be as normative in public worship as the sermons that were being proclaimed by the preacher. Eventually, this practice expanded within Keach's church to include the singing of hymns on public days of thanksgiving, and by 1690, hymn singing was practiced every Sunday.[43] Keach had a strong belief about the educational value of hymn singing, and he used hymns as a potent tool to expound Scripture texts, to elucidate parables, and to deconstruct metaphors.[44]

As public hymn singing in Keach's congregation increased in frequency, so did the opposition from some in his church who remained unconvinced at its propriety. Ultimately, a bitter controversy developed, led by Isaac Marlow, who in 1690 published *A Brief Discourse Concerning Singing in the Publick Worship of God in the Gospel Church*. Marlow was not a part of Keach's congregation, hence the difficulty in keeping the matter contained within his church.[45] Even though several prominent Particular Baptist leaders had made public their endorsement of congregational singing, the practice remained problematic for some. Keach responded to Marlow in his *The Breach Repaired in God's Worship or, Singing of Psalms, Hymns, and Spiritual Songs, proved to be an holy ordinance of Jesus Christ* (1691). Those who were uncomfortable with singing ultimately left Keach's congregation and established their own church.

In time, the public nature of the controversy resulted in even more worshippers who were willing to enter the arena of hymn singing. Although still slow in progress, many were steadily becoming favorable to hymns at the turn of the eighteenth century. This was not limited to Baptists only but included other groups and denominations.

41. Music, "Hymns of Benjamin Keach," 147.

42. Keach, *Spiritual Melody*, x.

43. Benson, *English Hymn*, 97.

44. Watson, *English Hymn*, 111.

45. Walker, *Excellent Benjamin Keach*, 284.

NOTABLE HYMNS

Other important and enduring hymns produced in this period include John Milton's "The Lord will come and not be slow," George Herbert's "King of glory, King of peace," Henry Vaughn's "My soul, there is a country," Richard Baxter's "Ye holy angels bright," John Mason's "How shall I sing that majesty," and Nahum Tate's "While shepherds watched their flocks by night."

BIBLIOGRAPHY

Benson, Louis F. *The English Hymn: Its Development and Use in Worship*. New York: George M. Doran, 1915.

Bunyan, John. *The Pilgrim's Progress*. 23rd ed. London: n.p., 1741.

———. *Solomon's Temple Spiritualized*. Edinburgh: n.p., 1786.

Clarke, Elizabeth. "Hymns, Psalms, and Controversy in the Seventeenth Century." In *Dissenting Praise: Religious Dissent and the Hymn in England and Wales*, edited by Isabel Rivers and David L. Wykes, 13–32. London: Oxford University Press, 2011.

Crossman, Samuel. *The Young Man's Meditation*. London: n.p., 1664.

Eskew, Harry, and Hugh T. McElrath. *Sing with Understanding: An Introduction to Christian Hymnody*. 2nd ed. Nashville: Church Street, 1995.

Gregory, Arthur E. *The Hymn-Book of the Modern Church: Studies of Hymns and Hymn-Writers*. London: Charles H. Kelly, 1905.

Herbert, George. *The Temple*. 9th ed. London: n.p., 1667.

Julian, John. *A Dictionary of Hymnology, Setting Forth the Origin and History of Christian Hymns of All Ages and Nations*. New York: Charles Scribner's Sons, 1892.

Keach, Benjamin. *Spiritual Melody*. London: n.p., 1691.

Ken, Thomas. *A Manual of Prayers for the Use of the Scholars of Winchester College*. London: n.p., 1715.

Music, David W. "The Hymns of Benjamin Keach: An Introductory Study." *The Hymn* 34 (July 1983) 147–54.

Rogal, Samuel J. "John Bunyan and English Congregational Song." *The Hymn* 28 (July 1977) 118–25.

Walker, Austin. *The Excellent Benjamin Keach*. 2nd ed. Kitchener, Ontario: Joshua, 2015.

Watson, J. R. *An Annotated Anthology of Hymns*. New York: Oxford University Press, 2003.

———. *The English Hymn: A Critical and Historical Study*. New York: Oxford University Press, 1999.

Watts, Michael. *The Dissenters: From the Reformation to the French Revolution*. New York: Oxford University Press, 1978.

Wither, George. *Preparation to the Psalter*. London: n.p., 1619.

Chapter 10

Richard Baxter

Trent A. Hancock

HISTORICAL BACKGROUND

Richard Baxter was born on Sunday, November 12, 1615, in Rowton, in the county of Shropshire, England, the son of Richard Baxter (d. 1663) and Beatrice Adeney (d. 1635). Due to the impoverished circumstances of his early childhood, Baxter lived with his maternal grandparents until age 11, when, upon his father's conversion, Baxter returned home. His father's conversion had a significant impact on the adolescent Baxter, who would later describe his father as "the Instrument of my first Convictions, and Approbation of a Holy Life."[1]

While Baxter would become a prolific writer, his education was largely informal and principally inadequate. Baxter later wrote that he had "four teachers in six years, all of whom were ignorant and two led immoral lives."[2] Nevertheless, Baxter was a voracious reader and motivated autodidact. When Baxter was fifteen, for example, he was deeply affected by Richard Sibbes's *The Bruised Reed*. Baxter later reflected: "Sibbes opened more the love of God to me, and gave me a livelier apprehension of the mystery of

1. Baxter, *Reliquiae Baxterianae*, 1.2–3.
2. Baxter, *Reliquiae Baxterianae*, 1.3–4.

redemption and how much I was beholden to Jesus Christ."[3] In addition to Sibbes, Baxter was also greatly influenced by the writings of William Perkins, and from age 16 until his ordination four years later, he engaged in a private, and largely self-directed study of the scholastics, including Aquinas, Scotus, and Ockham.

His early religious upbringing has been described as that of a "conforming moderate puritan," the perspective "that further reformation and the cause of the gospel should be furthered within the institutional and liturgical structures provided by the English church and from positions of cultural influence and political power secured within the various hierarchies that constituted the contemporary status quo."[4] Baxter's education and early experiences, then, set the stage for what Baxter himself would later describe as his "mere-nonconformity"—a dual commitment to reform, as well as a steadfast commitment to church unity amidst difference.

Baxter experienced frequent illnesses in childhood and throughout his life. Reflecting much later on his illnesses and near-obsession with his own mortality, Baxter acknowledges that these experiences had "a great operation" upon his soul "giving him a sense both of urgency in ministry and mercy from God."[5] This sense of urgency can be seen throughout his life, in his pursuit of improvements at Kidderminster, his indefatigable engagement in the theological disputes of his day, and his prodigious literary output.

Baxter was ordained on December 23, 1636. His first ministry was at Dudley, where he taught at the new school and preached regularly. It was at this time that Baxter "began a serious study of the issues of conformity, ceremonies and ecclesiastical discipline."[6] After less than a year in Dudley, Baxter accepted a call to minister at Bridgnorth, a parish "completely free of episcopal jurisdiction."[7] It was also at Bridgnorth that Baxter made his first public stand on a matter of ecclesiastical policy when, at a meeting of ministers in 1640, he spoke against the *et cetera* oath in the *Canons of 1640*, which constituted a pledge to uphold the office of bishop and the regnant Anglican hierarchy.

In March 1641, Baxter was invited to Kidderminster, Worcestershire, as a preacher or "lecturer." Shortly thereafter (August 1642) hostilities marking the beginning of the English Civil War commenced. Baxter was initially

3. Baxter, *Reliquiae Baxterianae*, 1.4–5.
4. Segger, *Richard Baxter's* Reformed Liturgy, 12–13.
5. Purves, *Pastoral Theology in the Classical Tradition*, 99.
6. Segger, *Richard Baxter's* Reformed Liturgy, 14.
7. Segger, *Richard Baxter's* Reformed Liturgy, 14.

"reluctant to take sides during the civil war,"[8] but that changed in 1645, when, visiting parliamentary troops, Baxter "was troubled by the religious state of the New Model army."[9] In the army, Baxter encountered "hot-headed Sectaries [who] had got into the highest places" and were Cromwell's "chief Favourites."[10] Baxter agreed to act as chaplain, with the express intention of countering the spread of antinomianism among the troops.

In 1647, Baxter's prolonged illnesses compelled him to leave the army. He recuperated at the Worcestershire home of Sir Thomas and Lady Rous, where he wrote the first part of *The Saints' Everlasting Rest*. After his recovery, Baxter returned to Kidderminster where he began to concentrate on writing and the concerns of "practical" piety. "My writings were my chiefest daily labor," he reflected, whereas "preaching and preparing for it, were but my recreation."[11] Baxter's fragile health "sharpened his pastoral sensibilities and empowerment. . . . Baxter himself noted that 'in all my labours at Kidderminster, after my return (from the Army) I did all under languishing weakness, being seldom an hour free from pain.'"[12]

It was during these years at Kidderminster that Baxter became a national figure, gaining great renown for the transformation of the community and church he helped to establish there. Baxter had initially arrived at Kidderminster following a petition by the congregation against its former pastor that resulted in his dismissal. Baxter later reflected on the dire conditions he faced at Kidderminster upon his arrival: "When I came thither first, there was about one Family in a Street that worshipped God and called on his name," but "when I came away there were some Streets where there was not past one Family in the Side of a Street that did not so; on the Lord's Day . . . you might hear an hundred Families singing Psalms and repeating Sermons, as you passed through the Streets."[13] In addition to regular preaching, Baxter catechized church members two days each week and encouraged families to sing psalms in their homes throughout the week.

Like Baxter's theology, the liturgy at Kidderminster was marked by the dual elements of the freedom embraced by radical puritanism as well as the prescriptiveness of his Presbyterian tradition and the *Book of Common Prayer*. Baxter employed a mix of written and extemporaneous prayers

8. Segger, *Richard Baxter's* Reformed Liturgy, 24.
9. Segger, *Richard Baxter's* Reformed Liturgy, 25.
10. Baxter, *Reliquiae Baxterianae*, 1.56.
11. Baxter, *Reliquiae Baxterianae*, 1.85.
12. Purves, *Pastoral Theology in the Classical Tradition*, 99.
13. Baxter, *Reliquiae Baxterianae*, 1.84–85.

in his leading of public worship, a practice that would later influence his contribution at Savoy and his *Reformed Liturgy*.

It was during this period, after his return to Kidderminster, that Baxter also began to write prolifically. There are more than 130 volumes attributed to Baxter, many of which were published posthumously, including several that remain in print to this day. Among these writings are his most well-known and enduring works: *Gildas Salvianus: The Reformed Pastor* (1656), *The Saint's Everlasting Rest* (1650), and *A Christian Directory* (1673).

The Reformed Pastor, Baxter's most well-known work, is a sustained reflection on the key commitments of his ministry at Kidderminster—the importance of conversion, catechesis, and community formation—first shared with the local association of ministers on a "day of recollection" held on December 4, 1655. Purves clarifies that, "By reformed pastor, Baxter did not intend to reference the Calvinist or Presbyterian pastor, but the quickened or renewed pastor, one who, in the words of the guiding text, keeps watch over himself, and over all the flock, of which the Holy Spirit has made one a pastor, to shepherd the church of God that he obtained with the blood of his Son (Acts 20:28)."[14]

In *The Saint's Everlasting Rest,* Baxter explores the "supreme joy of the Christian," which he understood as the contemplation and enjoyment of eternity in the present.

> [Baxter] exhorts the reader to re-create in himself a feeling of the joys of eternal life by painting as vividly as he can in his mind the physical and sensible analogues to inconceivable bliss. He suggests that we endeavor to conceive the joys of heaven by recollecting the joys of earth, "By arguing from sensitive delights as from the less to the greater." By recalling and imaginatively re-creating physical and sensitive pleasures we have known, we may gain a suggestion of the heavenly.[15]

This theme, of the hope of heaven as a balm to the struggles this earthly life, can be seen in Baxter's hymn, *Christ leads me through no darker rooms*:

> Christ leads me through no darker rooms
> Than He went through before;
> And he that in God's kingdom comes
> Must enter by this door.
>
> Come, Lord, when grace hath made me meet
> Thy blessed face to see;

14. Purves, *Pastoral Theology in the Classical Tradition*, 104.

15. Keeble, *Richard Baxter*, 102.

For if Thy work on earth be sweet,
What must Thy glory be!

Then I shall end my sad complaints,
And weary, sinful days,
And join with the triumphant saints
To sing Jehovah's praise.

My knowledge of that life is small;
The eye of faith is dim;
But 'tis enough that Christ knows all,
And I shall be with Him!

In *The Saint's Everlasting Rest*, Baxter also extols the "usefulness of self-examination, and concern for the actions of the heart.[16] Consider, for example, Baxter's evocation of a well-tuned heart, in the final stanza of his hymn *Ye holy angels bright*:

My soul, bear thou thy part,
Triumph in God above:
And with a well-tuned heart
Sing though the songs of love;
Let all thy days
Till life shall end,
What'er he send,
Be filled with praise.

In *A Christian Directory*, intended as a practical guide for ministers as they encountered the spiritual needs of their parishioners, Baxter sets out a theology of the Christian life "directing Christians how to use their knowledge and faith; how to improve all helps and means, and to perform all duties; how to overcome temptations, and to escape or mortify every sin."[17] Themes prevalent, as well, in Baxter's hymn *My soul, go boldly forth:*

My soul, go boldly forth,
Forsake this sinful earth;
What hath it been to thee
But pain and sorrow?
And think'st thou it will be More kind tomorrow?

Thy God, thy Head's above;
There is the world of love;
Mansions there purchased are

16. Lindberg, *Pietist Theologians*, 59.

17. Baxter, *Christian Directory* (from the subtitle).

By Christ's own merit;
For these He doth prepare
Thee by His Spirit.

Lord Jesus, take my spirit;
I trust Thy love and merit;
Take home Thy wandering sheep.
For Thou has sought it;
My soul in safety keep,
For Thou has bought it.

In 1653, Baxter established the Worcestershire Association "to bring unity, order, and discipline to the churches in Worcestershire"[18] in the midst of the unsettled ecclesiastical landscape of Interregnum England. In the creation of the Worcestershire Association we see Baxter's commitment to pastoral service combined with his passionate desire for unity among Christians of differing persuasions. As Baxter wrote in *The Reformed Pastor*, "God hath possessed my heart with such a burning desire after the peace & unity of the Churches that I cannot forget it, or lay it by. I feele a supernaturall power forceing my zeale, & thoughts that way."[19] Baxter developed twenty Resolutions which formed the basis for the Association. Significantly, nearly all of the Resolutions concerned matters of "practical divinity rather than doctrine" focusing on church discipline and unity rather than theological differences.[20]

At the Restoration of Charles II in 1660, Baxter found himself in political and ecclesiastical benefit.[21] Baxter enjoyed a brief period of royal favor, even preaching before the new king on one occasion and receiving an appointment as chaplain to the king. In June 1660, Baxter, along with some of the other London ministers, had an audience with the king in which "they expressed their desire to reconcile their differences with the episcopal party so that a comprehensive national church could be realized."[22] Baxter and his fellow divines were initially optimistic that some understanding might be reached. During the deliberations that followed, however, Baxter went well beyond the intended purview of the conference, proposing his own plan for church government. Baxter's plan was rejected by the other divines, as was the compromise plan suggested by the king. After a failed attempt to seek a

18. Segger, *Richard Baxter's* Reformed Liturgy, 32.
19. Baxter, *Gildas Silvanus.*
20. Segger, *Richard Baxter's* Reformed Liturgy, 35.
21. Purves, *Pastoral Theology in the Classical Tradition*, 100.
22. Segger, *Richard Baxter's* Reformed Liturgy, 40.

settlement by royal decree, Charles II called for the conference at Savoy to revise the *Book of Common Prayer* on March 25, 1661.[23]

Baxter continued to press for church unity as well as the continuing reformation of the church, especially in matters of discipline and liturgy. His ministry as a nonconformist was largely tolerated during this period, despite his frequent challenges to the established ecclesiastical authorities. Lacking a formal pastoral appointment, Baxter continued to preach and lead worship in the homes of his adherents on Sunday afternoons, always careful not to interfere with the public worship of his devotees. This pattern continued until his arrest on June 12, 1669, under the Five Mile Act of 1665. It is characteristic of Baxter's commitment to church discipline and ecclesial unity, that he continued his ministry despite the prescriptions of the Clarendon code.

When, in March 1672, Charles II's declaration of indulgence was issued, Baxter was initially reluctant to seek a license to preach. Baxter did eventually apply for a license, however, provided that it was issued to him as "a mere nonconformist," rather than in the name of a particular sect or denomination. The license was issued to him as "a Nonconforming Minister" on October 27, 1672, and, unusually, it authorized him to preach "in any licensed or allowed Place."[24] He preached publicly for the first time since 1662 on November 19, 1672.

Although parliament compelled the king to withdraw his declaration of indulgence the next year, Baxter's retirement was effectively over. For the rest of his life, Baxter, despite his lack of a formal appointment to serve as pastor of a congregation, continued to teach and preach. His commitment to preserving church unity, and his resistance to challenging the established church meant that his ministry was always understood as a supplement to, and not a replacement of, public worship and the parishioner's obligation to his or her church.

On September 10, 1662, Baxter married Margaret Charlton. Upon her death in 1681 Baxter wrote the poem that would become the hymn *Ye Holy Angels Bright.* Baxter died on December 8, 1691, after a long illness. He was buried, alongside his wife in Christ Church, Greyfriars.

THEOLOGICAL PERSPECTIVES

Baxter engaged in many of the theological, ecclesiastical, and liturgical debates of his time. His writings, however, did not share the characteristics of

23. See "Contribution to Liturgy and Worship" below.

24. Turner, *Original Records of Early Nonconformity*, 1.575.

most theological writing of his period. Instead, his work can be characterized by its focus on "practical Christianity"—theology written for the sake of the Christian struggling to live a life of faith and faithfulness. Above all, Baxter was concerned with providing a theological rationale for a practical piety meant to counter what he saw as the threat represented by the antinomians who held that with the accomplishment of salvation by Christ there was no longer a need to keep the law. This perceived threat of antinomianism—seen first among the soldiers and officers of the New Army—would continue to be a pervasive influence behind Baxter's "practical Christianity." It was in response to the threat of antinomianism that Baxter penned his first theological treatise on the doctrine of justification: *Aphorismes of Justification with Their Explication Annexed* (1649). His subsequent treatments of justification would span the next forty years.

Baxter charged that, to the antinomians, faith was "but the declaration of what has already occurred for the elect." Baxter, however, argued that "if the law's demands have been eternally met, we would have no need to keep the law a second time by our own acts. Faith would become, then, a search for confidence in salvation rather than for conversion."[25] Baxter's view, sometimes referred to "neonomian," was closer to Arminianism—the view that there was a human component in the economy of salvation—rather than the Calvinism of his inherited tradition. In fact, Baxter struggled "to maintain the priority appropriate to God's grace in Jesus Christ, while insisting on a legitimate place for human responsibility."[26]

In another departure from his received tradition, Baxter rejected the doctrine of imputed righteousness. For Baxter, there was no "great exchange"—the orthodox protestant view of the period that the sins of the elect were "exchanged" for the obedience of Christ by imputation. Instead, Baxter "held that Christ's righteousness caused a change in the demands of the law."[27] According to Baxter, two kinds of righteousness were required for entrance into the new covenant: "legal righteousness" understood as the righteousness of Christ, and "evangelical righteousness," Baxter's term for the faith of the particular Christian whose righteousness had been imputed by Christ.

Baxter understood justification as a continuous process. The Christian entered the state of grace by faith but remained only by continued faithfulness evident in one's keeping of the law. The decisive moment of justification, its beginning in faith, was termed "constitutive justification." An

25. Purves, *Pastoral Theology in the Classical Tradition*, 102.

26. Purves, *Pastoral Theology in the Classical Tradition*, 102.

27. Brown, "Not by Faith Alone," 146.

equally decisive moment came at the end of life's journey in the "declarative justification" of the last day when final judgment takes place. But throughout the journey of the Christian life, Baxter identified the process of "executive justification," or the giving of promised benefits and rewards along the way. Baxter emphasized the priority of God's covenant, but also the importance of "faithful covenant-keeping in order to reach the promised goal."[28]

Baxter rejected the imputed obedience of Christ as the ground of justification, embracing, instead, the legal views of Hugo Grotius, who "held the position that Christ's death was not an identical satisfaction for sins, but an equivalent one."[29] Baxter's indebtedness to the Grotian theory of the atonement can be seen in one of his hymns in the *Monthly Preparations* in which he has Love declare: "The Pleas of Justice I'll adjust / My only Son shall die."[30]

Baxter also departed, to a degree, from many of his contemporaries in his view of the atonement. His primary disputant on this score was the Calvinist John Owen. Baxter's view of the atonement can be seen as derivative of his unease with antinomianism. As we have seen, Baxter was concerned that Christians were in danger of ignoring the practical requirements of obedience that followed from the gift of God's covenant. Baxter's doctrine of the atonement is explained most fully in *Methodus Theologiae Christianae* (1681), but it is in his *Christian Directory* (1673) that one finds the practical implications of his view. Baxter's view of the atonement departed from traditional Calvinism in a number of ways. Consistent with his rejection of the traditional doctrine of imputation, Baxter argued that Christ died for *sins*, not for the *elect*, per se. The benefits of Christ's atoning sacrifice were made effective by faith and continuing faithfulness, rather than by the imputation of Christ's righteousness.

CONTRIBUTIONS TO LITURGY AND WORSHIP

Baxter's *Reformed Liturgy*, drafted during the Savoy Conference, provides important insights into the practices at Kidderminster and is indicative of Baxter's commitment to a practical piety richly resourced by Scripture.

The Savoy Conference (1661) was a meeting of twelve Presbyterian divines and twelve episcopal bishops gathered together at the request of Charles II to consider revisions to the *Book of Common Prayer*. The Presbyterian contingent was invited by the bishops to list proposed revisions.

28. Von Rohr, *Covenant of Grace in Puritan Thought*, 53.
29. Brown, "Not by Faith Alone," 145.
30. Coffey, *Heart Religion* 38.

Baxter, however, "retired from the others to draw up entirely new forms of worship" clearly exceeding the king's mandate to compose "some additional Forms in the Scripture phrase."[31] Baxter's proposal was published later that year as *A Petition for Peace: with the reformation of the Liturgy, as it was presented to the right reverend bishops, by the divines appointed by His Majesties commission to treat with them about the alternation of it.* It became known simply as the *Reformed Liturgy*. While largely rejecting the spirit of collaboration intended by the conference, Baxter hoped his contribution would serve as a "liturgy of compromise."[32] In fact, as Segger argues, one must understand the *Reformed Liturgy* in the "context of Baxter's theological endeavors during the time of the Commonwealth and protectorate" during which time he established the Worcestershire association, his ongoing effort to achieve unity within the church.[33]

Baxter's *Reformed Liturgy* is characterized by its thoroughgoing Biblicism. In defense of this approach, Baxter argues for the infallibility of Scripture, its ecumenical advantages, and the fact that "there is no other words that may be preferred before the words of God, or stand in competition with them."[34] In accordance with Baxter's commitment to the practical and to the promotion of personal piety, the participation and needs of the congregation were foremost, so that while the basic structure and outline of the service for the Lord's Day closely resembles the *Directory*, the level of congregational participation in the liturgy is more than doubled. Further, there is a "logical character" to the service:[35] The service began with a prayer asking for divine acceptance of the worship to be proffered, followed by a profession of obedience to God by means of the recitation of the Creed and the Decalogue. This profession was followed by a prayer of confession, and a declaration, by the minister, of absolution and a scriptural admonition to maintain a godly life. The congregation would then respond by the singing of a psalm of praise. The people, having been prepared to receive the Word, listened as the minister read Scripture and preached the sermon. The Word was followed by intercessory prayers, the singing of another psalm, and the dismissal with a blessing by the minister. When the Sacrament of the Lord's Supper was celebrated, the service followed the same liturgy and appended the Sacrament at the end.[36]

31. Segger, *Richard Baxter's* Reformed Liturgy, 1.
32. Segger, *Richard Baxter's* Reformed Liturgy, 4.
33. Segger, *Richard Baxter's* Reformed Liturgy, 4.
34. Davies, *Worship and Theology in England*, 429.
35. Chadwick and Nuttall, *Uniformity to Unity*, 121.
36. Segger, *Richard Baxter's* Reformed Liturgy, 51.

Baxter wrote frequently of his love of singing—especially the psalms—but also advocated for the composition of hymns for congregational worship. At the Savoy conference Baxter also emerged as a leader among post-Restoration Presbyterians in the introduction of hymn singing as part of the liturgy. Baxter presents his case in his *Reformed Liturgy*: "Concerning the Psalms for Publick use. We desire that, instead of the imperfect version of the Psalms in Meeter now in use . . . [hymns] may be received and corrected by some skillful men and both allowed (for grateful variety) to be Printed together on several Columes or Pages, and publickly used."[37] While Baxter continued to embrace psalm singing, he also argued, in the preface to his *Paraphrase on the Psalms* (1692) that hymns had been sung from the beginning and that,

> Doubtless Paul meaneth not only David's Psalms, when he bids men sing with grace in their hearts, Psalms, and Hymns, and Spiritual Songs; Yea, it is past doubt, that Hymns more suitable to Gospel-times, may and ought to be now used: And if used, they must be premeditated; how else shall Congregations sing them? And if premeditated, they must be some way imposed; How else shall the Congregations all joyn the same?[38]

Psalm singing continued to dominate, but in time Presbyterians began to supplement the psalms with hymns, and with the help of "lining out"—a process by which a leader presents each line of a hymn tune as it is to be sung—could facilitate the singing of hymns without providing additional books for the congregation.

Baxter recognized his limitations as a poet and hymnist, "acknowledging in the preface to his *Poetical Fragments* that it was only his grief at the loss of his wife that prevailed upon him to print what was otherwise unworthy, in his eyes, for publication."[39] Among his greatest influences, however, was the poet, George Herbert, who according to Baxter "speaks *to* God like one that *really believeth a God*, and whose business in the world is most *with God. Heart-work and Heaven-work* make up his books."[40]

This heart—and head—work are seen most clearly in Baxter's communion hymns, which he understood as a helpful way for the Christian to prepare to receive the sacrament. In his *Monthly Preparations for the Holy Communion* (1696), Baxter includes more than a dozen "hymns suited to

37. Benson, *English Hymn*, 82–83.
38. Benson, *English Hymn*, 85.
39. Martin, *Puritanism and Richard Baxter*, 100.
40. Coffey, *Heart Religion*, 34.

the Sacrament of the Lord's Supper."[41] In this, Baxter was representative of a larger movement among dissenters of composing hymns that "waxed lyrical about the wonders of God's love" and evoked a sense of "awe" that "God had become man and died a criminal's death." Consider the opening stanza of *Christ leads me through no darker rooms:*

> Christ leads me through no darker rooms
> Than He went through before;
> And he that in God's kingdom comes
> Must enter by this door.

As well as the opening lines of *My soul, go boldly forth*:

> My soul, go boldly forth,
> Forsake this sinful earth;
> What hath it been to thee
> But pain and sorrow?
> And think'st thou it will be
> More kind tomorrow?

Coffey explains that these hymns also served a polemical purpose: "The rise of anti-Trinitarianism in the later seventeenth-century may well have intensified pastoral frustration with exclusive psalmody. For orthodox pastors, Old Testament psalms were of little help in stemming the rising tide of Arianism and Socinianism."[42]

Baxter was a fervent advocate of the aesthetic and sensual. For, as Baxter argued, "God would not have given us, either our Senses themselves, or their usual objects, if they might not have been serviceable to his own praise"; hence, it is "a point of our Spiritual Prudence, and a singular help to the furthering of the work of Faith, to call in our Sense to its assistance."[43] Martin argues that while Baxter is often associated with logical arguments and reasoning "there is in him at times a mystical strain."[44] In the *Saint's Everlasting Rest* and in *Gildas Salvianus* Baxter writes with great appreciation for Bernard's sermons on the *Canticles*, "and so it is not surprising that several of Baxter's hymns also talked of ravishment, rapture and 'extasie,'"[45] a theme suggested in the second stanza of *Ye holy angels bright*:

> Ye blessed souls at rest,

41. Baxter, *Monthly Preparations*, 149–72.

42. Coffey, *Heart Religion*, 39.

43. Baxter, *Saints Everlasting Rest*, 757.

44. Martin, *Puritanism and Richard Baxter*, 137.

45. Coffey, *Heart Religion*, 42.

Who ran this earthly race,
And now, from sin released,
Behold the Saviour's face
God's praises sound,
As in his sight
With sweet delight
Ye do abound.

Baxter's hymns also frequently spoke of Christ's beauty as well as an intimacy with Christ, for example:

Come my Beloved, let me view
Thy beauteous lovely face;
Thee I would fold in arms of love,
Fain I would thee embrace.
I feel, I feel a flame within,
Dear Lord I the admire;
Thy sparkling beauty which I see,
Hath set me all on fire.[46]

NOTABLE HYMNS

Most of Baxter's hymn texts can be found in his *Poetical Fragments* (1681) and are sometimes accompanied by brief explanatory notes providing the historical context of their composition. As noted above, *Ye holy angels bright* was written upon the death of Baxter's wife. The hymn *Lord, it belongs not to my care* includes this note: "This Covenant my dear Wife in her former Sickness subscribed with a Cheerful will." Few of Baxter's hymns remain in print, and the exact dates of composition are largely unknown, as they are mostly found in collections of occasional works. Those most often included in modern hymnals include: *Christ leads me through no darker rooms*; *Lord, it belongs not to my care*; *My soul, go boldly forth*; and *Ye holy angels bright*.

BIBLIOGRAPHY

Baxter, Richard. *A Christian Directory*. London: Printed by Robert White for Nevil Simmons, 1678.

———. *Gildas Silvanus: The Reformed Pastor*. London: Thomas Parkhurst, Jonathan Robinson, and John Lawrence, 1707.

———. *Monthly Preparations*. London: Printed by Tho. Bunce, for Tho. Parkhurst, at the Bible and Three Crowns in Cheapside near Mercers Chapel, 1706.

46. Baxter, *Monthly Preparations*, 151.

———. *Saints Everlasting Rest.* Northampton [MA]: Simeon Butler, [Northampton?]: J. Metcalf, 1980; 1819.

Baxter, Richard, J. M. Lloyd Thomas, and N. H. Keeble. *The Autobiography of Richard Baxter.* London: Dent, 1985.

Benson, Louis F. *The English Hymn: Its Development and Use in Worship.* London: Hodder & Stoughton, 1925.

Brown, Michael G. "Not by Faith Alone: The Neonomianism of Richard Baxter." *Puritan Reformed Journal* 3.1 (2011) 133–52.

Chadwich, Owen, and Geoffrey F. Nuttall, eds. *Uniformity to Unity, 1662–1962.* London: Sheldon, *1962.*

Coffey, John. *Heart Religion: Evangelical Piety in England and Ireland, 1690–1850.* Oxford: Oxford University Press, 2016.

Davies, Horton. *Worship and Theology in England, 1.II: From Andrewes to Baxter and Fox, 1603–1690.* Grand Rapids, MI: Eerdmans, 1996.

Julian John. *Dictionary of Hymnology.* London: John Murray, 1907.

Keeble, N. H. *Richard Baxter: Puritan Man of Letters.* Oxford: Clarendon, 1982.

Ladell, A. R. *Richard Baxter: Puritan and Mystic.* New York: Macmillan, 1925.

Lindberg, Carter, ed. *The Pietist Theologians: An Introduction to Theology in the Seventeenth and Eighteenth Centuries.* Malden, MA: Blackwell, 2005.

Martin, Hugh. *Puritanism and Richard Baxter.* London: SCM, 1954

Nuttall, Geoffrey F. *Richard Baxter.* Camden: Thomas Nelson and Sons, 1965.

Purves, Andrew. *Pastoral Theology in the Classical Tradition.* Louisville, KY: Westminster John Knox, 2001.

Segger, Glen J. *Richard Baxter's* Reformed Liturgy: *A Puritan Alternative to the* Book of Common Prayer. Burlington, VT: Ashgate, 2014.

Turner, G. L., ed. *Original Records of Early Non-Conformity Under Persecution and Indulgence.* London: T. Fisher Unwin, 1911.

von Rohr, John. *The Covenant of Grace in Puritan Thought.* Atlanta: Scholars, 1986.

Wooten, Janet H. "The Wilderness and Christian Song." *International Congregational Journal* 10.1 (Spring 2011) 75–90.

Chapter 11

English Language Metrical Psalters of the Seventeenth Century

J. Michael Morgan

HISTORICAL BACKGROUND AND THEOLOGICAL PERSPECTIVES

The opening years of the seventeenth century saw significant resolution in the Catholic and Protestant conflict that resulted in the Reformation. At the same time, some amazing events prompted significant change, in both church and state, which set the course of English, Scottish, and American history for the next 400 years and beyond.

In 1603, Queen Elizabeth died without a direct heir to the throne, and the crown passed to her cousin James, who had reigned since infancy in Scotland, thus uniting the two monarchies as King James I. In 1604, King James assembled leaders from all factions of the church ("high church" and moderate Anglicans, Scots Presbyterians, Puritans, and English Reformed congregations) at Hampton Court Palace to join in seeking ways to come together. One of the major resolutions was to produce a new version of the Bible, which could be read in worship throughout the realm. Scholars worked for the next seven years comparing all previous English Bibles with each other, as well as versions in other languages. Their efforts resulted in the "King James Bible"—the most influential and widely circulated book ever published in the English language.

One reason for the literary success of the King James Bible was the fact that the English language itself was experiencing a tremendous creative "generation," which culminated with the work of William Shakespeare, who died in 1616. Through him, the vocabulary and possibilities of imagery and expression reached new heights, which found expression in the English Bible.

Protestant congregations began to expand from Europe to the New World, bringing with them their traditions and dreams. Among their essentials were a shared adoration for God and a mutual devotion to the practice of worship, which included the singing of metrical psalms.

The English and Scottish congregations continued to sing faithfully their praises and laments from the version of Sternhold and Hopkins (1562) and the Scottish variant (1564). The English-speaking Reformed Church in the Netherlands, however, sought a different direction in its congregational song.

Henry Ainsworth's Reformed Psalter and the Bay Psalm Book

Henry Ainsworth (1571–ca. 1622) was pastor of the Independent Reformed English Church in the Netherlands, where a number of Reformed congregations settled when the established Church of England became less tolerant of dissenters from their faith and practice. According to one author,

> Ainsworth was a fine type of Elizabethan puritan—learned, sincere, earnest, and uncompromising. He attached himself to those who were styled "Brownists" who, under the name of "Independents," afterwards played so important a part in English history, and who were the ancestors of the "Congregationalists" and other free churches of the present time. Their essential distinction was the claim that each church or congregation should be a religious republic, regulating its own affairs in entire independence of state control, whether episcopal or Presbyterian.[1]

As far as congregational singing in his church was concerned, Ainsworth stated in his *Defence of the Holy Scriptures, Worship and Ministrie Used in the Christian Churches*: "(We) do content ourselves with joint

1. Leslie, *Dictionary of National Biography*, 1:191.

harmonious singing of the Psalms of Holy Scripture, to the instruction and comforts of our hearts, and praise of our God."[2]

Ainsworth, a Hebrew scholar, held the belief that the earlier English and Scottish poets who had paraphrased the psalms in meter too often strayed from a strict fidelity to the original Hebrew text. Thus, he began his own version of the psalms, both in prose, with a commentary, and in meter for his congregation (first published in 1612), concentrating on how best to express the ancient Jewish sentiments in English contemporary with his Christian church. In the preface to his *Annotations upon the Book of Psalmes*, Ainsworth explains his devotion to the original:

> Now because many things, both for phrase and matter, are difficult to such as are not acquainted with David's language, I have (out of my slender store) annexed a few brief notes, comparing the Scriptures, and conferring the best expositors, especially the ancient Greek and Chaldee versions, whereby if any help of understanding may arise, the praise be to God, the comfort to his people.[3]

His paraphrase of Ps 23 begins strongly with his addressing God by his ancient Hebrew name:

> Jehovah feedeth me, I shall not lack.
> In grassy folds, he down doth make me lie;
> He gently leads me, quiet waters by.
> He doth return my soul, for his name's sake. . . .
>
> Doubtless, good and mercy shall all
> the days of my life follow me;
> also within Jehovah's house I shall
> to length of days, repose me quietly.

In Ps 98 Ainsworth speaks very strongly of our imperative to worship God through music:

> Unto Jehovah, all the earth, shout ye triumphantly;
> shout cheerfully, and joyful shout and sing melodiously.
> Unto Jehovah with the harp melodiously sing ye;
> even with the harp and with the voice of singing melody.
> With shrilling trumpets, also with the cornets' sounding voice
> before the King Jehovah's face, shout with triumphant noise.

2. Hanbury, *Historical Memorials*, 181.
3. Ainsworth, *Annotations upon the Book of Psalmes*, A2.

In addition to the Book of Psalms, Ainsworth published a new translation with commentary on the Five Books of Moses and the Song of Solomon. His devotion to the original Hebrew bordered on obsession, and he constantly bombarded his Jewish colleagues in Amsterdam with questions about their Scriptures and how they related to the Messiah. When he died under rather suspicious circumstances during the winter of 1622, many of his followers believed that he was poisoned by the Jewish leaders in the community who did not trust his motives, but this was never proven.

As the conflicts between the Anglicans and Presbyterians continued in Great Britain, the Reformed Church found itself in a comparable state of division. The Puritans generally represented the more educated, middle class members still holding some ties with the Church of England. The Pilgrims, on the other hand, were Independents ("independent" from the Anglican Church) and were less scholastic and financially independent. The Pilgrims held strongly to their psalm singing tradition. While they remained faithful to Henry Ainsworth's paraphrase, questions were raised as to the quality of the poetry, the faithfulness to the Hebrew original, and whether the Christians in the New World deserved a new psalter of their own.

John Cotton, the preeminent minister and theologian of the Massachusetts Bay Colony, in his analysis of singing psalms in worship, states his commitment to metrical psalms with these words: "The translating of the psalms into verse, in number, measure, and meter, and suiting the ditty with apt tunes, do help to stir up the affection; and the singing of psalms being appointed of God, they tend to make a gracious melody to the praise of God and edification of his people."[4]

A dozen of his colleagues shared Cotton's commitment to singing the psalms, and in 1640 appeared *The Whole Booke of Psalmes Faithfully Translated into English Metre*, popularly known as the Bay Psalm Book. More than its contents, its historical significance lies in the fact that it was the first book to be printed in the New World.

Many of the versions in the Bay Psalm Book are certainly inferior to the more secular verse of the period, particularly in the writings of John Milton, George Herbert, and John Dryden, among others. But then, the composers of the texts were more astute in theological rather than literary achievements. Zoltan Haraszti observes, "The ministers of the Bay Colony were under no illusion of having produced memorable poetry. They knew that their verses were 'not always so smooth and elegant' as might have been

4. Cotton, *Singing of Psalmes*, 60.

expected. But they were not abashed."[5] On the other hand, Richard Mather defended their perceived poetic flaws in the preface to the psalter itself:

> If therefore the verses are not always so smooth and elegant as some may desire or expect, let them consider that God's altar needs not our polishings, for we have respected rather a plain translation than to smooth our verses with the sweetness of any paraphrase, and so have attended conscience rather than elegance, fidelity rather than poetry, in translating the Hebrew words into English language, and David's poetry into English meter, that so we may sing in Sion the Lord's songs of praise according to his own will.[6]

The setting of Ps 24 from the Bay Psalm Book is one of its less-than-memorable settings:

> The earth Jehovah's is,
> and the fullness of it:
> the habitable world, and they
> that there upon do sit.

The expression of the imagery in Ps 23 is considerably more resonant to our contemporary ears, and, while the word order may be a bit irregular, there is an inherent strength which reflects the courage of the colonial refugees:

> The Lord to me a shepherd is,
> want therefore shall not I.
> He in the folds of tender grass
> doth cause me down to lie.
> To waters calm me gently leads,
> restore my soul doth he;
> he doth in paths of righteousness
> for his name's sake lead me.

While none of the texts from the Bay Psalm Book are sung in worship today, they were revised several times and often reprinted in America, England, and Scotland over the next 125 years.

5. Haraszti, *Enigma of the Bay Psalm Book*, 55.
6. Bay Psalm Book, *Bay Psalm Book*, preface.

English and Scottish Psalters of the Seventeenth Century

By far the most enduring work associated with singing the psalms in worship was not related to the texts but rather to the tunes to which they were sung, beginning with the harmonized settings composed by Thomas Ravenscroft (1592–1635). Ravenscroft grew up as a chorister at St. Paul's Cathedral and graduated from Cambridge's Pembroke Hall in 1605. Four years later, he published two important collections of English rounds, in which his famous "Three Blind Mice" appeared for the first time (*Deuteromelia*, 1609). In Ravenscroft's psalter (1621) the texts were taken from the "Old Version" of the psalms. Ravenscroft was both an editor and a musician, and his collection of tunes is described in his title as being "such severall Tunes as have beene, and are usually sung in England, Scotland, Wales, Germany, Italy, France and the Netherlands: never as yet before in one volume published."[7] For this project, he collected ninety tunes; thirty-seven of them identified as "proper psalm tunes," eight as "spiritual songs," and the remaining forty-five are "common tunes." The "proper tunes" are generally more difficult to sing for congregations who did not have a strong choir to support the vocal parts, while the "common tune are more accessible." He drew on the work of such prominent composers of church music as Richard Allison, Thomas Morley, John Dowland, Giles Farnaby, and John Milton. So good was his work that very little was added to the English hymn repertory for the next fifty years.

English Psalters in the Seventeenth Century

George Sandys (1577–1644) was the youngest son of Edwin Sandys, Archbishop of York. A widely traveled nobleman, he took great interest in the early colonization of America, and in 1621 became colonial treasurer of the Virginia Company. His paraphrase of the psalms, "set to new tunes for private devotion" by Henry Lawes of the King's Chapel Royal, was published in a collection entitled *A Paraphrase upon the Divine Poems* in London in 1638, along with his poetic versions of the book of Job, Lamentations of Jeremiah, Ecclesiastes, and a number of excerpts from the Old and New Testaments. Sandys's rendering of Ps 23 is a perfect example of the florid, uncommon language and imagery he employed in all of his paraphrases (spelling updated):

> The Lord my Shepherd, me his Sheep
> will from consuming famine keep.
> He fosters me in fragrant meads,

7. Ravenscroft, *Whole Booke of Psalmes,* title page.

by softly-sliding waters leads;
my soul refreshed with pleasant juice,
and lest they should his name traduce,
then when I wander in the maze
of tempting sin, informs my ways.

Scottish Psalters in the Seventeenth Century

Psalm singing had become a vital component of worship in the Scottish churches, particularly the Psalter of 1564. In 1615 the prominent Edinburgh printer and bookseller Andro Hart set the stage for Thomas Ravenscroft by publishing his own collection of harmonized psalm tunes, all identified by him as "common tunes," which had been granted official status by the Church of Scotland. Ten years later, in 1625, Edward Raban published his Aberdeen Psalter, which contained a number of psalm tunes "in reports," or composed as miniature anthems to be sung in worship.

King James died in 1624 and was succeeded by his son who was crowned King Charles the First. King James's attempts to reconcile the Churches of England and Scotland had been, for the most part, successful in the first quarter of the seventeenth century, but almost immediately upon coming to the throne, Charles began to widen the gap, strongly biased toward the "High Church" Anglicans led by William Laud, his Archbishop of Canterbury.

Charles and Archbishop Laud initially wanted Scotland to adopt the Book of Common Prayer. This met deep-seated opposition in Scotland, and in 1637, their attempt to impose the English liturgy led to riots in Edinburgh and elsewhere.

In their failed attempt, they were convinced that if the liturgy could be somehow linked with King James, who still held much allegiance from his fellow Scots, there would be little or no opposition to having it authorized. James had over the years paraphrased a few of the psalms in verse, and, since a metrical psalter was the accepted congregational songbook in the Scottish (and English) church, this seemed the perfect place to start. Thus, Sir William Alexander (1580–1640), the Earl of Stirling, employed a few of James's texts, with alterations, and contributed his own versions (which comprised the bulk of the psalter) in a volume entitled *The Psalmes of King David, Translated by King James* in 1631. The Scottish Privy Council in December 1634 passed an injunction that only the King James translation should be printed or imported, and Alexander was granted the exclusive right of publishing it for thirty-one years, very much to his own benefit. Because of the opposition created by the 1631 edition, he in great measure rewrote his original version, which was bound up and issued with Laud's Scottish Prayer Book of 1637. This liturgy was imposed on the Church of Scotland and prompted riots, which led up to the English/Scottish Civil War. The Scottish Church refused to accept any worship resource that dictated the language of the prayers of the people, and this new psalm version, being "attached" to the Prayer Book, suffered the same fate.

Alexander's rendering of Ps 100, sung to the "Old Hundredth" tune, could have ably competed with Scotsman William Kethe's setting in the "Old Version" of Sternhold and Hopkins, had it not been included with the Scottish Prayer Book:

> Make all ye lands a joyful noise,
> to him that is the Lord of might;
> with gladness ever serve the Lord,
> and come with singing in his sight.
> Know that the Lord is our great God,
> he us, not we, our selves did make;
> we are his people, and the sheep
> that he as his own flock did take.

His Ps 23 is of equal quality, and might well have endured had it not been coupled with the imposed "dictated" liturgy:

> The Lord of all, my Shepherd is,
> I shall from want be free;
> he makes me in green pastures lie,
> and near calm streams to be.
> He doth restore my soul, and leads
> the way that I should take:
> into the paths of righteousness,
> even for his own name's sake.

The Westminster Assembly of Divines was convened by Parliament in 1643 to reform the Church of England and its practices and, in the view of the Scots commissioners at least, to unite the two great churches of Britain "in one form of Kirk Government, one Confession of Faith, one Catechism, and one Directory for the Worship of God."[8]

Between the years 1640 and 1650, the Church of Scotland experienced great strides in the political and theological arenas. The power of

8. Wainwright and Tucker, *Oxford History of Christian Worship*, 478.

the monarchy under King Charles the First and his Parliament diminished greatly as Oliver Cromwell and the Scottish Puritans and Presbyterians pressed forward with their visions for a church and empire free from the domination of the British nobility. The civil war continued to rage and culminated in the execution of the king and the establishment of the Commonwealth at the end of the decade.

During this era, the Anglican Book of Common Prayer was banned in deference to the Directory for Worship. The Scottish metrical psalms, brought back from Geneva by the Marian refugees nearly a century before, was in serious need of revision, and no longer met their needs for music in worship. Two Puritan authors stepped forward to provide a new paraphrase of the psalms. Francis Rous (1579–1659) was an English lawyer and active member of the Long Parliament seeking action against King Charles and the bishops in the Church of England. He was appointed a member of the Westminster Assembly and held other appointments under Cromwell. His rival, William Barton (1598–1678), was a clergyman in the Church of England. For that reason, the House of Lords favored Barton's version, but the General Assembly of the Church of Scotland preferred the more accurate version composed by Rous, though they were not totally convinced that his paraphrase should become the standard in the church they hoped to establish.

The General Assembly began making extensive amendments, using Rous's psalter as its basis, published a final version in Scotland in 1650, and ordered it to be sung in both Scottish and English congregations to the exclusion of all other versions. With minor revisions, more of its texts are still sung in churches three and a half centuries later than any other versions.

Some of the settings did carry over from earlier psalters, like William Kethe's paraphrase of Ps 100, "All People That on Earth Do Dwell." But there was a wealth of new versions that first appeared in 1650, including the classic rendition of Ps 23:

> The Lord's my shepherd, I'll not want;
> he makes me down to lie
> in pastures green; he leadeth me
> the quiet waters by.

The virtues of the 1650 Scottish Psalter were well summed up by Dr. John Ker in his book, *The Psalms in History and Biography*: "No version has ever been made which adheres so closely to the Scripture. It proceeds on the principle of giving every thought in the original, and nothing more;

and in this it has succeeded to an extent which is marvelous, and which can be realized only by one who has tested it through careful comparison."[9] While the authorized Scottish Psalter of 1650 remained the most widely sung version for the remainder of the century in Scotland, the end of the Commonwealth period and the return of the monarchy under King Charles the Second opened the door to the reprinting of the "Old Version," most often bound with copies of the Book of Common Prayer. The number of independent versifications increased greatly to offer alternatives, but these were generally published in very small editions, often paid for by the author and circulated among friends, church members, and colleagues, never finding their way into the church at large.

Other Metrical Versions of the Seventeenth Century

Among the writers who penned a paraphrase of the complete book of Psalms were few noted poets indeed, but devout Christian representatives of a variety of occupations. George Wither (1632) was a noted poet and satirist who wavered as a Royalist and Puritan. His version of the psalms was printed in Amsterdam but banned in Britain. William Nicholson (1662) was a Royalist schoolmaster and priest, expelled from the church during the Commonwealth, but later appointed Bishop of Gloucester. Francis Roberts (1665) served as a priest and was appointed by Parliament to the Commission for the ejection of scandalous ministers and schoolmasters. Samuel Woodford (1667) was a musician and later a priest, famous for his verbose and flowery poetry. Miles Smyth (1668) was a Royalist and Secretary to the Archbishop of Canterbury. Thomas, Lord Fairfax (1669), served as Commander-in-Chief of the English military under King Charles and the Commonwealth military under Cromwell. Richard Goodridge (1684), also a musician, was known for the simplicity and neatness of expression in his poems. Richard Baxter (1692), a leading nonconformist minister, was a prolific author of practical theology, and even composed an alternative liturgy to the English Book of Common Prayer.

None of these psalm versions had a lasting influence on congregational song, most likely due to the quality of the poetry, which two hundred years later prompted Oscar Wilde to remark that there seemed to be a direct correlation between piety and poor rhyme!

9. Ker, *Psalms in History and Biography*, 207.

The Musical Edition of John Playford

Ravenscroft's harmonized version of the psalm tunes (1621) enjoyed a fifty-six-year monopoly on part-singing by choirs and individuals who wanted to sing in harmony, but in 1677 John Playford (1613–96) came out with his *Whole Book of Psalms . . . Compos'd in Three Parts: Cantus, Medius, and Bassus*. A few years earlier he had published a similar collection of selected psalm tunes along with some hymns, but his later volume was devoted solely to the metrical psalms, with the hope that his audience would be greatly enhanced by those congregations who professed to sing the Old Testament texts exclusively. It was frequently reprinted over the next century, and many congregants purchased copies and brought them to their worship. The actual influence of Playford's book was by way of prolonging the period of psalm singing, and adding money to his coffers as a prominent music publisher.[10]

The "New Version" by Nahum Tate and Nicholas Brady

The second major version of the psalms in meter for the Church of England appeared in the closing years of the seventeenth century and was the paraphrase executed by Nahum Tate, the noted Poet Laureate of England, and Nicholas Brady, vicar of Richmond in Surrey. It quickly became known as the "New Version," in opposition to Sternhold and Hopkin's psalter, which was called the "Old Version."

Tate was born in Dublin in 1652 and educated at Trinity College. He is said to have been a man of intemperate and improvident life, and died in London in 1715. While he brought the poetic skill to the table, Brady (1659–1726), who received his Doctor of Divinity degree from Trinity College as well, served more as the theological and biblical guide for the work. Both men had experienced some success as poets, but it is impossible to discern which author contributed which psalms to the "New Version."

By far the more prominent partner was Nahum Tate, described by a contemporary as being "a man of learning, candor, and courteous to all, with a good share of wit and a great deal of modesty."[11] In addition to his poetry, he wrote several dramatic productions, and revised Shakespeare's works in an attempt to improve them—so much for his sense of modesty![12]

10. Benson, *English Hymn*, 77.
11. Hadden, "Sternhold and Hopkins," 82.
12. Brown, *Oxford Handbook of the Psalms*, 576.

Their work was completed in 1696. Upon publication, however, it received significant criticism and it was virtually rewritten in 1698. In its revised state, the "New Version" was reprinted through the nineteenth century. The opening verse of the twenty-third psalm, in the original state from 1696 and the revised text of 1698, shows the extreme steps they took to make the version more acceptable.

Edition of 1696
Since God does me, his worthless charge,
protect with tender care,
as watchful shepherds guard their flocks,
what can I want or fear?

Edition of 1698
The Lord himself, the mighty Lord,
vouchsafes to be my guide;
the Shepherd by whose constant care
my wants are all supplied.

Apparently none of the prospective worshipers singing the "New Version" wanted to refer to themselves as God's "worthless charge" and the imagery transferred from the human to the divine!

CONTRIBUTION TO LITURGY AND WORSHIP

As the seventeenth century moved forward, there was an increase in the number of dissenting and nonconformist congregations who found it difficult to remain a part of the Established Church of England. One of the points of contention in their worship life centered around restrictions that limited congregational song to the Old Testament psalms alone, leaving little or no room for hymns drawn from the New Testament.

Dating back to the Reformation, paraphrases of the canticles from the Gospels—the Benedictus (Song of Zechariah), the Magnificat (Song of Mary), and Nunc Dimittis (Song of Simeon)—were frequently allowed to be sung, but the metrical psalms dominated congregational singing. This meant that the Christian Year was like living in a perpetual Advent with no celebration of the Nativity, and an endless Lent with no acknowledgement of the resurrection.

An obvious solution was to broaden the interpretation of psalm paraphrases to reflect more of what we experience in our lives as we live on this side of the cross. John Patrick (1632–95), preacher at the Charter House in London, believed strongly that portions of some of the psalms were not appropriate to be sung in Christian worship, that they dwelt too much on the wrath of a vengeful God, called too strongly for the destruction of the enemies of God's chosen people, and dealt too intimately with issues that were only associated with Jewish faith and culture. In his paraphrase, published for his congregation in 1694, he claimed the license to interpret the psalms in a more Christian light, thus setting the stage for Isaac Watts and his psalms "imitated in the language of the New Testament" some twenty-five years later.[13]

Timothy Duguid, in his treatise on singing the psalms, sums up the incomparable gift the tradition has brought to our worship:

> The metrical psalms and their melodies were shared by all conditions of men and women. Young and old, rich and poor, noble and commoner, learned and unlearned, all joined their voices together in these words and tunes that allowed them to give shared expression to their religious faith in psalms that voiced their pains, struggles, hopes, and beliefs and thus brought them closer to their God.[14]

Our congregational song in the twenty-first century certainly owes much to the metrical psalmody in the early years of Protestant worship in the English and Scottish traditions. It was the singing of psalms in the face of theological debate, heretical persecution, liturgical conflict, and religious turmoil that established the "firm foundation" upon which we proclaim and celebrate our faith today.

NOTABLE HYMNS

William Kethe's setting of Ps 100 from the Sternhold and Hopkins psalter and the first Scottish psalter continued to be reprinted in all but the independent versions. With only the alteration of the word "fear" to "mirth" in the first stanza, it remains virtually unchanged to this day.

The Scottish psalter of 1650, which underwent closer examination than any previous version, has only a few surviving settings. The most popular is Ps 23 ("The Lord's My Shepherd, I'll Not Want"), but a few others appear with substantial editing: Ps 46 ("God Is Our Refuge and Our Strength") and Ps 102 ("Lord, Hear My Prayer").

13. Brown, *Oxford Handbook of the Psalms*, 575.

14. Duguid, *Metrical Psalmody* 234.

From the more famous poets who never attempted to produce a complete psalter (John Donne, George Herbert, John Milton, and Richard Crashaw, to name a few), the only version we still sing is Milton's setting of Ps 136, composed in 1624, "Let Us With a Gladsome Mind." With a contemporary revision of the text in the interest of inclusive language, we sing today:

Let us with a gladsome mind praise the Lord who is so kind:
For God's mercies shall endure, ever faithful, ever sure.

BIBLIOGRAPHY

Ainsworth, Henry. *Annotations upon the Book of Psalmes*. Amsterdam, 1617.

Bay Psalm Book. *The Bay Psalm Book, Being a Facsimile Reprint of the First Edition, Printed by Stephen Daye at Cambridge, in New England in 1640*. New York: New England Society, 1903.

Benson, Louis F. *The English Hymn: Its Development and Use in Worship*. Richmond, VA: John Knox, 1962.

Brown, William P. *The Oxford Handbook of the Psalms*. New York: Oxford University Press, 2014.

Cotton, John. *Singing of Psalmes a Gospel Ordinance*. London: M. S., 1647.

Duguid, Timothy. *Metrical Psalmody in Print and Practice*. Burlington, VT: Ashgate, 2014.

Hadden, J. C. "Sternhold and Hopkins and Their Followers." *Gentleman's Magazine* 280 (January–June 1896) 77–88.

Hanbury, Benjamin. *Historical Memorials Relating to the Independents or Congregationalists: From Their Rise to the Restoration of the Monarchy A.D. MDCLX*. London: Printed for the Congregational Union of England and Wales [by] Fisher, Son, & Co. and Jackson and Walford, 1844.

Haraszti, Zoltan. *The Enigma of the Bay Psalm Book*. Chicago: University of Chicago, 1956.

Leslie, Stephen, ed. *Dictionary of National Biography*. New York: Macmillan and Company, 1885.

Ker, John. *The Psalms in History and Biography*. Edinburgh: Andrew Elliot, 1887.

Ravenscroft, Thomas. *The Whole Booke of Psalmes: With the Hymnes Evangelicall, and Songs Spirituall*. London: Thomas Harper, 1621.

Wainwright, Geoffrey, and Karen B. Westerfield Tucker. *The Oxford History of Christian Worship*. Oxford: Oxford University Press, 2006.

Chapter 12

Eucharistic Hymnody among British Dissenters

Bryan D. Spinks

HISTORICAL BACKGROUND[1]

David Wykes states, "Hymn-singing, as distinct from psalm-singing, was introduced by dissenters into their regular worship in the period after the 1689 Toleration Act and was adopted rapidly from the beginning of the eighteenth century."[2] In fact, some groups apparently were singing hymns during the Commonwealth and Protectorate period. The Presbyterian Thomas Edwards catalogued a whole number of sectarian abuses, amongst which was the view that the singing which Christians should use, is that of hymns and spiritual songs, framed by themselves, composed of their gifts. William Barton, whose metrical psalms were championed by the Cromwellian regime, also authored *A Century of Select Hymns,* one of which had the title "Sacrament of the Supper." It consisted of six parts and was a metrical version of a catena of different Scripture verses. Part three concluded:

1. Portions of this chapter first appeared in my work, Spinks, *Liturgy in the Age of Reason.*

2. David L. Wykes, "From David's Psalms to Watts's Hymns," 229.

To eat this bread and drink this cup
Holds forth a saviour slain
So often as we celebrate,
Until he come again.

Richard Baxter, who chose nonconformity and then dissent rather than accept the See of Hereford, wrote hymns, and his literary executor, Matthew Sylvester, published *Mr Richard Baxter's Paraphrase on the Psalms of David in Metre, with other Hymns* in 1692. In 1695 Matthew Henry, son of Phillip, published *Family-Hymns: Gather'd (mostly) out of the best Translations of David's Psalms.* Though designed for daily family worship, Henry noted in his Epistle to the Reader, "If Psalms were more sung in Families, they would be better sung in Congregations."[3] It may be that some of these might have been sung at celebrations of the Lord's Supper, but none of them seem to have been composed specifically for this purpose. Other dissenting ministers provided non-scriptural texts for congregational singing. At first these texts seem to have been used immediately after the Lord's Supper, in imitation of the synoptic Gospel accounts of the Last Supper, after which Jesus and the disciples sang a hymn. Though this may refer to the *hallel* psalms used at Passover, the Greek *humnesantes* (Mark 14:26) was imprecise enough to justify non-scriptural hymns. From this initial use at the Lord's Supper, hymns seem to have been introduced into regular Sunday worship.

In 1694, Richard Davis, Independent minister of Rothwell, Northamptonshire, published a second edition of *Hymns Composed on Several Subjects.* The fact that this was a second edition indicates that hymn-singing in this community was already an established practice. Davis included fourteen hymns for the Lord's Supper composed by his predecessor, Thomas Browning, which he found in Browning's study. The collection was divided into three books, the third being for the Lord's Supper. While the literary merit of these hymns is not great—"warm but artless" in Louis Benson's estimation—the context of their composition and the theology they reflect is of considerable interest.[4]

Richard Davis had been a schoolmaster until 1689, and a member of the Congregational Church of Silver Street, London, whose pastor was Thomas Cole. Realizing that there was to be no comprehension for Presbyterians, the latter turned to the idea of cooperation with the Independents, leading to the "Common Fund" of 1690, and the "Heads of Agreement" in 1691. The "Happy Union" was inaugurated April 6, 1691. Simultaneously, however, a controversy was taking place over the republication of the works

3. Henry, *Family-Hymns.*

4. Benson, *English Hymn,* 105.

of Dr. Tobias Crisp (1600–1643), which the Westminster Assembly had condemned as antinomian. Richard Baxter had condemned the theology of Crisp's works, and Thomas Cole had defended it. Davis apparently shared the convictions of his former pastor, and it is no accident that the publisher of Davis's hymns, W. Marshall, also republished Crisp's works.

The fact that Book III of his hymn collection included communion hymns by his predecessor suggests that hymn singing was first introduced in the Rothwell congregation at the Lord's Supper. By the time of the publication of the 1694 collection, hymns in Books I and II were sung at other parts or occasions of public worship, as indicated by a contemporary account of worship under Davis, published in 1700:

> When the Congregation is assembled, the Preacher (whether Pastor or Elder) begins with Prayer, the People generally standing, (they look upon those as lazy who sit and will not suffer any Man to be covered): When Prayer is ended, they cover their Heads, and sit or stand, as they please, during the Sermon. This is the whole of their Behaviour and service, unless they Sing a Hymn, which they ordinarily do.[5]

Baptists worshipped with some freedom in the 1650s, though they existed in several groupings. The General Baptists originated with John Smyth, and were regarded as Arminian; the Particular or Strict Baptists were staunchly Calvinist, as were the Seventh Day Baptists, though the latter were committed to worship on Saturday. There were also open communion Baptists such as John Bunyan, and the Fifth Monarchy Baptists typified by the Welshman, Vavasor Powell. Although worship services differed from congregation to congregation, the pattern outlined in the Church Book of the meeting at Paul's Alley, Barbican in 1695, provides some indications of Baptist practice:

> SEVENTHLY; That the publick Worship in the Congregation on the Lord's Day be thus performed, viz. In the morning about half an hour after nine, some Brother be appointed to begin the Exercise in reading a psalm, & then to spend some time in Prayer; & after yt to read some other Portion of H.Scripture, till the Minister comes into the Pulpit; and after Preaching 7 Prayer to conclude wth singing a Psalm. The afternoon exercise

5. *An Account of the Doctrine*, 20. There were four kinds of meetings: (1) On every Lord's Day, prayer, preaching and receiving the Lord's Supper when it was celebrated; (2) Certain solemn days, appointed by the congregation; (3) Church meetings, for covenanted members only, to regulate church matters; and (4) Messengers meetings, for the evangelists of the "sister churches" originating from Davis's itinerant preaching.

> to begin abt half an hour after One, & to be carried on & concluded as in the forenoon.
>
> EIGHTHLY; That on breaking-Bread-Days, the Psalm to be omitted in the Afternoon tell the Conclusion of the Lord's Supper.
>
> Pursuant to the aforesaid Agreemt the two Churches did unite on Wednesday the 12th of June, 1695, and also met together the next Lord's Day following, &c.[6]

This congregation had Calvinist pastors, but was technically independent of both the General and Particular Baptists.

The Lord's Supper, being a "supper," was celebrated in the afternoon according to General Baptist custom. The congregation also had a psalm sung. Not all Baptist congregations allowed singing. When the General Baptists met in Assembly in London 1689, singing was one of the items on the agenda, and according to the minutes recorded by Thomas Grantham, it was argued:

> As Prayer of one in the Church is the Prayer of the whole Church so the singing of one in the Church is the singing of the whole Church, and as he that prayeth in the Church is to pforme the Service as of the ability wch.God giveth even so he that singeth praises in the Church ought to pforme that Service as of the Ability reced.of God.[7]

This seems to have allowed soloist singing rather than congregational singing, though the material which might be sung remained undefined. Both Bunyan and Powell wrote hymns, and though it is doubtful that their own congregations sang them, it indicates that some Baptists were not averse to singing extra-biblical songs. One of the most prominent hymn writers to come from the seventeenth century Baptist tradition was Benjamin Keach, a General Baptist turned Particular Baptist.

Benjamin Keach (1640–1704) came from a Church of England family, but by 1655 had joined a General Baptist congregation, and in 1658 became pastor of a General Baptist congregation in Buckingshire.[8] In 1662, he was dragged from his pulpit and threatened with being trampled to death by the horses of the arresting troopers. In 1664, he was indicted for being "a Seditious, Heretical, and Schismatical Person, evilly and maliciously disposed

6. "Paul's Alley, Barbican, 1695–1768," 46–54.

7. Whitley, *Minutes of the General Assembly*, 27–28.

8. The earliest source, written by Keach's father-in-law, Thomas Crosby, is *History of the English Baptists* (London, 1738); a good modern treatment is Copeland, *Benjamin Keach and the Development of Baptist Traditions*.

and disaffected to his Majesty's Government, and the Government of the Church of England."[9] He had published a catechism, *The Child's Instructor*, in which he criticized the Church of England and the *Book of Common Prayer*, and was subsequently sentenced to prison and the pillory. In 1666, he published *Zion in Distress*, which was a verse lament for the state of religion in England voiced on behalf of dissenters:

> My Children, which both young and tender are,
> The fierce looks of these Beasts do greatly feare.
> And some they seiz upon as their own Prey,
> And them into to their Den do bear away;
> Where they are kept in sore captivity,
> Mourning for me, and their extremity.[10]

In the postscript Keach advised,

> *Break of all yoaks, set the oppressed free,*
> *And labour for Christian Liberty.*[11]

In 1672, he became a Particular Baptist, pastoring a congregation at Horsleydown, Southwark. One ritual distinction between General and Particular Baptists was that the former normally added a hand-laying immediately following baptism by submersion, and Keach continued to promote and defend this practice after becoming a Particular Baptist. In a work entitled *Darkness Vanquished*, 1675, Keach argued:

> It cannot be rationally concluded he [John] should, considering the lesser is blessed, of the greater . . . But the promised Spirit, which is the end of the Ordinance of the Laying on of hands, is said to be Christ's own gift, Ephes.4.7 . . . yet I may say, the Father laid his hands upon him, and the Spirit cam down visibly in the likeness of a Dove, and rested upon him, just after he came out of the water. . . . This way he was visibly by God the Father sealed, after he was baptised.[12]

Keach opposed the Seventh Day Baptists' observance of Saturday, though he remained on good terms with Joseph Stennett. He also wrote against Quakers, and with double entendre intended, one of his hymns began,

> O Quake ye who most guitly are,
> who love and live in sin;

9. Crosby, op. cit., book ii, 186.
10. Keach, *Zion in Distress*, 2–3.
11. Keach, *Zion in Distress*, 51.
12. Keach, *Darkness Vanquished*, 51, cited in Copeland, op. cit., 47.

For God will suddenly break forth,
As usual hath not been.

The shaking times that are at hand,
Will bring Great Babel down.
And then will God save this our Land,
And Saints with Blessings Crown.[13]

It appears that shortly after becoming pastor of the Horselydown congregation, Keach introduced hymn singing after the Lord's Supper. By 1691, he had introduced hymn singing into regular Sunday worship, though not without controversy; a number of his congregation seceded to found a separate church, which maintained its opposition to hymn singing until 1736.[14] Addressing the disagreement in 1691 Keach wrote,

> Hath not the Church sung at breaking of Bread always for 16 or 18 Years past, and could not, nor would omit it in the time of the late Persecution? . . . And have we not for this 12 or 14 Years sung in *mixt Assemblies, on Days of Thanksgiving*, and never any offended at it, as ever I heard? What is done more now? 'tis only practised oftner: and sure if it be God's Ordinance, the often practising of it, by such who find their Hearts draw out so to do, cannot be sinful.[15]

Keach became engaged in the controversy over hymn singing with Isaac Marlow. Marlow wrote a number of books and tracts arguing that since hymns were artificial rhymes, there was no difference between them and using set forms of prayer. In his *A Brief Discourse Concerning Singing* (1690), Marlow argued that the New Testament references to hymns and spiritual songs was an extraordinary spiritual gift limited to the New Testament times, that congregational singing compromised the elect, that in the early church there was a single cantor, and that mixed singing violated 1 Cor 14:34 and 1 Tim 2:11–12. In his 1691 work, *The Breach Repaired*, Keach countered these arguments, noting that Eph 5:19 and Jas 5:13 enjoined singing, that if hymns were extraordinary gifts, why were prayers and sermons not also limited to New Testament times, and that if mixed singing contaminated the elect, why not shared prayers? Furthermore, if women could give an account of their faith in public, why should they not be able to sing their faith?

13. Keach, *Spiritual Melody*, 9 (Hymn 3, though this heading seems to have been omitted).

14. Watts, *Dissenters*, 1:310.

15. Keach, *Breach Repaired in God's Worship*, viii–ix.

Keach's earlier publications contain verse compositions and an occasional hymn. In 1691, he published a collection of almost three hundred hymns and psalms, entitled *Spiritual Melody*. Keach was not the only hymn writer from the Baptist tradition. Joseph Stennett, a Seventh Day Baptist who worshipped with the Particular Baptists on Sundays, published *Hymns in Commemoration of the Sufferings of our Blessed Christ: Compos'd for the Celebration of his Holy Supper* (1697), and *Hymns Compos'd for the Celebration of the Holy Ordinance of Baptism* (1712). The Irish Presbyterian, Joseph Boyse, published a collection of twenty-five hymns for the Lord's Supper and Baptism in 1693.[16] Some of these were indeed suitable for the Lord's Supper, but do not make specific reference to the Supper.

THEOLOGICAL PERSPECTIVES

Book III of Richard Davis's collection was devoted to hymns for the Lord's Supper, including those by Browning. Davis's Eucharistic hymns simply reiterate the themes of the hymns of the other two books, and some of them seem no more specifically suited to the Lord's Supper than those in the other two books. The past tense, "We fed were," and "We Drunk the *Wine*" (III.3; III.6; cf.III.19), reinforce the fact that these were sung after the reception of communion, though the present tense as continuous is also used. "In the Eucharist we show forth Christ's death below as he shows it forth above" (III.4). "The 'daintyes' of free grace are offered to us at the communion" (III.6; III.3). The Supper is a banquet:

- Choicest Banquet! Rarest Wine!
- Soul-reviving Blood!
- Table well spread with Heav'nly Bread!
- delicatest Food! (III.12, stanza 1)

We eat "his most glorious Flesh," and "have communion with that Blood the *Son* of *God* for us did Bleed!," feeding on the "*Glorious Sacrifice*" (III.7). As has been noted elsewhere, hymn III.18 exhorts the congregation to "Behold the bleeding Lord of Life." It concludes:

> *This* Love the greatest torments bore;
> this *Love* did groan, this Love did Bleed;
> Our *Lover* thus wept bloody Tears:
> behold how *Jesus* lov'd indeed!

16. *Sacramental Hymns collected (chiefly) out of such passages of the New Testament.*

III.8, 9, 11 and 14 also reflects this intimate language, which freely draws on the imagery of the Song of Songs, and references "our pretious husband" who ravishes with grace, and the elements which are "ravishing Food" (III.5). Isaiah 53 forms the material for III.22, and Christ as the Lamb is a favorite image in these hymns. Thus:

> The *Lamb* i'th'midst o'th'Throne of Grace
> us now hath freely Fed;
> And by his *Spirit* down hath sent
> from Heav'n the *living* Bread. (III.10.stanza 2)

The work of the Holy Spirit in the Supper is again articulated in III.15:

> The *Blood* of *Christ*, that great high Priest
> the *Spirit* does apply.

Ultimately, for Davis the Lord's Supper is another testimony of grace:

> Most freely drank the *bitter Cup*
> my sin prepar'd for him;
> That I might have a *Cup* prepar'd
> top full of *Grace* to th'brim. (III.25.stanza 6)[17]

The hymns of Mr. Browning were numbered XXVI-XXXIX, and pre-date those of Davis. Thomas Browning became minister at Rothwell in 1662 until his death in 1685.[18] He had begun ministry during the Interregnum, and chose not to conform. His communion hymns, like those of Davis, center on the atonement. Stanza 5 of Hymn XXVI says:

> From Heav'n like Worms we crept away,
> Christ found us in his Grave;
> Next to his Heart he did us lay,
> And dying did us save.

Hymn XXVII has the idea that in the supper, we pledge ourselves to God:

> Christ drank to us in *Blood*, and then
> had us pledge him in *Wine*.

Though written for the Lord's Supper, few have any direct reference to it. "Board," "fare," and "dainties" are words he frequently used. Hymn XXXIX perhaps is the nearest we have to Browning giving an extended theology of the Supper:

17. For more on this see Spinks, *Liturgy in the Age of Reason*.

18. See Glass, *Early History of the Independent Church*.

Whence comes it that this *Bread* and *Wine*
Such Soul refreshing yield?
This Springs not from the *common* Vine
Nor grows in *ev'ry* Field.

'Tis curious Fare, this Childrens *Bread*
It is both *Bread* and *Meat*,
Whereby we are both Taught and fed,
Which we may safely eat.

It breeds no *Worms* not shall they dye
Who truly eat this *Bread*:
The *Feeder* is Transform'd thereby,
And no bad *Humour* Fed.

'Tis no *intoxicating* Cup
That is put in our Hand;
Which if we could but drink it up
Would all our *Cares* disband.

O blessed be that gracious *Hand*
That holds and fills the same!
And gladly would we see the *Land*
From whence this *Bread* first came.
Thou Lord, who art the God of Peace,
Who are our strength and stay,
Let *Comfort* by thy means increase
And let the *Flesh* decay.

Like all the hymns, it could end with a standard two-stanza doxology.

Benjamin Keach explained that his collection of hymns was aimed at three groups of people. First it was for "Such who like and approve of Books in Verse which treat of Divine Things, and would gladly have a little help in order to the understanding of *Metaphorical Scripture*." Secondly, it was for "*Parents* and *Masters of Families*" for whom it

> may prove of great advantage to their Children, who generally are taken with Verse, and are much addicted to learn such Songs and Ballads which generally tend to corrupt Youth . . . these Hymns being short, Children will soon get them by heart, as also full of varieties, and if instructed to sing, they may be the more affected with the matter, and receive the greater advantage.[19]

The third group were "those godly Christians who know 'tis their indispensible duty to sing *Psalms and Hymns*, &c.not only in their Families, but in

19. See Spinks, *Liturgy in the Age of Reason*, 99.

the publick Congregation."[20] Most of the hymns in this collection were in Common Metre of 8.6.8.6, and in a few Keach used material from other writers. David Music has noted that in addition to using John Patrick's "All Ye that Serve the Lord, His Name," Keach drew on William Barton's *Four Centuries of Select Hymns* of 1668. In 1696, Keach published a further collection, *A Feast of Fat Things*, and here he drew on the work of John Mason and Richard Davis.[21] In this collection he also used Long and Short Metre. Copeland appropriately notes that the hymns are "not the language of the ages," but nevertheless provide an insight into the spirituality of Keach and those who used his hymns.

Spiritual Melody was divided into thematic parts. Part I focused on the glory and perfections of God the Father, with Hymn 1 beginning,

A Father doth his Child beget,
So we begotten are,
By thy own Word and Spirit Lord,
And do thine Image bear.

A variety of themes were given expression: God as dwelling place of saints, a Husbandman, chief builder, and "a man of War." Hymn 12 depicts God as a woman in travail. Part II was christological, and included the favorite Calvinist themes of covenant and atonement. Hymn 18 proclaimed:

'Twas thou Lord Christ who in our room
To th'Father didst engage
To satisfie his justice, and
His wrath for to asswage. (stanza 8)

Hymn 19 was "set after the Sacrament," but its theme is the atonement and covenant, not the Lord's Supper *per se*. Stanza 5 asserted:

By that one single payment, Lord,
Laid down when thou didst die,
Relief to us thou didst afford,
Who dead in sin did lye.

Christ the Bridegroom, and (Luther's) testament and testator are also treated. Kingship was the theme of Hymn 17. Perhaps with the limits of the Toleration Act in mind, stanzas 6 and 7 announced:

Thou hast thy *Laws*, and 'tis by them
We must be rul'd alway;

20. Keach, *Spiritual Melody*, A2–A3.

21. Music, "Hymns of Benjamin Keach," 147–54.

And such who will not own thee king,
Thou wilt destroy one day.

Adore, and see ye reverence him,
All ye who love on Earth;
Obey his Laws, Saints sing his Praise.
And set his Glory forth.

And perhaps also stanza 2 of Hymn 48:

None understand all Rites and Laws
But, Lord, thy self alone,
And soon canst thou find out what flaws
There is in any one.

Keach asked his fellow worshippers the question, "Will it hold good i'th'Court above?" Hymn 66 took up the theme of Christ being all in all, and nearly every line begins with the name "Christ." The third section indicated Keach's commitment to Trinitarian belief, with the Holy Spirit being the theme. The Spirit was addressed,

O then come down, O blessed Dove,
Abide thou in our breast,
To be an Earnest of God's love,
And quietly we'll rest.

In other parts, Keach placed hymns which celebrated Word and Gospel, the graces of the Holy Spirit, the nature, work and office of the angels and souls, the church and several occasions, including after the sermon and the ordinances. A final part provided some metrical psalms. Hymn 154 noted that the Gospel is received by the elect:

Great Goodness thou, O Lord, hast wrought
Who can of it conceive?
And those thou dost regenerate,
'Tis thy do it receive. (stanza 1)

Hymn 157 proclaimed:

Thy Gospel is the means whereby
We, Lord, came to believe,
And in it does great Riches lye,
Which we by Faith receive. (Stanza 2)

A few hymns in the earlier parts of the collection would have been suitable for the Lord's Supper, but it is the last section that contains some specifically designed for the sacrament. More are to be found in *A Feast of Fat Things* (*FFT*). According to Keach,

In ev'ry Ordinance also
In which we should be found
O thou art all; for we well know
Grace in thee doth abound.

The Sacraments do hold thee forth,
And witness bear to thee;
And we by one to see by Faith
Thou nail'd was to the Tree;

Thy Body broke, and Blood was shed;
In Baptism we do espy
Thou is the Grave wast covered,
But long thou didst not lye. (Hymn 61, Part 4, stanzas 1–3)

FFT 88 provided a hymn of preparation for Ordinances:

'Tis thou, O God, that must *prepare*
our *Hearts*, we therefore cry,
Cleanse us from every Sin and Spot;
O purge Iniquity!

That we may hear and sing to Thee;
so as with thee to meet;
And find thy Word and Ordinance
to us exceeding sweet. (FFT 65, stanzas 1 and 2)

In *The Child's Delight*, Keach asked, "is the Bread and Wine in the Lord's Supper . . . the real Body and Blood of Jesus Christ?" to which the reply was "No, they are but Signs and Figures."[22] For Keach the efficacy of this Ordinance lay in remembering the act of atonement and the grace which flowed from it. Thus,

Bless'd be the Lamb that hither came
To be a Sacifice;
'Tis by thy Blood we have all good,
In thee all Blessings lyes. (Hymn 164, stanza 2)

In remembering, we recall the benefits of redemption:

Unto the Cross they did thee nail,

22. Keach, *Child's Delight*, 39, cited by Copeland in op. cit., 102.

Thy Sides they pierc'd also;
O let us all apply thy Blood
Which from thy Wounds did flow.

Its precious vertue we receive,
To purge and make us white,
That through it we might all indeed
Be lovely in thy sight. (Hymn 178, stanzas 6–7)

The Supper is the banquet of the Lamb and of the Bridegroom (*FFT* 86; Hymn 149):

A Banquet rich thou dost provide,
A Table of Fat things;
To feast our Souls, O let us eat
And drink of thy own Springs.

The Feast is thine, of thine own cost,
The Lamb is of thy Fold;
It is the best in all the Flock,
More precious far than Gold. (Hymn 155, stanzas 4–5)

It is the fatted Calf, the bread and precious wine, where the feast is free and grace is for all (Hymn 201). It is precious food (Hymn 151) where Christ is our meat and drink (*FFT* 84), and the elect are exhorted,

Eat, eat, O friends, on what is good,
And drink abundantly;
The best of Heav'n is your Food,
No fatness I deny. (Hymn 151 stanza 6)

Keach's fame rests in his advocacy of congregational song rather than the quality of his hymns. However, these hymns witness to the spirituality of those "peculiar people" who lived in close-knit communities on the margins of seventeenth century life.

Joseph Stennett's 1697 collection, for the Holy Supper, consisted of thirty-seven hymns. Some of these were concerned with salvation and atonement only (XVIII; XX; XXXIV), but others made explicit reference to the Lord's Supper. Hymn III, stanzas 2–4 read:

That ne're to be forgotten Night,
When our Redeemer was betray'd;
Before his Sufferings he took Bread,
Gave Thanks, then Brake't, and thus he said,

Take, eat, this is my Body broke
For you upon the Cursed Tree:

Perform this Ord'nance as I do,
And when you do't, remember Me.

He took the Cup too, crown'd with Wine,
Bless'd it, and to's Disciples said,
'Tis the New Test'ment in my Blood,
For you, and many others shed.

Hymn IV asserted that no common food God here presents, and no common drink, but

For Meat he gives his Flesh; for Wine
The Spear his Heart divides.

Hymn XIX spoke of Christ being both sacrifice and priest, and that communicants "sup *with* him and *on* him too." It is a celestial banquet, the wine being the Tincture of his veins and his body the bread (Hymn XXXV). At the table, we behold the all-sufficient sacrifice, and we ask that we might feel the virtue of Christ's blood. (XVII).

CONTRIBUTION TO LITURGY AND WORSHIP

What is strange is that these communities, who were so opposed to set forms of liturgical prayer, and who generally kept a low profile because of their dissent, should have authored these hymns, which, while inspired by Scripture, were not themselves Scripture. However, given that Scripture recorded the singing of a psalm or hymn after the Last Supper, and Paul spoke of hymns and songs, it was regarded as having a scriptural mandate which set forms of public prayer did not have. In services that were dominated by the minister's voice and extempore prayer, these hymns allowed congregational participation, and opened up thoughts and sentiments which metrical psalmody alone could not convey. They were the precursors of Watts, and were the foundations on which others could build.

BIBLIOGRAPHY

An Account of the Doctrine and Discipline of Richard Davis of Rothwell, in the County of Northampton, and those of his Separation. London: 1700.

Benson, Louis. *The English Hymn: Its Development and Use in Worship*. New York: Hodder and Stoughton, 1915.

Copeland, David A. *Benjamin Keach and the Development of Baptist Traditions in Seventeenth-Century England*. Lampeter: Edwin Mellen, 2001.

Crosby, Thomas. *History of the English Baptists*. London: 1738.

Edwards, Thomas. *The First and Second Part of Gangraena, or, A Catalogue and Discovery of many of the Errors, Heresies, Blasphemies and Pernicious Practices of the Sectaries of this Time, Vented and Acted in England in these Four Last Years.* London: 1646.

Glass, Norman. *The Early History of the Independent Church at Rothwell, alias Rowell, in Northamptonshire.* Northampton: Taylor and Sons, 1871.

Henry, Matthew. *Family-Hymns: Gather'd (mostly) out of the best Translations of David's Psalms.* London: Thomas Parkhurst, 1695.

Keach, Benjamin. *The Breach Repaired in God's Worship: Or, Singing Psalms, Hymns, and Spiritual Songs, proved to be an Holy Ordinance of Jesus Christ.* London: John Hancock, 1691.

———. *The Child's Delight.* 3rd ed. London: 1702.

———. *Darkness Vanquished.* London: 1675.

———. *Spiritual Melody,Containing near Three Hundred sacred Hymns.* London: John Hancock, 1691.

———. *Zion in Distress: Or, The sad and Lamentable Complaint of ZION and Her Children.* London: 1666.

Music, David W. "The Hymns of Benjamin Keach: An Introductory Study." *The Hymn* 34 (1983) 147–54.

"Paul's Alley, Barbican, 1695–1768." *Transactions of the Baptist Historical Society* 4 (1914) 46–54.

Sacramental Hymns collected (chiefly) out of such passages of the New Testament as contain the most suitable matter of Divine Praises in the celebration of the Lord's Supper. To which is added one hymn relating to Baptism and another to Ministry. By J.Boyse, with some other hands. London: Thomas Parkhurst, 1693.

Spinks, Bryan D. *Liturgy in the Age of Reason: Worship and Sacraments in England and Scotland 1662–c.1800.* New York: Routledge, 2014.

Watts, Michael R. *The Dissenters.* vol. 1. Oxford: Clarendon, 1978.

Whitley, W. T., ed. *Minutes of the General Assembly of the General Baptist Churches in England.* Vol. 1, *1654–1728.* London: Kingsgate, 1909.

Wykes, David L. "From David's Psalms to Watts's Hymns: The Development of Hymnody among Dissenters Following the Toleration Act." In *Continuity and Change in Christian Worship*, edited by R. N. Swanson, 227–39. Studies in Church History 35. Woodbridge: Boydell & Brewer, 1999.

Chapter 13

German Lutheran Hymnody (1650–1750)

Joseph Herl

HISTORICAL BACKGROUND

By the end of the Thirty Years' War in 1648, Germany had lost at least a third of its population (two-thirds in some places) from the combined effects of war, disease, and famine. In a society that seemed to be falling apart, an inner faith was sustained by intensely personal hymns that spoke deeply to the heart.

Chief among the hymn writers of the seventeenth century, and the most influential Lutheran hymn writer of any age after Martin Luther, was Paul Gerhardt (1607–76). He earned a theology degree in Wittenberg, then arrived in Berlin in 1642 or 1643 and obtained employment as a tutor in the household of a lawyer, whose daughter he eventually married. In 1647, the cantor of St. Nicholas Church in Berlin, Johann Crüger, published a hymnal called *Praxis Pietatis Melica* ("Musical Practice of Piety") that contained eighteen hymns by Gerhardt. The book appeared in nearly sixty editions through the middle of the eighteenth century, making it the best-selling German-language hymnal of the 1600s.[1] Its title is an allusion to *The Practice of Piety* by the Welsh divine Lewis Bayly (d. 1631), chaplain to Prince

1. The count is from Ameln, Jenny, and Lipphardt, *Das deutsche Kirchenlied*, *passim.*

Henry and later Bishop of Bangor. That book was published in 1611, and in 1630 it appeared in a widely read German translation called *Praxis Pietatis*. Bayly's book stressed the importance of meditation and application in one's devotional life: it was not sufficient, for example, to hear a sermon, but one should meditate on it and apply it to one's life.

Gerhardt was particularly influenced by the writings of Johann Arndt (1555–1621), pastor of St. Martin's Church in Braunschweig and later general superintendent of the duchy of Braunschweig-Lüneburg. His book *Vom wahren Christenthum* ("On True Christianity"), originally published in 1605 and expanded with three more volumes over the next several years, owes much to pre-Reformation mystical writers such as Bernard of Clairvaux (1090–1153), Angela da Foligno (1248–1309), Johannes Tauler (ca. 1300–61), and Thomas à Kempis (ca. 1380–1471). The book, which emphasized the need to be a Christian in deed and not only in name, appeared in more than 240 editions by 1800; a recent chronicler of Pietism calls it "the most widely read book in German Protestant history."[2] Another book by Arndt also became popular: the *Paradies-Gärtlein* ("Little Garden of Paradise") of 1612, a collection of meditations on various aspects of the Christian life set in the form of prayers. The headings to five of Gerhardt's hymns reference specific sections of this book.

Gerhardt's hymns have endured not only because of their devotional nature, but especially because of the quality of their poetry and the depth of their theology. The hymns follow the poetic reforms of Martin Opitz (1597–1639), with regular metrical stresses and careful attention to rhyme. Simplicity of language is key: uncommon words are rare, and words of one syllable predominate. This is not to say that the language itself is common: it abounds in devices that make it attractive and memorable, with especially powerful images and the use of similar vowels and consonants in close proximity to one another.

THEOLOGICAL PERSPECTIVES

In his theology, Gerhardt was careful that what he wrote reflected the understanding of God's work and humanity's place in it that he had learned through a study of the Lutheran confessions and other Christian writings. In 1694, Conrad Tiburtius Rango, general superintendent of Pomerania, objected to the introduction of new hymns into the church because so many of them contained poor theology. But he made an exception for those of

2. Shantz, *Introduction to German Pietism*, 29.

Gerhardt, "because they stem not from a fantastical kind of poetry, but from a theological spirit."[3]

Here are four stanzas from Gerhardt's fifteen-stanza Christmas hymn "O Jesu Christ, dein Kripplein ist," published in the 1653 edition of Crüger's *Praxis Pietatis Melica* (the version on the left is a literal translation; the one on the right is poetic):

Table 13.1: Christmas hymn "O Jesu Christ, dein Kripplein ist,"

1. O Jesus Christ, your manger is my paradise, where my soul grazes. Here is the place, here is the Word, clothed in person with our flesh.	O Jesus Christ, Thy manger is My paradise at which my soul reclineth. For there, O Lord, Doth lie the Word Made flesh for us; herein thy grace forth shineth.
2. The One whom the sea and wind obey gives himself to service and becomes a slave for sinners. You, Son of God, become earth and clay, lowly and weak, like ourselves and our children.	He whom the sea And wind obey Doth come to serve the sinner in great meekness. Thou, God's own Son With us art one, Dost join us and our children in our weakness.
6. His light and salvation heal everything; the treasure of heaven makes good again all loss. The source of joy, Immanuel, strikes down devil, hell, and their whole empire.	Thy light and grace Our guilt efface, Thy heav'nly riches all our loss retrieving. Immanuel, Thy birth doth quell The pow'r of hell and Satan's bold deceiving.
7. Therefore, devout Christian, whoever you are, be of good courage and do not allow yourself to be sad; for the Child of God binds you to himself. It cannot be otherwise: God must love you.[A]	Thou Christian heart, Whoe'er thou art, Be of good cheer and let no sorrow move thee! For God's own Child, In mercy mild, Joins thee to Him, how greatly God must love thee![B]

A. Crüger, *Praxis Pietatis Melica*, no. 191.
B. Translated by the editors of *The Lutheran Hymnal*, no. 81.

In this hymn, the Jesus in the manger is not a weak, helpless infant, but the immortal God who has come to earth to snatch sinners out of the

3. Rango, *Von der Musica*, 29. The literal translations in this chapter are by its author.

devil's grasp and who cares for the smallest details of the singer's life. In emphasizing the theology of the incarnation, Gerhardt follows such writers as Augustine ("Veni redemptor gentium" ["Redeemer of the nations, come"]) and Luther ("Vom Himmel hoch, da komm ich her" ["From heaven above to earth I come"]).

Gerhardt's theological position was that of Lutheran Orthodoxy, a theological movement that lasted from about 1580, when the most important Lutheran confessional documents were assembled into the *Book of Concord*, to at least 1730, although the most important Orthodox theologians were active before 1685; namely, Martin Chemnitz (1522–86), Johann Gerhard (1582–1637), and Abraham Calov (1612–86). Orthodox Lutherans stressed adherence to the teaching of Scripture and the Lutheran confessions, valued the witness of the early church fathers, maintained theological and liturgical traditions, emphasized the objective efficacy of Word and sacrament, and zealously opposed distinctive Catholic and Calvinist doctrines. The attention to doctrinal clarity in Orthodox writings has often led modern theologians to dismiss them as being devoid of any personal or devotional qualities. But this was hardly the case, as should be evident from the hymns of Gerhardt and other Orthodox writers. At their best, Orthodox Lutherans produced high-quality sermons, theological writings, and devotional works.

After 1650, Lutherans became more receptive to the ideas of other Christians. This happened partly because society was weary of religious battles after a devastating war that was, at least in theory, a conflict between Catholics and Protestants. At least as important was the simple fact that as the economy improved and more books were available, Lutherans were exposed to more writings by Christians of other confessions.

Such a free circulation of religious ideas created the intellectual climate in which Pietism developed. Pietism was a movement within late seventeenth- and early eighteenth-century German and Scandinavian Protestantism, both Lutheran and Reformed, that emphasized holy living as a reflection of one's Christian faith. It began around 1670 and continued in Germany through much of the eighteenth century and in Scandinavia through the nineteenth century. It was exported to Britain in the form of Methodism and to America in the revivalism of the nineteenth century. The American evangelicalism of today is its direct descendant.

The principal centers of German Pietism were Halle in Saxony and the duchy of Württemberg in southern Germany. Halle Pietism was the more important in the history of hymnody; its leader was August Hermann Francke (1663–1727), and Francke's son-in-law Johann Anastasius Freylinghausen (1670–1739) compiled the *Geist-reiches Gesang-Buch* ("Spirit-filled Songbook") of 1704. It was the most popular hymnal of the era, with nineteen editions appearing by 1759, and its contents placed it firmly in the Pietist camp.

Pietists insisted that the lives of true Christians be transformed by the Gospel, and their hymns are full of exhortations to avoid sin and live in a distinctly Christian manner. Here is an excerpt from a ten-stanza hymn by the Pietist writer Johann Burkhard Freystein (1671–1718):

Table 13.2: Hymn by Johann Burkhard Freystein (1671–1718)

1. Prepare yourself, my spirit, awake, stand, and pray, lest the evil time come upon you unexpectedly; for Satan's cunning has led many devout souls into temptation.	Rise, my soul, to watch and pray, From thy sleep awake thee, Lest at last the evil day Suddenly o'ertake thee; For the foe, Well we know, Oft his harvest reapeth, while the Christian sleepeth.
4. Watch, lest Satan's cunning come upon you sleeping, for otherwise he is quick to deceive you; and God often allows him [Satan] to punish those he loves when they are securely sleeping.	Watch against the devil's snares Lest asleep he find thee; For indeed! no pains he spares To deceive and blind thee; Satan's prey Oft are they, Who are soundly sleeping, And not watch are keeping.
8. He indeed desires to be asked if he is to give something; he demands our cries if we wish to live and overcome through him our mind, enemy, world, flesh, and sins.	Yea, indeed, He bids us pray, Promising to hear us, E'er to be our Staff and Stay, Ever to be near us. Ere we plead, Will He heed, Strengthen, keep, defend us, And deliv'rance send us.

10. Therefore let us always keep watch, stand, pray; for fear, need, and danger tread ever closer. For the time is not far off when God will judge and destroy the world.[A]	Therefore let us watch and pray Ever without ceasing, For we know, with every day Dangers are increasing; And the end, Doth impend, When the trumpet calleth, Earth in ruins falleth.[B]

A. This hymn, "Mache dich mein Geist bereit," was in Freylinghausen's hymnal; but it had previously appeared in *Geistliche Lieder und Lobgesänge*, 138–40.

B. The translation is from *Evangelical Lutheran Hymn Book*, no. 253.

The admonition to keep watch and pray is certainly biblical, reflecting 1 Pet 5:8 ("Be sober-minded; be watchful. Your adversary the devil prowls around like a roaring lion, seeking someone to devour"). But what will become of the Christian who tries to resist temptation but fails? This hymn has nothing to say on that subject; in Lutheran terms, the hymn is all Law with little Gospel.

Martin Luther's great realization was that God forgives those who are unworthy of forgiveness. That forgiveness is communicated to a fallen humanity through God's Word. When we hear a sermon or read a book containing the Gospel message, we learn that God has forgiven us. But some may doubt whether that forgiveness applies to them because they find themselves unable to conquer their sin or believe that their sins are too great. This is where the sacraments come in. In baptism, individuals are marked with the cross of Christ and baptized in the name of the Trinity, signifying that they belong to God. In the Lord's Supper, they receive the body and blood of Christ for the forgiveness of their sins, as the Lutheran formula for distribution says. Sacraments are given separately to individuals, and each individual hears, touches, and tastes the words of forgiveness, so there can be no doubt that the word of forgiveness applies to each person. But those who still are uncertain can enumerate the sins that trouble them to a pastor and receive absolution—God's forgiveness communicated by the pastor in the stead and by command of Jesus Christ. Those who still doubt that they are forgiven are in effect calling God a liar.

The Pietists, though, in their insistence that true Christians will produce good works, downplayed the efficacy of the sacraments and absolution. Whereas Luther, in hearing confessions, simply took penitents' word that they desired absolution and granted it on that basis, Philip Spener (1635–1705), the father of Pietism, taught that pastors should not grant absolution unless they had evidence that those coming to confession were sincere in their repentance.[4] This would have been unthinkable for Luther, because for him, the forgiveness of sins rested not on a penitent's worthiness, but solely on the promise of God. In other words, to answer the question, "How can I know whether I am forgiven?" the Pietists said, "Look to yourself and your works," while Luther and the orthodox Lutherans said, "Look to God and his promise."

The Pietist view of absolution is clear in Johann Adam Haßlocher's sixteen-stanza hymn "You say, 'I am a Christian.'" Most stanzas begin with a reason Christians might consider themselves forgiven: they have been baptized, they read and hear God's Word, they confess their sins to a priest and receive absolution, they participate in the Lord's Supper, they attend church, and so on. The second half of each stanza warns the singers that none of these things do Christians any good unless they prove their faith through holy living. As stanza 10 says:

10. You say "I am a Christian;
 I pray, read, and sing;
 I go into God's house;
 aren't these good things?"
 Yes, they are, but only if
 they are done in such a way
 that God is always seeing
 in those actions a pure heart.

The hymn ends with this terrifying thought:

16. O my God, give grace,
 that I might earnestly strive
 to be a true Christian
 and not just one in name.
 For whoever does not possess
 both name and deeds,
 he will never come
 into the kingdom of heaven.[5]

As with Freystein's hymn, there is no comfort to be found, only the admonition that Christians must lead holy lives if they wish to be saved. Once again, the hymn contains Law without Gospel.

4. Krispin, "Philip Jacob Spener," 24.

5. "Du sagst: ich bin ein Christ," in McMullen and Miersemann, *Geistreiches Gesangbuch*, no. 244 (vol. 1, part 1, pp. 332–33). The literal translation of these stanzas will also appear in the forthcoming companion to the 2006 *Lutheran Service Book*. No poetic translation is available.

Because for Pietists, the forgiveness of sins depended not on God's unconditional promise but on the sincerity of their repentance, no Pietist could be certain that his or her sins were truly forgiven. This led to doubt and despair concerning one's own salvation. But Pietism developed another way to assure Christians that they belonged to God; namely, a personal experience of him. Simply put, if God speaks directly to you, either through your mind or through your emotions, then you know you have an intimate relationship with him. To express that sort of relationship, many Pietist hymns address God as a friend or a lover. Here is an example by Johann Quirsfeld (1642–86) from Freylinghausen's hymnal:

1. The tender glances that Jesus gives me,
   that make me ache
   and press into my heart,
   so that I am completely in love with Jesus:
   for this my spirit is
   completely ripped from me
   and searches for You only,
   O Jesus, my "I."

5. My breast experiences a divine fire;
   I weep with joy
   and desire to feel such pain
   constantly in my heart with delight.
   O sweetest pain,
   how you capture me!
   Oh! Oh! I do not know,
   oh, how it happens to me![6]

The most desirable relationship was union with God, something expressed by this well-known eight-stanza hymn by the Reformed writer Gerhard Tersteegen (1697–1769):

6. "Die lieblichen blicke, die Jesus mir giebt," in McMullen and Miersemann, *Geistreiches Gesangbuch*, no. 453 (vol. 1, part 2, pp. 646–47). The literal translation of these stanzas will also appear in the forthcoming companion to the 2006 *Lutheran Service Book*. No poetic translation is available.

Table 13.3: Hymn by Gerhard Tersteegen (1697–1769)

1. God is present; let us worship and come before him in reverence. God is in our midst; let everything within us keep silent and bow before him. Whoever knows him, whoever names him, cast down your eyes; come, surrender yourself once again.	GOD reveals his presence; Let us now adore him, And with awe appear before him. God is in his temple, All within keep silence, Prostrate lie with deepest reverence. Him alone God we own, Him our God and Saviour; Praise his name for ever.[A]
5. Air that fills everything, in which we ever hover, foundation and life of all things, sea without floor or end, wonder of all wonders, I let myself sink down into you. I in you, you in me, let me disappear entirely, seeing and finding only you.[B]	[no suitable poetic translation of stanza 5 found]

A. Mercer, *Church Psalter*, no. 297.
B. Tersteegen, *Geistliches Blumen-Gärtlein*, 1729, no. XI.

Stanza 5 describes an individual's relationship with God in terms of a mystical experience. Tersteegen himself had such an experience in 1724 in the form of a dramatic conversion, following which he wrote out a covenant with God and signed it with his own blood. That experience served him well for a number of years, although late in life he felt that God had abandoned him, forcing him to trust only in God's promises rather than in his own experiences.[7] But when this hymn appeared in 1729, Tersteegen was at a spiritual high point, and the hymn is a remarkable expression of a mystical union with God.

Orthodox Lutherans would have nothing to do with these sorts of hymns and in fact roundly criticized them.[8] The following hymn by Erdmann Neumeister (1671–1756), chief pastor at the Jakobikirche in Hamburg and a fierce opponent of Pietism, answers the question that Freystein's hymn did not address: what recourse does a Christian have who tries to resist temptation but fails?

7. Shantz, *Introduction to German Pietism*, 65.

8. A notable document is a review of Freylinghausen's hymnal produced by the orthodox theology faculty at the University of Wittenberg in 1716 (see *Der Löblichen Theologischen Facultæt zu Wittenberg* in the bibliography).

Table 13.4: Hymn by Erdmann Neumeister (1671–1756)

1. Let me, full of joy, say "I am a baptized Christian," who in the midst of human frailties is nonetheless a child of God. Of what use is any treasure, since I possess a treasure that brings me every benefit and makes me eternally blessed?	God's own child, I gladly say it: I am baptized into Christ! He, because I could not pay it, Gave my full redemption price. Do I need earth's treasures many? I have one worth more than any That brought me salvation free Lasting to eternity!
2. No sin makes me anxious. I am a baptized Christian! For I am assured that as long as this comfort is in my heart, I can release myself from the fear of my sins, Jesus, through your blood, for the precious water bath has sprinkled me with it.	Sin, disturb my soul no longer: I am baptized into Christ! I have comfort even stronger: Jesus' cleansing sacrifice. Should a guilty conscience seize me Since my Baptism did release me In a dear forgiving flood, Sprinkling me with Jesus' blood?
3. Satan, listen to this: I am a baptized Christian. And with that I can strike you even though you are still so cruel, since when I was baptized all your power was taken away. And God's covenant frees me from your tyranny.[A]	Satan, hear this proclamation: I am baptized into Christ! Drop your ugly accusation, I am not so soon enticed. Now that to the font I've traveled, All your might has come unraveled, And, against your tyranny, God, my Lord, unites with me![B]

A. "Lasset mich voll Freuden sprechen," from Neumeister, *Evangelischer Nachklang*, no. 4. Two additional stanzas address the meaning of baptism for the dying Christian.

B. The translation by Robert E. Voelker was first published in *Evangelical Lutheran Hymnary*, no. 246, and was given a new tune in *Lutheran Service Book*, no. 594.

For a Lutheran, baptism "works forgiveness of sins, rescues from death and the devil, and gives eternal salvation to all who believe this, as the words and promises of God declare," as Luther says in his Small Catechism.[9] Christians who struggle with sin but have yielded to temptation are not thereby condemned, but rather look to their baptism, in which they were forgiven of their sins once and for all; and the assurance of that forgiveness gives them the courage to pick themselves up and try again to lead a life pleasing to God. Pietists found it difficult to accept that baptism had such power,

9. *Luther's Small Catechism with Explanation*, 23.

and so they needed something else—either reminders to live a holy life or the emotional high that comes from intimacy with Jesus—to assure them that they belonged to God. This is the key difference between Orthodox Lutherans and Pietists, one that is frequently seen in their respective hymns.

To sum up the period 1650 to 1750, we turn to a hymn by Salomo Franck (1659–1725). Franck was a lawyer, poet, and government official, but he is best known today as the author of a number of cantata texts set to music by Johann Sebastian Bach. The following hymn, published in 1714, includes several features popular in Lutheran hymns of the period: a focus on the individual rather than on the corporate church, a request for rescue from the power of sin and help in resisting temptation, a prayer for sanctification, and a concluding stanza that pleads for a blessed death. Four of the original five stanzas are presented here. The omitted fourth stanza asks for God's blessing on the good works done in the singer's everyday life.

Table 13.5: Hymn by Salomo Franck (1659–1725)

1. O God, do not forsake me! Give me your hands of mercy; lead me, your child, that I might run my race and in the end be blessed. Be the light of my life, my staff, my refuge, my shelter. O God, do not forsake me!	O God, forsake me not! But lead, full of compassion, With loving hands Thy child, That I may gain salvation, When here my course is run; Be Thou my Light, my Lot, My Staff, my Rock, my Shield. O God, forsake me not!
2. O God, do not forsake me! Control my turmoil; let me nevermore fall into sin and shame. Give me the good Spirit, give the confidence of faith, be my strength and power. O God, do not forsake me!	O God, forsake me not! Take not Thy Spirit from me, And suffer not the might Of sin to overcome me; Increase my feeble faith, Which Thou Thyself hast wrought; Be Thou my Strength and Power. O God, forsake me not!

3. O God, do not forsake me! I cry from the bottom of my heart: O Highest, strengthen me in every evil hour. Whenever temptation torments me and troubles my soul, do not leave my side. O God, do not forsake me!	O God, forsake me not! Lord, hear my supplication! In every evil hour Help me o'ercome temptation! And when the Prince of hell My conscience seeks to blot, Be Thou not far from me. O God, forsake me not!
5. O God, do not forsake me! I remain devoted to you. Help me, O great God, to believe rightly, to live a Christian life and have a blessed departure, and to gaze upon your face; help me in need and death. O God, do not forsake me![A]	O God, forsake me not! Lord, I am Thine forever; Grant me true faith in Thee, Grant that I leave Thee never. Grant me a blessed end, When my good fight is fought, Help me in life and death. O God, forsake me not.[B]

A. "Ach GOtt! verlaß mich nicht," from *Anderer Theil des Naumburgischen Gesang-Buchs, Anhang*, 106–7.
B. Translation by August Crull, from *Evangelical Lutheran Hymn Book*, no. 263.

The mention in stanzas 2 and 3 on sin and resisting temptation might suggest that Franck was a Pietist, but in fact he was not. These were concerns for both Orthodox and Pietist writers, but where Pietists tended to focus on the expectation of a life free from conscious sin, Orthodox authors were more realistic: knowing that Christians could not in this world escape sin entirely, they offered the comfort of the Gospel.

CONTRIBUTION TO LITURGY AND WORSHIP

Before the end of the seventeenth century, Lutherans were cautious about allowing newly written hymns in church services, fearing that they might contain heterodox teachings, and a number of Lutheran localities actually forbade their introduction.[10] But as the hymns of Paul Gerhardt gained wide acceptance, this attitude softened, and more new hymns were introduced.

Five developments in hymn performance characterized the period 1650 to 1750. First, singing tempos slowed considerably during the seventeenth century, with the sprightly rhythms of sixteenth-century tunes being evened out to produce long notes of equal duration. Second, in the late seventeenth and early eighteenth centuries those attending church services

10. Herl, *Worship Wars*, 161.

began to bring hymnals they had purchased to church with them. This allowed congregations to have a larger repertoire of hymns, since complete hymns no longer had to be memorized. Third, organ accompaniment of congregational singing, which was first mentioned around 1600, was becoming more popular by 1700, and by 1800 it was widely practiced. Fourth, by the late seventeenth century a new style of tune, with an ornamented melody that resembled a solo aria, was being written. Fifth, in many localities by the second quarter of the eighteenth century organists were beginning to play interludes of about two measures between every phrase of a hymn. This, coupled with slow tempos and the large number of stanzas in many hymns, meant that hymns took a long time to sing.[11] With all these changes, hymn singing was quite different in 1750 from what it had been in 1650.

NOTABLE HYMNS

A genre popular during and after the Thirty Years' War was the hymn of consolation, with the message that no matter how bad things are in one's life, God is still in charge and in the end will make everything right. One of the most popular consolation hymns was "Wer nur den lieben Gott läßt walten" ("If thou but trust in God to guide thee"), written in 1642 (but not published until 1657) by the twenty-one-year-old Georg Neumark (1621–81), who later became a court official in the Duchy of Saxe-Weimar. Paul Gerhardt also wrote a number of consolation hymns, the most enduring being "Befiehl du deine Wege" ("Commit whatever grieves thee"). The first words of its twelve stanzas form Ps 37:5 in Luther's German translation: "Commit your way to the Lord and hope in him; he will make it good." Gerhardt's best-known hymn, though, is not a hymn of consolation, but the ten-stanza Passion hymn "O Haupt voll Blut und Wunden" ("O sacred head, now wounded"). But that is not an original hymn by Gerhardt, but rather a translation of a Latin text from the late Middle Ages.

Other significant hymn writers, other than those named above, include the Orthodox Lutherans Johann Olearius (1611–84), author of "Gelobet sei der Herr" ("The Lord, my God, be praised"), and his nephew Johann Gottfried Olearius, who wrote "Es war die ganze Welt" ("When all the world was cursed"). Several non-Lutheran Pietist writers wrote hymns sung by Lutherans, including Nicolaus von Zinzendorf (1700–60), founder of the group that became the Moravian Church and author of "Christi Blut

11. For more information on musical developments, see Herl, *Worship Wars*, 104–6, 134–47, and 167–72.

und Gerechtigkeit" (translated by John Wesley as "Jesus, thy blood and righteousness"), and the Reformed pastor Joachim Neander (1650–80), author of "Lobe den Herren, den mächtigen König der Ehren" ("Praise to the Lord, the Almighty, the King of creation"). The Catholic Angelus Silesius (birth name Johann Scheffler, ca. 1624–77), a former Lutheran who following his conversion to the Catholic faith produced polemical works against the Lutherans, wrote, "Ich will dich lieben, meine Stärke" ("Thee will I love, my strength, my tower"). His hymns exhibit a mysticism similar to that found in Pietist hymns.

BIBLIOGRAPHY

Ameln, Konrad, Markus Jenny, and Walther Lipphardt. *Das deutsche Kirchenlied: Verzeichnis der Drucke von den Anfangen bis 1800*. 1 vol. in 2. Kassel: Bärenreiter, 1975–80.

Anderer Theil des Naumburgischen Gesang-Buchs. Naumburg: Boßögel, 1714.

Axmacher, Elke. Johann Arndt und Paul Gerhardt. Mainzer hymnologische Studien 3. Tübingen: Francke, 2001.

Bunners, Christian. *Paul Gerhardt: Weg—Werk—Wirkung*. Göttingen: Vandenhoeck & Ruprecht, 2007.

Crüger, Johann. *Praxis Pietatis Melica*. 5th ed. Berlin: Runge, 1653.

Evangelical Lutheran Hymn Book. Published by order of the General English Lutheran Conference of Missouri and Other States. Baltimore: Lang, 1889.

Evangelical Lutheran Hymnary. Prepared by the Worship Committee of the Evangelical Lutheran Synod. St. Louis: MorningStar, 1996.

Geistliche Lieder und Lobgesänge, Aus der lebendigen und reinen Quelle des Geistes Gottes entsprungen. [N.p.], 1695.

Herl, Joseph. *Worship Wars in Early Lutheranism: Choir, Congregation, and Three Centuries of Conflict*. Oxford: Oxford University Press, 2004.

Hewitt, Theodore Brown. *Paul Gerhardt as a Hymn Writer and His Influence on English Hymnody*. 2nd ed. St. Louis: Concordia, 1976.

Krispin, Gerald S. "Philip Jacob Spener and the Demise of the Practice of Holy Absolution in the Lutheran Church." *Logia: A Journal of Lutheran Theology* 8.4 (Reformation 1999); reprinted in vol. 21, no. 3 (Holy Trinity 2012), 19–27.

Der Löblichen Theologischen Facultæt zu Wittenberg Bedencken über das zu Glauche an Halle 1703. im Waysen-Hause daselbst edirte Gesang-Buch. Frankfurt and Leipzig: Zimmermann, 1716. Translated by Dianne Marie McMullen, in "The *Geistreiches Gesangbuch* of Johann Anastasius Freylinghausen (1670–1739): A German Pietist Hymnal," 568–99. PhD diss., University of Michigan, 1987.

The Lutheran Hymnal. Authorized by the synods constituting the Evangelical Lutheran Synodical Conference of North America. St. Louis: Concordia, 1941.

Lutheran Service Book. Prepared by the Commission on Worship of the Lutheran Church—Missouri Synod. St. Louis: Concordia, 2006.

Luther's Small Catechism with Explanation. St. Louis: Concordia, 2017.

McMullen, Dianne Marie, and Wolfgang Miersemann, eds. *Johann Anatasius Freylinghausen: Geistreiches Gesangbuch: Edition und Kommentar*. 3 vols. in

7. Halle: Verlag der Franckeschen Stiftungen Halle im Max Niemeyer Verlag Tübingen, 2004–.

Mercer, William. *The Church Psalter and Hymn Book*. London: Jewell and Letchford, 1855.

Neumark, Georg. *Fortgepflantzter Musikalisch-Poetischer Lustwald*. Jena: Sengen, 1657.

———. *Thränendes Haus-Kreutz*. Weimar: Müller, 1681.

Neumeister, Erdmann. *Evangelischer Nachklang, Das ist: Neue Geistreiche Gesänge* über die ordentlichen Sonn- *und Festtags-Evangelia aufs gantze Jahr*. Hamburg: Gennagel, 1718.

Rango, Conrad Tiburtius. *Von der Musica, alten und neuen Liedern, Sende-Schreiben, nebst einer, Anno 1675, vor sehl. Johann Krügers Gesang-Buch, Stettinischer Edition, publicirten Vor-Rede, zum Unterricht und Rettung der Warheit*. Greifswald: Starcke, 1694.

Shantz, Douglas H. *An Introduction to German Pietism*. Baltimore: Johns Hopkins University Press, 2013.

Tersteegen, Gerhard. *Geistliches Blumen-Gärtlein Jnniger Seelen*. Frankfurt and Leipzig: Böttiger, 1729.

Part 6

Eighteenth Century

Chapter 14

Isaac Watts

Composer of Psalms and Hymns

Rochelle A. Stackhouse

HISTORICAL BACKGROUND

At the time of Isaac Watts's birth in Southampton, England, on July 17, 1674, persecution afflicted religious nonconformists, like his parents, Isaac and Sarah. Watts's father spent time in prison on multiple occasions for worshipping with an independent church led by a priest named Nathaniel Robinson. While the Church of England was the only legally established church, numerous smaller congregations met regularly, affiliated with each other under the independent or nonconformist labels. Baptists, Quakers, Presbyterians, and other non-established congregations defied the establishment laws by worshipping together. Not until Watts's twenty-fourth year did King James proclaim the "Declaration of Indulgence," which opened the door to independent churches worshipping openly, at which time Watts's father served as a deacon in Robinson's congregation.

In the established Church of England and many nonconformist congregations in Watts's childhood, the traditional singing of the psalms was increasingly supplemented with hymns on scriptural themes. Under the influence of Calvin, however, the Presbyterian and independent churches clung to the psalms as the only appropriate music for worship, particularly metrical psalmody. In metrical psalmody, a psalm, translated from the Hebrew into English, is rendered into poetry to fit a specific meter for a tune, so both exact translation and poetic beauty often were sacrificed to strophic form. The average parishioner knew less than a dozen tunes, which they sang over and over to different sets of words. Most popular among English Independents were Thomas Sternhold and John Hopkins's *The Whole Booke of Psalms Collected into English Metre* (1562) and Thomas Ravencroft's *The Whole Book of Psalms with the Hymns Evangelicall and Songs Spirituall* (1621).

The Puritans who had come to Massachusetts firmly promoted a more literal translation of psalms for singing in worship, producing the 1640 Bay Psalm Book, *The Whole Book of Psalms Faithfully Translated into English Metre*. The introduction to the book made plain their intentions: "wee . . . have not soe much as presumed to paraphrase to give the sense of his [David's] meaning in other words; we have therefore attended herein as our chief guide the orignall, shunning all additions."[1] The result, though, is that translations are wooden and often incomprehensible as they are shoehorned into metrical tunes.

In 1679, John Patrick initiated a sea change in shaping the paraphrasing of the psalms to fit current events, something Watts would later perfect. Patrick's *A Century of Select Psalms and portions of the Psalms of David, especially those of praise* included a hymn commemorating the defeat of the Spanish Armada in 1588. Patrick also made a move toward "Christianizing" the psalms, a choice that had enormous influence on Watts, as he acknowledged in his preface to his own Psalter.[2] Patrick's version found a welcome home among many nonconformist congregations over the next several decades.

Although not a nonconformist like Watts, Joseph Stennett, a Baptist pastor in London, found the music to be sung in conjunction with the Lord's Supper to be lacking. He published *Hymns in commemoration of the Sufferings of our Blessed Saviour Jesus Christ, compos'd for the celebration of his Holy Supper* in 1697, a book that went into multiple additions in before 1709. Stennett certainly influenced Watts, for he used some of Stennett's lines for his own hymns.[3] Baptists, who would go on to adopt Watts's work enthusiastically, thus were primed for hymns and relevantly paraphrased psalms.

1. Bay Psalm Book, sig.**2-**3.
2. Watts, *Psalms of David Imitated*, preface.
3. Benson, *The English Hymn*, 100–101.

In 1698, Nahum Tate and Nicholas Brady published *A New Version of the Psalms of David.* Their take on the psalms, like Patrick's, included much freer translations and metrical settings; many of them would be recognizable to modern singers as "hymns." Many current hymnals across Protestant traditions still include two Tate hymns, "While Shepherds Watched Their Flocks by Night," and the paraphrase of Ps 42, "As Pants the Hart." Some purists criticized Tate and Brady as taking too many liberties in paraphrases rather than literal translation, but their "New Version" became popular in the established churches and beyond.

Watts entered the musical fray slowly, and mostly out of frustration with the lack of beauty and sensibility in the psalms sung at his home congregation in Southampton. When he complained to his father, the elder Isaac suggested he try to do better! He wrote his first hymn, "Behold the Glories of the Lamb," in response, a hymn that would later appear in his *Hymns and Spiritual Songs* (1707).[4]

Watts left Southampton in October 1696 for London to prepare for ministry in an Independent church, studying at the nonconformist academy led by the Rev. Thomas Rowe. He continued to write poetry and hymns. In 1700, he received a letter from his brother, Enoch, complaining heartily about the music being sung at their church in Southampton. He wrote that both Patrick and Tate and Brady's versions of the psalms had a "mighty deficiency of that life and soul, which is necessary to raise our fancies and kindle and fire our passions. I have been persuaded to a great while since, that were David to speak English, he would choose to make use of your style."[5]

That letter, along with support from the congregation in London where he worshipped, and would eventually pastor, Mark Lane Chapel, moved Watts to begin to lay out his "System of Praise." He had already published his poetry (*Horae Lyricae*, 1705, both in England and America, a volume which included some hymns), and he had used some of his paraphrases in the Mark Lane Chapel. In 1707, he published the first edition of *Hymns and Spiritual Songs.* This included 210 hymns, including paraphrases of Scripture and "free composures," such as "When I Survey the Wondrous Cross." After releasing the book, he solicited critical response from others and then published a second edition in 1709.

At the time Watts published his hymns, the English Independent congregations suffered from declining numbers and lackluster worship in many places. Congregations were therefore poised to be receptive to music that felt more relevant to their lives and spoke in words they could understand.

4. Fountain, *Isaac Watts Remembered*, 34.

5. Fountain, *Isaac Watts Remembered*, 55.

Over the next few years, Watts's hymns (and later the psalms) came to dominate in many Independent congregations throughout England.

Watts followed up on *Hymns* by going back to the psalms project once inspired by Patrick's work and his brother's suggestion. In 1719, he published *The Psalms of David Imitated*, a work so popular that seven editions were published in ten years. He aimed to make David sing not only as a Christian, but as an Englishman. Except for the twelve psalms he felt were unsuited to Christian singing,[6] Watts paraphrased or "imitated" each psalm at least once and often multiple times in different meters. Wherever the Hebrew psalms mentioned "Israel" or "Zion," Watts often substituted "Britain" or "England." Like Patrick, Watts wrote paraphrases dedicated to historical events (Ps 115 dedicated to the memory of Guy Fawkes Day). He adjusted other psalms to refer directly to Jesus (as in the paraphrase of Ps 98 today known as "Joy to the World! The Lord is come").

As with his book of Hymns, the Psalter found a welcome in Independent churches throughout England. Not only was it used in public worship, but many people had personal copies to use in devotions in the home. "It is calculated that in its first twenty-five years a new edition appeared every year, and claimed that as late as 1864 60,000 copies were sold within the year."[7] Baptists and Presbyterians, in addition to Independent churches, also adopted Watts almost exclusively. By the mid-eighteenth century, copies of the *Hymns* and the Psalter appeared bound together, coming to be known as *Psalms and Hymns*.

Both Watts's *Hymns* and the Psalter crossed the Atlantic to the growing Congregational, Baptist, and Presbyterian churches in North America. Certainly, he had the market in mind, as he entitled Ps 107 "A Psalm for New England." Benjamin Franklin published the Psalter in America in 1729, but it remained largely unsold, until a few years later two circumstances opened America to Watts.[8] In the 1730s and '40s, the First Great Awakening bloomed in New England and the Mid-Atlantic region, and at about the same time, the controversy over the method of singing in churches, including the rise of "Singing Schools."

The First Great Awakening came about through revival preaching and growing evangelical and emotional worship. George Whitfield, though often associated with the Wesleys, preferred Watts's music, and introduced it at his large revival meetings. As a result, Jonathan Edwards, then pastor in

6. The twelve psalms include those most dark and violent: 28, 43, 52, 54, 59, 64, 70, 79, 88, 108, 137, 140.

7. Benson, *English Hymn*, 125–26.

8. Benson, *English Hymn*, 162.

Northampton, Massachusetts, returned from a long journey away from his church in 1742 to discover that his congregation wanted to sing nothing but Watts, especially the hymns. Edwards, a great lover of the psalms, convinced them to add in the psalms alternating with the hymns![9] Watts quickly overtook the Bay Psalm Book in popularity among New England congregations.

As in England, singing in most congregations in the American colonies is often described as a painful affair. A precentor, or cantor, would sing a line of a psalm and then the congregation repeated it. The average Psalter broke up the lines in odd ways so that it was hard for any clear idea of the thoughts of the psalmist to come through. Watts tried to paraphrase the psalms in such a way that the sense of the line contained a complete idea. Many congregations did not have a precentor with musical ability, and the tunes could change mid-psalm. In the mid to late eighteenth century, Singing Schools arose, which resulted not only in trained precentors, but in the rise of choirs, which sought more interesting music to be sung in parts. Watts's hymns, along with the work of William Billings and others, provided more possibilities for choral singing. As churches slowly opened worship to music other than the psalms, Watts's popularity grew.

With the publication of *Psalms*, Watts's "System of Praise" was complete. Though changes and small additions appeared in subsequent editions of both books, Watts produced no other musical work of this size in his lifetime. He suffered from ill health most of his life, and the filth of the London of his era contributed to his disability. However, other hymn writers and psalm-paraphrasers continually revised his work, taking seriously his methodology of making congregational singing relevant to its times, especially as the American Revolution soured relations with England. John Wesley, John Mycall, Joel Barlow, and Timothy Dwight revised many of Watts's psalms and hymns for the American churches. For example, Watts's version of stanza 4 of Ps 19 begins "Ye British Lands rejoice." Wesley changed this to "Ye happy lands rejoice." Mycall changed "British" to "America" when he published his version of Watts's Psalter in 1781. Barlow in 1785 made it "Christian lands," and Dwight in 1801 revised it to "Western lands."[10]

For the rest of his life and ministry, Watts continued to write and publish poetry, but he focused most on a revival of worship in the Independent, Baptist, and Presbyterian churches in England. He wrote theological treatises and worked to support Whitefield and other revivalists both in England and in America. By the end of his life he had published over 800 hymns. Long an invalid, Watts died on November 25, 1748, directing that

9. Benson, *English Hymn*, 163.

10. Stackhouse, *Language of the Psalms in Worship*, 141.

his funeral be conducted by "two Independent ministers, two Presbyterian and two Baptist,"[11] reflecting the ecumenical nature of his theology as well as his understanding of how broadly his hymns and psalms had been accepted.

THEOLOGICAL PERSPECTIVES

In the early- to mid-seventeenth century, English Independent, Presbyterian, and Baptist churches largely held to Calvin's instruction that the only words fit for singing in worship came from the psalms of the Hebrew Bible. Calvin differed from Luther in his opinion of both the words and the tunes best suited to Christian worship, which did not allow repurposed drinking tunes. Wanting to differentiate music in worship from his experience of "the frivolity of current French song,"[12] Calvin determined that only the words of Scripture should be sung. Unlike Luther, who wrote hymns and "baptized" German secular tunes, Calvin wanted to separate worship music from popular culture. Thus, the English metrical psalm, sung to a handful of approved tunes, came to dominate those churches formed in the Calvinist tradition. Calvinist congregations, often in contrast to Lutherans, saw the singing of the psalms as a duty in worship, not as an occasion for joy or boisterous singing. Until Independent churches of all kinds could legally worship openly, they also had to sing quietly or not at all, thus cementing an understanding of the restrictive and somber place of music in worship, both in performance and in content, which endured in some places even into freedom.

In the years before Watts, words other than those directly from Scripture had begun to make their way into the church's singing. Sternhold and Hopkins, and Tate and Brady, contained hymns based on Scripture, and members of the established Church of England sang hymns freely. Patrick's paraphrases of the psalms began the move Watts continued, believing that the music sung should reflect the times in which the people lived and their situation as Christians, not just biblical history. The theological hold from Calvin concerning the psalms as the *only* words to be sung in worship remained stronger in America than in any part of Great Britain. "The Puritans followed Calvin in their insistence that *sola Scriptura* (Scripture alone) was the paramount and exclusive liturgical criterion."[13] Even in America, however, the seeds were sown that would later open the churches' leaders to agree to freer psalm paraphrases and eventually to hymns. Those seeds came

11. Fountain, *Isaac Watts Remembered*, 98.

12. Benson, *English Hymn*, 23.

13. Davies, *Worship of the American Puritans*, 24.

from a theological understanding of the importance of free, Spirit-inspired, preaching and prayer.

The Puritans (and their descendants in the Congregational, Presbyterian, and Baptist churches in New England and the Middle Atlantic region) practiced free prayer as opposed to reading the prayers of the Book of Common Prayer, or any other Prayer book. They objected to a set group of prayers to be used at each service and the same in every congregation on a variety of grounds, including the fact that Scripture did not model this way of praying. They also believed each pastor, knowing his flock, should pray as they had need. This became so specific as to include people handing "prayer notes or bills to the minister . . . including personal petitions . . . and therefore democratizing the worship."[14] Since the Puritans (and their nonconformist colleagues in England and Scotland) also believed clergy should be free to preach as the Spirit led, and not to read sermons given to them by church officials, the theology of liturgy in these traditions showed an openness to local custom, local need, and timely relevance that certainly prefigures a change in practice from singing only stilted translations of the psalms to freer, more relevant songs in worship as well.

Watts's "System of Praise"[15] brought the liturgical theology of the free church, long applied to preaching and praying, into the singing of the people. He strove to make the psalmists "always speak the common sense and language of a Christian."[16] While the New Testament sang in the sermons and prayers of the preachers of the time, the words of the Hebrew Bible predominated in song. Watts's liturgical theology understood David as prefiguring Christ, and so he made the logical move, from his point of view, into making David (and Asaph, etc.) sing as a Christian. "In the older metrical versions, there was a concern for a re-presentation of the psalm, but in Watts the concern was for re-interpretation."[17] Sometimes Watts made subtle changes to psalms to "Christianize" them. One example is the Christmas hymn "Joy to the World," a paraphrase of Ps 98. We sing this at Christmas and so assume that the "Lord" and "Savior" who comes is Jesus. Yet nowhere in the actual hymn do we find the name of Jesus. Watts's "imitation" carries the mood and many of the actual words of the psalm, but sets them in a new context so that singers in churches would assume they refer

14. Davies, *Worship of the American Puritans*, 144.

15. Watts's system sought to simplify the metrical singing of the psalms to make it simpler for the average worshipper to follow. His original motivation for revising the Psalter came from his disgust with how people could not sing complex metrical versions led by a precentor. He hoped for clear, united, congregational singing.

16. Watts, *Psalms of David Imitated*, xvi.

17. Leaver, "Isaac Watts's Hermeneutical Principles," 58.

to Jesus. This hymn also reflects Watts's desire for the singing in worship to be full of praise and sung with passion. He makes liberal use of exclamation points to make sure the singers understand. "Joy to the world! the Lord is come." At other times, Watts made changes that more directly brought Christ into the psalms. Psalm 103 becomes the hymn "Bless, O My Soul! The Living God." The third verse of the hymn reads, "Tis He, my soul! Who sent his Son to die for crimes which thou hast done." His version of Ps 19 includes this verse: "Nor shall Thy spreading gospel rest / Till through the world Thy truth has run / Till Christ has all the nations blest / That see the light, or feel the sun."

In addition, Watts saw the need for free-composed hymns on Christian themes. As he wrote in his 1707 *Essay towards the improvement of Christian Psalmody, by the use of evangelical Hymns in worship, as well as the Psalms of David*, "The Scriptures themselves . . . command us to sing and give thanks in the name of Christ. Why shall we pray and preach in that name, and sing under terms of the Law?"[18] If, as Calvin wrote, only the words of Scripture are fit to be sung, then why not use all parts of Scripture and not exclusively the psalms? He also observed that if the Spirit is to be invoked and expected in preaching and prayer, why not in the composition of songs for worship? The same year, Watts wrote and published a hymn illustrating exactly this point: "Come, Holy Spirit, Heavenly Dove." The second stanza seems rather pointed in context: "In vain we tune our formal songs / In vain we strive to rise / Hosannas languish on our tongues / and our devotion dies."

One of the theological breaks Watts made from current belief and practice concerned the purpose of music in worship. Watts began to pair sermons with hymns, thus moving toward a theology of hymns as proclamation of the gospel and not simply words of praise. Hymns became words *to* the congregation, to teach and inspire, and not only words *from* the congregation to God. Thus, a worship service began to have a theme that developed not only in preaching and praying, but also in congregational song. His seasonal hymns and psalm paraphrases, for example, clearly proclaimed theology to the people and not just the praises of the people. "Alas and Did My Savior Bleed" lays out the theology of substitutionary atonement succinctly in just the first two verses: "Alas! And did my Savior bleed, and did my Sovereign die! / Would He devote that sacred head for sinners such as I! / Was it for sins that I have done He suffered on the tree? / Amazing pity! Grace unknown! And love beyond degree."

18. For his complete theology on the use of hymns, see Watts, *Hymns and Spiritual Songs*, 256–66.

Finally, Watts felt that not all the experiences of the Christian person, and especially contemporary Christians, were covered in the psalms, and so new words, based in Scripture but not limited to the words of Scripture, should be written to allow contemporary Christians to praise God out of their lived experiences. Watts read the psalms discerning that they were composed about very specific situations in the lives of specific people and the nation in biblical times. His theology of "imitation" meant that he sought to write words which would do the same thing for people of his time and for his nation. "David must be made to play the part of an orthodox and patriotic English Christian of the early XVIIIth century."[19] Watts's original version of Ps 75 in *Psalms of David Imitated* bears the description "Power and Government from God Alone. Applied to the glorious Revolution by King William, or the Happy Accession of King George I to the Throne," and contains this verse: "Britain was doomed to be a slave / Her frame dissolved, her fears were great; / When God a new supporter gave / To bear the pillars of the state." Unabashedly political in his reimagining of the psalms, Watts actually echoed the original Psalter's many themes of the national life of Israel. For the ancient psalmists, politics and worship were not mutually exclusive. "From the Restoration of the Monarchy and the Church in 1660, to the coming of William and Mary and the Toleration Act, to the establishment of the Hanoverian line in 1714, questions of church and state and the identity of both occupied the minds of many Britons. . . .Watts used the occasion of the public singing of the psalms to contribute to these discussions."[20]

This practice of concretizing the psalms to the present day was not always in support of the government, however. An excellent example of Watts's hermeneutic of relevance appears in his "imitation" of Ps 90, perhaps Watts's best-known hymn today: "Our God, Our Help in Ages Past." For a number of years before Watts wrote this hymn, circa 1714 (later published in his 1719 Psalter), nonconformists had coexisted peacefully with the established Church of England. In 1714, however, Parliament passed the Schism Act, which forbade Independents to operate schools and foreshadowed a return to persecution, especially after the death of Queen Anne in August of that year. Many Independents, Baptists, and Presbyterians (as well as Quakers and other smaller groups) once again feared that the old days would return. Amidst that anxiety, Watts wrote this hymn, which, ironically, has been

19. Benson, *English Hymn*, 112.

20. Stackhouse, *Language of the Psalms in Worship*, 37.

used ever since in times of national anxiety in Great Britain, Canada, and the United States.[21]

The hymn makes clear that the "throne" to which the faithful should be looking does not exist in London, but with God. "Under the shadow of thy throne / Thy saints have dwelt secure; / Sufficient is thine arm alone / and our defense is sure." Verse 8, which no longer appears in hymnals, makes Watts's context and theology even clearer: "Like flow'ry fields the nations stand / Pleas'd with the morning light / The flowers beneath the Mowers hand / Lie withering e'er 'tis night."[22]

In general, however, Watts believed hymns should not contribute to divisions among people, especially in doctrine, rather seeking to express beliefs generally held in common by Independent Christians. His hymns do not delve into complex theological disputes. He writes in the preface to the 1707 *Hymns* that he seeks to avoid "the more obscure and controverted Points of Christianity."[23] His hymns expressed "loyalty to the Protestant principle that every part of public worship should be conducted in a language understood by the people."[24] Due in part to this theological stance, Watts's hymns quickly moved into a wide variety of denominations, including the Church of England.

Watts's hermeneutic of relevance and his abiding belief that the Holy Spirit works not only in the spoken word but in the sung word grounds all his hymns, as does his belief that beauty is as important as literal translation and a gift from God.

CONTRIBUTION TO LITURGY AND WORSHIP

At one time, historians spoke of Watts as the inventor of the English Hymn, but that would be denying the work of people like Tate, Brady, Sternhold, Hopkins, and John Patrick, among others. Without question, however, Watts popularized the hymn and freer translations of the psalms among a people whose theology seemed to reject both. Independents, Congregationalists, Presbyterians, Baptists, and others eagerly sang his music because they heard their own yearnings, fears, hopes, and beliefs reflected in them. "Purposing to construct Church Song anew, [Watts] sought for the true

21. For example, the hymn was sung in the service at the National Cathedral in Washington following the September 11, 2001, attacks.

22. For more on "Our God Our Help," see Stackhouse, "Hymnody and Politics," 47–52.

23. Watts, *Hymns*, vii–viii.

24. Benson, *English Hymn,* 210.

basis of a sympathetic devotion. He found it not in a poet's mind, but in the thoughts and feelings and aspirations held in common by the largest number of Christians."[25] For this reason, his books became common in homes to be used for family devotions. The hymns and psalm "imitations" served the prayer life of countless worshippers by being read in homes as well as sung in churches.

In a time when lengthy and passionate sermons dominated worship services, Watts made a case for music's importance as a method of Scripture interpretation, a vessel for proclamation of the word, and heartfelt prayer. In fact, Watts often attached hymns to the printed versions of his own sermons. Watts believed in the importance of thematic unity to all parts of a worship service.

The revivals in both England and America in the time of the Great Awakening proved this point most fully. Music took center place in these revivals. The hymns of the Wesleys and of Watts, used by evangelists such as George Whitfield, impacted worship in local congregations as well as in these special events. Both the psalm paraphrases and the free-composed hymns had a contemporary and personal nature to them, which appealed to those experiencing the emotional spirituality of the revivals, though Watts did not write for revivals nor intend his hymns to be used for anything other than parish worship. His Passion hymns especially picked up the emotional context of faith. "When I Survey the Wondrous Cross," for example, swells to the verse "Were the whole realm of nature mine, that were a present far too small / Love so amazing, so divine demands my soul, my life, my all."

The influence of Watts hymns came to be felt not only in the words being sung, but in how they were being sung. Watts believed in singing the "regular way," with the congregation all singing together as opposed to lining out, one line at a time, with the congregation repeating what a precentor (cantor) sang. Singing in unison allowed a congregation more fully to enter into praise and joy instead of being slowed down by continual repetition, line after line. The arrival of hymns brought the demise of the precentor, which in most congregations meant singing became not only livelier, but more prayerful, as the sense of the words now could be communicated clearly. In America, as Singing Schools arose, Watts's hymns and psalm paraphrases helped fuel the rise of church choirs.

Watts's hymns inspired others to begin writing free-composed hymns. "Watts's hymns became a direct model for the construction of other hymns, and he became unconsciously the founder of a school of hymn writers."[26]

25. Benson, *English Hymn*, 207.

26. Benson, *English Hymn*, 210.

John Wesley had copies of Watts's books with him when he came to America, and he reprinted them (and often revised them). In England, Joseph Addison and Philip Doddridge, among others, acknowledged their debt to Watts as they wrote hymns. In America, the first great native hymn-writer, Timothy Dwight, began by revising and adding to Watts's 1719 Psalter, for a book commissioned by the established Congregational Church in Connecticut.[27]

Watts's influence on liturgy and worship can continue to be measured by the great numbers of his hymns and psalm paraphrases still present in contemporary hymnals of numerous denominations in the United States and Great Britain. The most recent hymnal published by the United Church of Christ (the descendants of Dwight's Congregationalists) includes fourteen Watts hymns. In Great Britain, *The New English Hymnal* contains eleven Watts hymns.

NOTABLE HYMNS

By far the most well-known and continuously sung of Watt's hymns is "Our God Our Help in Ages Past." The hymn first appeared as the second of five "imitations" of Ps 90 in *Psalms of David Imitated.* John Wesley changed the first word to "O," which still appears in many hymnals. In Great Britain, the hymn has been used on so many occasions of national struggle or grief that it appears under the category of National Hymns. Close to "Our God" in popularity would be Watts's seasonal hymns: "Joy to the World" (Ps 98) for Christmas and "When I Survey the Wondrous Cross," "It Was a Sad and Solemn Night," and "Alas and Did My Savior Bleed" (from *Hymns*) for Holy Week.

Other psalm paraphrases that have lasted include his version of Ps 117, "From All That Dwell Below the Skies," and his version of Ps 72, "Jesus Shall Reign Where'er the Sun." "I Sing the Mighty Power of God," "Come Holy Spirit, Heavenly Dove," and "Come We That Love the Lord" from the 1709 Hymnal continue to be sung. In most hymnals in the English speaking churches more than 300 years after Watts's first published hymn appeared, his hymns appear more often than most authors who have succeeded him.

BIBLIOGRAPHY

A Facsimile Reprint of the first Edition of the Bay Psalm Book. New York: Burt Franklin, 1973.

27. Dwight's most famous hymn, "I Love Thy Kingdom, Lord," versifies Ps 137, which Watts omitted. Stackhouse, *Language of the Psalms*, 59–69.

Benson, Louis. *The English Hymn.* Richmond: John Knox, 1962.

Davies, Horton. *The Worship of the American Puritans, 1629–1730.* New York: Peter Lang, 1990.

Fountain, David. *Isaac Watts Remembered.* Oxford: Oxford University Press, 1978.

Leaver, Robin A. "Isaac Watts's Hermeneutical Principles and the Decline of English Metrical Psalmody." *Churchman* 92 (1978) 56–60.

Stackhouse, Rochelle A. "Hymnody and Politics." In *Wonderful Words of Life,* edited by Richard Mouw and Mark A. Noll, 42–66. Grand Rapids: Eerdmans, 2004.

———. *The Language of the Psalms in Worship.* Lanham, MD: Scarecrow, 1997.

Watts, Isaac. *Hymns and Spiritual Songs with an Essay Towards the Improvement of Christian Psalmody by the Use of Evangelical Hymns in Worship as well as the Psalms of David.* London: Humfreys, 1707.

———. *The Psalms of David Imitated in the Language of the New Testament.* London: J. Clark, 1719.

Chapter 15

The Wesleys

Charles and John

Erika K. R. Stalcup

HISTORICAL BACKGROUND

This chapter addresses the hymnological contributions of John Wesley (1703–91) and Charles Wesley (1707–88), two of the founders of Methodism. During Charles's lifetime and the majority of John's, Methodism was not its own denomination but rather an evangelical movement rooted in the Church of England. This movement was characterized by its outdoor preaching, social outreach, the lively singing of new hymns, and a tightly organized structure of small groups for the purposes of worship, devotion, and "holy conversation."[1]

While both John and Charles were priests within the Church of England, and while both insisted that Methodists attend the established church to receive the sacraments, the link with the Church of England became increasingly tenuous throughout the eighteenth century. Though Methodism did attract many people who already frequented the Church of England, it also proved attractive to those who had little church background or who

1. From John Wesley's sermon, "The First-fruits of the Spirit," reproduced in Outler, *Works of John Wesley*, 236–37.

had distanced themselves from religion. For these persons, participation in the Church of England was often much less interesting than attending specifically Methodist events with music that stirred the emotions and fiery preaching that struck at the hearts of audience members. Theologically speaking, Methodism did not represent a departure from the Church of England (at least according to the Wesleys)—rather it emphasized particular concepts such as assurance of faith, the possibility of direct encounter with the divine, and the necessity of conversion. These ideas contributed greatly to the evangelical revival of the eighteenth century and led individuals to feel that God held not only collective but also personal interests at heart.

While the sermons of Charles Wesley, John Wesley, and other Methodist leaders played a starring role in the expansion of the movement and in the promotion of Methodist theological emphases, hymns played an equally important part in engaging the minds and hearts of those who sang, heard, and read them. This chapter explores the place of hymnody within the Methodist movement—not only the "emotive" function of melody and the poetic quality of text, but also the experiential theology of singing and other means of engaging with hymns. Such an investigation requires not only attention to the Wesley brothers, but also a foray into the experiences of Methodist lay people and the devotional role of hymns in the lives of early Methodists. This chapter will first address eighteenth-century Methodist music including brief biographies of John and Charles Wesley, after which theological perspectives will be explored along with the function of hymns in the spiritual progress of Methodist lay people.

Biographical Background

Charles and John Wesley were raised in a devout household headed by a father who was a Church of England priest and poet, and a mother with exemplary religious and organizational zeal. Samuel Wesley, Sr. served the parish of Epworth, and all the Wesley children would have shared certain musical experiences in common, such as singing metrical psalms at school and with the family as well as hearing the parish choir each Sunday.[2] Neither boys were particularly musical, it seems, though both John and Charles are both reported to have played the flute.[3] Both attended Christ Church College at Oxford University, both were ordained priests in the Church of Eng-

2. Temperley and Banfield, *Music and the Wesleys*, xiii; and Young, *Music of the Heart*, 33.

3. Temperley and Banfield, *Music and the Wesleys*, xiii; and Young, *Music of the Heart*, 33–34, 116.

land, both traveled to the American colony of Georgia as missionaries, both experienced evangelical conversion within days of one another (Charles on May 21, 1738, followed by John three days later) and both were intimately involved in the organization and maintenance of Methodist societies. Yet for all this, the two brothers had very different temperaments as well as distinctive theological tendencies, pastoral mannerisms, and family situations.

In general, Charles displayed a greater ecumenical openness through his willingness to reconcile theological differences with the Moravians and the Calvinists, while John appeared to take conflicts much more personally, showing little flexibility for those who did not share his viewpoints or accept his organizational authority. Spiritual narratives of Methodist lay persons reveal that many found Charles to be the more pastoral of the two brothers.[4] While John enjoyed robust health and exercised a rigorously itinerant ministry throughout his lifetime, Charles was plagued with poor health and was prone to bouts of melancholy. While Charles eventually settled into a seemingly happy family life, John had at least two thwarted relationships in his younger days and eventually entered into a disastrous marriage with a widow in 1751. One additional source of tension between the brothers was the facility with which Charles mixed with higher society, particularly musicians.[5]

Musical Background

Given their distinctive personalities, it is not surprising that the two brothers brought distinctive but complementary contributions to the music of Methodism. Perhaps predictably, John tended to establish the structure and *raison d'être* of hymn publications while Charles furnished the poetic soul through his texts. The two brothers published jointly and independently numerous hymn collections during their lifetimes.[6] Some of the collections were clearly meant as resources for congregational song, while other text-

4. These authors may have naturally been biased toward Charles, however, as they were writing their spiritual narratives at his request. See for examples Mrs. Plat to Charles Wesley, 1740, Early Methodist Volumes 10; and Sarah Middleton to Charles Wesley, May 1740, Early Methodist Volumes 5. The Early Methodist Volumes (hereafter EMV) are found in the Methodist Archives and Research Centre (hereafter MARC) at the John Rylands University Library, University of Manchester.

5. See for example Alyson McLamore's chapter "Harmony and Discord in the Wesley Family Concerts" in Temperley and Banfield, *Music and the Wesleys.*

6. Refer to The Center for Studies in the Wesleyan Tradition website for comprehensive lists of the works of John and Charles Wesley: https://divinity.duke.edu/initiatives/cswt.

only collections were published according to a theme and were destined for a particular context or time.[7] Before examining the contents of these collections, it is worth reflecting on the Wesley brothers' philosophy of music as well as the singing practices of Methodists.

It is fitting that Charles Wesley's apologia should come in hymn form. The primary indices of his thoughts on music were expressed in two hymns under the heading, "The True Use of Musick" published in the second volume of *Hymns and Sacred Poems*, 1749. The first hymn, "Listed into the Cause of Sin," defends the goodness of music in asserting that Jesus rather than the devil constitutes the soul of music.[8] The second hymn, "Jesus, Thou Soul of all our Joys," affirms that the chief end of music is God's glory and not our own.[9] At the same time, music is a gift which must be used wisely. In the ideal circumstance, music incites us to join our voices in one accord to praise God and to affirm our hope of living according to God's will.[10]

True to his own character, John elaborated his ideas in a formal treatise entitled "Thoughts on the Power of Music," published in 1779. According to John, music ought to serve as a "handmaid of religion."[11] Music is therefore subservient to text. Its function is to "enhance and intensify the ideas and (especially) the feelings that those words articulate."[12] He looked to the music of the ancient Greeks, and concluded that it was superior to modern music in its capacity to stir the passions because it employed the melody only. John argued that counterpoint engaged merely the ear as opposed to the passions. For this reason, he strongly opposed fugal textures, for example, complaining that the practice of singing different words at once made it impossible to understand the text.[13]

While John remained unconvinced about vocal harmony, Charles approved it without question. Another source of musical contention between the two brothers centered on the usefulness of organs. John strongly disapproved and instructed that organs should not be used among the Methodists.

7. See Robin A. Leaver's chapter "*Psalms and Hymns* and *Hymns and Sacred Poems*: Two Strands of Wesleyan Hymn Collections" in Temperley and Banfield, *Music and the Wesleys*, for a discussion of two types of hymn collections in early Methodism.

8. Wesley, *Hymns and Sacred Poems*, 253–55.

9. Wesley, *Hymns and Sacred Poems*, 255–56.

10. J. R. Watson, "The Music of Poetry," in Temperley and Banfield, *Music and the Wesleys*, 29.

11. Temperley and Banfield, *Music and the Wesleys*, xiii.

12. Temperley and Banfield, *Music and the Wesleys*, 3.

13. "Thoughts on the Power of Music, 1779" reproduced in Hildebrandt and Beckerlegge, *Works of John Wesley*, 766–69.

Even so, it seems that a few organs were purchased and placed in Methodist spaces during his lifetime. John appears to have softened his position enough to publish *Sacred Harmony*, a tunebook intended for harmonized voices, harpsichord, and organ, in 1781. The subject continued, however, to be disputed until over thirty years after both Wesley brothers had died.

Despite their loyalty and reverence for the Church of England, both Charles and John Wesley deemed existing church music insufficient for the purposes of Methodist societies. Within the established church at this time, laity generally did not participate much in singing. What congregational singing that did occur was often led very slowly by the parish clerk.[14] Methodist singing, however, seemed to be quite a different thing. Firstly, it took place in alternative spaces. As the Wesley brothers never had their own parish within the Church of England (except John during his brief time in America), Methodists met in whatever spaces could accommodate their preaching, prayer meetings, and other group events—in barns, in fields, in homes, and in other buildings lent to them—until they were able to build their own chapels. Unlike the music of the established church, Methodist singing was "free, informal, lively, well led, and open to all."[15] It may have reminded people of other spaces in which all sang together—perhaps at the tavern or while working in the fields.[16] Early Methodists often wrote about having sung in small groups on many different occasions, including informal moments among friends. For instance, Elizabeth Halfpenny recalled being "in some measure supported under [her] heavy burthen" when she heard Mr. Richards and Mr. Ellison singing "O thou who when I did complain" during breakfast.[17]

In the preface to the hymnal, *Select Hymns: With Tunes Annext* (1761), John Wesley offered seven guidelines for congregational singing. He exhorted Methodists to first learn the tunes contained therein before learning any others, and to sing them exactly as indicated on the page. Regarding the manner of singing, he encouraged Methodists to sing all together, to sing in time, and to sing neither too loudly nor too softly. One must not "bawl," but neither must one be afraid of one's voice. Lastly, John emphasized the importance of singing spiritually—to attend to the meaning of the text and

14. Nicholas Temperley, "John Wesley, Music, and the People Called Methodists," in Temperley and Banfield, *Music and the Wesleys*, 5.

15. Nicholas Temperley, "John Wesley, Music, and the People Called Methodists," in Temperley and Banfield, *Music and the Wesleys*, 5.

16. Nicholas Temperley, "John Wesley, Music, and the People Called Methodists," in Temperley and Banfield, *Music and the Wesleys*, 5.

17. Elizabeth Halfpenny to Charles Wesley, May 1742, EMV 87.

not to let one's heart be distracted by the music. In this way, music remains a means to an end rather than an end in itself.

Most people reported that Methodist singing was of good quality, that it was warm and full of emotion. Some tunes featured sections where the women sang alone, without the men. A Swedish visitor to the Foundry Chapel in 1769 remarked admiringly that this greatly enhanced the "harmonious charm" of the singing.[18] Not everyone shared such a positive opinion about Methodist music, however. In 1745, William Roberts wrote a comic performance sub-titled "The Scourge of the Methodists" in which a Methodist preacher is portrayed as teaching someone how to be a successful exhorter. He says:

> In the first place you must sing and shout hymns by the score if you would be devout, then you must frighten to death with your roar the people asleep in the house next door. Fools there will be just like unbridled horses, snorting away as they sing through their noses, turning both this way and that for to find the verses that send the land out of its mind.[19]

As mentioned above, Charles and John Wesley published numerous hymn collections independently and together. The majority of the texts in these publications were authored by Charles, who wrote between 6,000 and 9,000 hymns depending on what one deems a "hymn" as opposed to a "poem." This prolific output has earned Charles the title of "poet laureate" of Methodism.[20]

A few text collections merit special attention. For instance, the 1737 *Collection of Psalms and Hymns* was not only the first Wesleyan hymn publication but also the only one to be published in America.[21] It also has the distinction of being the first hymnbook published in America, having been printed during John's missionary voyage. The first two collections (both entitled *A Collection of Psalms and Hymns* though with different content) do not include any Charles Wesley texts, as Charles's prolific hymn writing began after his conversion in 1738. The first publication to include Charles's texts was the first volume of *Hymns and Sacred Poems* (1739). From this time on, the majority of eighteenth-century Methodist hymnody came from Charles's pen. The 1780 *Collection of Hymns for the Use of the People Called Methodists* is often considered by scholars to be the epitome of eighteenth-century Methodist hymnody and the forerunner of future authorized

18. Bretherton, "John Wesley and Professor Liden," 3.

19. Cited in Luff, *Welsh Hymns and Their Tunes*, 92.

20. Tyson, *Assist Me to Proclaim*, 252.

21. See Baker and Williams, *John Wesley's First Hymn-book*, 1964.

Methodist hymnals. This historical significance is due to its size, its organizational schema (according to spiritual state rather than liturgical periods) and the fact that it was destined specifically for the use of Methodist laity.[22]

In addition to text collections, John Wesley also published the following tune books: *A Collection of Tunes, Set to Music, As They are commonly Sung at the Foundery* (1742);[23] *Select Hymns: with Tunes Annext, Designed chiefly for the Use of the People called Methodists* (1761 and 1765, also referred to as *Sacred Melody*);[24] and *Sacred Harmony: a choice Collection of Psalms and Hymns set to Music in two or three parts for the Voice, Harpsichord and Organ* (1781 and 1790). According to John, these books were supposed to represent tunes already in common use among the Methodists. Many melodies had been previously published in non-Methodist collections, so they were not necessarily new in themselves. Within these three "authorized" tunebooks, five major tune sources can be distinguished: 1) English psalm melodies already in common use among Anglicans and dissenters; 2) German melodies that John had learned from the Moravians; 3) melodies descended from English art-music; 4) parody tunes in which the melody had been taken from a secular source and given new words; and 5) melodies written for the Methodists by John Frederick Lampe.[25] Other non-Wesleyan tunebooks that circulated among Methodists include *Hymns on the Great Festivals and Other Occasions* by John Frederick Lampe (1746),[26] *Harmonia Sacra* edited by Thomas Butts (1754, followed by further editions) and *Divine Musical Miscellany* edited by George Whitefield (1754).

THEOLOGICAL PERSPECTIVES

Methodist hymns proved extremely versatile in their usage. They were read and sung for private devotions, for group worship, in homes, in fields, and in prisons. The texts spoke to a wide range of life circumstances, and the act of singing served to reinforce and incorporate the meaning of the words. When considering the theology of these hymns, one first readily turns to the contents of the texts. What messages are conveyed through the poetry?

22. See the chapter on authorized hymnody in Clarke, *British Methodist Hymnody*, for further discussion of this collection.

23. See Kimbrough and Young, *John Wesley's First Tune Book*.

24. See Kimbrough and Young, *John Wesley's Second Tune Book*.

25. See Temperley's chapter "John Wesley, Music, and the People Called Methodists," in Temperley and Banfield, Music and the Wesleys, 10ff.

26. See Martin V. Clarke's chapter "John Frederick Lampe's *Hymns on the Great Festivals and Other Occasions*," in Temperley and Banfield, *Music and the Wesleys*, 52–62.

This section focuses largely on the hymns of Charles Wesley, particularly those hymns that were sung as opposed to those poems written for specific, non-liturgical circumstances. While the Wesley brothers did occasionally employ hymnody as polemic (particularly in promoting Arminianism over Calvinism, for example), the hymns that had the most popular impact were those that focused on personal conversion and spiritual growth.[27] It appears to be these hymns that helped the Methodist movement to gain momentum rather than those used for the Wesley brothers' personal and political interests.

One first notices that the hymns are permeated with biblical references and allusions. Charles Wesley knew his Bible, and he was skillfully generous in his use of Scripture. For Methodists who did not frequent the Church of England (and perhaps for those who did), hymns became their catechism. The hymns carried so much scriptural weight that they were more than capable of conveying the essentials of biblical and church teachings, as well as particularly Methodist emphases.[28] As Bernard Manning mused romantically, "The hymns . . . set forth, not the amiable generalization of natural religion in which Wesley's contemporaries delighted, but the peculiar and pungent doctrines of uncompromising Christianity."[29]

Despite the scriptural richness of Charles Wesley's texts, this is not necessarily a distinguishing feature of Methodist hymnody. As Stevick observes, there are no real doctrinal innovations. This is perhaps logical given Charles's loyalty to the Church of England. What renders his hymns so distinctive is their personal appeal, their sense of immediacy, and their ability to transport the individual into the biblical narrative.[30] Hymns do not merely tell—they transform. They are not only a means of transmitting theology, but a means of doing theology. This experiential ("experimental") theology was a key feature of early Methodism, and hymns a key means of embodying and enacting that theology.

Within evangelicalism, there existed an individualistic tendency: Jesus died not for an anonymous crowd, but for each individual. Consequently, one's salvation experience must be uniquely personal. Charles's hymns are filled with the language of "I" and "me." In adopting the first person, Charles ensures that the singer cannot remain an anonymous, passive observer of a

27. This assertion is based on the comments of Methodist lay persons as found in their spiritual narratives. See Stalcup, "Sensing Salvation."

28. Nuelsen, *John Wesley und das Deutsche Kierchenlied*, 3, 10; and Bett, *Hymns or Methodism*, 71ff.

29. Manning, *Hymns of Wesley and Watts*, 27.

30. Stevick, "Altar and the Cross," 62.

biblical scene. Instead, one is an active participant, a particular recipient of God's grace.

Within the conversion experience, one accepted a personal relationship with Jesus, a savior who knew them by name. In this sense, the fact of being a particular someone was essential. Early writers recounted specific details that distinguished their conversions from those of others. They recalled mystical experiences in which Jesus spoke directly to "me," in which hymns and sermons seemed expressly intended for "me," in which the eye of the preacher was fixed intently on "me." For example, Thomas Middleton wrote of a worship service at the Foundery in which "the hymns and the preaching seemed to be directed immediately to me."[31] These personal experiences were not only encouraged, but in fact created by the intensely individual nature of the hymns and sermons.

Rather than retelling biblical stories as past events, Charles renders scriptural narratives in the present. To further draw the individual into the narrative, Charles frequently emphasizes that God's salvific action happens "now," that Christ is calling individuals to repentance "now." There is an immediacy and an urgency in the text that leaves no room for spiritual complacency. These hymns are not meant to gently encourage but to radically transform.

As Joanna Cruickshank and others have observed, Charles actively directs the emotions of the singer.[32] He describes (or prescribes) the emotional state of the believer: the blissful unawareness of the unconverted, the despair of the almost-converted, and the intense joy of the newly converted. Feelings, therefore, become an important—even essential—part of religious experience. Intellectual assent is no longer enough; one must also feel one's way to salvation, passing through guilt, anguish, and ecstasy to a calm but joyful assurance.

Charles achieves this emotional guidance in part by appealing to the senses. By using highly visual imagery, Charles acts as an artist who shows rather than a theologian who convinces. He described colors, textures, and sounds in order to render the message incarnate in the bodies and hearts of individuals, intentionally directing the believer's gaze toward a particular aspect of the scene.[33] Cruickshank affirms, "[Charles] Wesley's hymns are distinctive in their detailed and insistent construction of the relationship

31. Thomas Middleton to Charles Wesley, October 8, 1743, EMV 111.

32. Cruickshank, "Singing at the Scaffold," 133.

33. Cruickshank, "Appear as Crucified," 317; and Stevick, "Altar and the Cross," 70.

between sight, feeling and spiritual change, particularly in the explicit emphasis given to the power of sight."[34]

Beyond their capacity to depict, the hymns engage the imagination in order that the singer/reader/hearer might generate her own imagery.[35] Indeed, a number of Methodists reported that their engagement with hymns resulted in visions and visualizations that alternately produced comfort, terror, or sympathy. One might see oneself on the brink of hell, or witness Jesus saving one from a fiery pit, or gaze upon the body of the suffering Christ.[36] Following the vocabulary utilized in Methodist circles, early Methodist laity spoke of the "eye of faith" to describe the means by which they apprehended these spiritual truths that eluded the weaker physical eye.[37] For them, these visions were far from delusions—rather they were glimpses into spiritual realities or possibilities that could not be apprehended by the physical senses.

It is fortunate for the historian that Charles Wesley solicited spiritual accounts from several Methodist societies, for these accounts provide a glimpse into the experiences of laity and how they utilized and interpreted hymns in their daily lives. Paul Chilcote observes in the spiritual writings of Methodist women that hymns were more frequently quoted earlier in the eighteenth century rather than later. Indeed, the spiritual accounts written in response to Charles Wesley's invitation were produced mainly in the early 1740s. Authors frequently quoted memorable lines in exclamation, and they also recounted circumstances in which texts spoke particularly to them.[38]

In addition to "official" publications, Charles distributed hymns to individuals he thought might benefit from them. For instance, Fanny Cowper expressed her gratitude for the "sweet hymns" sent by Charles Wesley, "wich we have sung every day since we have had 'em."[39] One imagines that these hymns were sung in a domestic setting. Another woman perused her hymnbook while in "deepest distress," turning randomly to "Who is the humbling sinner who." Charles reports in a letter to his wife that the woman immediately received a promise applied to her heart and continued "unspeakably happy for 2 years."[40] Others recounted powerful experiences of hymns in the context of group worship. It was while singing the words "Thy mercy never shall remove, thy nature and thy name is love" that William Holder received

34. Cruickshank, "Appear as Crucified," 320.
35. Cruickshank, "Appear as Crucified," 327.
36. Cruickshank, "Singing at the Scaffold," 137.
37. Cruickshank, "Appear as Crucified," 329.
38. See Chilcote, "Songs of the Heart," 99–114.
39. Fanny Cowper to Charles Wesley, March 8, 1741, EMV 43.
40. Charles Wesley to Sarah Wesley, September 7, 1766, DDCW 7/13, MARC.

confirmation of God's work in his soul. He averred, "I could not doubt the truth of it, the Lord shone so clear upon his work."[41]

Methodists often commented on the personal nature of the hymns, asserting that they seemed destined specifically for them. Such was the case of Thomas Middleton, who confessed a particular hymn of mercy and deliverance "was so suitable to me that it reached my very heart." He later quotes from Charles Wesley's hymn, "Depth of Mercy! Can there be," presumably the same hymn that he felt to be meant for him.[42]

It is often speculated that hymns may have at times been more effective at reaching souls than sermons. This was at least the case for John Walsh. Though a sermon preached at the chapel on West Street failed to move him, the two last lines of a hymn instantly freed him from his "besetting temptation." He recalled, "To the best of my remembrance, I heard only this: 'Mourning's o'er, look up for thou shalt weep no more.' And instantly lifting up my soul in strong hope, I wished for the repetition of those lines, but when sung again could only hear, 'Thy warfare o-er, look up, for thou shalt weep no more.'"[43]

As a testimony to their transformative potential, hymns occasionally generated physical responses such as crying, trembling, and out-of-body experiences. Both men and women reported having wept copiously after singing a hymn. Dennys DeBeret wrote of his wife "weep[ing] savourly" after singing.[44] Thomas Middleton recalled wanting to "weep my life away at the saviour's feet" and to "mourn and weep continually."[45] Charles Wesley also recorded in his journals and letters many instances of himself crying, in addition to his exhortations for others to do so.

Others reported even more extreme responses to hymns. Elizabeth Downes provides an example of some of the more intensely physical language in the early Methodist spiritual accounts. She wrote of numerous occasions in which she experienced great pain, fluttering, and sinking. For instance:

> After the sacrament was ended Mr. Diaper gave out the hymn, and att mentioning the cross perticular, I felt as itt were a change

41. William Holder journal, November 4, 1768, Diaries Collection, MARC.

42. As quoted in the narrative: "Whence to me this wast[e] of love / Ask my advocate above / See the cause in Jesus' face / Now before the throne of grace." Hymn published in John Wesley and Charles Wesley, *Hymns and Sacred Poems* (London: Strahan, 1740).

43. John Walsh to Charles Wesley, August 11, 1762, EMV 134.

44. Dennys DeBeret to William Seward, April 24, 1739, DDSe 39, MARC.

45. Thomas Middleton to Charles Wesley, October 8, 1743, EMV 111.

> as I thought inward and outward. My heart fluttered as though itt would have tore out of my body. I seemed as though I had been convulsed. . . . I was immediately caught as itt were out of the body.[46]

The effects of evangelical transformation did not go unnoticed by the public. As part of his ministry to prisoners, Charles Wesley sang hymns with those awaiting execution. On one occasion he led a hymn of his father's "Behold the Saviour of Mankind," noting that all were "delightfully cheerful."[47] Indeed, the authorities believed some recent converts to be *too* cheerful, complaining that their comportment did not help to discourage others from a similar fate.[48]

Hymns were not, of course, the only catalyst for transformative experiences—rather they worked in tandem with the other "means of grace" (such as prayer, receiving Holy Communion, engaging in "holy conversation," etc.) to guide individuals through the necessary steps leading to a full assurance of salvation. Due to the physical nature and collective energy of singing, the personal nature and immediacy of the text, and the power of music to "stir the passions," hymns were a particularly potent tool of Methodist evangelism.

CONTRIBUTIONS TO LITURGY AND WORSHIP

In considering the Wesleyan contributions to liturgy and worship, one first notices the features on the surface: alternative locations for singing (i.e., outside of church walls); an increased participation in singing; a greatly expanded repertoire of hymns thanks to the poetic gifts of Charles Wesley and the musical selections of John Wesley. One might then examine the poetic quality of Charles Wesley's texts, noting his astute use of Scripture and the

46. Elizabeth Downes to Charles Wesley, April 13, 1742, EMV 53.

47. This hymn would become a classic execution hymn throughout the eighteenth century, continuing its popularity into current hymnals. See Kimbrough and Newport, *Manuscript Journal*, 133, 136–39.

48. "I have often thought that great hurt has been done to Society by the Methodist preachers, both in town and country, attending condemned Malefactors, as by their fanatical conversion, visionary hymns, bold and impious applications of the Scriptures, &c., many dreadful offenders against law and justice, have had their passions and imaginations so worked upon, that they have been sent to the other world in such raptures, as would better become martyrs innocently suffering in a glorious cause, than criminals of the first magnitude. . . . [Instead,] notorious offenders [are] encouraged to persevere, trusting sooner or later, to be honoured with a similar degree of notice, and thus by a kind of hocus pocus, be suddenly transformed into saints." Lackington, *Memoirs of the First Forty-five Years*, 271–73.

way in which he pushes the limits of space and time with the repeated use of the words "all" and "now." If one searches a bit deeper, however, one will begin to ask not only "What do the hymns say?" but "What do the hymns do?" Indeed, the value of Methodist hymns resided not in the information that they transmitted, but in the transformation that they effected. Through the singing, hearing, and reading of hymns, early Methodists found themselves active participants in the biblical narrative. Through song and verse, they not only learned about God—they also communicated with God and received revelation. For early Methodists, both the reading of the text and the bodily experience of singing, hymns "enabled communication between self and community and between self and God, [standing as] models of sincere speech and authentic emotion."[49]

NOTABLE HYMNS

Charles Wesley

Of the many Charles Wesley texts that still exist in present-day hymnals, I have selected six noteworthy hymns—three associated with particular times in the liturgical year and three appropriate for any season.

"And Are We Yet Alive"

Written during a period of persecution, this hymn praises God's care and protection between Christian gatherings. It first appeared in *Hymns and Sacred Poems* (1749) and is often sung at yearly Methodist meetings today.

"Christ the Lord Is Risen Today"

This classic Easter hymn rejoices in love's ultimate triumph over death. It is the only Charles Wesley text in the current hymnal of The United Methodist Church (1989) that appears with the same tune with which it was originally paired. [FN Foundery]

49. Mack, *Heart Religion*, 48.

"Come, Thou Long-Expected Jesus"

First published in *Hymns for the Nativity of Our Lord* (1745), this hymn is still sung during Advent today. Consisting of just two stanzas, the hymn proclaims that Christ has been born to liberate humanity from its "fears and sins."

"Hark! the Herald Angels Sing"

This renown Christmas hymn celebrates the newborn Christ child and God's promise of peace on earth. Originally beginning "Hark how all the welkin rings," the text first appeared in *Hymns and Sacred Poems* (1739).

"Love Divine, All Loves Excelling"

Written in the first-person plural, this hymn describes the immensity of God's love, which leaves the singer "lost in wonder, love, and praise." It is commonly used as part of marriage ceremonies. The text was first published in *Hymns for those that seek and those that have Redemption in the in the blood of Jesus Christ* (1747).

"O For a Thousand Tongues to Sing"

The present-day version begins with the seventh stanza of the original hymn, which begins, "Glory to God, and praise and love." The hymn was originally published in *Hymns and Sacred Poems* (1740) under title "On the Anniversary Day of One's Conversion" to commemorate the first anniversary of Charles Wesley's own conversion. It is the first hymn in many Methodist hymnals.

John Wesley

Though John Wesley did write a few texts, it is difficult to know exactly how many since the two brothers agreed not to designate authorship of their jointly published hymns. Some scholars have attempted to define criteria that would distinguish the brothers from each other, though it is generally agreed that Charles was primarily author while John was primarily translator and editor. At present, there are only seven undisputed original titles attributed to John.[50] Of these seven works, only one is religious in nature and none were published for the purposes of congregational singing. John Wesley's textual contributions come rather in the form of translations and adaptations of preexisting hymns. Because of his early association with the German Moravians, John translated over thirty texts from German into English, three of which appear in the current *United Methodist Hymnal*.[51] Scholars have praised the fluidity of John's translations, even going so far as to say that they were regarded not as "imported foreign wares," but as "genuine English possessions."[52] One can distinguish John's theological tendencies in his translations from the German as well as his adaptations of English poets, such as George Herbert and Isaac Watts. For example, in modifying one of his father's texts for publication in the *Foundery Collection* (1742), John demonstrates a preference for addressing God in the second person as opposed to simply speaking about God. He therefore changes "How good and just! How large his grace" to "How good thou art, how large thy grace."[53] Like Charles, John intended for the singer/reader to be an active participant in (rather than passive recipient of) the salvation story.

BIBLIOGRAPHY

Adams, Nelson F. "The Musical Sources for John Wesley's Tune-Books: the Genealogy of 148 Tunes." SMD diss., Union Theological Seminary, 1973.

Baker, Frank. *Charles Wesley's Verse: An Introduction*. London: Epworth, 1964.

Baker, Frank, and George Walton Williams, eds. *John Wesley's First Hymn-book:* A Collection of Psalms and Hymns, *a facsimile with additional material*. Charleston: The Dalcho Historical Society and London: The Wesley Historical Society, 1964.

Bett, Henry. *The Hymns of Methodism*. London: Epworth, 1913.

Bretherton, F. F. "John Wesley and Professor Liden, 1769." *Proceedings of the Wesley Historical Society* 17, no. 1, 1929.

Chilcote, Paul. "Songs of the Heart: Writings of Early Methodist Women." *Proceedings of The Charles Wesley Society*, vol. 5, 1998.

Clarke, Martin V. *British Methodist Hymnody: Theology, Heritage and Experience*. New York: Routledge, 2017.

Cruickshank, Joanna. "Appear as Crucified: Sight, Suffering, and Spiritual Transformation in the Hymns of Charles Wesley." *Journal of Religious History* 30.3 (October 2006) 311–30.

50. "John Wesley's Poetry, Hymn, and Verse," https://divinity.duke.edu/initiatives/cswt/john-wesley.

51. "Give to the Wind Thy Fears" from Paul Gerhardt (#129), "Jesu, Thy Boundless Love to Me" from Paul Gerhardt (#183), and "Thou Hidden Love of God" from Gerhard Tersteegen (#414).

52. Nuelsen, *John Wesley und das Deutsche Kierchenlied*, 53.

53. Wesley, *Holy Communicant Rightly Prepar'd*, 258.

Cruickshank, Joanna. "Singing at the Scaffold: Charles Wesley's Hymns for Condemned Malefactors." *Proceedings of the Wesley Historical Society* 56.3, October 2007.

Hildebrandt, Franz, and Oliver A. Beckerlegge, eds. *The Works of John Wesley*. Vol. 7, *A Collection of Hymns for the use of the People called Methodists*. Nashville: Abingdon, 1989.

Kimbrough, S. T., Jr., and Kenneth G. C. Newport, eds. *The Manuscript Journal of the Reverend Charles Wesley, M.A.* Vol. 1. Nashville: Abingdon, 2007.

Kimbrough, S. T., and Carlton R. Young, eds. *John Wesley's First Tune Book:* A Collection of Tunes, Set to Music, as they are commonly sung at the Foundery, *A Facsimile Edition with Introduction and Critical Notes.* Madison: The Charles Wesley Society, 2011.

Kimbrough, S. T., and Carlton R. Young, eds. *John Wesley's Second Tune Book:* Select Hymns: with Tunes Annext: Designed chiefly for the use of the People Called Methodists, *A Facsimile Edition with Introduction and Critical Notes.* Madison: The Charles Wesley Society, 2015.

Lackington, James. *Memoirs of the First Forty-five Years of the Life of James Lackington.* London, 1792.

Lightwood, James T. *Methodist Music in the Eighteenth Century.* London: Epworth, 1927.

Luff, Alan. *Welsh Hymns and Their Tunes.* Carol Stream: Hope; London: Stainer and Bell, 1990.

Mack, Phyllis. *Heart Religion in the British Enlightenment: Gender and Emotion in Early Methodism.* New York: Cambridge University Press, 2008.

Methodist Archives and Research Centre (MARC), The John Rylands Library, The University of Manchester.

Manning, Bernard L. *The Hymns of Wesley and Watts: Five Informal Papers.* London: Epworth, 1942.

Nuelsen, John L. *John Wesley und das Deutsche Kierchenlied.* Nashville, TN: The Historical Society of the Methodist Episcopal Church, 1938. Translated by Theo Parry, Sidney H. Moore, and Arthur Holbrook, as *John Wesley and the German Hymn.* Yorkshire: A. S. Holbrook, 1972.

Outler, Albert C., ed. *The Works of John Wesley.* Vol. 1, *Sermons I,* 1–33. Nashville: Abingdon, 1984.

Stalcup, Erika K. R. "Sensing Salvation: Accounts of Spiritual Experience in Early British Methodism, 1735–1765." PhD diss., Boston University, 2016.

Stevick, Daniel B. "The Altar and the Cross: The Atonement in *Hymns on the Lord's Supper.*" *Proceedings of the Charles Wesley Society* Vol. 5, 1998.

Temperley, Nicholas, and Stephen Banfield, eds. *Music and the Wesleys.* Urbana: University of Illinois Press, 2010.

Tyson, John R. *Assist Me to Proclaim: The Life and Hymns of Charles Wesley.* Grand Rapids: Eerdmans, 2007.

Wesley, Charles. *Hymns and Sacred Poems.* Vol. 2. Bristol: Farley, 1749.

Wesley, John. *Select Hymns: with Tunes Annext: Designed Chiefly for the Use of the People Called Methodists.* London, 1761.

Wesley, Samuel. *The Holy Communicant Rightly Prepar'd.* London: Charles Harper, 1700; 2nd ed., 1716.

Young, Carlton R. *Music of the Heart: John and Charles Wesley on Music and Musicians.* Carol Stream: Hope, 1995.

Chapter 16

Nikolaus von Zinzendorf and Moravian Song

Neal Campbell

HISTORICAL PERSPECTIVES

The Moravian Church, formally known as the Unitas Fratram or Unity of Brethren, is one of the oldest protestant denominations in the world. In fact, it is understood by many to be *the* oldest protestant denomination, its history being traced to persons and events some one hundred years before Martin Luther nailed his theses to the chapel door at Wittenburg in 1517. Moravians are the spiritual descendants of the martyr John Hus, who was condemned by the Council of Constance and burned at the stake on July 6, 1415.

Even though 1517 is the accepted date for the beginning of the Reformation, the events leading to Luther's denunciation had been brewing for at least a century prior. It is also generally understood that the Reformation did not necessarily end in 1555 with the Peace of Augsburg or in 1648 with the Treaty of Westphalia. Political and religious distribution of power fluctuated and triggered wars over periods of time, including persecutions and the Catholic Church's response to the Protestant movement, the Counter-Reformation.

John Wycliffe may be thought of as the theorist of ecclesiastical Reformation, but Hus is considered the first church reformer, the antecedent of Luther, Calvin, and Zwingli. His teachings had a strong influence on the states of Western Europe in the formation of a reformist Bohemian religious denomination and, more than a century later, on Martin Luther himself. Hus was burned at the stake for heresy against the doctrines of the Roman Catholic Church, including those on ecclesiology, the Eucharist, and other theological dogma. The ancient Unitas Fratrum, as followers of Hus, almost became extinct following his death and the resulting wars and Counter-Reformation. Small pockets of followers known as the "remnant of the seed" were found, however, throughout eastern Europe, but their activities were contained in small secret groups.

The Moravian Church of today (as opposed to the older Unitas Fratrum) derives from a group of these exiles who fled Moravia escaping persecution and arriving at the Berthelsdorf estate of Count Nikolaus von Zinzendorf in 1722. The heritage of the church dates to followers of Hus in Bohemia and its crown lands Moravia and Silesia, which were then an autonomous kingdom within the Holy Roman Empire, and today known as the Czech Republic. The renewed church, which settled in Berthelsdorf, is now known as the Moravian Church, but it also retains the ancient secondary name: Unitas Fratrum.

The modern Moravian church has about 750,000 members worldwide and continues to draw on the traditions and manifestations established in its eighteenth-century revival, the primary attributes being personal piety, ecumenism, education, missionary work, liturgy and music, with emphasis on strong congregational and choral singing, and brass bands and other instruments. The motto of the denomination is, "In essentials, unity; in non-essentials, liberty; in all things, love."[1]

Nikolaus Ludwig Zinzendorf (1700–1760) is frequently cited as being the founder of the Moravian Church and that is true in a practical sense. In this regard, his life trajectory is similar to that of John Wesley, who is referred to as the founder of the Methodist Church. Like Wesley, who remained an Anglican priest all his life, Zinzendorf remained a Lutheran, eventually becoming an ordained minister and bishop. It was no more his intent to found another denomination (the Moravians) than it was Wesley's to found Methodism. Zinzendorf was an eclectic theologian who emphasized a personal growth and relationship with the historic Jesus. He also believed strongly in Christians living in community, a community based

1. Website of the Moravian Church in North America: http://www.moravian.org/the-moravian-church/the-moravian-church-is/.

on familial relationships as opposed to a monastic principle. In an era of precisely defined religious and political boundaries he was radically ecumenical in his understanding of God's unique plan for the individual, and his ecumenism was evident in the company he sought and kept. He is today commemorated in the liturgical calendars of the Lutheran and Episcopal churches as a hymn writer and church leader.

Zinzendorf was heir to one of Europe's leading families and was destined for high duties as a nobleman in eighteenth-century Europe. His father died shortly after he was born, and the boy was reared by his mother, her sister Henrietta, and his grandmother, Lady Gersdorf, on her estate sixty miles east of Dresden. The family was devout in its religious fervor and subscribed to the wing of the Lutheran Church influenced by Pietism, seeking to know Christ in a personal way and considering themselves separate and apart from the secular world. From a very early age, the young count was drawn to the religious life at home, in an atmosphere of prayer, Bible reading, and hymn singing. Even though he was raised in a pious milieu, he was still raised as a young count. When he professed a desire to enter the ministry, it was made clear that he was to follow the path of public service his nobility dictated. He studied at the Paedagogium in Halle under the staunch pietist disciple August Francke (1663–1727). He spent six years there during which time he mastered several languages and showed poetic gifts. From Halle he went to Wittenburg University, a stronghold of Lutheran orthodoxy that was not particularly friendly to those of pietistic leanings, but was a proper place for a young nobleman preparing for service. Upon completion of his studies, he undertook in 1719–20 a grand tour of Europe as was typical of someone of his noble background, and he was exposed to the rich culture it afforded.[2]

The most significant experience in Zinzendorf's time in France was undoubtedly his intense friendship with the Cardinal Archbishop of Paris, Louis de Noailles (1651–1729), which was facilitated by Father de la Tour, the head of the Fathers of the Oratory in Paris. Upon meeting Zinzendorf, Father de la Tour was impressed with the young count's interest in things religious, introduced him to the Cardinal, and accompanied him at their first visit, which lasted some two and a half hours.

There was a growing movement in the Roman Catholic Church, primarily in France, known as Jansenism, which centered on the teaching of the Dutch theologian Cornelius Jansen, who died in 1638, but left a treatise based on the teaching of Augustine that attracted many adherents in the wake of the Enlightenment. Throughout the seventeenth and into the eighteenth centuries Jansenism was a distinct movement within the Roman

2. Weinlick, *Count Zinzendorf*, 45.

Catholic Church that was especially strong in France. Jansen's treatise espoused several attributes that were strikingly similar to those of the Reformation, Calvin in particular, on matters of free will, predestination, grace, and the necessity and frequency of receiving Holy Communion. As the movement grew it became controversial and divisive. Many in the church hierarchy, the Jesuits in particular, were opposed to Jansenism, as they derisively called it; to their thinking it was heretical. Had Pope Clement XI not intervened with his decree *Unigenitus Dei Filius* in 1713–19, schism within the church in France was probable.

Cardinal de Noailles was a strong proponent of Jansenism and it seems likely that his leanings toward its concepts eased the path of his friendship with Count Zinzendorf or, at the least, provided a common ground from which their friendship evolved. The two discussed at length, in person and in correspondence, topics of mutual interest and quickly came to openly respect each other's traditions, even though they also were quick to realize that neither of them was likely to capitulate in favor of the other's denomination.

It was against this backdrop that the growing tension reached a climax and Cardinal de Noalles, being at heart loyal to the church and not wishing to cause a lasting rupture—together with the increasing infirmities of age, accepted the *Unigenitus* decree in 1720. Zinzendorf was disappointed in this and even wrote the Cardinal a farewell letter as he felt their relationship had been irrevocably severed. Indeed, the two never met again, but they did soon resume their correspondence, which continued until Cardinal de Noalles died in 1729.

Their friendship was a remarkable manifestation of Zinzendorf's ecumenical nature. The details of denomination doctrine and the various matters of tradition were of only passing interest to him. Zinzendorf's biographer Weinlick states it best:

> The mutual attraction between the count and the cardinal lay in the fact that they were kindred spirits in their concept of Christianity. Both had a deeply Christocentric faith expressed in personal obedient devotion to the Savior.[3]

While in Düsseldorf, upon seeing Domenico Fetis's painting *Ecce homo* (Behold the Man) and reading the inscription under the thorn-crowned Christ, "I have done this for you; what have you done for me?" Zinzendorf confessed inwardly that he had done very little and from that point on he vowed to do whatever God led him to do.[4] For the rest of his life, he looked

3. Weinlick, *Count Zinzendorf*, 45.

4. Weinlick, *Count Zinzendorf*, 42.

to this event in his young life as a turning point, something akin to being born again, in his resolve to devote his life to things religious. This did not deter him from continuing his worldly travels, but as he continued to visit the busy commercial cities of Gouda, Rotterdam, Haarlem, and Amsterdam his interests increasingly leaned toward meeting persons of differing religious denominations in the free atmosphere of the tolerant nation. He met and worshiped with his Lutheran colleagues, as well as with Reformed, Mennonites, and Anglicans, and found compelling aspects to each of their points of view.

In 1721, he began work as the king's judicial counselor in Dresden. His duties were light and required his presence only at intermittent times of the year, which left him ample opportunity to pursue his religious interests. He opened his apartment for informal religious devotions on Sundays and soon attracted a circle of adherents. It was during this time that he wrote what is his best-known hymn, "Jesus, still lead on" which, at thirty-three stanzas, has been translated into many languages and is sung throughout the world.[5]

Even while doing his secular work at state, he envisioned setting up a Christian community in a manner akin to a modern-day retreat center. Upon obtaining his majority, he purchased his grandmother's estate, Berthelsdorf, in April 1722, which contained a parish church that had existed since 1346. Shortly after obtaining the estate, the incumbent pastor of Berthelsdorf died and Count Zinzendorf was instrumental in securing the new pastor, John Andrew Rothe, and from that time forward his life was inexorably intertwined with the spiritual affairs of the community. On September 7, 1922 he married Countess Erdmuth Dorothea von Reuss, a sister of a friend, who was as devout as he was and became his partner in his religious pursuits.

Even though he was still living in Dresden, word had gotten around that Zinzendorf had in mind establishing a religious community in Berthelsdorf. So it was that when a small group of exiles inquired of the manager of the estate, Johann Georg Heitz, Zinzendorf agreed to give them space. Heitz showed them a plot at one corner of the estate where they could establish residence and gave it the name Herrnhut, meaning "under the Lord's watch." In 1724, Zinzendorf made the trip to Herrnhut to see his vision taking shape and laid the cornerstone for an academy, the first large building of the new community. While he was there, five young men from Zauchtenthal in Moravia, who were fleeing persecution and arrest, arrived to visit. These five men were part of the "hidden seed" of the ancient Unitas Fratrum and

5. "Zinzendorf and the Moravians."

were so moved by the fervor of Herrnhut that they decided to remain. By 1725, there were ninety Moravian brethren living at Herrnhut.

Meanwhile John Andrew Rothe, pastor of the local Lutheran parish on the estate, through force of his preaching, drew many people of various backgrounds to worship, to the point where many Lutheran pietists became regulars at Herrnhut, together with former Roman Catholics, Separatists, Reformed, and Anabaptist Christians. In spite of the religious nature of the community, most of the residents were craftsmen and tradesmen who contributed to a thriving economy on the estate. By 1726, the population had grown to 300. Given the considerable variation in secular and religious backgrounds represented in Herrnhut, it was not long before serious tensions developed over styles of worship and liturgy at the Sunday services, leadership, and other aspects of communal living. In an attempt to provide spiritual oversight and focus to the community, Zinzendorf and his family moved to Herrnhut in 1727 and he worked as a councilor and advisor to his flock, visiting each family and organizing the community by way of a "Brotherly Agreement," which codified the guidelines under which the community lived and worshipped. Shortly a spirit of cooperation and love began to evidence itself. The community elected twelve elders and appointed a night watchmen (who announced the hours with a hymn), a caretaker for the sick, and almoners to supervise distribution of goods to the poor. They also organized small groups of various kinds. For example, it was not uncommon for there to be a town meeting type of gathering following a service at which Roth would assign duties to individuals and groups. On other occasions duties would be relegated by the drawing of lots, which increasingly became a typical way of settling routine matters at Herrnhut.

In July 1727, Zinzendorf journeyed to Zittau and in the library there discovered, quite by accident, a copy of the constitution of the ancient Unitas Fratrum with a preface written in 1660 by Bishop John Amos Comenius. It was then that Zinzendorf realized that the five young men from Zauchtenthal in Moravia who arrived at Herrnhut were the spiritual descendants of the Unitas Fratrum, which was in fact a fully established Christian church predating the Lutheran church. Amazed at the similarities between this constitution and his newly adopted "Brotherly Agreement," he copied portions of it into German and shared them with his people on the return to Herrnhut. By the following summer, the people had developed into a prayerful, united community, to the point where on Wednesday, August 13, at a communion service in the Berthelsdorf church, such a powerful manifestation of the Spirit came upon them that Zinzendorf afterward referred to that day as the "Pentecost" of the renewed Moravian Church. This date continues to be observed in Moravian churches as the date of the restored Unitas Fratrum and the birth of the Moravian Church as it exists today. The *Ratio Disciplinae* continues today, many times revised from the original "Brotherly Agreement," and is known as the "Covenant for Christian Living."[6]

Zinzendorf continued to be the guiding presence at Herrnhut, though he remained a Lutheran, even being ordained as a clergyman in 1734, and a bishop in 1737. He hosted John Wesley on his visit to Herrnhut in 1738. He oversaw missionary work and the founding of churches throughout Europe, the West Indies, and eventually in America, where the denomination established early centers in Pennsylvania and North Carolina, several of which remain today, such as those in Bethlehem begun in 1742 in Pennsylvania, followed closely by Nazareth, and Lititz, each of which were formed on the Herrnhut model. Founded in 1766 it was Salem (now Winston-Salem) that was destined to be the center of Moravian life in the South. Three congregations from the Colonial era exist to this day in Forsyth County, North Carolina: Friedberg, Friedland, and Hope. In 1756, Zinzendorf's wife died, he remarried and abdicated his position of nobility in the Empire to his nephew and devoted his activities entirely to the work of the Moravian church. He died May 9, 1760, at Herrnhut.

Zinzendorf's influence was ultimately felt throughout the Christian Protestant world. His emphasis on the "religion of the heart" deeply influenced John Wesley. He is remembered today, as Karl Barth put it, as "perhaps the only genuine Christocentric of the modern age."[7] Scholar George Forell put it more succinctly: Zinzendorf was "the noble Jesus freak."[8]

THEOLOGICAL PERSPECTIVES

Zinzendorf intended for hymns to be a form of direct communication with God; this he makes clear in his writings. They are not elaborations of theological concepts, or enlargements upon dogma. In his own words, they were to be "a kind of response to the Bible, an echo and an extension thereof. In the Bible one perceives how the Lord communicates with mankind; and in

6. "Zinzendorf and the Moravians."

7 Galli, quoted in *Christianity Today*, November 2017.

8 Galli, quoted in *Christianity Today*, November 2017.

the hymnal, how mankind communicates with the Lord."[9] Included in the preface to each successive hymnal of the Moravian Church are Zinzendorf's own words:

> May all who use these hymns experience at all times the blessed effects of complying with the Apostle Paul's injunction in Ephesians 5:18–19, "Be filled with the Spirit, as you sing psalms and hymns and spiritual songs among yourselves, singing and making melody to the Lord in your hearts." Yea, may they anticipate, while here below, though in a humble and imperfect strain, the song of the blessed above, who, being redeemed out of every kindred, and tongue, and people, and nation, and having washed their robes, and made them white in the blood of the Lamb, are standing before the throne, and singing in perfect harmony with the many angels round about it. "Worthy is the Lamb that was slain, to receive power, and riches, and wisdom, and strength, and honor, and glory, and blessing, for ever and ever. Amen."[10]

It was Zinzendorf's deeply felt "heart religion" that informed his understanding of theology and its various manifestations, including his religious poetry and hymnody, which he felt quite specifically was the proper vehicle for the congregation's addressing the Almighty. Like many of his era and milieu he grew increasingly dissatisfied with the formulas and dogmas of the orthodox Lutherans and felt a strong affinity for the wing of the denomination that was similarly informed, the Pietist movement. He was also unmoved by the humanist views of the Enlightenment that were being espoused broadly during the era. He felt that only a personal relationship with Jesus would ensure salvation of the soul. In this way, his understanding was not dissimilar to the fundamentalists of a later age in their understanding of being born again. At the same time, he retained an appreciation for the liturgical, musical, and poetic legacies of his noble upbringing as a Lutheran, and he and the fledgling renewed Moravian community relied on and drew strength from the considerable existing canon of hymns and the tunes composed for them, including many of the Latin hymns of Roman Catholicism in translation. However, in the end, "Zinzendorf insisted that the truest language for heart religion is song . . . the truths of the Christian religion are best communicated in poetry and song, not in a systematic theology and polemics."[11] From an early age, Zinzendorf himself felt called to the ministry or, more likely, a call to serve Jesus, if we are to believe his own

9. *Moravian Book of Worship*, i.

10. *Moravian Book of Worship*, iii.

11. Attwod, "Blood, Sex, and Death," 136.

account on first seeing Fetis's *Ecce homo*. All commentary on him refers to his life of devotion to Christ, at each stage of his life, even when he was very young and perhaps was not even able to articulate its practical implications. Such was the household in which he was brought up and of the prevailing ethos of the Pietist wing of the Lutheran church into which he was born and to which his mother, aunt, and grandmother were devout adherents.

As the *de facto* pastor of Herrnhut, he cultivated singing to a very high degree in terms of quantity and quality, elevating it almost to the level of a sacrament—it was an essential component of the communal worship on par with, or even surpassing, the sermon. To him is attributed the origin of a unique service, the *Singstunde* a communal song service at which hymns, or more specifically, selected stanzas of hymns (sometimes as many as one hundred), were chosen to amplify a spiritual theme with the same deliberateness as a preacher selecting his biblical texts. This *Singstunde* became foundational for his practice of public worship, as Weinlick has commented:

> In it the brother in charge selected with care individual stanzas from various hymns in such a manner that they would develop some demonstrable facet of Christian truth as the singing progressed. The congregation, which possessed an unusual command of the hymnal, would fall in with the leader before he reached the end of the first line of each stanza, singing by heart. No address was given on such occasions; none was needed.[12]

It is not by accident that the Moravian hymnals throughout the twentieth century in America, including the hymnal still in use, contain an index of first lines *of all stanzas* of each hymn in the hymnal, not just the first lines of the *first* stanzas or of a refrain by which a hymn might be popularly known. This allows those planning services to be very specific in the thematic content of the hymns chosen.

Commenting on the central part singing had at Herrnhut, Weinlick notes that although the Moravians produced several hymnbooks, these were not usually used in services—"the count [Zinzendorf] was of the conviction that a hymn must be memorized in order to express adequately the individual's Christian experience."[13] This exemplifies Zinzendorf's belief that true religion must be a religion of the heart and be part of a personal relationship with Jesus.

A good example of Zinzendorf's theology and piety is expressed in his hymn:

12. "Zinzendorf and the Moravians."

13. Weinlick, *Count Zinzendorf*, 85.

The Saviour's blood and righteousness
Can be the only proper dress
In which I dare approach that place,
Where God shall judge our human race.

Bold shall I stand in that great day,
For who aught to my charge shall lay?
Fully through thee absolved I am
From sin and fear, from guilt and shame.

Lord, I believe thy precious Blood,
Which at the mercy-seat of God
Forever doth for sinners plead.
For me, e'en for my soul, was shed.

When from the dust of death I rise
To claim my mansion in the skies,
E'en then shall this be all my plea,
'Jesus hath lived, hath died for me.'
14

CONTRIBUTIONS TO LITURGY AND WORSHIP

The body of hymns indigenous to the Unitas Fratrum and the Moravian Church is modest by comparison with the total of those from the Lutheran, Roman Catholic, or Anglican tradition. There are no iconic hymns, beloved of all, across denominational lines throughout the world such as Charles Wesley's contemporaneous "Hark, the herald angels sing" or "Jesus Christ is risen today," or Luther's "A mighty fortress" from the sixteenth century, or of Samuel John Stone's "The church's one foundation" in the nineteenth century. Although, there are hymns of Moravian origin which are well-known and beloved within the denomination that are, perhaps, iconic to Moravians.

It cannot be said that Moravians invented or inaugurated a new style of hymnody or the musical tunes associated with it. Rather, they liberally used existing material, and enlarged and expanded on it to a recognizable degree mainly through the copious amounts of music used in the services and communal activities. Denominational uniqueness was not something that was sought or deemed necessary in the tenets of Moravianism, and this is true of its hymnody as well. From the outset, persons of various backgrounds and religious persuasions found their way to the Brethren and they borrowed liberally from existing materials indigenous to their own heritage. This was true in the ancient Unitas Fratrum and particularly so in the renewed Zinzendorf era, a golden era of hymn writing and of associated music to go with it. Even though relatively few indigenous Moravian hymns found their way into hymnals of other denominations of the time, Zinzendorf's

14. Stanza 1 tr. Madeleine Forell Marshall, *Moravian Book of Worship*; Stanzas 2–4, tr. John Wesley, *Service Book and Hymnal*, 376.

hymns were known and admired by John and Charles Wesley. The most lasting Moravian contribution to Christian hymnody might actually be that of precursor or handmaiden.

> The Moravian Church's contribution began with the new emphasis on congregational singing through John Hus. . . . The renewed Moravian Church added its emphasis on the Christian's living relationship to his crucified and risen Lord, the joy of salvation and of Christian fellowship. When we sing the great hymns of our heritage of Christian faith, we come near to fulfilling our Lord's prayer for unity.[15]

The liturgies of the Moravian Church and the music associated with it are a logical outgrowth of the services of the Lutheran church in post-Reformation Eastern Europe and Germany. The Lovefeast is a tradition unique to Moravians. Although it may appear to be an obvious descendant from the ancient Eucharist or Lord's Supper, it is more correctly a holdover from the Herrnhut *Singstunde* in that in consists of much singing, no sermon, and only brief spoken words, to which is attached a simple meal. It is more of an elevated form of sacred fellowship than a sacrament, which it is not. The music associated with it is typically choral and congregational, or sometimes instrumental, a good deal of which is predicated by the practical need to cover the physical actions of distributing and collecting the components of the simple meal, buns and coffee in modern American observances.

Through their missionary endeavors, which were a significant part of the earliest manifestations of the renewed Unitas Fratrum (in which Zinzendorf himself participated, both in his travel and physical presence, and in his financial support), an international element emerged in the traditions of the Moravian church, including a particularly strong presence in America. Musical traditions have flourished there in the communities of Bethlehem, Pennsylvania, and Salem (now Winston-Salem), North Carolina, where the music associated with the Lovefeast was developed to a significant degree.

NOTABLE HYMNS

Zinzendorf wrote more than 2,000 hymns during his lifetime, in varying circumstances and for various occasions, including some that were spontaneous. Most of them have been consigned to obscurity. The most notable exception is "Jesus, still lead on" which appears in many translations throughout the world, and which is sung to the tune *Seelenbräutigam*

15. *Hymnal and Liturgies of the Moravian Church* 1969, iv.

by Adam Drese (1620–1701). It is contained in many hymnals of varying denominations in America and throughout the world and comes the closest to being an iconic contribution by Zinzendorf. Its familiarity is enhanced by many organ compositions based on the hymn tune, such as those by Sigfrid Karg-Elert (1877–1933) in Germany and Robert Elmore (1913–85), organist of the Central Moravian Church in Bethlehem from 1955–68, and other contemporary composers. A close second, in terms of familiarity across denominational lines, is his hymn "The Saviour's blood and righteousness," also in varying translations. Another, "O thou whose all-searching sight" in a translation by John Wesley, is also found across denominational lines in many American hymnals. These three hymns may rightly be thought of as Zinzendorf's lasting contribution to the canon of Christian hymnody since the Reformation.

In the three Moravian hymnals of the twentieth century in America, those dating from 1923, 1969, and 1995 (the hymnal currently in use), Zinzendorf is represented with between twenty-four and thirty-eight hymns in each which, with the exception of the three aforementioned, are unfamiliar to most non-Moravians. Many of them are paired to tunes of various older composers such as Joachim Neander (1650–80), Claude Goudimel (1508–72), and Johann Crüger (1598–1662). But most of them are linked to tunes composed or arranged by Christian Gregor (1723–1801) for the hymnal he compiled for the Herrnhut community where he worked and lived. Gregor, who ultimately was made a bishop, was instrumental in refining the liturgical and musical life of Herrnhut. He edited and compiled its hymnals and chorale books, and composed much music, specifically its services, to the degree that he is generally thought of as the "father of Moravian Music."[16]

After Zinzendorf himself, probably the best-known Moravian hymn writer was James Montgomery (1771–1854), whose global influence as a hymn writer was greater than Zinzendorf given the continuing use of his hymns, the most popular of which are better known across international denominational boundaries down to the present time. Montgomery was born in Sheffield, England, the son of a Moravian minister. He attended seminary with the intent of joining the clergy, but various secular enterprises and forays into journalism intervened. He became the assistant to the owner of the Sheffield *Register,* a radical newspaper. When its owner fled the country to avoid political persecution, Montgomery took it over and renamed the paper *The Iris* and its political content became even more radical. Montgomery was himself imprisoned twice for writing subversive material

16. Asti, "Moravian Music of Christian Gregor (1723–1801)," 1.

and he became an outspoken critic of existing child labor and slave trade practices. He became associated with the Wesleyan Methodists and was particularly supportive of Thomas Cotterill, the rector of St. Paul's in Sheffield, who was a strong proponent of congregational singing. Montgomery wrote over 400 hymns, many of them published in Cotterill's *Selections of Psalms and Hymns for Public and Private Use* (London, 1819). He also compiled his own collections of hymns: *Songs of Zion* (London, 1822), *The Christian Psalmist* (Glasgow, 1822), and *Original Hymns for Public, Private and Social Devotion* (London, 1853).[17] Montgomery's best-known hymns are "Angels from the realms of glory" and "Go to dark Gethsemane," each of which are included in the current hymnals of several American denominations.

BIBLIOGRAPHY

Asti, Martha Secrest. "The Moravian Music of Christian Gregor (1723–1801): His Anthems, Arias, Duets, and Chorales (Germany)." PhD diss., University of Miami, 1982.

Attwood, Craig D. "Blood, Sex, and Death: Life and Liturgy in Zinzendorf's Bethlehem." PhD diss., Princeton Theological Seminary, 1995.

Galli, Mark. *131 Christians Everyone Should Know.* Nashville: B & H, 2000.

Glover, Raymond, ed. *The Hymnal 1982 Companion.* 3 vols. New York: Church Hymnal Corporation, 1994.

Moravian Book of Worship. Bethlehem and Winston-Salem: Moravian Church in America, 1995.

Weinlick, John R. *Count Zinzendorf.* New York: Abingdon, 1956.

"Zinzendorf and the Moravians. 250th Anniversary of Protestant Missions," and other articles in *Christian History*, Vol. 1, No. 1, 1982.

SOURCES CONSULTED

Atwood, Craig D. *Community of the Cross: Moravian Piety in Colonial Bethlehem.* University Park: Pennsylvania State University Press, 2004.

Fogleman, Aaron Spencer. *Jesus Is Female: Moravians and the Challenge of Radical Religion in Early America.* Philadephia: University of Pennsylvania Press, 2007.

Freeman, Arthur J. *An Ecumenical Theology of the Heart: The Theology of Nicholas Ludwig von Zinzendorf.* Bethlehem, PA: The Moravian Church in America, 1998.

Hamilton, Taylor. *A History of the Moravian Church or the Unitas Fratrum of the United Brethren during the Eighteenth and Nineteenth Centuries.* Bethlehem, PA: Time, 1900.

Hymnal and Liturgies of the Moravian Church (Unitas Fratrum). Bethlehem: Provincial Synod, 1920.

17. Glover, *Hymnal 1982 Companion,* 2:537.

Hymnal and Liturgies of the Moravian Church. Chicago: The Moravian Church in America Northern and Southern Provinces, 1969.

Kinkel, Gary Steven. *Our Dear Mother the Spirit: An Investigation of Zinzendorf's Theology and Praxis.* New York: University Press of America, 1990.

Knouse, Nola Reed, ed. *The Music of the Moravian Church in America.* Rochester: University of Rochester Press, 2008.

Langton, Edward. *History of the Moravian Church: The Story of the First International Protestant Church.* London: George Allen & Unwin, Ltd., 1956.

Lewis, A. J. *Zinzendorf the Ecumenical Pioneer: A Study in the Moravian Contribution to Christian Mission and Unity.* Philadelphia: Westminster, 1962.

Merritt, Jane T. *At the Crossroads: Indians and Empire on a Mid-Atlantic Frontier, 1700–1763.* Chapel Hill: University of North Carolina Press, 2004.

Podmore, Colin. *The Moravian Church in England, 1728–1760.* Oxford: Clarendon, 1998.

Sawyer, Edwin Albert. *All About the Moravians: History, Beliefs, and Practices of a Worldwide Church.* Bethlehem and Winston-Salem: The Moravian Church in America, 2000.

Sawyer, Edwin Albert. *The Religious Experience of the Colonial American Moravians.* Nazareth, PA: Moravian Historical Society, 1961.

Service Book and Hymnal of the Lutheran Church in America. Minneapolis: Augsburg, 1958.

Sensbach, Jon. "Searching for Moravians in the Atlantic World." In *Self, Community, World: Moravian Education in a Transatlantic World*, edited by Heikki Lempa and Paul Peucker, 35–53. Bethlehem: Lehigh University Press, 2010.

Weinlick, John R., and Albert H. Frank. *The Moravian Church Through the Ages.* Bethlehem and Winston-Salem: The Moravian Church in America, 1966.

Westmeir, Karl-Wilhem. "Becoming All Things to All People: Early Moravian Missions to Native North Americans." In *International Bulletin of Missionary Research* 21.4 (October 1997) 172–76.

Wheeler, Rachel. *To Live Upon Hope: Mohicans and Missionaries in the Eighteenth-Century Northeast.* Ithaca: Cornell University Press, 2008.

Zinzendorf, Nikolaus L. von. *Hymns Composed for the Use of the Brethren by the Right Reverend and most illustrious C. Z.* London: Printed for James Hutton, 1749.

Chapter 17

Evangelical Anglican Hymnists

Karen B. Westerfield Tucker

HISTORICAL BACKGROUND

The evangelical movement within the Church of England grew throughout the eighteenth century and contributed to but also addressed the social, economic, and ecclesiastical upheaval occurring in England at that time. Satirist William Hogarth (1697–1764) portrayed through his engravings and paintings these challenges as well as his skepticism of the experiential religion associated with the minority evangelicals. "Gin Lane" (1751) captures the rampant societal problems provoked by industrialization and urbanization—poverty, prostitution, infanticide, mental illness, and suicide—and fed, in part, by the overconsumption of alcoholic spirits. "The Sleeping Congregation" (1736) shows a near-sighted cleric in the elevated pulpit of an Anglican parish church reading from either *The Book of Common Prayer* or the text of a published sermon while the congregation below slumbers. "Enthusiasm Delineated" (1760, never published) and its revision "Credulity, Superstition and Fanaticism" (1762) ridicule Catholicism and "enthusiastic" religion. Both depict a meetinghouse with clear glass windows, a raised pulpit, and a reading desk beneath which hangs a paper that reads, "Only love to us be giv'n / Lord we ask no other Heav'n / Hymn by G. Whitefield / p. 130." In "Enthusiasm Delineated," a howling dog bearing a collar engraved with the name "Whitfield" sits beneath the reading desk and, in the right hand corner, a thermometer listing several emotional states rests on "A Methodist Brain." There is a new list of emotional states on the thermometer in the 1762 version and the brain now rests on a book labeled "Wesley's sermons."[1]

Hogarth's suspicions related to the rise of enthusiastic religion associated with Anglican clergymen John Wesley (1703–91) and George Whitefield (1714–70) were widely shared. England was not too distant in time from the "late unhappy confusions"[2] of the English Civil War, and there was fear of political and social consequences arising from a people's movement. The Church of England was dealing with multiple theological shifts within its ranks that pressed in new ways against its self-understanding as a *via media*. Enlightenment rationalism caused some clergy and learned laity to reconsider the doctrine of the Trinity and other confessions of faith delineated in the church's Thirty-nine Articles. The discovery or rediscovery of early Christian texts, among them the *Apostolic Constitutions* (c. 380) with an apparent low Christology, influenced and supported Unitarian or Arian perspectives. *Apostolic Constitutions* figured in the Unitarian orientation of *Book of Common Prayer* revisions made by Cambridge professor William Whiston (*The Liturgy of the Church of England reduc'd nearer to the Primitive Standard* [1713]), Samuel Clarke of Saint James, Westminster, and others. The second generation of non-jurors, those unable to swear an oath of allegiance to William of Orange, also engaged in their own liturgical experimentations, some of which drew upon ancient sources including *Apostolic Constitutions*, the liturgies of eastern churches, and/or the Roman Catholic mass.[3] Other proposed revisions of the prayer book had the enthusiasts in mind. Samuel Roe of Bedfordshire encouraged purging from the prayer book the "corrupt Errors and extravagant Notions of the Holy Spirit" to avoid "adding Fuel to the Flames of Enthusiasm" manifest among "vain Bigots and Sceptic Methodists."[4]

1. Krysmanski, "We See a Ghost," 292–310. Krysmanski includes images of "Enthusiasm Delineated" and "Credulity, Superstition and Fanaticism" in his essay.

2. *Book of Common Prayer* (1662), preface.

3. For a study of prayer book revisions, see Peaston, *Prayer Book Reform Movement*.

4. Roe, *Another Pertinent and Curious Letter*, 23–26.

One critic of enthusiasm, identified only as "Eusebius" in the dedication of *A Fine Picture of Enthusiasm* (1744), posited, "religion is a *wise*, a *still*, and *silent* Thing, that consists not in *Frisks* of *Fancy*, and *Whirlwinds* of *Passion*; but in a *divine* Temper of Mind, and an universal *Resignation* of our Wills to God."[5] Later in the book, the author contrasted this definition with the song and singing of the "Methodists."

> [A]s to their *Singing*, they, perhaps, have got some of the *most melodious* Tunes that ever were composed for *Church Music*; there is *great Harmony* in their Singing, and it is very *inchanting* [sic]. I say very *inchanting*; because the Hymns they Sing, i.e. all I have seen or heard of, are not *rational* Compositions, nor do they accord with the first Principles of all Religion, but like their Prayers, dwell upon a Word, or are immediate Addresses to the *Son of God*, as the supreme Object of Worship: And do represent him as much *more* friendly and compassionate to the human World than God the Father ever was—So that their *Singing* is calculated to engage the *Passions* by nothing more than Words, and the Melody of the Sounds, or Voices; but, if you would sing with *Understanding*, or have a Reason of Praise, or pray with the *Understanding*, you must have other Sorts of Compositions both for *Psalmody* and *Prayer*, than what the Foundery or the Tabernacle do afford you.[6]

The term "Foundery" here refers to the building in Moorfields, London, used by John Wesley and his followers from 1739 onward, and "Tabernacle" to the structure also at Moorfields built in 1741 by the followers of George Whitefield. In the eighteenth century, the terms "enthusiast" and "Methodist" were often synonymous. "Methodist," as a "stigma of reproach," was "first applied to Mr. Wesley's, Whitfield and their followers," for though they claimed attachment to the established church and disavowed designation as dissenters, they were "not conformists in point of parochial order, but had separate seasons, places and assemblies of worship." The term then broadened beyond Wesley and Whitefield in the description to include "all persons, whether clergy or laity, who preach or profess the doctrines of the reformation, as expressed in the articles and liturgy of our church."[7] Thus, "Methodists" were also (for the most part) "Anglicans." To these persons the term "evangelical" also applied as active participants in the wider evangelical revival that during this time transcended denomination and geography.

5. [Eusebius], *Fine Picture of Enthusiasm*, 14.
6. [Eusebius], *Fine Picture of Enthusiasm*, 24.
7. Scott, *Force of Truth*, 22. Scott was an evangelical clergyman.

Though loosely organized for most of the eighteenth century and a minority (and often persecuted) group within the Church of England, it was not until the nineteenth century that Evangelical Anglicans would constitute a more formal or official party. Such an informal alliance led to some fluidity as evident by the distinction made by "Eusebius" between Foundery and Tabernacle. Evangelical Anglicans defied simple definition: they were clergy and laity, men and women, persons who worked inside and outside of the Church of England's formal parish structures, and those who theologically tended more in the direction of Calvinism or inclined toward Arminianism.[8] Yet all held to what David Bebbington indicates as the four common features of Evangelicalism from the eighteenth century to the present: "*conversionism*, the belief that lives need to be changed; *activism*, the expression of the gospel in effort; *biblicism*, a particular regard for the Bible; and what may be called *crucicentrism*, a stress on the sacrifice of Christ on the cross."[9] Of these four, conversion took primary place because of the perceived need for the salvation of individual souls and with them the salvation of England, which in turn could be a means for the alleviation of the nation's social ills.

Most Evangelical Anglicans valued the liturgy of the Church of England's *Book of Common Prayer* (1662), and attended—or presided at, if clergy—the church's Lord's Day gatherings or morning and evening prayer. Sunday worship in most parish churches consisted of morning prayer, litany, ante-communion, and sermon; the Lord's Supper might be offered monthly, quarterly, or less. Evangelical Anglicans typically added other occasions for worship outside of church hours, including services with preaching and/or exhortation as well as prayer meetings. For these gatherings, clergyman John Berridge (1716–93) advised:

> When ye are assembled, behave with the same Gravity, as if ye were in God's House, avoiding all Compliments and Chit-chat, and how do-ye-do Questions. Let some one give out an Hymn or two; then read a Portion of the Scripture, and if any is able, let him give a Word of Exhortation; afterwards sing a few Hymns more; then *kneel* down, and offer up your Prayers unto God; afterwards, sing again, and depart.[10]

Hymn singing was usual at these extra liturgical sessions and, in some cases, made an irregular appearance during the church's liturgy—irregular,

8. On the theological and political complexities within Evangelical Anglicanism during the eighteenth century, see Danker, *Wesley and the Anglicans.*

9. Bebbington, *Evangelicalism in Modern Britain*, 2–3.

10. Berridge, *Collection of Divine Songs*, ix.

because a standing injunction of Elizabeth I (1559) only permitted hymns prior to or following common prayer; metrical psalmody was the approved liturgical repertoire. Permission for hymn singing in the liturgy proper came in 1820 with the Archbishop of York's approval of Thomas Cotterill's *A Selection of Psalms and Hymns*. However, not all evangelical clergy warmed to hymn singing to the exclusion of psalmody, among them William Romaine (1714–95). Romaine's *An Essay on Psalmody* (1775, second ed. 1778) intended to clarify the subject of the psalms "to restore the singing of them in the congregation to their primitive usefulness" especially at a time when hymn writers "thrust out the psalms to make way for their own compositions."[11]

Despite Romaine's reluctance, hymns "of human composure" flourished among the Anglican Evangelicals, either by the collection of hymns from previous sources, especially the texts of Congregationalist Isaac Watts (1674–1748) and Anglican Charles Wesley (1707–88), or the writing of original texts. Many new texts had a first printing in tracts or popular magazines and later found a place in larger collections. One such magazine was *The Gospel Magazine* begun in 1766 with the stated purpose of "the uncompromising declaration of the Gospel of Free Grace, both in belief and in practice." From December 1775 to June 1776, Evangelical Anglican clergyman Augustus M. Toplady (1740–78) served as the editor and used his position to rail against those Evangelicals who took a strong Arminian theological position, in particular John Wesley and his colleagues. Toplady was an outspoken Calvinist, and to serve notice on the Wesleyans had already published *The Church of England Vindicated from the Charge of Arminianism* (1769) and the two-volume *Historic Proof of the Doctrinal Calvinism of the Church of England* (1774). John Wesley's response in print came in several forms, including the establishment in 1778 of the *Arminian Magazine: Consisting of Extracts and Original Treatises on Universal Redemption* to counter the stress on predestination from other Evangelicals, and to provide a forum for the publication of new hymns Arminian in orientation.

THEOLOGICAL PERSPECTIVES

The original hymns of the Evangelical Anglicans, not surprisingly, took up the theological perspectives that so identified them. Scripture undergirded the theology articulated in the hymns and was textually present via quotation, paraphrase or allusion; some texts were a catena of biblical references drawn from different parts of the canon. A prominent theme was the saving

11. Romaine, *Essay on Psalmody*, iii, 104.

work of God revealed in the entirety of Scripture, but especially through the atonement wrought by Christ's crucifixion. These authors affirmed the consubstantial Trinity and their hymns assumed such, yet overall the hymns tend toward christocentricism because of the crucicentrist orientation. Numerous hymns contributed to the Church of England's annual liturgical cycle, with particular emphasis on Christ's incarnation/nativity, passion, and death. Hymns that prepare for, attend to, or reflect afterward upon the Lord's Supper appeared in several collections, but baptism hymns were rare likely because that sacrament was strongly associated with infancy. Conversion of heart or a new birth that claimed full assurance of faith, however, were common themes, and some compilers of hymnals incorporated autobiographical conversion narratives in prefaces to their hymn books. Christian experience, liberty, and work were regular topics. Hymns also circulated that assessed theologically the events or issues of the day, from the London earthquakes and the unrest in the American colonies, to England's drift toward Unitarianism/Arianism and scientific advancements such as electricity. In these texts, the author's or collector's own theological convictions relative to Arminianism or Calvinism are evident amidst the common themes. Most of the hymnals do not offer a systematic arrangement of hymns under groups of headings, though many do supply a thematic heading specific to a text.

The brothers John and Charles Wesley had not practiced their crafts of hymn writing, translating, and editing in the days of the Holy Club at Oxford, but began doing so in earnest following a brief stay in the American colonies. Already by 1744, Evangelicals in connection with the Wesleys were to "sing no hymns of your own composing"[12] lest they convey inappropriate teachings or create competition for the sales of the Wesleys' hymn tracts and pamphlets. Even so, a few Wesley associates circumvented these restrictions, among them Thomas Olivers (1725–99), who wrote "The God of Abraham Praise" inspired by the Jewish *Yigdal* that originated with Maimonides, and John Bakewell (1721–1819), whose name often appears with "Hail Thou once despised Jesus."

George Whitefield joined the Holy Club while a student at Oxford, and after leaving the university exercised his significant talent as a preacher. Whitefield too found his way to the colonies—multiple times—where he became a leader there in the Great Awakening. In England, he soon drew like-minded associates who favored his strategies for proclaiming the gospel and appreciated the content of his message that favored predestination. Whitefield's Calvinistic leanings precipitated a break with the Wesleys,

12. *Minutes of the Methodist Conferences*, 20.

symbolized by the construction of the Moorfields Tabernacle in 1741. Yet Whitefield retained the practice of singing and drew upon metrical psalms as well as the texts of Isaac Watts and the Wesleys for his gatherings outdoors and indoors, "society" meetings, and small-group devotions. He encouraged hymn writing and the publication of hymn collections among his coworkers. John Cennick (1718–55), who was a participant in the joint Methodist-Moravian society at Fetter Lane in London and one of Wesley's first lay preachers, aligned with Whitefield in 1741. In that same year, Cennick brought out *Sacred Hymns for the Children of God, in the Days of their Pilgrimage* with a lengthy autobiographical conversion account in the preface. A thematic heading stands above each hymn text, for example, "Going out, or Coming in" for his original "Be with me, Lord, where're I go," and "Grace before Meat" for his single stanza text "Be present at our Table, Lord: / Be Here, and Ev'ry Where ador'd; / Thy Creatures bless, and grant that we / May feast in Paradise with Thee."[13] Two years later, Cennick compiled *Sacred Hymns for the Use of Religious Societies: Generally composed in Dialogues* (1743), which provides several hymns where the words appear in plaintext or italics for male and female voices in alternation.[14] Thus, the first stanza of Hymn 7, "The Pilgrims Hymn, in a Dialogue" reads, "Tell us, O Women! We wou'd know / Whither so fast ye move? / *We call'd to leave the World below, / Are seeking one above*," and the song concludes, "Friends of the Bridegroom we shall reign: / Saviour, we ask no more: / *Hail Lamb of God for Sinners slain! / Whom Heaven and Earth adore!*" The headings in the collection indicate that Cennick had in mind ongoing use by the Wesleys' followers: Hymn 13 is "Compos'd for the Society in Kingswood" and Hymn 14 "An Hymn for the Feast of Charity" (or Lovefeast); both are in dialogue form, which enjoyed popularity at the time.[15] By 1745, Cennick joined the Moravians, and later may have played a role in the compilation of hymnbooks for that denomination.

Extra-parochial clergyman Robert Seagrave (1693–1760?), who worked with the Wesleys and Whitefield, and in *A Letter to the People of England* (1735) lamented what he perceived as the collapse of Anglican Calvinism, published his *Hymns for Christian Worship, Partly Composed, and Partly Collected from Various Authors* in 1742. Seagrave's primary intention was to use the book for singing at Loriners' Hall, London, where he served. The preface is remarkable for its defense of the singing of psalms and hymns in which Seagrave claimed, "[e]xercises of this sort, properly conversant

13. Cennick, *Sacred Hymns for the Children of God*, 161, 75.

14. Lightwood, "Tune Books of the Eighteenth Century," 107.

15. Cennick, *Sacred Hymns for the Use of Religious Societies*, 12–13, 19–23.

on the Subject of Free-Grace, are the most acceptable religious Service Believers can possibly offer." He then asserted, contrary to the stance of John Wesley: "In my Opinion every religious Assembly, with Reverence and Sobriety, may lawfully use even their own Compositions, provided they speak a Language altogether agreeable to Scripture, and such as arises from true Christian Experience. This I conceive a Part of Christian Liberty, as much as to pray or preach in our own Words."[16] True to this sentiment, Seagrave included his own compositions over the course of four editions, notably among them the eschatologically oriented "Rise my Soul, and stretch thy Wings" and "Now may the Spirit's Holy Fire," which stresses the Comforter's work in making songs more than "vain addresses." Daniel Sedgwick republished the entire corpus of Seagrave's hymnic work in 1860 as *Hymns and Spiritual Songs for Christian Worship*.

The year 1745 marked the departure of William Hammond (1719–93) from Whitefield for the Moravians as well as the printing of his *Psalms, Hymns, and Spiritual Songs*. A table of contents that lists topics shows attentiveness to the liturgical calendar, e.g., Christ's birth ("What Good News the Angels bring?"), circumcision ("See, my Soul, with Wonder see"), and other aspects of ecclesiastical life, including the consecration or dedication of a church building. A hymn with the heading "Steps or Degrees of Faith" placed into poetry what Hammond developed theologically in the preface and identified as his method for including texts: "some are fitted for those who are *Babes in Christ*, others for *Perfect Men*; some are adapted to the Condition of Souls who are *weak in Faith*; others are calculated for them that enjoy *a full Assurance of Faith*."[17] Hammond's hymn "Before Singing of Hymns" ("Awake, and sing the Song") concludes with a declaration of the role of singing on these steps leading to salvation: "Sing till you feel your Hearts / Ascending with your Tongues, / Sing till the Love of Sin departs, / And Grace inspires your Songs. / Sing till you hear CHRIST say / 'Your Sins are All forgiv'n.' / Go on rejoicing All the Way, / And sing your Souls to Heav'n."[18] Unusual for the time, some of the texts in the collection are translations made by Hammond from Latin originals.

Inspired by the hymnic output of his colleagues, and desirous of a book designed for his London Tabernacle, Whitefield published *A Collection of Hymns for Social Worship* (1753). The hymnal borrows heavily from Watts and the Wesleys.[19] Other writers figure as well, including Cennick and Sea-

16. Seagrave, *Hymns for Christian Worship*, iii–iv.

17. Hammond, *Psalms, Hymns, and Spiritual Songs*, iv.

18. Hammond, *Psalms, Hymns, and Spiritual Songs*, 86.

19. Charles Wesley's (not Whitefield's) hymn "Partners of a Glorious Hope" on p.

grave, with the former providing the last hymn ("Children of the heav'nly King") in the collection and the latter the first ("Now may the Spirit's Holy Fire"). There is no evidence to confirm that Whitefield wrote any of these, or any other, hymns. The headings that divide the collection into two parts indicate the intentions for the book's use—"Hymns for Public Worship," with the majority of texts, followed by "Hymns for Society and Persons meeting in Christian-Fellowship"—though both parts include texts that stress the personal and corporate experiences of salvation. The second part includes dialogue hymns, chosen since "something like it is practised in our Cathedral Churches, but much more so because the Celestial Choir is represented in the Book of the Revelations, as answering one another in their heavenly Anthems." Concerned that singers not be "obliged to sing Lies," some texts Whitefield "altered in some Particulars" including abbreviation, for he found three to four stanzas with a doxology sufficient lest weariness replace edification.[20] The original authors sometimes objected to these alterations, John Wesley among them, who complained that many of the brothers' texts now leaned more toward Calvinism.[21] Ignoring their distress, Whitefield's *Collection* appeared in multiple editions and, after 1756, the title page indicates use at Whitefield's chapel in Tottenham Court Road, London. Long after Whitefield's death, Matthew Wilks "corrected and enlarged" an edition in 1798, which itself went through several editions. Hymnal compilers—Evangelical Anglican and other—throughout the eighteenth century turned to Whitefield's book as a source for their own collections.

An ascription on the title page of the 1753 *Collection* linked Whitefield with "the Rt. Hon. the Countess of Huntingdon." Countess Selina Hastings (1707–91) became involved with the Wesleys, Whitefield, and their associates in the late 1730s and frequently offered her properties for their worship and meetings. She built chapels on her own land and elsewhere (e.g., Bath, Brighton, and Bristol), and invited Evangelicals who shared her Calvinist theological commitments to serve as chaplains, among them Whitefield. Appreciative of the value of hymn singing, Lady Huntingdon encouraged her chapels to publish their own hymn collections, many of which likely no longer exist. Her direct involvement in creating these collections is not clear, though one book with 289 hymns declared in its title *A Select Collection of Hymn to be universally sung in all the Countess of Huntingdon's Chapels, Collected by her Ladyship* (1780). Unclear also is her capacity as a hymn writer

130 in *Collection of Hymns for Social Worship* is the source for Hogarth's hymnic quotation quoted above.

20. Whitefield, *Collection of Hymns*, preface.

21. See Wesley's comments on textual emendation in his preface to *A Collection of Hymns for the Use of the People Called Methodists* (1780), dated 1779.

since no specific or confirmed text exists. By 1783, she had broken with the Church of England and accordingly registered her chapels as the dissenting Countess of Huntingdon's Connexion, and thereby at least formally severing her association with the Evangelical Anglicans.

Martin Madan (1725/26–1790) came into the orbits of the Wesleys, Whitefield, and the Countess of Huntingdon prior to ordination as an Anglican priest, contacts that shaped his service as chaplain at Lock Hospital in London's West End. As a charitable institution founded for the treatment of venereal diseases, Lock Hospital attracted benefactors from the musical arts, some of whose compositions inspired the melodies sung in the hospital chapel and eventually figured in Madan's *A Collection of Psalm and Hymn Tunes, Never Published Before* (1769, "The Lock Collection"). Madan contributed a few of his own tunes to the compilation, but there is no indication that he wrote completely original texts. He brought out in 1760 *A Collection of Psalms and Hymns* largely based on Whitefield's 1753 *Collection*, and exercised his own Calvinistic editorial hand to produce "scriptural" texts "most Useful for Edification in respect of Plainess and Simplicity of Expression" that "avoid inserting any thing that could tend to doubtful Disputations." He insisted on preserving in the hymns Christian fundamentals incompatible with Deist, Arian, Socinian, Papist, Antinomian, and Formalist viewpoints, and included as Hymn 142 a text "For the Arians, Socinians, Deists, Pelagians, &c." placed prior to the section "Gloria Patri" that contained trinitarian doxologies.[22] A section of "Sacramental Hymns" comprising twenty-seven texts and a single hymn "at dismission" concluded the book. Madan's *Collection* went through multiple editions and itself became a source for other hymn compilations, among them *A Collection of Psalms and Hymns, from Various Authors: for the Use of Serious and Devout Christians of all Denominations* (1767) by clergyman Richard Conyers (1725–86). More importantly, Madan's textual revision of hymns by Watts, the Wesleys, and others became the standard form for later hymnals.

By far one of the most systematically arranged hymnbooks was *A Collection of Divine Songs* (1760) of the aforementioned John Berridge, who intended the book for religious societies near his parish at Everton, Bedfordshire. A nine-part organizational system identified hymns for society gatherings; hymns prior to preaching; hymns for those seeking redemption; hymns for believers; hymns for backsliders; hymns for morning, evening, and the church's festivals; hymns for the Lord's Supper; hymns for the sick and for funerals; and hymns related to daily and pastoral life (e.g., mealtime, traveling). The majority of hymns came from the Wesleys, and these along

22. Madan, *Collection of Psalms and Hymns*, ii–v, 144–45.

with other texts were subject to revision especially in the instance of "hard words." Ultimately dissatisfied with *Collection*, particularly because of its "Levitical twang,"[23] Berridge during a sustained illness engaged further in the editing of existing texts and in his own hymn writing, with *Sion's Songs or Hymns* (1785) the result. *Sion's Songs* included some of Berridge's original hymns first published in *The Gospel Magazine*, including "Our [Since] Jesus freely did appear" for a wedding, which survived in numerous nineteenth-century hymnals.

While most of John Berridge's original hymns did not pass the test of time, the story is different for the texts of John Newton (1725–1807) and William Cowper (1731–1800), the latter cousin to Madan. Newton, former master of slave ships, in 1764 became curate of the parish in Olney, where he attended to parish duties, society meetings, and weekday preaching services. Cowper arrived in Olney in 1767 and took up responsibilities as Newton's lay assistant in spite of periodic episodes of mental instability. Each man encouraged the other in writing hymns principally for the praise and prayer of Christians at Olney, though they published some texts in *The Gospel Magazine* and Newton appended hymns by both of them to his *Twenty Six Letters on Religious Subjects* (1774). *Olney Hymns* (1779) contained their combined poetic efforts, the vast number by Newton, and came into print to "promote the faith and comfort of sincere Christians" but also as a memorial to their friendship. Since the intended recipients of the collection were "plain people," "[p]erspicuity, simplicity and ease" were of utmost concern.[24] *Olney Hymns* comprised three distinct "books" ("On Select Texts of Scripture," "On Occasional Subjects," On the Progress and Changes of the Spiritual Life"), each of which concluded with a table identifying the order and subjects of the hymns. The topics in the third book speak to the way of salvation, from "solemn addresses to sinners" and "seeking, pleading, and hoping" finally to "praise." The hymns themselves express a moderate Calvinism, which may in part explain their longevity and use by different Christian communities as well as the continued publication of *Olney Hymns* in numerous editions. Among Newton's widely known hymns in the collection are "Amazing Grace! (How Sweet the Sound)," "Glorious Things of Thee are Spoken," "How Sweet the Name of Jesus Sounds," and "Safely thro' another Week." Cowper's "God moves in a Mysterious Way" figures in the collection as do "Oh! For a closer Walk with God," "Sometimes a Light Surprizes," and "There is a Fountain fill'd with Blood."

23. Berridge, *Sion's Songs or Hymns*, iii.

24. [Newton and Cowper], *Olney Hymns*, vi, vii.

Evangelical clergy and laity continued to produce hymn collections in the last decades of the eighteenth century. Notable among these hymnbooks is Augustus Toplady's *Psalms and Hymns for Public and Private Worship* (1776) that, despite the compiler's theological disputes with the Wesleys, contained some of their (edited) texts. Toplady insisted that hymns and their collections keep in view that "God is the God of *Truth*, of *Holiness*, and of *Elegance*," especially since the "best Christians, in all ages, have been Hymn-Singers." In this light, he defined the singing of hymns as an ordinance of God, since it "has proved a *converting* Ordinance, to some of his people; a *recovering* Ordinance, to others; a *comforting* Ordinance, to them all: and one of the divinest Mediums of communion with God, which his gracious benignity has vouchsafed to his church below."[25] A hymn writer as well as a compiler and editor, Toplady is best known for "Rock of Ages, Cleft for Me." Another significant collection was *Carmina Christo* (1792) by Thomas Haweis (1734–1820), who at one time had been an assistant to Madan at the Lock Hospital and a chaplain to Lady Huntingdon. Multitalented, Haweis wrote both texts and tunes, for he found that "no other method of communicating the knowledge of religious truths hath been attended with happier effects, or serves to leave deeper impression of them on the memory and conscience of the common people, than sacred songs."[26]

CONTRIBUTION TO LITURGY AND WORSHIP

Despite the objections to "enthusiasm," the popularity of hymns of the Evangelical Anglicans that emphasized both the praise of God and the "real" experience of a person from awakened sinner to born anew believer pressed the Church of England to permit hymn singing as part of the official liturgy. Already in the eighteenth century, many of the hymns easily permeated other ecclesial and ecclesiastical barriers, so that hymns by Evangelical Anglicans became part of the repertoire of congregational and choral song in the worship offered by Moravians, Congregationalist, Baptists, and others. English-speaking immigrants brought these songs with them, where texts and tunes implanted in new soil and spread widely. Most English-language hymnals in the twenty-first century contain a good representation of texts produced by these eighteenth-century hymnists.

25. Toplady, *Psalms and Hymns*, preface.

26. Haweis, *Carmina Christo*, preface.

NOTABLE HYMNS

Many notable hymns come from the Evangelical Anglican corpus. In addition to the texts already mentioned, others with the long histories are Cennick's "Jesus, My All, to Heav'n is Gone"; Newton's "Approach, my Soul, the Mercy Seat" and "One there is, above all Others"; and Cowper's "Jesus, where'er thy People Meet."

BIBLIOGRAPHY

Bebbington, David W. *Evangelicalism in Modern Britain: A History from the 1730s to the 1980s*. Boston: Unwin Hyman, 1989.

Berridge, John. *A Collection of Divine Songs, Designed Chiefly for the Religious Societies of Churchmen, in the Neighbourhood of Everton, Bedfordshire*. London: 1760.

———. *Sion's Songs or Hymns: Composed for the Use of them that Love and Follow the Lord Jesus Christ in Sincerity*. London: Printed for Vallance and Conder, 1785.

Cennick, John. *Sacred Hymns for the Children of God, in the Days of their Pilgrimage*. London: Printed and Sold by B. Milles, 1741.

———. *Sacred Hymns for the Use of Religious Societies: Generally composed in Dialogues*. Part 1. Bristol: Printed by Felix Farley, 1743.

Danker, Ryan. *Wesley and the Anglicans: Political Division in Early Evangelicalism*. Downers Grove, IL: IVP Academic, 2016.

[Eusebius]. *A Fine Picture of Enthusiasm, Chiefly Drawn by Dr. John Scott, formerly Rector of St. Giles's in the Fields*. London: Printed for J. Noon, 1744.

Hammond, William. *Psalms, Hymns, and Spiritual Songs*. London: Printed by W. Strahan, 1745.

Haweis, T[homas]. *Carmina Christo; Or, Hymns to the Saviour: Designed for the Use and Comfort of Those who Worship the Lamb that was Slain*. Bath: Printed and Sold by S. Hazard, 1792.

Krysmanski, Bernd. "We See a Ghost: Hogarth's Satire on Methodists and Conoisseurs." *The Art Bulletin* 80.2 (June 1998) 292–310.

Lightwood, James T. "Tune Books of the Eighteenth Century." *Proceedings of The Wesley Historical Society* 5.4 (1905) 101–8.

Madan, Martin. *A Collection of Psalms and Hymns, Extracted from Various Authors*. London: 1760.

Minutes of the Methodist Conferences, from the first, held in London, by the Late Rev. John Wesley, A.M. in the Year 1744. Vol. 1. London: Printed at the Conference Office by Thomas Cordeux, 1812.

[Newton, John, and William Cowper]. *Olney Hymns, in Three Books*. London: Printed and Sold by W. Oliver, 1779.

Peaston, A. Elliot. *The Prayer Book Reform Movement in the Eighteenth Century*. Oxford: B. Blackwell, 1940.

Roe, Samuel. *Another Pertinent and Curious Letter Humbly offered to the Public in Favour of a Revisal, and the Amendment, of our Liturgy*. Cambridge: Printed by Fletcher and Hodson, 1768.

[Romaine, William]. *An Essay on Psalmody*. London: 1775.

Scott, Thomas. *The Force of Truth: An Authentic Narrative*. London: Printed for G. Keith, 1779.

Seagrave, Robert. *Hymns for Christian Worship, Partly Composed, and Partly Collected from Various Authors*. 2nd ed. London: 1742.

Toplady, Augustus. *Psalm and Hymns for Public and Private Worship*. London: Printed for E. and C. Dilly, 1776.

Whitefield, George. *A Collection of Hymns for Social Worship*. London: Printed by William Strahan, 1753.

Chapter 18

Roman Catholic Hymnists

JONATHAN JAKOB HEHN

HISTORICAL BACKGROUND

THE ARCH OF HYMNODY in the Roman Catholic tradition between the Council of Trent (1545–63) and the present day can be represented by an inverted bell curve. At the beginning of the curve, that is, in the period following the liturgical reforms of the Council of Trent, there was a quick and precipitous decrease in the number of newly created hymns in the Catholic tradition, as well as a decrease in the amount of hymnody, vernacular or otherwise, that was sung in the context of liturgical or extra-liturgical celebrations. By the middle of the nineteenth century, that trend had been reversed, as a new flowering of hymnody coincided with a significant and fervent liturgical reform movement. That flowering, represented as the end of the curve, continued to the end of the twentieth century thanks to the work of the Second Vatican Council (1962–65). The eighteenth century, by contrast, represents the bottom of the curve, in which there was comparatively little activity. Nonetheless, some important figures and well-known hymns were penned during this period, some of which are still in popular use today. Latin and vernacular hymns, both newly composed and those previously existing, continued as an important part of Catholic worship. This chapter sketches that period of hymnological history for the Roman

Rite[1] of the Catholic Church and seeks to put in into a liturgical context, in order that scholars and practitioners of today might better understand this somewhat neglected segment of Catholic Church music history.

Latin Hymnody

Though vernacular hymnody had been sung in churches of the Roman Rite since the Middle Ages, it should be understood that Latin has nearly always been the officially preferred language of the Roman Catholic Church, including its hymnody. The best examples from the substantial corpus of Latin hymns written for the church over its first seventeen centuries continued to be sung in the eighteenth century. However, new Latin hymnody was also written during this time period, and those new works were incorporated into the worship life of the church, especially during the Divine Office, as local dioceses tended to produce breviaries for regional use that contained content by local authors. Cathedrals, monasteries, and large parishes with more substantial liturgical life and/or larger numbers of resident clergy or religious would have been most likely to use this Latin hymnody.

The Council of Trent (1545–63) had previously called for a revision of the liturgical books of the Roman Rite, including the breviary[2] and the missal.[3] In the Roman Catholic tradition, these books contain both liturgical text and music for the rites. Since hymns in this period were most often sung during the celebration of the Divine Office, the breviary would have comprised the main, or at least the official "hymnal" for the Roman Catholic liturgy in the post-Trent era.

Unlike the Vatican's new edition of the breviary, the new missal promulgated during the pontificate of Pius V (1566–72) was almost universally adopted after its publication. That missal had a significant (negative) impact on Roman Catholic hymnody. Sequences, for example (referred to in Latin variously as *sequentiae* or *prosae*), were a genre of hymns that had prior to Trent often been sung during the Mass, just after the Alleluia. By the latter part of the Middle Ages, these sequences numbered in the thousands, and were an important musical part of most Sunday and feast day Masses. Yet

1. This chapter does not address the Eastern Rite Catholic churches of this period, which have a very distinct history, one rich with its own hymnody.

2. The breviary is the liturgical book for the Divine Office.

3. Nathan Mitchell says that "strictly speaking, therefore, neither Trent nor Vatican II 'reformed' Roman Catholic worship. Instead, each called for the creation of papally appointed commissions to carry out that task." Foreward to White, *Roman Catholic Worship*, x.

after Trent, the number of sequences allowed was reduced to just five. These five sequences remained an important part of the Mass liturgy in the eighteenth century, mostly because they were sung on major feast days, when members of the general public were more likely to show up to worship.[4]

Although hymnody in the strict sense was very much still part of Catholic worship during this period, congregational hymn singing was not common, except in German-speaking areas as discussed below. The hymns of the Mass and the Divine Office were supposed to be sung exclusively by the clergy and choir. The congregation, when they were present, were largely spectators at these liturgical events. This was especially true in monastic churches, which not only had liturgical but sometimes also physical barriers separating the choir and presbytery areas from the nave, where the congregation would have been standing or seated. This separation between the congregation and the liturgical ministers[5] in the post-Trent era is often misunderstood to mean that there was only clergy participation in worship, which is not exactly the case. Though the congregation as a whole did not actively participate, at least in the singing, James White reminds us that choirs of the eighteenth century were commonly comprised of lay people rather than clergy as had been the case in earlier centuries.[6] Thus, at least with regard to hymn singing, one might more correctly say that in the eighteenth century there was a participation gap between the liturgical ministers and the congregation, rather than between the laity and the clergy.

Vernacular Hymnody

Vernacular hymnody in the Western Church by no means began with the Reformation, but is known to have begun already in the late Middle Ages. Pre-Reformation vernacular song was most commonly practiced in German-speaking areas of central Europe (*das Deutsche Sprachraum*),[7] and has been

4. These are *Lauda Sion* for the feast of Corpus Christi, *Stabat Mater* for the feast of Our Lady of Sorrows, *Victimae Paschali Laudes* for Easter, *Veni Sancte Spiritus* for the day of Pentecost, and *Dies Irae* for funerals/Masses for the Dead.

5. "Liturgical ministers" is here meant to indicate all of those nonordained leaders in worship, including both lay musicians as well as all of the "minor orders" that were abrogated after Vatican II.

6. White, *Roman Catholic Worship*, 42.

7. It is not proper to speak of "Germany" during this era, since those areas of central Europe now comprising Germany were at the time independent states, not to mention that there were other German-speaking areas such as Austria, Switzerland, parts of present-day Poland, the Alsace, etc.

most thoroughly documented by scholars writing in German.[8] However, vernacular hymn singing was common throughout the continent by the end of the Middle Ages, as well as in Britain, whose English-speaking residents still today cherish the medieval tradition of singing vernacular Christmas carols. Another rich tradition of vernacular carols exists in France, and one can see these in common usage still in the twentieth century. Similarly, Spanish-speaking regions of North America have a tradition of *alabados*, folk hymns that are often sung at para-liturgical events throughout the year.

In most cases in the late Middle Ages, vernacular hymns were incorporated "unofficially" across the liturgical spectrum; that is, at Mass, into the Divine Office, and at para-liturgical events such as processions on major feast days or services such as Benediction.[9] Such was the liturgical milieu regarding congregational song leading up to the Council of Trent. The council's attempt to achieve greater uniformity across the Roman Catholic Church and react to the burgeoning Protestant communities in Europe, the council fathers crafted policies regarding sacred music that, when later implemented, severely restricted the use of hymnody, especially vernacular hymnody, during worship.[10] At the same time, the council also set in motion a serious effort to revitalize the use of Gregorian Chant, including the hymns of the breviary and missal. Robert Hayburn reminds us that the revival of chant was slow at first, not culminating until the late nineteenth and early twentieth centuries. In the first two centuries following Trent, "the Chant of the Church was used principally by those who were obliged to recite or to sing the Divine Office in the canonical choir. At Mass in public it was little used."[11]

The perceived neglect of the chant was seen by the Catholic bishops at the Council of Trent as a deficit in need of correcting. Thus, as rites were revised up through the beginning part of the seventeenth century, Latin chant was increasingly promoted while restrictions were wrought on vernacular song. The most well-known document of this era to address vernacular hymnody in that way (as well as any extra-liturgical hymnody in Latin)

8. Detailed work can be found in Hochstein and Krummacher, *Geschichte der Kirchenmusik*, as well as the somewhat older Fellerer, *Geschichte der katholischen Kirchenmusik*.

9. See, for instance, Harnoncourt, *Gesamtkirchliche und teilkirchliche Liturgie*. Also see Beck, "Die Musik des liturgischen Gottesdienstes im 18," 186–88.

10. The implementation of liturgical reforms begun at Trent were actually achieved later via papal decree; the work of revision itself was done largely by a commission appointed by Pope Pius V.

11. "Sixteenth, Seventeenth, and Eighteenth Centuries," in Hayburn, *Papal Legislation*, 69–114.

was the 1749 encyclical *Annus Qui* promulgated by Pope Benedict XIV. In this work, Benedict speaks at great length about the perceived abuses in liturgical music in the Roman Catholic Church, and addresses the issue of vernacular music as part of his section on "motets."

> Suarez seems to be in favor of the chant [singing] of motets, even those written in the vernacular as long as they are serious and devout. To prove his assertion he invokes the habit and practice of some churches governed by wise prelates who do not condemn these canticles or rhythmical chants. He also adds that in the early stages of Christianity the faithful sang in Church those pious and devout hymns that sprang from their own piety and devotion; and that such an ancient practice serves in a certain way to approve the use of motets.
>
> But . . . in 1657, the Supreme Pontiff Alexander VII issued a Constitution . . . beginning with *Piae sollicitudinis,* in which he ordered not to sing during the Divine Office and during the exposition of the Blessed Sacrament for the public adoration of the faithful any hymn which is not formed from the words taken from the *Breviary* or *Roman Missal*. . . .
>
> Moreover, he willed and ordered musicians to follow all the rules of the Choir and to be always in perfect conformity with it. As it is not allowed in Choir to add anything to the Office of Mass, he also forbade musicians to make changes and allowed only some verses or motets to be taken without changing the words from the Office and the Mass.[12]

The promulgation and implementation of documents like *Annus Qui,* and of the already-mentioned Tridentine liturgical reforms, resulted in a great waning of vernacular hymnody in the seventeenth century across the Catholic Church. This was true both for the Office and for the Mass. However, the reforms of Trent and teaching of subsequent popes notwithstanding, there emerged in the seventeenth and also eighteenth centuries many local liturgical books that restored the pre-Reformation practice of allowing vernacular hymnody in the Mass and Office.[13] In some cases, bishops allowed for vernacular hymns to stand alongside a Low Mass or even replace

12. *Annus Qui*, as found in Hayburn, *Papal Legislation*, 100. The Suarez mentioned in this quote is Francisco Suarez, a Jesuit theologian to whose work De Religione Benedict XIV is referring.

13. Jungmann documents this practice with regard to the Mass, both in the pre-Reformation era and the late sixteenth century. Jungmann, *Mass of the Roman Rite*, 146–47.

the singing of the Latin propers.[14] With regard to the Office, the important breviary known as *Manuale Ecclesiasticum*, first published in Mainz in 1701 and reprinted throughout the eighteenth century, instructs that on some days German chorales are to be sung alongside the Latin antiphons.[15] During Second Vespers on Ascension Day, for instance, after the singing of the Latin antiphon *Ascendo ad Patrem* by a select group of singers, an instruction asks that the choir sing the German chorale *Christ fuhr gen Himmel.*[16] Likewise, after the sequence *Veni Creator Spiritus* is sung at Pentecost vespers, the *Manuale Ecclesiasticum* suggest the singing of *Nun bitten wir den Heiligen Geist* as the choir goes back to its place.[17]

Other areas of Europe seem not to have pushed for vernacular hymnody in the same way that German speaking areas did after the Council of Trent. This could be, perhaps, due to the fact that the other largely Catholic areas—France, Spain, Portugal, Italy—spoke Romance languages rather than Germanic ones, and so did not experience as large a discrepancy between the language of the liturgy and their spoken language. Scandinavian areas at this point in history were officially Lutheran and like Britain had not yet become open to Catholics, so any discussion of Catholic Hymnody in these areas is moot.

THEOLOGICAL PERSPECTIVES/CONTRIBUTIONS TO LITURGY AND WORSHIP

Many local breviaries were created and/or used during the eighteenth century, and there seem to have been two major reasons for their presence. The first and more basic reason is that many of the late-medieval Office hymns which populated breviaries of the sixteenth century were simply of substandard quality. The Council of Trent had called for a revision of the breviary

14. Jungmann, *Mass of the Roman Rite*, 154–55.

15. *Manuale Ecclesiasticum, pro Archdioecesi Mogutina.*

16. *"His peractis, reditur ad chorum, cantando: Christ fuhr den Himmel." Manuale Ecclesiasticum*, 139. It is uncertain what the exact performing forces of the choir [here "chorus"] are, but it is most likely that this was indeed a separate group of singers (whether lay or clergy) who sat and sang separately from the other liturgical ministers. This supposition is supported by the illustrations found in 1600 edition of the *Caeremoniale Episcoporum*, 134, 141.

17. "*Sequitur* Collecta. *Veni Creator Spiritus, ut sopra in Vesperis, fol. 146. Deinde duo superius, cantant tertio, elevando vocem: 'Accipite Spiritum Sanctum'* . . . *In regressum ad choram canitur 'Nun bitten wir den Heiligen Geist.'' Manuale Eceliasticum*, 154. The chorales in this book are part of the pre-Reformation collection of German chorales, and thus held in common by both Roman Catholics and Lutherans.

to correct the perceived errors of those late-medieval hymns, whether they be grammatical or theological.[18] It was of the utmost importance to the so-called "Counter Reformation" that Catholic Church teaching be clear and theologically accurate, including the teachings found in hymns sung during liturgy. Catholics, like their Protestant counterparts, recognized the ability of hymns and other music to foster faith and to teach its tenets. The Vatican itself produced the first new versions of both the breviary and missal in the decades after the council. However, as Hayburn relates:

> Pope Pius V promulgated the [post Trent] Missal and Breviary without giving attention to the chants contained therein. There had been no thought given to alterations in the melodies of the chant as a whole, the only changes were minor and involved the adaptation of corrected texts to the melodic line.[19]

That is, while texts had indeed been revised for the new Roman breviary, the melodies themselves had not. For Gregorian chant, which features such an intimate relationship between the text and a monophonic musical line, this has obvious negative implications.[20] Bishops concerned with the quality of worship in their diocese would have good reason to pursue a local revision that incorporated intelligent textual as well as musical revisions. Moreover, doing so kept with a centuries-long precedent of creating local "usages" of the Roman Rite. Pronouncements about liturgical uniformity from the Vatican after the Council of Trent, while seriously heeded in some places, seemed to carry little weight in others. Already in the late sixteenth century, some Spanish and Italian printers had produced chant books for their own local use that were "in conformity" with those produced by the Vatican. In some other places, such as France and Germany, the work of breviary revision was not only slow but also ongoing; many books initially printed in the early seventeenth century continued to be revised into the eighteenth century.

The second reason for the breviary revisions in the eighteenth century arose somewhat later, and is in a way at odds with the first. The philosophical/theological effects of the Enlightenment, known as the *Aufklärung* in German, cast a newly negative light on the theological emphases of

18. Hayburn, *Papal Legislation*, 27–30.

19. Hayburn, *Papal Legislation*, 34.

20. Bishop Blancicampianus of Vienne articulated the issue already in 1543, when he said that "even one vowel, incorrectly written, is able to make the sense of the words and prayers perverse and heretical, therefore those most important books which are accustomed to be used, which they call missals and breviaries, ought to be most carefully written and edited." Hayburn, *Papal Legislation*, 26.

late-medieval and even some Counter-Reformation hymns. The great flurry of textual revisions to the chant made through the seventeenth century had largely been concerned with improving medieval works that still reflected that era's theological emphases. Even in 1749, Benedict XIV's *Annus Qui* continues to reflect Trent when he speaks of sacred music in these rather medieval terms:

> This is the chant that excites the souls of the faithful to devotion and piety; it is also this chant which, if executed in God's churches according to the rules and with decorum, is more willingly listened to by devout men, and more rightly preferred to chant called figurative.[21]

For Benedict, fostering a sentiment of piety and dutifully following the rules of the liturgy are of high importance; he thus reflected the type of late-medieval thought to come out of the Council of Trent's calls for chant reform. Enlightenment thought, which was starting to emerge even at the beginning of the eighteenth century, promoted more rationalist, educational, and overtly moral/ethical ideals that conflicted with more mystical and devotional medieval sensibilities. Leonard Swidler gives a good summation of how this theological shift affected hymnody:

> The emphasis in Aufklärung church music on moral instruction and motivation for the most part produced music and hymns that were "free from fanaticism and exaggeration in both thought and expression." The titles themselves of many of the hymns indicate this characteristic. They included such as the following: On an Understanding Reading of the Bible, On the Love for Virtue, On the Growth in Virtue, On the Knowledge of Oneself, On the Overcoming of Faults in Charity, On Friendship, On Mercy, On the Avoidance of Pious Pride, and On the Enjoyment of Life.[22]

Though the two main impetuses for the revision of the breviaries in the eighteenth century seem to be at odds with one another, they together resulted in a significant process of hymnody reform across the Catholic Church. Such reform is most notable in France and the German *Sprachraum.*

In France, a new breviary published in 1736 for the diocese of Paris was adopted by more than fifty local dioceses and thus saw widespread use. It contained only twenty-one hymns from the age before the Council of Trent and well over two hundred newly composed hymns by French authors, thus

21. *The Liturgy*, 51.

22. Swidler, *Aufklärung Catholicism*, 31.

making it a thoroughly local and decidedly contemporary book. Samuel Willoughby Duffield, in his book *The Latin Hymn Writers and Their Hymns,* carefully details the story and contents of this breviary at its associated personalities.[23] A few of the contemporary writers from the Paris breviary remain important figures in hymn writing even today. Charles Coffin is the foremost of these; others include Guillaume de la Brontière, Nicolas le Tourneux, Sebastian Benault, Isaac Habert, and Jean Comire.

Some German bishops also made revised breviaries for their dioceses that contained both Latin hymns and some vernacular hymns.[24] Mainz seems to have been the most important location for the production of books in the German *Sprachraum* in this time period, though it was by no means the only one. Because German-speaking areas continued to use vernacular hymnody in the Office and at Mass into the eighteenth century, it is that vernacular repertoire that is considered here. In addition to brevaries, German-speaking areas produced a host of books for general use in the eighteenth century. These *Gesangbücher* contained German hymns for use at Mass as well as other liturgies, and were doubtless used for devotional or paraliturgical activities as well. Some examples include Nickolaus Beuttner's *Catholische Gesang-Buoch* (Graz, 1602–1718), the *Catholische Cantual oder Psalmbüchlein* (Mainz, 1605–1780), *Alt vnd newe Geistliche/Catholische/Ausserlesene Gesäng* (Würzburg, 1628–1716), *Geistliche Gesänger Und Gebetter* (Heidelberg, 1717), Martin von Cochem's *Catholisches Cantual* (Mainz, 1745), and many others.[25] Michael Härting provides a comprehensive list of individually notable figures in his article on Enlightenment hymnody in *Geschichte des katholischen Kirchenmusik.*[26]

It is no surprise that when collections of vernacular hymns began to appear for use by German Roman Catholics, Lutheran hymnody was well represented. Andrea Neuhaus has clearly documented that by the end of the sixteenth century, the plethora of Roman Catholic hymnals that had appeared in the German speaking areas were full of "Protestant" hymns.[27] Neuhaus also believes that the presence of Protestant hymns in Catholic books at the end of the seventeenth century was not born out of a great ecumenical desire, but rather so that Protestants might be lured back into the Roman Catholic communion. Swidler also documents a substantial

23. Duffield, *Latin Hymn Writers,* 328–46.

24. Chupungco, *Handbook for Liturgical Studies,* 164.

25. A detailed list and history of this type of book can be found in Neuhaus, "Barockzeit (17. and 18. Jahrhunderts)," in Fugger and Scheidgen, *Geschichte des katholischen Gesangbuchs,* 11–18.

26. Fellerer, *Geschichte der katholischen Kirchenmusik,* 2:174.

27. Fugger and Scheidgen, *Geschichte des katholischen Gesangbuchs,* 16.

and purposeful borrowing of Protestant hymns by Catholics in his book on Enlightenment-era Catholicism, but unlike Neuhaus is of the opinion that seventeenth century compilers found these hymns to actually resonate with their own beliefs:

> In their publishing of new church hymnals Aufklärung Catholics did not hesitate to include many Protestant hymns. While the Aufklärung Catholics obviously thought that they were improving the religious quality of the Catholic worship service by drawing upon these Protestant hymns, conservative Catholic writers since that time have very often treated such action in itself as very close to treason. However, in speaking on this matter, the open, but cautious, Waldemar Trap wrote: "Nevertheless both prayer books [which included a large number of hymns by Protestant authors] almost throughout also contained many valuable and beautiful hymns."[28]

Swidler goes on to quote the hymnal editor Benedict Maria von Werkmeister, who included some forty-eight Protestant hymns in his 1784 hymn book for the Catholic Court Chapel in Duchy of Württemberg. The introduction to that book says the following: "In this collection only such hymns have been chosen which recommend practical Christianity and which can be sung by all Christians of our country without their being disturbed in their devotion by the presentation of a foreign belief."[29] Based on this assessment, one can see how Werkmeister and others assembling general-use Catholic hymnals in this period were just as sensitive to how well the hymns in their collections reflected Enlightenment values as they were to how "Catholic" the theology was. Such an open, ecumenical approach to religion is typical of Enlightenment values.[30] Moreover, many Lutheran chorales served not only as ready-made vernacular substitutes for traditional Latin liturgical texts, but there was a plethora of freely composed chorales also appointed for specific Sundays and feasts of the liturgical year. Thus it's appropriate to mention in this chapter on Catholic hymnody such Lutheran hymnists as Christian Fuerchtegott Gellert and Friedrich Gottlieb Klopstock.

In the areas just mentioned there was a fair bit of liturgical consonance between Lutherans and Catholics. However, the situation was different in

28. Swidler, *Aufklärung Catholicism*, 32.

29. Swidler, *Aufklärung Catholicism*, 32.

30. The most obvious case making this point is the series of reforms led by the Holy Roman Emperor Joseph II (1741–90), who despite being the emperor of that most Roman Catholic of kingdoms, issued an Edict of Tolerance in 1782 that extended significant new freedoms to Protestants, Orthodox, and even Jews.

majority Reformed or Anglican communities. Not only was the liturgy in both these traditions less parallel to the Roman Rite, but they also restricted their congregational singing to metrical psalmody in the eighteenth century, a repertoire that is not particularly useful in the Roman Rite. That being said, Anglican parishes had begun introducing some non-Scripture based hymnody into worship by the eighteenth century. Certainly some of the flowering of vernacular hymns from Anglican circles in the decades following made its way into the repertoire of English-speaking Roman Catholics. At least by the time of the Oxford Movement in the early- to mid-nineteenth century, one sees extensive borrowing of hymns between Anglicans and Roman Catholics. However, before the Roman Catholic Relief Act of 1791, Catholics in England worshipped in secret, so it's nearly impossible to ascertain what exactly the practices of hymnody were for English Catholic communities in the eighteenth century. Reformed communities on the continent also began introducing hymnody into worship in the eighteenth century, and some of that Reformed repertoire may have been incorporated into Roman Catholic worship in those areas, especially where Germanic languages were spoken. Lutheran hymns were present in a number of European *Sprachräume*, too, not just German ones, especially those populated by both Lutherans and Roman Catholics.

NOTABLE HYMNISTS

The important aspects of eighteenth century Roman Catholic hymnody have mostly to do with various liturgical books and regulations rather than with individual hymnists. However, a handful of influential figures do bear mentioning. They and their works have had a lasting impact on Roman Catholic hymnody, insofar as the works continue to be sung by Catholics of today.

Charles Coffin (1676–1749) was the rector of the University of Paris and a noted Jansenist who contributed around one hundred new hymns to the 1736 Paris breviary.[31] These same hymns were published in separately that same year in the book *Hymni Sacri Auctore Carolo Coffin.* Many of Coffin's hymns were later translated into English and appeared in Henry Newman's *Hymni Ecclesiae* (1838), William Henry Monk's *Hymns Ancient and Modern* (1861) and Ralph Vaughan Williams's *The English Hymnal*

31. Jansenism was a Catholic theological movement, primarily in France, that emphasized original sin, human depravity, the necessity of divine grace, and predestination. The movement originated from the posthumously published work of the Dutch theologian Cornelius Jansen, who died in 1638.

(1906). By far the most commonly known of Coffin's hymns today is "*Jordanis oras praevia*," known in English as "On Jordan's Bank the Baptist's Cry." Other commonly translated texts are the two Advent/Christmas hymns "*Quem stella sole pulchrior*" ("What star is this, with beams so bright") and "*Instantis adventum Dei*" ("The advent of our King"), and the evening hymn "*Labente jam solis rota*," ("As now the sun's declining rays"). Though Coffin's theological predilections are not too readily apparent in his hymnody, one can detect the Jansenist emphasis on God's providence and grace in a number of the hymns listed above. More obvious is the liturgical orientation of Coffin's hymns. They were, after all, meant to be sung in the context of the Divine Office, to which the cycles of the liturgical year are of the utmost importance.

Ignaz Franz (1719–90) was a Catholic priest who was born in Protzan bei Frankenstein, Silesia, a small town also known as Protzau in what is now Southwest Poland. He was educated at the University of Breslau and ordained a priest in 1742. He is known to have edited more than one hymn book that shows the influences of the Enlightenment. Though his overall output isn't particularly notable, he is credited with the ubiquitous text "*Grosser Gott, Wir Loben Dich*," which is based on the ancient Latin hymn *Te Deum laudamus.* "Grosser Gott" is often translated as "Holy God, We Praise Thy Name." That hymn was first found in one of the hymnals he edited, the *Katholisches Gesangbuch* of 1744.

John Frances Wade (1711–86) is commonly given attribution for both of text and tune of the universally known hymn "Adeste Fidelis," sung in English as "O Come, All Ye Faithful." From a hymnological standpoint, it is really the hymn that is more notable than Wade himself. Wade was noted as one of the Jacobites, a large and heavily Catholic political group that supported restoration of the Stuart line of monarchs in Britain. Bennett Zon has opined that this hymn is really an ode to Charles Edward Stuart, the Jacobite pretender known as "Bonnie Prince Charlie," and that it contains a veiled call for his restoration to the throne.[32] Taken from a strictly theological perspective, "*Adeste Fidelis*" does a wonderful job knitting together Christmas liturgical themes with the texts of the Nicene Creed and *Gloria in Excelsis.*

A notable Marian hymn from this era is "*O Sanctissima.*" Popularly known as the "Sicilian Mariner's Hymn," "*O Sanctissima*" is a Latin hymn of unclear origin that first appeared in truncated form in 1792 in an issue of *The European Magazine and London Review.*[33] It has since become one of the most widely used Marian hymns, still sung in Latin by many

32. Durham University News, "O Come All Ye Faithful."

33. *The European Magazine*, 22:342

Catholic congregations. While Marian devotion among both Catholics and Protestants may have waned during the eighteenth century due to Enlightenment influences, Marian hymnody nonetheless remained an important Roman Catholic tradition for most. In fact, Stephanie Budwey reminds us, "In the Enlightenment period Rome became even 'more defensive' in light of rationalism . . . and 'restraints' on popular devotions, including those to Mary."[34] That is, though some circles of the Roman Catholic Church openly embraced the Enlightenment, other circles manifested their strong allegiance to traditional Catholic teaching in the form of an intense Marian devotion.

Though not actually written in the eighteenth century, one might also mention the hymn "Hail Queen of Heaven, the Ocean Star" as a notable example of Marian devotion from this era. "Hail Queen of Heaven" is one of the oldest vernacular English hymns of any genre stemming from the Roman Catholic tradition.[35] It is loosely based on the Latin hymn *Ave Maris Stella*, and was written by the English Catholic Priest John Lingard, who was born in 1771 and died in 1851. In addition to being a well-noted theologian, Lingard was a highly respected and influential historian of England who was trained in present-day France at the English College at Douai.

Finally, the composers from the First Viennese School are worth mentioning for tunes they composed that are now in common usage as hymn tunes. First is Joseph Haydn (1732–1809), who in 1797 composed the anthem "Gott erhalte Franz den Kaiser," which is known by the tune name AUSTRIAN HYMN. That tune has since fallen out of favor because of its use as a national anthem by Hitler's Third Reich. Second is Wolfgang Amadeus Mozart (1756–91), who is attributed with the tunes ELLESDIE and ARIEL. Lastly, though he composed it in 1824, Ludwig von Beethoven's (1770–1827) tune HYMN TO JOY ("An die Freude") is an important tune both for its widespread use and its association with music of the Enlightenment.

BIBLIOGRAPHY

Beck, Hermann. "Die Musik des liturgischen Gottesdienstes im 18. Jahrhundert (Messe, Offizium)." *Geschichte der Kirchenmusik*. Vol. 2: Das 17. und 18. Jahrhundert. Laaber: Laaber-Verlag, 2012. 186–88.

Budwey, Stephanie A. *Sing of Mary: Giving Voice to Marian Theology and Devotion*. Collegeville, MN: Liturgical, 2014.

Caeremoniale Episcoporum: Editio Princeps (1600). Vatican City: Libreria Editrice Vaticana, 2000.

34. Budwey, *Sing of Mary*, 93.

35. Budwey, *Sing of Mary*, 31.

Chupungco, Anscar. *Handbook for Liturgical Studies: Introduction to the Liturgy.* Collegeville, MN: Liturgical, 1997.

Duffield, Samuel Willoughby. *The Latin Hymn Writers and Their Hymns.* New York: Funk and Wagnalls, 1889.

Durham University News. "'O Come All Ye Faithful'—Bonnie Prince Charlie and the Christmas Carol." December 19, 2008. https://www.dur.ac.uk/news/newsitem/?itemno=7328.

Fellerer, Karl Gustav, ed. *Geschichte der katholischen Kirchenmusik.* Vol. 1: Von den Anfängen bis zum Tridentinum. Kassel: Bärenreiter, 1972.

Fellerer, Karl Gustav, ed. *Geschichte der katholischen Kirchenmusik.* Vol. 2: Von Tridentinum bis zur Gegenwart. Kassel: Bärenreiter, 1976.

Fugger, Dominik, and Andres Scheidgen, eds. *Geschichte des katholischen Gesangbuchs.* Göttingen: Francke, 2008.

Harnoncourt, Philipp. *Gesamtkirchliche und teilkirchliche Liturgie: Studien zum liturgischen Heiligenkalender und zum Gesang im Gottesdienst unter besonderer Berücksichtigung des deutschen Sprachgebiets.* Freiburg: Herder, 1974.

Hayburn, Robert F. *Papal Legislation on Sacred Music: 95 A.D. to 1977 A.D.* Collegeville, MN: Liturgical, 1979.

Jungmann, Josef. *The Mass of the Roman Rite: Its Origins and Development.* Vol 1. New York: Benziger Bros, 1951.

The Liturgy: Papal Teachings. Boston: Daughters of St. Paul, 1962.

Manuale Ecclesiasticum, pro Archdioecesi Mogutina. Mainz: Joannis Mayeri, 1701.

The Philological Society of London. *The European Magazine and London Review: Containing the Literature, History, Politics, Arts, Manners, and Amusements of the Age* 22 (July-December 1792).

Swidler, Leonard. *Aufklärung Catholicism 1780–1850: Liturgical and Other Reforms in the Catholic Aufklärung.* Missoula, MT: Scholars, 1978.

White, James. *Roman Catholic Worship: Trent to Today.* 2nd ed. Collegeville, MN: Liturgical, 2003.

Chapter 19

George Friedrich Händel

Musical Theology that Is Christological, Soteriological, and Supernatural

Michael F. Lloyd

HISTORICAL BACKGROUND

Although born in the same year, the careers of Johann Sebastian Bach (1685–1750) and George Friedrich Händel (1685–1759) went in different directions. Unlike Bach, Händel was not a church musician—apart from a brief spell in "the prestigious post of organist of the Domkirche"[1] in Halle from 1702 to 1703. He went from being organist in Halle to working at the opera house in Hamburg, and remained first and foremost a composer of dramatic music (opera and oratorio) for the rest of his life. He therefore had far less influence on the hymn *per se* than did Bach. Indeed, we know of only three hymns for which Händel himself composed tunes, of which only one is in common liturgical use today, and even these were "composed in a genre that was probably intended for private devotions rather than public worship."[2] These three hymns, the words of which were all written

1. Keates, *Handel*, 10.

2. Burrows, *Handel*, 393. However, in a personal communication, Andrew J. Newell writes: "I would be tempted to challenge this. It's not an incorrect statement,

by Charles Wesley (1707–88), are probably more important for what they contribute (cumulatively) to an understanding of Händel's religious views than for what they contribute to any history of the development of hymnody. A number of tunes written by Händel for other contexts have been put to service as hymn tunes,[3] and there exists in Händel's hand the opening line of one chorale tune (usually sung today in the Anglican tradition to the words, "The duteous day now closeth"), which he did not compose. That is the sum total of Händel's contribution to hymnody, strictly understood, and it is far less significant than his contribution either to the Church Anthem[4] (through the Chandos Anthems and the Coronation Anthems) or to the choral singing tradition in the UK. If, however, one allows a somewhat wider definition of hymnody as the communication of theological conviction through musical means, and if one considers a wider cultural context than the ecclesiastical, then, as we shall see, the contribution of Händel was arguably immense.

No meeting is known between Händel and either John or Charles Wesley. The connection seems to have been through the family of John Rich (1692–1761). John Rich was an impresario who inherited Lincoln's Inn Fields Theatre from his father, introduced pantomime to the English stage, and acted the (silent) part of Harlequin in such a way as to win the admiration of David Garrick. He was a friend of Alexander Pope—and the butt of Pope's satirical humor.[5] The success of *The Beggar's Opera*, with words by John Gay and music by Johann Christoph Pepusch, at the Lincoln's Inn Fields Theatre, famously made Rich very gay and Gay very rich. Rich was an important figure in Händel's life, and in his business dealings in particular. Many of Händel's operas and oratorios were put on at Rich's opera houses, and he left Rich his "Great Organ" in his will.[6] According to Charles Wesley's daughter, Sarah (or Sally), Händel taught Rich's daughters music.[7]

---

insofar as it is attempting to distance the hymns from the liturgical setting in which they came to be used—the hymns of the evangelical movement were not written for use in the church necessarily. But they were written for public worship, in the form of the *koinonia*—the methodist societies which gathered together in corporate, informal worship (which one might call public). The hymns were used for private devotions by individuals, but this was neither their primary function nor intention."

3. See Temperley, "Adaptations," in Landgraf and Vickers, *Cambridge Handel Encyclopedia*, 5–7.

4. For a study of Händel's English church music, see Burrows, *Handel and the English Chapel Royal.*

5. See Pope's *Dunciad Variorum* (1732) lll.1.257–260, where Rich appears in the role of the angel of the goddess Dulness!

6. See Burrows, *Handel*, 378, fn. 103.

7. See *The Wesleyan-Methodist Magazine* for December 1826, 11. It should be

Rich's third wife, Priscilla, is known to have had Methodist sympathies, and it seems to have been through her that Händel became aware of the Wesley texts. The connection between Priscilla Rich and the Wesleys appears well established: Charles Wesley's journal entry for Saturday, October 26, 1745 says: "Dined at Mrs. Rich's. The family concealed their fright tolerably well. Mr. Rich behaved with great civility. I foresee the storm my visit will bring upon him."[8] It is also clear that music played a significant role on the occasions when Charles Wesley visited the Riches socially: his journal reveals that he met there both Mr. Lampe[9] (the composer of the tunes to which the three hymns were set in the publications where Händel probably first encountered them) and Dr. Pepusch[10] (the composer of *The Beggar's Opera*).

Händel seems to have taken the texts for all three hymns from *Hymns on the Great Festivals and Other Occasions*, published in 1746[11]—"the first Methodist collection to have both words and music."[12] In these publications, the music was written by a Saxon called J. F. Lampe (1703–51), who played the bassoon in the opera house orchestra (and may therefore have played under Händel's conducting). Lampe clearly knew John Wesley, as well as Charles, as the former's journal for November 29, 1745, contains the note: "I spent an hour with Mr. Lampe, who had been a Deist for many years, till it pleased God, by the 'Earnest Appeal' to bring him to a better mind."[13]

Deism was, of course, one of the great intellectual movements of Händel's day, and constituted a considerable threat to orthodox Christian belief, not least in its rejection of miracles. The robust and joyful reassertion (pace the Deists) of belief in the ascension in "Rejoice, the Lord is King!" would have been knowing on the part of Charles Wesley, and setting such words would have presented an attractive opportunity to one such as Lampe who had seen cause to leave Deism behind—and, indeed, I shall argue, to Händel

noted that Sarah was not born until 1759—the year Händel died—so her knowledge of this is clearly second-hand.

8. Wesley, *Manuscript Journal*, 451. (It seems as if the editor has added the full name, and that the manuscript simply refers to "Mrs. R's." and "Mr. R." Thomas Jackson, in his 1849 edition, regards the identification of Mr. and Mrs. Rich as merely probable.) John Wilson comments: "We must not forget the hostility, both intellectual and physical, that the early Methodists and their sympathisers could then experience"—Wilson, "Handel's Tunes for Charles Wesley's Hymns," 34.

9. See the entry for March 29, 1746, in Wesley, *Manuscript Journal*, 456.

10. See the entry for April 29, 1748, in Wesley, *Manuscript Journal*, 529.

11. See Burrows's edition of *Complete Hymns and Chorales*, 2.

12. Wilson, "Handel's Tunes for Charles Wesley's Hymns," 32.

13. Wesley, *Works of John Wesley*, 1:523. The reference to the "Earnest Appeal" is to his publication, *An Earnest Appeal to Men of Reason and Religion*, first published in three parts, in 1743.

himself.[14] We shall explore this further in the section on the significance of these three hymns for the light they can shed on Händel's theology.

THEOLOGICAL PERSPECTIVES

One of the many difficulties in attempting to reconstruct Händel's theological views is that any reference to the texts he set is open to the objection that jobbing composers cannot be choosers, and therefore little can safely be read into his "choice" of texts. One of the interesting aspects of his setting of these three hymns is that it is unlikely that there was any pecuniary motivation to do so, and I suggest that more, therefore, may be read into the fact that he nevertheless agreed to set them. Even allowing for some sense of social obligation to Mrs. Rich, it is, I suggest, implausible that Händel would have set words with which he was significantly out of sympathy theologically. This consideration is the more compelling when we bear in mind John Wilson's urging that "We must not forget the hostility, both intellectual and physical, that the early Methodists and their sympathisers could then experience."[15] That Händel nevertheless allowed his name to be associated with the writings of Charles Wesley and the worship of the early Methodist movement suggests a degree of personal investment in the (albeit minor) project.

Methodologically, it would be safest to proceed by restricting ourselves to those theological aspects of these hymns that are common to other texts that he chose to set. Ruth Smith locates the libretti of the oratorios against the "background of energetic debate" between Deists and orthodox Christians, arguing that, when seen against that background, the libretti "appear more polemical, more committed and more complex than we had realized. When they are read alongside the topics of the debate and the arguments of the orthodox defense they are seen to bear so close a relation to that defense as to seem part of the response to contemporary freethinking."[16] The implications to be drawn from Händel's setting of these Wesley hymns support that contention in three ways.

14. For a discussion of John Wesley's attitude to Deism, see Chapter 4, on Deism and "True Christianity," in Ewbank, *John Wesley*, 51–67. For a discussion of the attitude to Deism demonstrated in Händel's oratorios, see Chapter 6, on the defense of Christianity, in Smith, *Handel's Oratorios*, 141–56. I have also argued that Händel's theology was *historical* to an extent that could be read as consciously constituting a defense of orthodox Christian faith against the Deists' ahistorical faith. See Lloyd, "Towards an Outline of Handel's Theology," 151–66.

15. Wilson, "Händel's Tunes," 34.

16. Smith, *Handel's Oratorios and Eighteenth-Century Thought*, 142.

First, they support the contention that Händel's theology was essentially *christological*.[17] Lord Herbert of Cherbury distilled the essence of Deism into five principles, which he believed would be common to all deists. They have been summarized as follows:

> First, is their belief in one supreme God. Second, this supreme God is the one who ought to be worshipped by all men. Third, the two chief parts of worshipping this God are virtue and piety. Fourth, we ought to be sorry for the sins that we have committed, and repent of them. Fifth, the goodness of God relates to man by His giving rewards and punishments to men, both in this life and the life to come.[18]

Notice how, in this Deist schema, there is no mention of Christ. How different from all three of the Wesley hymns that Händel set! *The Invitation* introduces Christ into the narrative of His parables, and is even explicitly Trinitarian in its appeal to the sinner:

> The Father, Son, and Holy Ghost
> *Is* ready with Their shining Host.

The Trinity, too, was the target of Deist attack.[19] "Rejoice, the LORD is King!" focuses on Jesus as King, as Ascended Savior, as Ruler and as Judge. *Desiring to love* is all about "The Love of CHRIST to me." That which the Deists rejected is made the cornerstone of Wesley's theology and devotion. Given the way in which *Messiah* may be seen as a defense of biblical prophecy against the assaults of the Deists,[20] and an insistent reading of the Old Testament through the lens of Christ, Händel's setting of these hymns suggests that it was the cornerstone of his, also.

Second, just as there is nothing christological in Lord Herbert of Cherbury's Deist schema, so there is nothing *soteriological*. As we shall see, Wesley's hymns express an objective understanding of the atonement, which, I have suggested, is reflective of Händel's substitutionary view of the cross.[21] This is undoubtedly the view embodied in *Messiah*—"All we like sheep have gone astray; we have turned every one to his own way. And the LORD hath laid on Him the iniquity of us all"[22]—and his operas and oratorios are full

17. See Lloyd, "Towards an Outline of Handel's Theology," 156–58.

18. Ewbank, *John Wesley*, 52.

19. Smith, *Handel's Oratorio*, 142.

20. See the final section of this chapter, on Händel's "Contribution to Liturgy and Worship."

21. See Lloyd, "Towards an Outline of Handel's Theology," 159–61.

22. Isaiah 53:6. See also, "Surely He hath borne our griefs, and carried our sorrows!

of people who die, or seek to die, for another, such as Didymus and Theodora.[23] Indeed, John Wesley believed this to be the fundamental point of disagreement between Deism and Christianity. In a letter to Mary Bishop on February 7, 1778, he wrote that the doctrine of the atonement

> is the distinguishing point between Deism and Christianity. "The morality of the Bible" (said Lord Huntingdon to me) "I admire; but the doctrine of atonement I cannot comprehend." Here, then, we divide. Give up the atonement, and we are all agreed.[24]

Third, as we noted earlier, Charles Wesley's joyful affirmation of the miraculous, in his celebration of the ascension, would have been self-consciously divergent from the Deist rejection of miracle. And, as I have suggested elsewhere, "Handel seems to have maintained a belief in the miraculous to the end of his life, if the passion, profundity and poignancy of the music he gave to 'He saw the lovely youth' (*Theodora* Act ll, Scene 6) is anything to go by."[25]

Händel's setting of these three hymns by Charles Wesley thus supports Ruth Smith's assertion that "the connections between the matter of the oratorios and arguments of the freethinkers are so strong that we can confidently assign the librettos as contributions to the defense of Christianity."[26] Conversely, it might also suggest that her strong delineation between the thought world of the oratorios and that of Charles Wesley's hymns[27] might be overdrawn. Having said that, it does need to be remembered that he who set these three Wesley hymns is the same composer who set these words:

> As steals the morn upon the night
> And melts the shades away:
> So Truth does Fancy's charm dissolve
> And rising Reason puts to flight
> The fumes that did the mind involve
> Restoring intellectual day.[28]

He was wounded for our transgressions, He was bruised for our iniquities; the chastisement of our peace was upon Him. And with His stripes we are healed" (Isa 53:4–5.)

23. See Lloyd, "Towards an Outline of Handel's Theology," 159–61.

24. Wesley, *Works of John Wesley*, 13:34.

25. See Lloyd, "Towards an Outline of Handel's Theology," 154, fn. 14.

26. Smith, *Handel's Oratorios*, 156.

27. Smith, *Handel's Oratorios*, 358–59.

28. From Part Three of Charles Jennens's libretto for *L'Allegro, Il Penseroso ed Il Moderato.*

Neither Jennens (who wrote the libretto for both works) nor Händel (who composed the music for both works) seem to have felt any tension between the christological, soteriological, and supernatural worldview of orthodox Christian faith, and a high view of the role of reason in the life of the state and of the ordinary believer. They clearly did not believe that reason was on the side of the Deists. In this, they were at one with the spirit of Bishop Butler's *Analogy of Religion*.[29]

NOTABLE HYMNS

We have argued so far that Händel's theology was christological, soteriological, and supernatural—and that all three categories side with orthodox Christian belief over against the revisionist agenda of his Deist contemporaries. We have suggested that he held to these traditional tenets of Christian belief without retreating into any obscurantist irrationalism. And we have posited that these three theological contours can be seen in the overlap between the themes of the three Charles Wesley hymns and the themes of other texts he chose to set. In this section, we shall look more closely at the theology implicit in those three hymns: *The Invitation*, *On the Resurrection*, and *Desiring to Love* (all published in 1746).[30]

The Invitation

Typical of Charles Wesley's style, this poem is a patchwork quilt of biblical allusions, but it applies those biblical allusions directly to the individual eighteenth century listener. The first stanza alludes to the parable of the Wedding Banquet in Matt 22. It places the listener/singer directly into the story of the parable. The invitation of the king in Matt 22:4 (AV)—"Behold, I have prepared my dinner: my oxen and my fatlings are killed, and all things are ready: come unto the marriage"—becomes:

29. Bishop Butler's *The Analogy of Religion, Natural and Revealed, to the Constitution and Course of Nature* was published in 1736, and is generally credited to be one of the most effective, and reprinted, responses to Deism. The book is a cumulative, probabilistic argument, which does not rely upon any premises not shared by his Deist opponents. He thereby sought to undermine the Deist claim that their natural religion was more rational than traditional revealed religion.

30. When they were written is, of course, a different question. However, Donald Burrows argues that "the paper of the autograph suggests a very narrow time-margin, because it is of a type used regularly by the composer only in 1746–7." See Burrows, *Complete Hymns and Chorales*, 2.

Sinners, obey the Gospel[31] Word;
Haste to the Supper of my LORD;
Be wise to know your gracious Day;
All things are ready; come away!

Four points are noteworthy in this biblical quantum. First, there is the sense of urgency, which the Wesleys are concerned to stress—both John in his preaching and Charles in his writing. The Authorized Version's "Come" is replaced with "Haste." Secondly, it is indeed invitation, but it is also command: "*Obey* the Gospel Word." This is justifiable within the narrative of the parable, as, when it comes from a king in antiquity, there is a thin line between invitation and command. Thirdly, the note of warning that is present within the parable itself is accentuated by an allusion to Luke 22:41–44 (AV):

> And when he was come near, he beheld the city, and wept over it, saying, "If thou hadst known, even thou, at least in this thy day, the things which belong unto thy peace! but now they are hid from thine eyes. For the days shall come upon thee, that thine enemies shall cast a trench about thee, and compass thee round, and keep thee in on every side, and shall lay thee even on the ground, and thy children within thee; and they shall not leave in thee one stone upon another; because thou knewest not the time of thy visitation."

What in the parable is said to the city of Jerusalem in the context of the Roman threat to its very existence—a threat that was found not to be empty in 70 CE, when Roman troops under Titus destroyed the city and its temple—is applied here to the individual listener in the context of our susceptibility to judgment: "Be wise to know your gracious Day." Fourthly, there is the interesting use of pronoun in the second line of the poem: "Haste to the supper of *my* LORD." Throughout the poem, the second person pronoun is used—"Be wise to know *your* gracious Day"—except here and in verse 9 ("The Wonder, why such Love to me!"). In seeking to persuade the singer to accept the invitation, the hymn seeks to ease the way to such an acceptance by already putting the language of personal relationship into the mouth of the singer. The hymn begins by emphasizing that the King of the parable is *my* LORD, and ends by stressing the wonder of such love to *me*. The singer of this hymn is invited to see themselves within the stories that are being told.

31. I have rendered the long "S" as an ordinary "s" throughout.

The second stanza applies the parable of the prodigal son (Luke 15) to similar effect:

> Ready the Father is to own
> And kiss his late-returning Son;
> Ready the loving Saviour stands,
> And spreads for you his bleeding Hands.

It is a telling of the parable to which the cross has been appended. Objective understandings of the atonement are sometimes criticized on the grounds that, in the parables of Luke 15, the sheep and the coin are found, and the prodigal welcomed home, without any apparent need for atonement to be made. The repetition of "Ready" to apply both to the image of the welcoming Father and to the image of the self-sacrificing Son is an attempt to tie the two metaphors so closely together as to forestall such a criticism.

The third stanza applies the New Covenant promise of a new heart (in Ezek 36:25–26) to the sermon-listener and hymn-singer:

> Ready the Spirit of his Love
> Just now the Stony to remove;
> T'apply and witness with the Blood,
> And wash and seal the Sons of GOD.

Again, the cross is introduced as the means by which the stony heart is replaced by a fleshy one. I have elsewhere suggested that "Handel was first and foremost a composer and theologian of the cross." Admittedly, "That may sound a surprising claim, given that his only setting of the Passion is arguably one of his least inspired works. But the themes to which he keeps returning are themes that are anchored in the failure and uncertainty of the cross, as befits a Lutheran."[32] The fact that he chose to set this hymn, which makes the cross central to parables and passages from which it is ostensibly absent, supports that claim.

The fourth stanza begins with the fourth "Ready," and is perhaps the most theologically adventurous image of the poem:

> Ready for you the Angels wait,
> To triumph in your blest Estate;
> Turning their Harps, they long to praise
> The Wonder of redeeming Grace.

It is theologically adventurous because it places the singer, not just into the narrative of a parable or into the imagery of an Old Testament prophecy, but into the event of the ascension. Into this unique event, often interpreted

32. Lloyd, "Towards an Outline of Handel's Theology," 159.

in Christian theology as the "coronation" of Christ, Wesley inserts the responding singer (and sinner): "Ready for *you* the Angels wait." So close, for Wesley, is the bond between believer and Lord; so closely has the Christ identified himself with his people, that what is true of him becomes true of them. This is a point that St. Paul makes in his letter to Col 3:1: "If ye, then, be risen with Christ, seek those things that are above, where Christ sitteth on the right hand of God."

The fifth stanza continues the ascension imagery—this time, not just with the *angels* awaiting the returning sinner, but the Trinity himself:

> The Father, Son, and Holy Ghost
> *Is* ready with Their shining Host;
> All Heaven is ready, to resound
> The Dead's Alive, the Lost is found!

Note the Trinitarian conflation of plural and singular in line 2. Note, too, the skillful way in which the poet returns us to the world of the prodigal son: "For this my son was dead, and is alive again; he was lost, and is found" (Luke 15:24).

There are another five stanzas in the hymn, but this striking use of ascension imagery seems an appropriate point at which to turn to Wesley's great ascension hymn, "Rejoice, the LORD is King!" For, despite being first published in a collection of Easter hymns, and despite being published, with Händel's tune, under the title "On the Resurrection," all the imagery points to the ascension rather than to the resurrection.

On the Resurrection

The first stanza is perhaps too general to be easily applied to either resurrection or ascension, though the context of Phil 4:4 (which the refrain quotes) is moving from the current presence of Christ in heaven to the future return of Christ to earth (3:20). It is the apostle's (and the poet's) confidence in that current location and future return of Christ that constitutes the (otherwise ungrounded) exhortation to rejoice:

> Rejoice, the LORD is King!
> Your Lord and King adore:
> Mortals, give thanks, and sing,
>
> And triumph evermore;
> Lift up your Heart, lift up your Voice,
> Rejoice, again I say, rejoice.

However, all the other imagery of the hymn points to the ascension as the prime event being celebrated here. Verse 2: "When he had purg'd our Stains, He took his Seat above." Verse 4: "He sits at God's Right-hand." Verse 6: "JESUS the Judge shall come, And take his Servants up To their Eternal Home." Such arguably dualistic language is open to significant criticism from a biblical and theological perspective,[33] but the word "take" clearly demonstrates that the hymn "locates" Christ in heaven, and celebrates his current rule "o'er Earth and Heaven." In other words, it is the Ascended Christ who is being lauded here, with glances back to the redemptive work of the cross ("When He had purg'd our Stains") and forward to the final victory of God ("Till all his Foes submit, And bow to His Command And fall beneath his Feet"). There is no direct reference to the resurrection at all.[34]

Two further points about this hymn are worth noting for their relevance to any attempted reconstruction of Händel's theological views. First, the poem clearly takes for granted an objective understanding of the atonement. "When He had purg'd our Stains" uses Old Testamental cultic imagery to suggest an objective shift both in our status before God and in the viability of our relationship with Him. I have argued elsewhere that Händel was himself comfortable with such an understanding of the atonement.[35]

Second, I have also argued that Händel was uncomfortable with militaristic imagery being used too directly of God. Certainly, he declined to set a section of Jennens's libretto for *Belshazzar*. As Hamish Swanston writes: "'You may believe,' he wrote to Jennens on receiving the final installment of the text, 'that I think it a very fine and sublime Oratorio, only it is really too long.' He refused to make any attempt to set a passage in which Jennens associated the prophet Isaiah with satisfaction in military conquest. Handel cuts and shapes and cuts until the emphases are placed at the end of the battle on a father's tears for his dead son and the general's rejection of 'destructive war.'"[36] The fifth stanza of *On the Resurrection* might seem a counter-example to this argument. In some ways, "He all his Foes shall kill" seems worse than the attribution to the (human) prophet, Isaiah, of

33. See Wright, *Surprised by Hope*.

34. I have no explanation to offer of why it was given the title it was, nor why it was placed in the "Easter" ("resurrection") section of *Hymns on the Great Festivals and other occasions*, rather than the "ascension" section.

35. See Lloyd, "Towards an Outline of Handel's Theology," 159–61. There I suggest that Händel believed in substitutionary atonement, which is one of the possible variants of an objective understanding of the atonement.

36. Swanston, *Handel*, 121–22. For another example of Händel declining to set words that applied militaristic imagery to the work of God, see Lloyd, "Towards an Outline of Händel's Theology," 163–64.

satisfaction in (human) military conflict, for the simple reason that it has the (human, but also divine) Christ doing the killing. However, it is likely that the "foes" of stanzas four and five are the personified forces of Death and Hell (as in stanza three), rather than human opponents of Christ. After all, the very next line (almost in poetic parallelism with the first line of the stanza) interprets the enemy as human sin rather than human beings:

> He all his Foes shall kill,
> Shall all our Sins destroy,

The destruction of the personified trio of Death, Hell and Sin—enemies both of God and of humanity—seems to have been acceptable to Händel in a way that glorification of warfare, or ascription of militaristic imagery to God, were not. As Donald Burrows comments, "Perhaps he had a well-grounded suspicion of extravagant claims for the palliative effects of military enterprise, as a result of the tales that he had surely heard in his youth concerning the sufferings of Halle during the Thirty Years War."[37]

Desiring to Love

Desiring to love (as first published with Händel's tune) has seven stanzas—the number (in biblical imagery) of perfection and completeness. However, it is a consummate articulation of *in*completeness and longing. The first line demonstrates that the "I" of the poem has tasted the love of God: the next two lines demonstrate that that taste has intensified (rather than satisfied) the desire. (Augustine famously gave voice to the same experience: "I tasted you, and I hunger and thirst."[38]) The immediate asking of a question (after the initial exclamation of delight) keeps the poem looking forward to resolution rather than experiencing or expressing it:

> O Love Divine, how sweet Thou art!
> When shall I find my longing Heart
> All taken up by Thee?
> I thirst, I faint, and die, to prove
> The greatness of redeeming Love,
> The Love of CHRIST to me.

Having set up the forward-driving dynamic of the poem, with its roots in dissatisfied (because unconsummated) desire, the poem faces the impossibility of plumbing the infinite depths for which the "I" longs. To underline

37. Burrows, *Handel*, 425–26.

38. Augustine, *Confessions*, Book X, 38, 262.

that impossibility, Wesley refers to Eph 3:17–19, where Paul prays "that ye, being rooted and grounded in love, may be able to comprehend with all saints, what is the breadth, and length, and depth, and height; and to know the love of Christ, *which passeth knowledge*" [my emphasis]. What the apostle and the poet long to know is beyond knowing:

> Stronger his Love, than Death or Hell;
> Its Riches are unsearchable:
> The first-born Sons of Light
> Desire in vain its Depths to see;
> They cannot reach the Mystery,
> The Length, and Breadth, and Height.

Not only is the love for which the hymnist longs infinite (and therefore never fully knowable by finite creatures), it is also inaccessible (unless "shed abroad"). Wesley here refers to 1 Cor 2:11, where Paul asks: "For what man knoweth the things of a man, save the spirit of man which is in him? Even so the things of God knoweth no man, but the Spirit of God." Therefore,

> GOD only knows the Love of GOD.
> O that it now were shed abroad
> In this poor stony Heart!
> For Love I sigh, for Love I pine:
> This only Portion, LORD, be mine,
> Be mine this Better Part!

There follow three stanza-length biblical vignettes, focusing on Mary in Luke 10, Peter in John 21, and John at the Last Supper—all of them expressing a desire for the intimacy and physical accessibility to Jesus that they experienced. Again, however, such accessibility is not possible, and each stanza begins "O that . . ." The near-ecstatic expression of frustrated longing finds outlet, if not relief, in request:

> Thy only Love do I require,
> Nothing on Earth beneath desire,
> Nothing in Heaven above:
> Let Earth and Heaven, and all Things go,
> Give me thine only Love to know,
> Give me thine only Love.

Love is the theme of themes, for both the Wesleys. For John Wesley, "there is nothing higher in religion; there is, in effect, nothing else."[39] And many

39. Wesley, *A Plain Account of Christian Perfection*, quoted in Hildebrandt and Beckerlegge, *Works of John Wesley*, 19. See Watson, *English Hymn*, 220.

of Charles Wesley's hymns move toward the theme of love. For example, "Come, O thou Traveller unknown" places the singer in the persona of Jacob, as he wrestles with the angel:

I need not tell thee who I am,
  My misery or sin declare;
Thyself hast called me by my name;
  Look on thy hands, and read it there:
But who, I ask thee, who art thou?
Tell me thy name, and tell me now.

The man who wrestles with him is read through a christological and soteriological lens: "Art thou the Man that died for me?" And, through that lens, it is love that comes into sharp focus:

Speak, or thou never hence shalt move,
And tell me, if thy name is Love.

'Tis Love! 'tis Love! Thou diedst for me;
  I hear thy whisper in my heart;
The morning breaks, the shadows flee,
  Pure, Universal love thou art:
To me, to all, thy bowels move:
Thy nature, and thy name is Love.[40]

CONTRIBUTION TO LITURGY AND WORSHIP

I have argued that Händel's theology was christological, soteriological, and supernatural. I suggested, too, that we are on safest ground when what we learn from the theology of these hymns coincides with the theology of other texts that he chose to set.[41] *Messiah*, for instance, contains all three charac-

40. Charles Wesley, from *A Collection of Hymns, for the use of the people called Methodists*, edited by John Wesley, The Third Edition corrected, printed by J. Paramore, London, 1782, No. CXXXVI.

41. It is also true to say that the theological characteristics of these hymns coincide with the theological characteristics of the Lutheran Pietism that was so prevalent in the land and period of Händel's birth. Consider, for instance, the chorale, "O Mensch, bewein dein Sünde groß," in Bach's *St. Matthew Passion*: all three characteristics are clearly present. It is christological ("Christ from his Father's bosom went forth and came to earth"), soteriological ("to carry the heavy burden of our sins"), and supernatural ("To the dead he gave life"). http://www.gbt.org/music/St_Matthew_text.pdf. This overlap with the dominant religious ethos of Händel's youth builds up the historical plausibility of this suggested reconstruction of the basic contours of his theology. (Note, again, how all three characteristics move in a different direction from Deism.)

teristics. First, it is christological. In Part One of *Messiah*, Jennens essentially weaves the story of Jesus' birth into Second Isaiah's prophecy (in Isa 40) of Yahweh's return to Zion,[42] thus making an implicit, but high, christological claim. Not only did the Deists not admit the deity of Jesus: they also denied the validity of the whole category of the prophetic. Richard Kidder, Bishop of Bath and Wells, defended the concept, looking at eighty verses of Scripture as test cases. His *A Demonstration of the Messias* "reads like a blueprint for the libretto of *Messiah*," writes Ruth Smith.[43] And well it might. Not only do we know that Jennens had a copy of the book in his library, but forty-one of the eighty Bible verses that Kidder considers are included in the libretto of *Messiah*, in the same overall order. *Messiah* is not "an oratorio of cobbled together texts from the Old Testament and New Testament," as Betsy Weber suggests.[44] *Messiah* is essentially a work of christological apologetics set to music.

Secondly, *Messiah* is soteriological. We have already noted the substitutionary nature of "Surely He hath borne our griefs" and "All we like sheep." But "And with His stripes" and "He was cut off" are no less so. Händel, elsewhere, even inserts the concept of substitution into contexts that are devoid of it. In *Esther*, the heroin prays:

> Take, O take my Life alone;
> And thy chosen people spare.[45]

Thirdly, *Messiah* embodies a supernatural and interventionist understanding of God. He is the God who can open the eyes of the blind, unstop the ears of the deaf, enable the lame to leap as an hart and the tongue of the dumb to sing—and He is the God of bodily resurrection, who offers hope for worm-eaten bodies.

Händel's contribution is not merely to have written hymn-tunes, some of which are still being used liturgically and some are not—and to have his Hallelujah Chorus sung in North American churches on Easter Sunday. His contribution is the far more architectonic one of having composed a huge body of choral music embodying an orthodox Christian conception of God in the face of what was arguably the most significant intellectual threat to the veracity, integrity, and survival of that faith (in the West, at least) since Arianism. In the battle of ideas against Deism, Bishop Butler engaged the

42. "Comfort ye, my people," "Ev'ry valley shall be exalted," "And the glory of the Lord," "O thou that tellest," and "He shall feed his flock" are all from Isa 40.

43. Smith, *Handel's Oratorios*, 150.

44. Betsy Weber, Director of Choral Studies at Houston University, quoted in Kadifa, "Handel's Iconic Hallelujah Chorus."

45. Act ll, Scene 1.

mind, the Wesleys appealed to the heart, and Händel captured the imagination. His hymn-settings offer us a tiny triangulation point into his thinking and his theology, which helps us discern the theological contours of this creative force of nature.

BIBLIOGRAPHY

Augustine. *Confessions*. Translated by Maria Boulding, OSB. Hyde Park, NY: New City, 1997.

Burrows, Donald. *The Complete Hymns and Chorales: Facsimile Edition with Introduction*. London and Sevenoaks: Novello, 1988.

———. *Handel*. 2nd ed. Oxford: Oxford University Press, 2012.

———. *Handel and the English Chapel Royal*. Oxford: Oxford University Press, 2005.

Ewbank, J. Robert. *John Wesley, Natural Man, and the "Isms."* Eugene OR: Wipf and Stock, 2009.

Hildebrandt, Franz, and Oliver A. Beckerlegge, eds. *The Works of John Wesley*. Vol. 7, *A Collection of Hymns for the use of the People called Methodists*. Nashville: Abingdon, 1989.

Jenkins, Terry. *John Rich: The Man Who Built Covent Garden Theatre*. Bramber, West Sussex: Barn End, 2016.

Kadifa, Margaret. "Handel's Iconic Hallelujah Chorus Is a challenge—and an Inspiration—for Choirs at Easter." *Houston Chronicle*, April 14, 2017. https://www.houstonchronicle.com/life/houston-belief/article/Handel-s-iconic-Hallelujah-Chorus-is-a-challenge-11074063.php.

Keates, Jonathan. *Handel: The Man and His Music*. London: The Bodley Head, 2008.

Kidder, Richard. *A Demonstration of the Messias. In which the Truth of the Christian Religion is Proved, against all enemies of Christianity thereof; But especially against the Jews. In three parts*. London, 1726.

Landgraf, Annette, and David Vickers. *The Cambridge Handel Encyclopedia*. Cambridge: Cambridge University Press, 2009.

Lloyd, Michael. "Towards an Outline of Handel's Theology." In *Händel-Jahrbuch*, 151–66. Kassel: Bärenreiter, 2013.

Marissen, Michael. *Tainted Glory in Handel's Messiah: The Unsettling History of the World's Most Beloved Choral Work*. New Haven: Yale University Press, 2014.

Rooke, Deborah W. *Handel's Israelite Oratorio Libretti: Sacred Drama and Biblical Exegesis*. Oxford: Oxford University Press, 2012.

Smith, Ruth. *Handel's Oratorios and Eighteenth Century Thought*. Cambridge: Cambridge University Press, 1995.

Stapert, Calvin R. *Handel's Messiah: Comfort for God's People*. Grand Rapids, MI: Eerdmans, 2010.

Swanston, Hamish. *Handel*. Outstanding Christian Thinkers Series. London: Cassell, 1990.

Thicknesse, Robert. "Dying of the Light." *The Tablet* (February 28, 2009).

Watson, J. R. *The English Hymn: A Critical and Historical Study*. Oxford: Oxford University Press, 1999.

Wesley, Charles. *The Manuscript Journal of The Reverend Charles Wesley, M.A.* Vol. ll, edited by S. T. Kimbrough Jr. and Kenneth G. C. Newport. Nashville: Kingswood, 2007.

Wesley, John. *The Works of John Wesley*. 3rd ed. Grand Rapids, MI: Baker, 1996, reprinted from the 1872 Edition issued by the Wesleyan Methodist Book Room, London.

Wilson, John. "Handel's Tunes for Charles Wesley's Hymns." The Hymn Society of Great Britain and Ireland, Bulletin 163, 11.2 (May 1985) 32–37.

Wright, Tom. *Surprised by Hope*. London: SPCK, 2007.

Chapter 20

Hymnody in Missionary Lands

A Decolonial Critique

Becca Whitla

HISTORICAL BACKGROUND

The history of hymnody in what became known as missionary lands goes back to the earliest days of conquest in the Americas beginning with Cristóbal Colón's arrival to the Caribbean in 1492. It gathered greater momentum with the expansion of Protestant missions in the eighteenth century, galvanized by the post-reformation expansion of congregational singing in general and grew exponentially in the nineteenth century. This blossoming corresponded with an enormous growth in hymn singing in Europe and the US, particularly in Protestant contexts. This chapter focuses on Protestant hymnody in English-speaking contexts, even as it acknowledges the broader contexts of hymnody in "missionary lands," a vast and complex topic that warrants an entire volume unto itself. The chapter adopts a decolonial approach in two ways. First, it explores how colonialism is interconnected with the history of missionary endeavors, and second, it celebrates the prolific and rich hymnic expressions from former "missionary lands," which in turn illustrates how the global South began to reconfigure and remap global Christianity.

Colonialism and Expansionism

During the first wave of European colonialism, which involved the conquering of the Americas by the Spanish and Portuguese beginning in 1492, the conquistadors were accompanied by clergy from the Roman Catholic Church. The military, economic, political, and cultural conquest of what is now Mexico, Central and South America, and the Caribbean was accomplished through the violent overthrow and the enslavement of the original peoples of those lands. The Spanish and Portuguese understood themselves to be superior human beings whose responsibility was to civilize and Christianize the "inferior" indigenous peoples they encountered. At the same time, some Christians, especially among the Jesuits, protested the mistreatment of the colonized from the beginning. Justo González traces in the development of early colonial encounters the "two faces to the Roman Catholic Church in Spanish America," those who exploited "the native population for the benefit of the Spanish settlers" and those who resisted such exploitation.[1] In this complex context, clergy introduced Western European versions of Roman Catholic rites and music to the people they encountered as part of their work to "save souls."

The second wave of European colonialism, while initiated shortly after in the sixteenth century by the French and English, was not really in full swing until the eighteenth century. France, England, and other European nations, including the Netherlands, Germany, Belgium, Italy, Sweden, and Denmark, also expanded their interests in various parts of the world. By the end of the nineteenth century, the whole rest of the world was understood by these European nations, and by the US, as territories that were available to be conquered and controlled. Examples of how this imperial attitude was carried out were embodied in the Berlin Conference in 1884 (also known as "the scramble for Africa"), where control of the African continent was divided up among European nations. It was epitomized by the fact that Britain's Queen Victoria was declared Empress of India in 1877.

This Euro-North Atlantic expansionism was accompanied by a growing missionary zeal among Protestants in which missionaries sought to take the message of the Good News of Jesus Christ's salvation to the rest of the world. The work of evangelizing was professionalized and a number of organizations were founded to train lay Christians for mission work, including, among many others, the Society for the Propagation of the Gospel in Foreign Parts (1701), the London Missionary Society (1795), the Church Missionary Society (1799), and the American Board of Commissioners

1. González, *Story of Christianity*, 451.

for Foreign Missions (1810). The web of Protestant missionary work was also enriched, expanded, and complicated by the growing diversity of denominational influences. With a view to convert those they encountered, missionaries felt motivated and justified by the Great Commission in which Jesus commands the disciples to "Go therefore and make disciples of all nations, baptizing them in the name of the Father and of the Son and of the Holy Spirit" (Matt 28:19–20, NRSV).

Missionary Impulses

The dominant Euro-North Atlantic historical narrative which describes this missionary work of the eighteenth and nineteenth centuries, emphasizes the *good intentions* of missionaries who sacrificed themselves out of a sense of calling and vocation to individually convert as many souls as possible in work that was "great and marvellous, a work of most noble Christian devotion and industry."[2] For these missionaries, however, their home culture was inextricably linked with the Christianity to which they sought to convert non-Christians. They saw it as their duty to bring the light to the "heathen," sharing their "cultural tradition [which] was providentially tied to Christianity. As a result, European cultural superiority went hand-in-hand in the evangelizing project."[3]

British missionary impulses in the eighteenth century were initially dominated by nonconformist denominations. In fact, John Wesley's encounter with Moravians on his first voyage to the Americas, and the fact that he was so moved by their hymn singing, encapsulates the missionary zeal that was in the air and that not only galvanized clergy and others to minister abroad, but also, as with the Wesley brothers, to minister at home. This missionary zeal was embodied in the religious fervor of the two Great Awakenings (1730s and early 1800s), which also corresponded with the shift of the U.S.A. from being a principle site for missionary activity to being a key player in the work of evangelization. As the U.S.A. gained political and economic power, its doctrine of manifest destiny based on the "belief that it was Anglo-Saxon Americans' providential mission to expand their civilization and institutions [including religious] across the breadth of North America," was used first to "fuel western settlement, Native American removal and war with Mexico" and then to expand its imperial interests

2. Stevenson, "Foreign Missions," 759.
3. Medina, "From Cultural Theologies."

beyond the North American continent.[4] Manifest destiny was intertwined with the conviction that Christianity justified this expansion.

As the eighteenth century wore on, Anglicans joined their nonconformist colleagues by embracing a more evangelistic approach. It is certainly true that "there were no simple connections between this religious [missionary] expansion and a specifically British influence and Empire overseas."[5] The web of interconnections was complex and Christian missionaries had a range of motivations, practices, and outcomes. Many appreciated and respected the people among whom they ministered, advocated on their behalf, and were themselves converted to other ways of seeing the world that changed the way they understood and lived their Christian faith. But the argument that "missionary thinking was profoundly egalitarian . . . [that] 'race' was immaterial," and that government institutions and the church were not intertwined in the common goals of Christianizing and civilizing—even though there was often an official separation between church and state—is unsustainable.[6]

Interrogating Missionary History

More recently a second historical narrative, from post and decolonial historical perspectives, acknowledges the fact that "the blending of Western European cultural theologies and Christianity into the work of evangelization turned mission work into an effective mechanism of imperial and Western cultural expansion."[7] Proponents of this perspective interrogate Christian complicity with colonial and imperial projects arguing that

> Christian *mission* has always been associated with power. . . . [In a] five-hundred-year claim to moral superiority, the conversion of peoples to Christianity was achieved by a combination of voluntary, social, legal, and violent compulsions . . . [in which] populations . . . were overwhelmed, subjugated, and frequently destroyed.[8]

Despite the complex reality of mission contexts, including, in some cases, resistance to oppressive colonial structures by missionaries, Christian missions were bound up with Euro-North Atlantic economic, political,

4. Pinsker, "Manifest Destiny."
5. Porter, "Religion, Missionary Enthusiasm, and Empire," 229.
6. Porter, "Religion, Missionary Enthusiasm, and Empire," 229.
7. Medina, "From Cultural Theologies."
8. Ransom and Bonk, "Mission and Power," 87–88.

cultural, and colonial interests. In W. R. Stevenson's article on hymnody in "Foreign Missions" in John Julian's 1892 *Dictionary of Hymnology*, nearly every part of the globe with the exception of Europe is named in four all-encompassing categories: "various parts of America; North, Central and South"; "the Islands of the Pacific, in New Guinea and Borneo"; "Asia, from Japan westward to Turkey"; and "Africa, East, South and West."[9] Interestingly, Stevenson articulates mission work in Canada and the US only in terms of mission among Indigenous peoples, and he does not mention Australia, an indication of the racialized parameters of how humanity was conceived. The scope and extent of the expansion of Christianity worldwide includes understanding the whole world as "missionary lands," defined by a Eurocentric optic, which saw that the "world and its various peoples were 'lost'; they therefore had to be 'found,' or rescued, by means of the gospel of Jesus Christ."[10] Added to this imperative was a sense that European versions of Christianity were synonymous with European culture and that both were the superior expressions of human achievement. This expansion was motivated and rationalized by biblical passages like Acts 1:8 in which, at the moment of Jesus' ascension, he proclaims that through the power of the Holy Spirit the disciples will become Jesus' witnesses at home in Jerusalem and "to the ends of the earth."

The other important facet of telling mission history from this perspective is that it opens up alternative ways to understand and interpret history through the stories of the conquered peoples from their own perspectives. An emphasis on the agency of conquered and subjugated peoples includes an acknowledgement of the multi-directionality of flows of influence. It affirms that there was an exchange both ways between missionaries and those they sought to "save."[11]

9. Stevenson, "Foreign Missions," 738. Stevenson's article is an admirable piece of scholarship for its breadth and detail. It demonstrates a global view, however much it was also influenced by the fact that it was written from the perspective of the height of England's powers at the end of the nineteenth century.

10. Leaver, "Theological Dimensions," 320.

11. There are some contexts where specific structures have been put in place to affirm narratives from this perspective, like the Truth and Reconciliation process in South Africa after the abolishment of Apartheid in 1994 and more recently, the Truth and Reconciliation Commission in Canada, which addressed the racially based cultural genocide inflicted against indigenous peoples in government-sponsored, church-run, missional, residential schools, to use just two such examples among many others. These processes have meant that "the memory and the testimony of the indigenous peoples operate as counter-narratives that reconstruct the history of these peoples and of these countries out of the historical debris of their collective memories." Medina, "Abya Yala."

Mechanisms of truth and reconciliation along with post and decolonial perspectives on mission history also expose the central role of doctrines of racial superiority that gained momentum in the eighteenth century. These doctrines gathered a full head of steam during the nineteenth century and played a central role in justifying European imperial interests, colonial conquests, and evangelization. As González notes, "The colonizers—including many devout Christians—were convinced that their enterprise was justified by the benefits the colonized would receive. As they saw matters, God had placed the benefits of Western civilization and Christian faith in the hands of white people—both Europeans and North American settlers."[12] At the same time, many of those who accepted and embraced Christianity in "missionary lands"—and who today comprise the majority of the Christian population worldwide—are proud of this missionary inheritance, including hymns. Those who embraced Christianity in the global South appropriated and reconfigured it in profound ways. The resulting diverse expressions of Christianity are touched on briefly in relation to liturgy toward the end of this chapter.

Role of Hymnody

The role of hymnody in Protestant missions was central. Along with the translation of the Bible, missionaries translated and composed hymns and prepared hymn books. In this monumental and complex task, they were aided by the local people. Beloved hymns from the motherland were translated. Hymns that explicitly supported the missionary cause were penned. And a third group of hymns were created by missionaries and their converts with new texts and new music. All of these activities had theological implications, which will be considered in the next section. As we shall see, there was a paradox at play in the role hymns played in missionary efforts. On the one hand, hymn singing, especially the singing of hymns about mission, were often "a text inscribing the act of colonialism itself."[13] On the other, paradoxically, hymn singing provided a way to make meaning in local contexts and often embodied resistance to the colonial experience. Thus, hymn singing was transformed by the colonized "into a means of responding to domination."[14] Of course, many hymns, perhaps most, fall between these two poles of the paradox. What remains clear is that the spread of hymnody

12. González, *Story of Christianity*, 417.

13. Bohlman, "World Musics," 71.

14. Bohlman, "World Musics," 71–72.

globally and the proliferation of hymns that were created in "missionary lands" is immense and widely varied.

THEOLOGICAL PERSPECTIVES

The hymns that travelled with missionaries in the eighteenth and nineteenth centuries reflected the theological currents and historical contexts in Europe and North America, which included a great diversity of biblical and theological themes as well as denominational and doctrinal approaches. In Protestant contexts, for instance, denominational approaches ranged from Calvinism, with emphases on "doctrines of providence and election" to the much more missional Arminianism of Moravians and Methodists.[15] As "at home," hymns were understood to be pedagogical tools that bolstered Christian belief. In so-called "missionary lands," this formational role of hymn singing was augmented by the drive to convert, colonize, enculturate, and sometimes "civilize," all of which were understood under the banner of Christianizing. Given the enormity of the scope of potential theological themes in mission hymnody, this section is divided into two parts: the imperial/colonial theology of mission hymns and the reconfiguration of hymn singing through contextualization and indigenization.

Imperial/Colonial Perspectives of Missionary Hymns

A present-day discussion of hymns in missionary lands, particularly those that fall under the purview of English Protestantism, must contend with its theological underside. Three such hymns, which will be analyzed from this perspective, are "Jesus Shall Reign" by Isaac Watts (1674–1748), "O'er the Gloomy Hills of Darkness," by William Williams Pantycelyn (1717–91), and "From Greenland's Icy Mountains" by Reginald Heber (1783–1826). When viewed from this perspective, these mission-focused hymns express a theology that undergirded the relationship between missionary activity and British imperial interests. Imperialism/colonialism is seen in the language, which had at its heart the view that European, and in this case British, cultural expressions of Christianity, were *the* superior religious cultural expression known to humanity. The hymns displayed notions of divine providential chosen-ness and were marked by racialized and gendered language, all of which was endorsed scripturally.

15. Leaver, "Theological Dimensions," 316.

Nonconformist Isaac Watts, often dubbed the father of English hymnody, wrote "Jesus Shall Reign," his version of Ps 72, in 1719. No doubt Watts was expressing what he saw as the noble intent and passionate desire to spread the good news so that the "whole earth be filled with God's glory" (Isa 6:3). At the same time—and though it was written before the peak of British imperialism and the height of Protestant missionary activity in the mid-nineteenth century he was nevertheless also expressing a growing coalescence between prevailing European, and especially English, imperial desire and a vision of God's reign thriving around the world.

As Michael Hawn notes, "Regardless of the author's intent, this hymn certainly coincided with the rise of the British Empire, and it would have been likely that a congregation in England who sang this psalm paraphrase in the eighteenth century would have made a link—consciously or subconsciously—between the Empire and phrases like 'his kingdom spread from shore to shore' in stanza one."[16] Such a link is reinforced by Watts's substitution of the biblical place names from the psalm (Tarshish, Sheba, and Seba) with Persia and India, which were "places of economic importance in the British Empire in the eighteenth century."[17] The original hymn of fourteen verses also included sentiments, which are no longer palatable—and no longer sung—in most church settings. For instance, in verse three, the unnamed barb'rous nations "submit, and bow" to the Lord: "And barb'rous nations at His word / Submit, and bow, and own their Lord." In language typical of the era, verse 13 refers to the "heathen lands," which were to be conquered for Christ.[18]

Certainly the hymn as it is sung today, usually with only verses 1, 5, 6, and 8, represents what can be understood as a faithful obedience the spirit of the biblical text. After all, the language of the king's dominion from "sea to sea and from the River to the ends of the earth," which Watts articulates as Jesus' universal reign stretching triumphantly from shore to shore (in verse 1) comes from Scripture (NRSV Ps 72:8).Yet, at the same time, biblical texts like this were widely used to justify colonialism. In the original verse 2, Watts writes, "Europe her best tribute brings." Though not explicit, the connection between the evangelizing task, Europe's religious tribute, and the establishment of Christ's reign on earth is nonetheless suggested. Watts's version accentuates the view that was becoming increasingly prevalent that Jesus' reign was also an affirmation of Europe's dominion and the belief that

16. Hawn, "History of Hymns."

17. Hawn, "History of Hymns."

18. See Watts, "Jesus Shall Reign," for the full fourteen-verse version.

European Christianity is the best expression of how God's "universal sway" (verse 9) was to be lived out.

There are countless other hymns that reflect a more blatant imperial/colonial theology, like Williams's "O'er the Gloomy Hills of Darkness," written in 1772. It displays a missiology that endorses earthly conquest intertwined with a doctrine of racial superiority, in the name of spreading the gospel from "Pole to Pole." Verse 2 is a particularly racialized proclamation of this view: "Let the Indian, let the Negro, / Let the rude Barbarian see / That divine and glorious Conquest / Once obtain'd on Calvary; / Let the Gospel, Loud resound from Pole to Pole." The final verse from the original 1792 version is clear about how such an evangelization should take place: "O let Moab yield and tremble, / Let Philistia never boast, / And let India proud be scatt'red / With their numerable Host; / And the Glory, / Jesus only be to thee." The spread of the Gospel was to be brought about by conquering the "other": "the Indian," "the Negro," and the "rude Barbarian."[19]

Hymns like this explicitly espoused an imperial/colonial theology based on an ideology of European superiority in which Christianization, imperial and colonial projects, and notions of civilizing the "heathen" were inseparable. They helped to justify Euro-North Atlantic domination all over the world and are exemplified in the many hymnals that were explicitly produced to support the mission cause.[20] A celebration of the spread of hymnody in the following 1892 quotation from Stevenson's article indicates just how much missions were intertwined with the geographic reach of colonialism. Here, the imperial interests (China, South Africa, etc.) of European nation states are celebrated for being places where the Gospel banner is uplifted—and the best hymns are sung:

> The fact is, that the best hymns of Watts, Doddridge, Cowper, Newton, Wesley, Heber, Lyte, Keble, Bonar, Miss Steele, Miss Havergal, and other English authors,—the best German hymns,—the best hymns of American composition,—are now sung in China and South Africa, in Japan and Syria, among the peoples of India, and in the isles of the Pacific Ocean,—indeed, in almost every place where Protestant missionaries have uplifted the Gospel banner and gathered Christian churches.[21]

Some hymns that were exported with missionaries but not necessarily understood as "mission" hymns *per se*, like "Lift High the Cross" (1887, George W. Kitchin) and "Onward Christian Soldiers" (1865, Sabine

19. Richards, *Imperialism and Music*, 388.
20. Mauney, "Mission Hymnody, USA."
21. Stevenson, "Foreign Mission," 759.

Baring-Gould), accentuated this kind of missiology by championing a triumphalist militaristic Christology. "Onward Christian Soldiers" for instance, though written as a children's processional, evokes the long held metaphor of the cross as a righteous battle shield going back to Constantine, echoes the Crusades, and highlights the extent to which the culture of the day was militarized in aid of the military imperial expansion of the British Empire. Drawing its key military imagery from 2 Tim 2:3 ("good soldier of Christ Jesus") and Eph 6:13–17 (images of battle and armor), this hymn emphasizes hierarchical images of Christ as royal master (verse 1) and triumphant king (verse 5). The church is likened to an undivided, unquestioning ("one in . . . doctrine," verse 3) army.[22]

Since it was written as a children's processional and not "intended for use in church,"[23] interpretations that grapple with its imperial underside can be viewed as somewhat anachronistic. Still, over the long history and popularity of this hymn, it *has* been used as a hymn to be sung in church *and* in battle. Moreover, as a children's processional, it is also a concrete example that demonstrates the potential power of hymns to form children—as Christians to be sure—but also as subjects of the British Empire who celebrate British militarism and a biblically justified triumphalist theology. In short, it contributed to the zeal for the British Empire that was culturally pervasive at the time.

Contextualization and Indigenization

"From Greenland's Icy Mountains" was written by Reginald Heber in 1819 for an event to support the Society for the Propagation of the Gospel in Foreign Parts. No doubt he had in mind Pauline theology, which celebrates those who represent the new creation, the new age "in Christ" (2 Cor 5:17). Heber, who wrote fifty-seven other hymns including "Holy, Holy, Holy, Lord God Almighty," became Bishop of Calcutta in 1823, where he was known for his advocacy with the East India Company on behalf of Indians who were overlooked for higher-ranking positions within the company.[24] Yet the hymn still encapsulates the colonizing theology described above, reflecting the prevailing sociocultural norms. Phrases like "The heathen in his blindness bows down to wood and stone" in verse 2 and "Can we, whose souls are lighted with wisdom from on high" in verse 3, make clear the contrast between the "blind heathen" and the self-perceived superiority of the

22. Baring-Gould, "Onward Christian Soldiers."

23. Bradley, *Abide with Me*, 100.

24. Hughes, *Bishop Sahib*, 170–72.

divinely sanctioned European Christian "we" of the hymn, whose "souls are lighted with wisdom from on high."

Not surprisingly, this hymn was not only sung "at home" in England to bolster the mission cause. It also travelled around the world and was translated into other languages by missionaries and those with whom they worked. Ironically, in the process of being translated the hymn was also reconfigured. For example, in its translation into Ojibwe, a North American Indigenous language, the original version with its triumphalist, expansionist vision of a superior Christianity is transformed instead into a proclamation of an inclusive theology that emphasizes a collaborative relationship between the creator and all of humanity. God's mercy is described as the immediate and intimate act of a loving creator and not as bestowed from on high by a distant, unreachable, king-like figure, as in the English version.

Theologically speaking, singing the hymn in Ojibwe and with an Ojibwe style reveals a hermeneutic undercurrent; "underneath what we see and hear is a dynamic of life which is unveiled and released in singing."[25] A different cosmovision emerges that reflects Indigenous spirituality in an immanent eschatology made present *through* singing. In the third verse in English, for instance, the focus is on bringing salvation to those ("men") who are benighted, or intellectually and morally backward. Meanwhile, the Ojibwe version encourages all who are wise to help people. Salvation is translated as *bimaadiziwin,* a term that can mean heavenly life, but can also include the here and now, "the good life, lived well in proper relationship to human and nonhuman persons."[26]

25. MacDonald, personal conversation, 2016.

26. McNally, *Ojibwe Singers*, 61.

Table 20.1: Ojibwe Hymn and Retranslation

Verses 1–3 in English:	**Retranslation from Ojibwe:**
From Greenland's icy mountains From India's coral strand, Where Afric's sunny fountains Roll down their golden sand; From many an ancient river, From many a palmy plain, They call us to deliver Their land from error's chain.	Those who are in the North And also in the East Those living there There where it is hot And also those who harpoon [and those among] Palms that bend You who have heard us Have great mercy for that reason.
What though the spicy breezes Blow soft o'er Ceylon's isle; Though every prospect pleases, And only man is vile: In vain with lavish kindness The gifts of God are strown; The heathen in his blindness Bows down to wood and stone	How they sleep It is handsome/beautiful, Those who live there Those who would pray. Have mercy on them They live well there They who salute Wood and also stone
Can we whose souls are lighted With wisdom from on high; Can we to men benighted The lamp of life deny? Salvation, O salvation! The joyful sound proclaim, Till each remotest nation Has learnt Messiah's Name.	All of us who have wisdom, Who have light, Will you be discouraged/afraid To help people O restoration of *bimaadiziwin* Tell the news everywhere, Until everyone They have listened to you.
	From the retranslation by the late Larry Cloud Morgan

Clearly the English version of "From Greenland's Icy Mountains" illustrates the colonial underside of the colonizing theological vision of nineteenth century missiology. Yet through the process of translation, it has been transformed, as we see in this example in Ojibwe, into a different kind of hymn, one that espouses an alternative theology and affirms local religious and cultural ways of understanding the world. This one example epitomizes a widespread process of hymnic—and theological—reconfiguration that came to pass as many hymns were translated, embraced, and, as a result, reinterpreted by the new people groups—new Christians—who claimed them as their own. A rich and robust process of theological reconfiguring ensued.

Collaborations between missionaries, translators, and hymn writers—both foreign (Euro-North Atlantic) and local—also produced new hymns along with the above-mentioned new ways of understanding inherited hymns. Increasingly, missionaries and local Christians wrote texts and tunes in Indigenous musical styles that reflected a wide range of spiritual and theological perspectives that made sense in each local context. The earliest known hymn in Canada, for instance, is the result of such processes. "Twas in the Moon of Wintertime," or *Jesous Ahatonhia* in Wendat, was said to have been written and set to a French tune by Jesuit missionary Jean de Brébeuf in 1643 when he lived near what is now called Midland, Ontario, among the Wendat-Huron peoples. It was not written down until about 150 years later, having been carried orally by the Huron people as they migrated east to the Québec city region.[27] A retranslation of the original Wendat words reveals an incarnational theology that integrates Indigenous understandings of the spirits—okie—with the celebration of the birth of Jesus. The final verse in Wendat, retranslated into English, places an emphasis on the "will of the spirits" and family: "They say, [three men of great importance] 'Let us place his name in a position of honour / Let us act reverently towards him for he comes to show us mercy / it is the will of the spirits that you love us, Jesus, / and we wish that we may be adopted into your family.' / Jesus, he is born"—*Jesous Ahatonhia.*[28] In 1927, English words were written by Jesse Edgar Middleton that are not a direct translation, but nonetheless contextualized the hymn to a Canadian context: "the shepherds became hunters; the swaddling clothes became rabbit skins; and the Magi, chiefs with valuable fox and beaver pelts."[29] For example, verse two reads: "Within a lodge of broken bark, / The tender Babe was found / A raged robe of rabbit skin enwrapped His beauty round / And as the hunter braves drew nigh, / The angel song rang loud and high: / Jesus your King is born, Jesus is born / In excelsis gloria." The hymn is still sung widely in both Catholic and Protestant settings.

In other instances, hymns arose almost entirely from local settings. A well-known example of this type of hymn is "Ulo Tixo mkulu" or the "Great Hymn," composed by Gaga Ntsikana (1780–1821), in South Africa at the time of his conversion to Christianity (c. 1815). According to David Dargie, Ntsikana's conversion occurred "without the presence of any missionary or white person."[30] "Great Hymn" was subsequently transcribed from the

27. McKellar, "'Twas in the Moon."
28. Cockburn Project, "Iesus Ahatonnia/The Huron Carol."
29. McKellar, "'Twas in the Moon."
30. Hawn, "Ntsikana Gaga."

oral tradition by J. K. Bokwe and was published in 1876.[31] The hymn is an expression of early Xhosa Christianity, contextualized for the local Xhosa context. To give just one example, the last line of the second stanza, "You created the blind—did you not create them for a purpose?" refers to the fact that "blind people were thought to have specific powers of discernment in Xhosa culture."[32]

As time went on and the former "missionary lands" became the center of Christianity worldwide, congregational singing diversified and flourished in the global South with the creation of more and more songs/hymns like "Ulo Tixo mkulu."[33] Whether hymns were adopted wholeheartedly, adapted through translation, and/or by mixing some combination of Western European and local elements, or contextualized as new local expressions, the direction of influence shifted and began to flow from the global South toward the "West" (the Euro-North Atlantic), from the "missionary lands" back to the "motherland," as we shall see in the next volume.

CONTRIBUTION TO LITURGY AND WORSHIP

The processes of contextualization just described point to the fundamental theological importance of the cultural dimension in any consideration of hymns from missionary lands. The good news that missionaries sought to share, and in some cases impose, was clothed in the garments of Euro-North Atlantic cultural expressions and especially hymns—in text and tune, instrumentation, and performance style. In the nineteenth century, as the connection between imperial and colonial projects and missions was culturally and politically entrenched, conversion meant assimilation into the "cultural expression of Christianity exhibited by the missionaries who had brought the gospel."[34] In fact, to this day, many in the global South still believe that following Jesus includes the abandoning and renunciation

31. Interestingly, Michael Hawn notes that "Ntsikana's hymn was the only example of this kind included in the earlier editions of *Cantate Domino* (the first four editions for the World's Student Christian Federation), 1924, 1930, 1938, 1951." E-mail correspondence with the author, November 17, 2017.

32. Hawn, "Ntsikana Gaga."

33. Hawn also notes that "Erik Routley's smaller monograph, *Ecumenical Hymnody* (c. 1955) is ground breaking" for its move away from mission hymnody toward ecumenical hymnody. Routley edited the 1974 version of *Cantate Domino*. Hawn, "Ntsikana Gaga."

34. Leaver, "Theological Dimensions," 318.

of one's local cultures and traditions as unworthy to bear Christian faith expressions.[35]

In its most egregious forms, missionary cultural influence presumed the adoption of Christian/Eurocentric cultural ways and resulted in a "corresponding denial of the culture from which the convert came."[36] It bears repeating that many missionaries had the best of intentions to share their love for Christianity; many also sacrificed much and endured great hardship. Still, in too many other cases, the denial of one's cultural tradition was forced upon entire people groups, as was the case with Residential Schools in Canada or the removal of Aboriginal children from their families in Australia to mission schools, for example. But, the cultural flow was not unidirectional—from Europe and the US to the rest of the world. From the moment of first contact, the cultures of the peoples who were encountered, however inferior they were perceived to be, also influenced the cultures of the colonizers.

The Transformation of Hymns and Liturgy

As we have seen, hymn singing began to be transformed, through the translation, interpretation, and performance of traditional hymns and in the creation of new hymns. Similarly, liturgical and worship practices were adapted to new settings, by being translated, but more importantly, by being culturally translated so that Christian practices (and theologies) would make sense in local contexts. Missionaries and denominations varied in their ability to be adaptive, but over time the balance of world Christianity gradually shifted toward the global South, in large part because of the work missionaries initiated, for good and/or ill. Those missionaries who were able to be open to Christianity's new expressions were aware that "spirituality and worship need to be earthed into the consciousness of each individual's cultural roots: language, thought-forms and artistic expressions."[37] As Robin Leaver asserts, "To do otherwise is to misunderstand the meaning of the incarnation."[38]

The repercussions of this shift of balance toward the global South has had a profound impact on the way liturgy is practiced and understood, just as it has reconfigured theology and ecclesiology. Shifts and processes of change continue to unfold. One of the signs of these reconfigurations

35. Lim, "Sacred Songs," 139–54.

36. Leaver, "Theological Dimensions," 320.

37. Leaver, "Theological Dimensions," 329.

38. Leaver, "Theological Dimensions," 329.

liturgically is in the rich and diverse hymnic contributions from churches in the global South, which are changing what is sung (and how it is sung) all over the world. These shifts are also embodied in ecclesial trends in the twentieth century which include: fuller congregational participation, local/indigenous Christian expressions, and an awareness of global Christianity through worship. Four key historical moments signify these trends: the revolutionary liturgical Catholic edict for "fully conscious active participation" from *Sacrosanctum concilium* of the Second Vatican Council in 1963; the prominence of global music at the World Council of Churches meeting in Vancouver in 1983; the Lutheran affirmation that worship must be transcultural, contextual, counter-cultural, and cross-cultural in the 1996 Nairobi Statement on Worship culture; and the United Methodist "Global Praise" program begun in the 1990s in the US.

These trends have also been put into practice in ecumenical settings that focus on congregational singing, like the Taizé community in France and the Iona community in Scotland, and are embodied by organizations and gatherings around the world that celebrate a diversity of liturgical practices and foster the creation of new hymns. For instance, the London Missionary Society, now known as the Council for World Missions and based out of Singapore, is developing a liturgical resource, including hymns, on themes of global concern such as violence, human trafficking, and environmental destruction. Today's map of global Christianities traces its roots to missionary activities that were set in motion 500 years ago. The rapid expansion of missions in the eighteenth, nineteenth, and eventually twentieth centuries accelerated this process. Just as Christian missionaries influenced the peoples they encountered, so too did the people they encounter begin to reconfigure Christianity. These processes are ongoing and live on in the remarkable and prodigious hymnic contributions from the global church.

NOTABLE HYMNS

As we have seen, the scope of hymnody in "missionary lands" is simply enormous. It includes: the vast canons of hymnody of each denominational tradition; explicitly mission-focused hymnody; and new hymns written in "missionary lands" amidst the diverse expressions of Christianity that began to unfold throughout the global South. For instance, the popular song "I Have Decided to Follow Jesus" is attributed to Sadhu Sundar Singh (1889–1929) of India, which, along with "Je Jone Apon Pan" ("O thou my soul, forget no more") by Krishna Pal (1764–1822) and many other hymns represent the rich tradition of hymn composition in India.[39] There are countless other examples of hymnody written or created in "missionary lands," which can be found in the hymn books and song books that began to proliferate in local languages. For example, *cancioneros* (song books) began to be produced throughout Latin America and included a mix of new compositions and translations from the "so-called 'traditional hymns' from Europe and the United States [of America]."[40] Pablo Sosa's *Cancionero Abierto* is one example of such a collection.[41] Another example is the *Shansi hymn book*, published in the Shanshi Province of China in 1901 by the China Inland Mission, which highlighted local composer Sheng-mo Hsi (席勝魔, 1835–96),[42] or *Sambika*, which was published in Japan in 1903.[43] In short, autochthonous historic Christian hymnody in former missionary lands is a vibrant and exciting emerging scholarly field and it is impossible to do it justice in such a short space.

BIBLIOGRAPHY

Baring-Gould, Sabine. "Onward Christian Soldiers." Hymnary.org. http://www.hymnary.org/text/onward_christian_soldiers_marching_as.

Bohlman, Philip V. "World Musics and World Religions: Whose World?" In *Enchanting Powers: Music in the World's Religions*, edited by Lawrence E. Sullivan, 61–90. Cambridge: Distributed by Harvard University Press for the Harvard University Center for the Study of World Religions, 1997.

Bradley, Ian. *Abide with Me: The World of Victorian Hymns*. London: SCM, 1977.

Cockburn Project. "Iesus Ahatonnia/The Huron Carol." *The Cockburn Project: Songs*. http://cockburnproject.net/songs&music/ia.html.

Ewald, Werner. "South American Hymnody." *The Canterbury Dictionary of Hymnology*. http://www.hymnology.co.uk/s/south-american-hymnody.

Foner, Eric, and John A. Garraty. "Manifest Destiny." In *The Reader's Companion to American History*, edited by Eric Foner and John A. Garraty. Boston: Houghton Mifflin Harcourt, 1991.

González, Justo L. *The Story of Christianity: The Early Church to the Dawn of the Reformation*. New York: Harper Collins, 2010.

Hawn, C. Michael. E-mail correspondence with the author. November 17, 2017.

———. "History of Hymns: Jesus Shall Reign." *Resources: Discipleship Ministries of the United Methodist Church*. https://www.umcdiscipleship.org/resources/history-of-hymns-jesus-shall-reign.

———. *Gather Into One: Praying and Singing Globally*. Grand Rapids: Eerdmans, 2003.

39. Thangaraj, "Indian Christian Hymnody."

40. Ewald, "South American Hymnody."

41. Hawn, *Gather Into One*, 32–71.

42. Hsieh, "Chinese Christian Hymnody."

43. Yokosaka, "Japanese Hymnody."

———. "Ntsikana Gaga." *The Canterbury Dictionary of Hymnology*. http://www.hymnology.co.uk/n/ntsikana-gaga.

Hsieh, Fang-Lan. "Chinese Christian Hymnody." *The Canterbury Dictionary of Hymnology*. http://www.hymnology.co.uk/c/chinese-christian-hymnody.

Hughes, Derrick. *Bishop Sahib: A Life of Reginald Heber*. West Sussex, Great Britain: Churchman, 1986.

Leaver, Robin A. "Theological Dimensions of Mission Hymnody: The Counterpoint of Cult and Culture." *Worship* 62.4 (July 1988) 316–31.

Lim, Swee Hong. "Sacred Song for All God's Children." In *Complex Identities in a Shifting World: Practical Theological Perspectives*, edited by Pamela Couture and Natalie Wigg-Stevenson, 139–54. Zürich: LIT, 2015.

Mauney, Richard S. "Mission Hymnody, USA." *The Canterbury Dictionary of Hymnology*. http://www.hymnology.co.uk/m/mission-hymnody,-usa.

MacDonald, Mark. Personal conversation with the author. June 2016.

McKellar, Hugh D. "'Twas in the Moon of Wintertime." *The Canterbury Dictionary of Hymnology*. http://www.hymnology.co.uk/t/'twas-in-the-moon-of-wintertime.

McNally, Michael. *Ojibwe Singers: Hymns, Grief, and a Native Culture in Motion*. St. Paul, MN: Minnesota Historical Society, 2009.

Medina, Néstor. "Abya Yala, Aztlán, Turtle Island, or Weesakajack." In *Decolonial Christianities: Latinx and Latin American Perspectives*, edited by Raimundo Barreto and Roberto Sirvent. New York: Palgrave McMillan, forthcoming.

———. "From Cultural Theologies to Theologies of Culture I: The Collapse of the European Cultures." In *Christianity, Empire and the Spirit: (Re)Configuring Faith and the Cultural*, by Néstor Medina. Leiden: Brill, 2018.

Morgan, Larry Cloud. "Retranslation of 'From Greenland's Icy Mountains.'" From the private collection of Michael McNally.

Pinsker, Matthew. "Manifest Destiny." history.com. http://www.history.com/topics/manifest-destiny.

Porter, Andrew. "Religion, Missionary Enthusiasm, and Empire." In *The Oxford History of the British Empire*. Vol. 3, *The Nineteenth Century*, edited by Andrew Porter, 222–46. Oxford: Oxford University Press, 1989.

Ransom, Lori, and Jonathan Bonk. "Mission and Power." In *Edinburgh 2010: Witnessing to Christ Today*, edited by Daryl Balia and Kirsten Kim, 86–115. Eugene, OR: Wipf & Stock, 2010.

Richards, Jeffrey. *Imperialism and Music: Britain, 1876–1953*. Manchester: Manchester University Press, 2002.

Stevenson, W. R. "Foreign Missions." In *A Dictionary of Hymnology: Setting Forth the Origin and History of Christian Hymns of All Ages and Nations*, edited by John Julian, 738–59. New York: Dover, 1892.

Thangaraj, M. Thomas. "Indian Christian Hymnody." *The Canterbury Dictionary of Hymnology*. http://www.hymnology.co.uk/i/indian-christian-hymnody.

Watts, Isaac. "Jesus Shall Reign." *Cyber Hymnal*. http://www.hymntime.com/tch/htm/j/s/r/jsreign.htm.

Yasuhiko Yokosaka. "Japanese Hymnody." *The Canterbury Dictionary of Hymnology*. http://www.hymnology.co.uk/j/japanese-hymnody.

Timeline for Volume 2

Mel R. Wilhoit

Note: There are timelines for the appropriate eras contained also in Volumes 1 and 3.

In most surveys of hymnody, a *topical approach* that focuses on one idea at a time (such as psalmody, Reformation hymnody, or African-American hymnody) is the logical way of organizing information, tracing the history of each development from its inception through its maturity, decline, or the present day.

The approach of this timeline seeks to trace a *chronology of hymnological developments*, often combining or juxtaposing events that normally would not be related under a topical approach (such as the year 1926 with the founding of the Stamps-Baxter Music Company and the beginnings of the American Liturgical Movement, or the year 1940 with the founding of the monastic Taize community in France, and the publication of Southern Baptist's *Broadman Hymnal*).

However, rather than just produce long lists of hymn writers or hymnal publications, there has been some attempt to group items where they share a common subject or time-period (such as the 1833 Oxford Movement, 1850s Sunday School Songs, or 1978–99 grouping of "Hymn Renaissance" hymnals).

There has also been an attempt to compile related information, such as subsequent editions of hymnals, under the first date of publication (1549 lists the Church of England's *Book of Common Prayer* and refers to subsequent editions through the present era).

To provide a larger historical context for hymnological developments, dates of a few major historical events have also been provided. Obviously, a timeline purporting to cover the entire history of hymnody must be *selective* rather than *comprehensive*—which means that a great deal of important information has been omitted. Hopefully such omissions will drive the reader to further study.

INTERPRETIVE KEY TO THE TIMELINE

EVENT: Regular type
PERSON: **Bold typeface**
HYMN TEXTS: "In Quotation Marks"
HYMN TUNES: CAPITAL LETTERS
PUBLICATION such as Hymnal/Collection/Book: *Italics*

YEAR	
1517	**Luther** posts 95 Theses; introduces Protestant Reformation
1519	**Zwingli** guides Reformation in Switzerland
1524–34	**Martin Luther** credited with 37 hymntexts including "Aus tiefer Not" ("Out of the depths," 1524), "Christ lag in Todesbanden" ("Christ lay in death's strong bonds," 1524), "Nun komm der heiden Heiland" ("Savior of the nations, come," 1524), "Ein' feste Burg" ("A mighty fortress," 1527–29), "Von Himmel hoch" ("From heaven above," 1534); **Luther** also credited with some of the tunes (EIN' FESTE BURG)
1524	*Etlich Cristliche Lider* [*sic*], commonly called *Achtliederbuch* (*Book of Eight Songs*); first Lutheran hymn collection with 4 texts by **Martin Luther**
1535	**Henry VIII** breaks with Church of Rome, beginning Reformation in England
1537	**William Tyndale**'s partial translation of Bible into English
1541	**John Knox** leads Reformation in Scotland
1539	**Miles Coverdale**'s *Goostly Psalmes and Spirituall Songes*—considered first English hymnal, containing early translation of **Luther**'s "Ein'feste Burg"

1545 *Geystlich Lieder* commonly called *Babst* hymnal with **Luther** preface and considered most representative hymnal of early Reformation

1545–63 Roman Catholic Council of Trent meets to develop responses to Reformation—ushers in the Catholic Counter-Reformation (until 1648)

1549 Issuance of *Book of Common Prayer*, containing complete forms of daily and Sunday worship in English, for what becomes Church of England; many later editions issued, including 1662 which became official edition for centuries, being supplemented by *Common Worship* in 2000

1551 OLD 100TH credited to **Louis Bourgeois** published in *Pseaumes Octante Trois de David* (earlier edition of Genevan *Psalter*) later coupled with **Thomas Ken**'s "Praise God from Whom all blessings flow"

1558 **Queen Elizabeth I** establishes Church of England (Anglican Church); era of **Shakespeare**

1562 Genevan *Psalter* (complete) for **John Calvin**'s congregation; versifications by **Clement Marot** and **Theodore Beze**; music by **Louis Bourgoise** and **Pierre Davantes**; contains tunes **OLD100TH** and **OLD113TH**; 1587 revision considered official psalter

The Whole Book of Psalms collected into English metre; versifications by **Thomas Sternhold** and **John Hopkins**; generally called *Sternhold-Hopkins* Psalter (later called *Old Version*); official psalter of Anglican Church

1563 **John Day**'s edition of *English Psalter* with 65 tunes in 4-part harmony, melody in soprano

1564 First edition of a *Scottish Psalter* whose various editions used into twentieth century

1565 *Ausbund* hymnal (words only) published by Swiss Anabaptists (including "Lob Lied" or "Our Father God, Thy name we praise" still sung by Old Order Amish)

1566 Tune MIT FRUEDEN ZART (later coupled with "Sing praise to God who reigns above")

1567 **Thomas Tallis**' tune TALLIS CANON or EIGHTH TUNE published in **Matthew Parker**'s Psalter (later coupled with text "All praise to thee, my God, this night")

1570 Revised Roman Missal (reflecting Council of Trent reforms) retains only 4 historic Sequences (e.g., "Dies irae"), discarding a vast body of medieval musical additions

1582 *Piae Cantiones* (*Sacred Songs*): early Scandinavian Lutheran collection including DIVINUM MYSTERIUM (coupled with "Of the Father's love begotten," 1851) and TEMPUS ADEST FLORIDUM (coupled with "Good King Wenceslaus," 1853)

1586 **Lukas Osiander**'s hymnal, *Funfzig geistliche* (*Fifty Spiritual Songs and Psalms*), in Homophonic or Kantional style of 4 parts with melody in soprano part (rather than tenor)

Pope Gregory VIII implements (modern) Gregorian calendar; adopted in England, 1752

1599 **Phillip Nicolai**'s words and music for "Wachet auf, ruf uns die Stimme" ("Wake, awake, for night is flying" called "Sleepers, awake") to WACHET AUF! and "Wie schoen leuchtet" ("How brightly shines") to WIE SCHOEN LEUCHTET. Barform tunes (AAB) reflect Meistersinger tradition

1601 **Hans Leo Hassler**'s tune PASSION CHORALE

1607 Jamestown colony established

1609 **Melchior Vulpius**' tune GELOB SEI GOTT

1611 Publication of **King James** Bible (Authorized Version for Church of England)

1615 **Melchior Teschner**'s tune ST. THEODULPH

1618–48 Thirty Years' War in Germany. Prolific period of hymn writing

1642–51 English Civil War

1620 **Pilgrims** bring Dutch *Ainsworth Psalter* (1612) to settlement at Plymouth

1623 Tune LASST UNS ERFREUEN (popularized in 1906 *The English Hymnal* with text "Ye watchers and ye holy ones"; later with "All creatures of our God and King" and "Praise God from whom all blessings flow")

1628 Puritans bring *Sternhold-Hopkins* psalter to settlement in Massachusetts Bay

1630 **Johann Heermann**'s "Herzliebster Jesu" (generally sung as "Ah, holy Jesus") to **Johann Cruger**'s tune HERZLIEBSTER JESU

1636 **Martin Rinkart**'s "Nun danket alle Gott ("Now thank we all our God"; in Germany called "Te Deum") coupled with **Johann Cruger**'s NUN DANKET ALLE GOTT

1640 *Whole Book of Psalms Faithfully Translated into English Metre* (called *Bay Psalm Book*) published in Cambridge, Massachusetts; first book printed in British North America; 9th edition of 1698 is first to contain tunes (13)

1641 **Georg Neumark**'s text and tune "Wer nur den lieben Gott" ("If you will only let God guide you")

1644 **Johann Cruger**'s tune collection, *Praxis Pietatis Melica* (*Practice of Piety in Song*); most important Lutheran hymnal of century (ultimately 45 editions); employing Kantional Style—4 parts with melody in top voice

1653 **Johann Franck**'s "Jesu, meine Freude" ("Jesus, my joy") and **Cruger**'s tune JESU MEINE FRUEDE

1656 **Paul Gerhardt**'s "O Haupt voll Blut" ("O sacred Head") to PASSION CHORALE and "Froelich soll mein Herze springen" ("All my heart this day (night) rejoices")

1661 **John Eliot**'s translation of Psalms into Algonquin language, *Wame Ketoohomae Uketoohomaongash David*, bound with Bible in translation

1670 Beginning of Lutheran Pietism by **Philipp Jakob Spener** emphasizing personal experience in conversion

1674 **Thomas Ken**'s "Praise God from Whom all blessings flow" published in *Manual of Prayers for the Use of Scholars* as third stanza to his hymns "Awake, my soul, and with the sun" and "All praise to thee (you), my God, this night"

1675 **Johann Jakob Schutz**' "Sei Lob und Ehr" ("Sing praise to God who reigns above")

1684 **John Bunyan** publishes *Pilgrim's Progress* from which hymn "He who would valiant be" derived

1696 *A New Version of the Psalms of David, fitted to the tunes used in Churches*; versifications by **Nahum Tate** and **Nicholas Brady**; generally called *Tate and Brady* (or *New Version*)

1691 Congregational hymn singing officially adopted by Baptist Church in Southwark, England, led by pastor/hymnwriter **Benjamin Keach** who authors *The Breach Repaired in God's Worship; or, Singing of Psalms, Hymns and Spiritual Songs, proved to be an Holy Ordinance of Jesus Christ*

1707–50 **J. S. Bach**'s extensive use of chorales (hymns) in his cantatas (JESU, JOY OF MAN'S DESIRING), passions (PASSION CHORALE), motets (JESU, MEINE FRUEDE), and organ works (*Schubler Chorales:* WACHET AUF)

1707 **Isaac Watt**'s *Hymns and Spiritual Songs* containing hymns "Alas, and did my Savior bleed," "Am I a soldier of the cross," "Come we that love the Lord," "I sing the mighty power of God," "When I survey the wondrous cross"

1708 *Supplement* to **Tate** and **Brady**'s *New Version* psalter: tunes ST ANNE and HANOVER attributed to **William Croft**; Lukan paraphrase, "While shepherds watched their flocks by night"

1712 **Joseph Addison**'s "The spacious firmament on high" (generally set to **Joseph Haydn**'s music for chorus, "The Heaven's are telling" from oratorio, *The Creation*, 1798)

1715 Beginning of Enlightenment (Aufklarung) which (re)constructed hymns in rationalist (non-supernatural) terms using isorhythmic ("same rhythm" quarter-note style) approach (rather than more complex rhythms of original chorales)

1719 **Isaac Watts**' *Psalms of David Imitated in the Language of the New Testament* containing Psalm paraphrases "My shepherd will supply my need," "Jesus shall reign," "O(ur) God, our help in ages past," "Joy to the world," "I'll praise my maker while I've breath"

1721 **John Tufts**' *An Introduction to the Singing of Psalm Tunes* initiates Singing School Movement in American colonies

1722 Moravians established at Herrnhut, Germany; led by **Nicholas Ludwig von Zinzendorf**, hymnwriter and Singstunden (hymn meetings) leader where **Zinzendorf** improvised hymns: "Christi Blut und Gerechttigkeit" ("Jesus, your blood and righteousness," **J. Wesley** trans.), "Jesu, geh voran" ("Jesus, still lead on") published in *Das Gesangbuch der Gemeine in Herrnhut* (1735)

1729 **Gerhard Tersteegen**'s "Gott ist gegenwartig" ("God himself is with us") American printing of **Watts**' *The Psalms of David Imitated* by Ben Franklin; almost 50 editions (by others) appear over next 50 years: *Barlow's Watts, Dwight's Watts, Winchell' Watts, Worcester's Watts*

1736/7	Beginning of First Great Awakening in Britain and colonies—opening door to hymn singing among previously Psalm-singing-only churches
1737	**John Wesley**'s *Collection of Psalms and Hymns* (called *Charlestown Collection*) printed in colonies
1738–88	Hymnwriting career of **Charles Wesley** including 6500 hymns: "And can it be," "Come, thou long-expected Jesus," "Christ the Lord is risen today," "Hark! the herald angels sing," "Jesus, lover of my soul," "Lo, he comes with clouds descending," "Love divine, all loves excelling," "O for a thousand tongues to sing," "Rejoice, the Lord is king," "Soldiers of Christ, arise," "Ye servants of God"
1741	Great Psalmody Controversy (on propriety of singing hymns rather than only Psalms) begins among colonial Presbyterians and continues in various denominations for a century
1742	Methodist *Collection of Tunes, set to Music, as they are commonly sung at the Foundery* (called *The Foundery Collection*)
1745	**William William**'s "Guide me, O Thou great Jehovah" (trans. 1771) coupled with **John Hughes**' Welsh tune CWM RHONDDA (1907)
	Anonymous lyrics for "God Save the King (Queen)" appear in *Gentleman's Magazine*, set to anonymous tune appearing in *Thesaurus Musicus* (1744)
1756	*Psalmodia Germanica*, first Lutheran hymnal published in colonies
1757	Anonymous hymn "Come, Thou almighty King" set to **Felice di Giardini**'s tune ITALIAN HYMN (1769)
1759	**Joseph Hart**'s "Come ye sinners, poor and needy"
1761	**James Lyons** compiles *Urania*, tunebook including Psalm tunes, hymntunes, and "fuging" tunes
1769	**C. P. E. Bach**'s publication of his father **Johann**'s collection of chorales that he arranged or harmonized, *Vierstimmige Choralgesange* (called "Bach Chorales")
1770	**William Billings**' *New England Psalm Singer* containing "Let tyrants shake their iron rods" to his tune CHESTER
	Thomas Oliver's paraphrase of Jewish "Yigdal," "The God of Abraham praise" set to **Meyer Lyon**'s tune LEONI

1772	**John Fawcett**'s "Blest be the tie that binds" set to **Johann Nageli**'s DENNIS (1845)
1774	Tune GROSSER GOTT (coupled with text "Holy God, we praise your name")
1776	**Augustus Toplady**'s collection, *Psalms and Hymns for public and private worship*, containing hymn "Rock of Ages" coupled with **Thomas Hasting**'s tune TOPLADY (1832)
1776–83	*Declaration of Independence* and American Revolutionary War
1780	**John Wesley**'s comprehensive *Collection of Hymns for the People Called Methodists*
1787	Anonymous hymn "How firm a foundation" (attributed to "K"—perhaps **Robert Keene** or **George Kieth**) published in **Rippon**'s *A Selection of Hymns from the Best Authors*, later coupled with anonymous tune FOUNDATION (1832)
1779	Collection *Olney Hymns* by **John Newton** ("Amazing Grace, how sweet the sound," Glorious things of Thee are spoken," "How sweet the name of Jesus sounds") and **William Cowper** ("God moves in a mysterious way," "O for a closer walk with God," "There is a fountain filled with blood")
1780	**Edward Perronet**'s "All hail the power of Jesus' name" generally sung to **William Shrubsole**'s MILES LANE (1779) or **Oliver Holden**'s CORONATION (1793) or **James Ellor**'s DIADEM (1838)
1782	**Matthias Claudius**' "Wir pflugen und wir struene ("We plow the fields and scatter") coupled with **Johann A. P. Schultz**' tune WIR PFLUGEN, ca 1800
	Lewis Edson's tune LENOX (coupled with **Wesley**'s "Blow ye the trumpet, blow!")
1789–99	French Revolution
1790	*Prayer Book*, the American version of Anglican *Book of Common Prayer*, published for new Episcopal Church, containing 27 hymns (reflecting American acceptance of singing hymns, well before Anglican Church)
1792	**William Carey** sparked creation of the Particular Baptist Society for the Propagation of the Gospel Amongst the Heathen, with an explosion of mission agencies soon to follow: London Missionary Society (1795), Scottish and Glasgow Missionary Societies (1796), Church Missionary Society

(1799), Religious Tract Society (1799), and the British and Foreign Bible Society (1804). English hymnody soon carried around the world, some by hymnwriters such as **Reginald Heber**, missionary to India (1823); his "From Greenland's icy mountains to India's coral strands" (1819) became the most sung missions hymn of nineteenth century

1793 **Oliver Holden**'s *Union Harmony* containing tune CORONATION (oldest American tune still in use)

Contributor Biographies for Volume 2

Alphabetical Listing

Alexander Blachly (PhD, Columbia University) is Professor of Music at the University of Notre Dame and the founder/director of the Renaissance vocal ensemble Pomerium, which has released fourteen commercial recordings of Renaissance polyphony. His most recent article compares two canonic rondeaux from Reims: Machaut's Ma fin est mon commencement and Baude Cordier's Tout par compas. He is currently writing a book on Pythagorean music of the Middle Ages and Renaissance.

Neal Campbell (DMA, Manhattan School of Music, New York) held church, synagogue, and college positions in Washington, DC, Philadelphia, New York, New Jersey, Connecticut, and Virginia, including ten years on the adjunct faculty of the University of Richmond, before assuming his present position. He served three terms on the National Council of the American Guild of Organists.

Trent A. Hancock (DMin/MDiv, Princeton Theological Seminary) is the author of *Meaningful and Faithful*, an examination of the relationship between the proclamation of the Gospel and the sharing of personal experiences of loss in the context of the funeral sermon, and a contributor to the *Encyclopedia of Christianity in the United States*.

Jonathan Jakob Hehn, OSL (DM/BM, Florida State University; MSM, theology, University of Notre Dame (MSM)), is a Presby-Lutheran musician and liturgist currently serving Saint Leo University and Good Shepherd Lutheran Church in Tampa, Florida.

Joseph Herl (PhD, University of Illinois; MMus, North Texas State University) is Professor of Music at Concordia University, Nebraska. His 2004 book *Worship Wars in Early Lutheranism* was awarded the Roland Bainton Prize of the Sixteenth Century Society and Conference. More recently, he was coeditor of a historical companion to the Lutheran Service Book.

J. Christopher Holmes (PhD, The Southern Baptist Theological Seminary) serves as the Pastor of Discipleship at Yellow Creek Baptist Church in Owensboro, Kentucky, and has taught classes on preaching at Covenant Baptist Theological Seminary. His studies and research interests have focused on the use of metaphor in preaching and seventeenth-century Baptist history.

Benjamin Kolodziej (MSM, MTS, Southern Methodist University, Dallas) is Director of Music at Lord of Life Lutheran Church in Plano, Texas, and serves as organist at Perkins Chapel at Southern Methodist University. As an organist, he has performed throughout the US and Europe and his musical compositions are published by CPH and GIA. He publishes frequently on liturgical and musical topics, particularly in the realm of Lutheran hymnody and liturgy.

Christina Labriola (ThD, Regis College of the Toronto School of Theology, University of Toronto; BM, Sacred Music at Emmanuel College) focuses on the interchange between music and theology, particularly theological aesthetics, mysticism, and the spiritual dimension of music. Christina ministers as a church music director at Roman Catholic parishes in downtown Toronto.

Michael F. Lloyd (DPhil, University of Oxford) is Principle of Wycliffe Hall, Oxford. He was educated at Downing College, University of Cambridge (BA, English Literature), Cranmer Hall, University of Durham (BA, Theology) and Worcester College Oxford (DPhil, Theology). Lloyd's research area is the problem of evil, and he is the author of a popular-level systematic theology entitled Cafe Theology.

Scott A. Moore (DrTheol cand., Liturgical Studies, University of Erfurt; MDiv, Lutheran Theological Seminary at Gettysburg) is an ordained pastor of the Evangelical Lutheran Church in America and is now a priest of the Episcopal Church (USA). He served a number of parishes in the United States and recently moved to Germany, where he has lived and worked in the "Luther" cities of Eisleben, Wittenberg, and Erfurt. Moore writes and teaches in the areas of Martin Luther, liturgy, sacramental theology, and ritual space.

J. Michael Morgan (DLitt, King University; MSLS, Atlanta University; BMus, Florida State University) is the Musician at Columbia Theological Seminary in Atlanta, and Organist Emeritus at Central Presbyterian Church, Atlanta. He is author of *Psalter for Christian Worship* (1999; rev. ed., 2010) and a contributor to *Psalms for All Seasons, People's Psalter, Oxford Handbook of the Psalms,* and the new Presbyterian hymnal.

David W. Music (DMA/MCM, Southwestern Baptist Theological Seminary) is Professor of Church Music in the School of Music at Baylor University. He served as editor of *The Hymn* (1991–96) and has written extensively on congregational song and sacred choral music.

Anthony Ruff (DrTheol, University of Graz; STM, Yale University; MDiv, St. John's University School of Theology) is Associate Professor of Theology at St. John's University in Collegeville, Minnesota, and an ordained monk of St. John's Abbey. He has been on the board of the National Association of Pastoral Musicians, the Hymn Society, and the Catholic Academy of Liturgy. He is founding director of the National Catholic Youth Choir and blogs at Pray Tell.

Corneliu C. Simuț (PhD, Aberdeen; ThD, Tilburg; DD, Pretoria, Dr. Habil, Debrecen) is Professor of Historical and Systematic Theology at Emanuel University and associate research fellow at the University of Pretoria. His scientific interests include the Protestant and Catholic Reformations, Western esotericism and theosophy, German idealism and liberalism, religious radicalism and secularism, ecodomy in Eastern Orthodox nationalistic rhetoric and indigenous African religions.

Bryan D. Spinks (DD, Examined Higher Doctorate, University of Durham) is the Bishop F. Percy Goddard Professor of Liturgical Studies and Pastoral Theology at Yale Institute of Sacred Music and Yale Divinity School. His areas of specialism include Church of the East, Syrian Orthodox and Reformed worship as well as Anglican rites. Spinks' most recent book is *Do This in Remembrance of Me: The Eucharist from the Early Church to the Present Day* (2013).

Rochelle Stackhouse (PhD, Liturgical Studies, Drew University; MDiv, Princeton Seminary) is Senior Pastor at the Church of the Redeemer UCC, New Haven, Connecticut, and Lecturer in Preaching at Yale Divinity School. Her scholarly writings have focused on Isaac Watts, American hymnody, and Jonathan Edwards.

Erika K. R. Stalcup (PhD, History of Christianity, Boston University; MDiv, Yale Divinity School) is pastor of the Eglise Evangélique Méthodiste in Lausanne, Switzerland. She specializes in early Methodist history and liturgy. Stalcup is currently involved in the training of French-speaking Methodist pastors through the Centre Méthodiste de Formation Théologique.

Karen B. Westerfield Tucker (PhD, University of Notre Dame) is Professor of Worship at the School of Theology, Boston University, where she teaches courses related to liturgical studies and church music. She is the author of *American Methodist Worship* (2001), and the editor for *The Sunday Service of the Methodists: Twentieth-century Worship in Worldwide Methodism* (1996) and (with Geoffrey Wainwright) *The Oxford History of Christian Worship* (2006; rev. and exp. ed. online).

Becca Whitla (MsMus, Emmanuel College, University of Toronto; BFA, York University) is a doctoral candidate at Emmanuel College. For her dissertation, she is working with liberationist, decolonial, and postcolonial theories and theologies to propose a liberating of congregational singing. She has recently published on Cuban hymnody and decolonial theology and is interim Director of Chapel at Emmanuel College in Toronto.

Mel R. Wilhoit (DMA, Southern Baptist Theological Seminary) served as Professor of Music and Department Chair at Bryan College, Dayton, Tennessee, for over thirty years. His popular and scholarly works on music have appeared in numerous traditional and online publications.

Index of Scripture

OLD TESTAMENT

Psalm

Isaiah

Ezekiel

NEW TESTAMENT

Matthew

Mark

Luke

Index of Names and Subjects

Index of Hymns

The Earliest Christian Hymnbook
The Odes of Solomon

By James H. Charlesworth (translator)

An introduction to and translation of the The Odes of Solomon, one of the earliest collections of Christian and proto-Christian odes and hymns.

Nearly two millennia ago a gifted poet in the Middle East composed the earliest Christian hymnbook, and this anonymous Odist became the early poet laureate of Christianity.

That the earliest followers of Jesus wrote poetry, hymns, and odes is evident already in the New Testament. This volume is a translation of The Odes of Solomon, a collection of early Christian hymns or odes dating from the 2nd Century; some are obviously Christian, others perhaps Jewish. The beauty of these poems is a tribute to the depth of spirituality in early communities of Christians, some of whom were perhaps also Jews or converted Jews. Professor Charlesworth offers an informative and insightful introduction and a translation of this work that is both engaging and true to the original languages. Having studied the Odes since 1966, Charlesworth believes the Odes express unique spiritual truths.

Invaluable as a resource for scholars and students of the religious literature of the period, the richness and spirituality of the Odes will also appeal to a wider audience. An Index of Ancient Sources also provides the reader with easy access to the wide range of references in the notes.

James H. Charlesworth is George L. Collord Professor of New Testament Language and Literature and Director and Editor of the PTS Dead Sea Scrolls Project.

Print Paperback ISBN: 9780227173558 / PDF eBook ISBN: 9780227903070
229x127mm, 170pp / Published: June 2011

9780227177211

BV - #0031 - 250222 - C0 - 229/152/19 - PB - 9780227177211 - Gloss Lamination